METHODS OF KNOWLEDGE

METHODS OF KNOWLEDGE

Perceptual, Non-perceptual, and Transcendental

According to Advaita Vedānta

By
Swami Satprakashananda

Foreword by
DR. HUSTON SMITH
Professor of Philosophy
M.I.T., U.S.A.

Introduction by
T.M.P. MAHADEVAN, M.A., PhD.
Professor of Philosophy
University of Madras, India

Advaita Ashrama
(Publication Department)
5 Dehi Entally Road
Kolkata 700 014

Published by
Swami Mumukshananda
President, Advaita Ashrama
Mayavati, Champawat, Himalayas
from its Publication Department, Kolkata
Email: mail@advaitaonline.com
Website: www.advaitaonline.com

First Published, 1965, George Allen & Unwin Ltd., London
First Indian Edition 1974
Fourth Indian Reprint, May 2001
1M1C

ISBN 81-7505-065-9

Printed in India at
Trio Process
Kolkata 700 014

Dedicated to

The Blessed and Revered Memories of

SWĀMĪ VIVEKĀNANDA

and

SWĀMĪ BRAHMĀNANDA

Two Illustrious Exemplars of

The Religion and Philosophy of Vedānta

in the Modern Age

On the occasion of their

One-hundredth Birth Anniversaries

January 12 and 21, 1963

CONTENTS

FOREWORD *page* 11

INTRODUCTION 13

PREFACE 15

NOTE ON THE PRONUNCIATION OF TRANSLITERATED SANSKRIT ALPHABET 21

ABBREVIATIONS 23

SYNOPSES OF CHAPTERS 25

PART ONE

Perception, Three Means of Non-Perceptual Knowledge, and the Way of Apprehending Non-Existence

I. Perception; its Scope and Means 35

II. The Metaphysical Background of the Sensible Universe 61

III. Perceptual Knowledge; its Distinctive Character and Process 85

IV. The Validity of Knowledge 110

V. Illusion; its Nature and Cause 124

VI. Three Means of Non-Perceptual Knowledge: Inference, Comparison, and Postulation 141

VII. Non-Apprehension: the Way of Apprehending Non-Existence 163

PART TWO

Verbal Testimony
(A Means of Valid Knowledge, Sensuous and Suprasensuous)

VIII. Verbal Testimony, a Unique Method of Valid Knowledge 173

IX. Verbal Testimony as the Means of Suprasensuous Knowledge; the Speciality of the Vedic Testimony 193

X. Sense-Perception, Reason, and the Vedic Testimony 219

XI. 'Thou art That', the Truth of truths 246

XII. 'The Knower of Brahman Attains the Highest' 274

Appendix A A Short Account of the Vedic Texts 305

Appendix B The Six Vedic Schools of Philosophy and their Notable Sanskrit Works (with available English Translations) 311

Appendix C The Yōgic Dualism and the Vedāntic Non-Dualism 335
Appendix D The Yogic Method of Meditation leading to Self-realization 337

Bibliography I (English Works quoted from in this book) 339
Bibliography II (Sanskrit Works quoted from in this book) 342

Index 347

FOREWORD

It has been less than a decade since I heard the chairman of one of the leading departments of philosophy in America claim that rigorous philosophy has been an exclusively Western phenomenon. That his statement passed unchallenged shows how far thought has moved in a brief ten years. A man who made such a claim today might not be hooted off the platform, but it would be widely felt that his education needed to be up-dated.

Early in our century Oswald Spengler called for a Copernican revolution in history which would relieve Westerners of their habit of equating what happened in Europe during the last 2500 years with history as a whole and place it in the perspective of *world* history. A comparable Copernican revolution in philosophy is, fortunately, under way. Bertrand Russell has not stood out during his lifetime as an admirer of Asian thought, but long after his contributions to mathematical logic have been forgotten his *History of Western Philosophy* may be remembered, not for its contents but for its title which, in the Western world, was the first to have the grace to recognize that Western philosophy is not synonymous with philosophy generally. The Honolulu conferences and companion journal, Philosophy East and West, have kept alive the distinction implied by Russell's title, and have made it more explicit.

By now it is pretty well recognized that Asia generally, and India in particular, has a philosophical heritage as rich, subtle, and variegated in its own ways as is that of the West. The next step will be to see that its merits do not belong wholly to the past; that they are not simply those of an historical monument. Even among Indians there is a disposition today to view the glories of Indian philosophy as gracing a bygone epoch; the future is entrusted, if not to science exclusively, at least to Western modes of thought. If Indians themselves succumb to this view, it is not surprising that few Westerners are aware of how relevant is much in classical Indian thought to the philosophical problems that occupy us today, to say nothing of the problems that don't occupy us but should. This is regrettable. Classical Indian thought presents a rich field for investigation not merely to the historian, not merely to the Orientalist, but to the constructive philosopher grappling with issues of current import.

This brings us to the book in hand—an exposition of Indian epistemology conceived in a resolutely scholarly spirit by one of the most qualified and enlightened spirits of that great land. That it contains a warehouse of information on the classical schools of Indian philosophy will be evident to the reader at once. But I have also been struck by how contemporary and 'Western'—the precise word would be one with which Indological studies in the West began, namely 'Indo-European'—are many of the themes it treats. Conspicuous instances are the relative merits of correspondence, coherence, and verification theories of truth, and the significance of language, or the 'word', in human thought. The author addresses himself to the modern scene without forcing comparisons with its transient currents. The themes to which he speaks are perennial.

It is now twenty-five years that Swāmi Satprakāshānanda has been among us, wearing his ochre robe each Sunday morning as, in the heart of America, he voices and exemplifies the primal richness of India's mind and spirit. It is an honour to preface these few lines to his meticulous account of the fundamental principles of Indian epistemology, authored (as it is) by the one who has taught me virtually everything I know about the thought of that extraordinary sub-continent. The reader will quickly sense that he is a thorough and painstaking scholar. It has been one of the great good fortunes of my life to have known him also as a spiritual leader of men; a man filled with insight and charity and totally dedicated to the service of the Lord.

HUSTON SMITH

Professor of Philosophy
Massachusetts Institute of Technology

INTRODUCTION

Advaita epistemology is not easy to expound. How the one non-dual consciousness that is the self appears split into cognizer, cognition and object cognized, it is not possible to explain. To say that this apparent splitting is the work of māyā is to say that it is inexplicable. The purpose for which a study of the problem of knowledge is undertaken is not to solve the problem but to go beyond it. The empirical situation in knowledge which demands the distinction of three factors, cognizer, cognition, and object cognized, does not admit of a satisfactory explanation. While the systems of philosophy that are opposed to Advaita imagine that they have offered an explanation, Advaita shows that the problem is inexplicable on the level of relative experience. When this level is transcended in the plenary non-dual experience, there is no longer any problem to be solved. Any epistemological analysis can be useful only in so far as it makes us become awake to this truth. An exposition of the various means of valid knowledge (pramāṇas) has for its aim, in the context of Advaita, the demonstration of their insufficiency and relative nature, paving the way for their transcendence in the unconditioned self which is pure knowledge. This difficult task, Swāmī Satprakāshānanda performs in a dexterous manner in this lucidly written work, *Methods of Knowledge*.

The classical manual of Advaita epistemology is the well-known text, *Vedānta-paribhāṣā* of Dharmarāja Adhvarin. In empirical matters, Advaita is said to follow the Bhāṭṭa School of Mīmāṁsā. In the latter school, six means of valid knowledge are recognized: perception (pratyakṣa), inference (anumāna), verbal testimony (śabda), comparison (upamāna), postulation (arthāpatti), and non-apprehension (anupalabdhi). Dharmarāja deals with these six means of valid knowledge, but from the standpoint of Advaita, Swāmī Satprakāshānanda follows closely, in this work, Dharmarāja's exposition.

Perception is of special importance because the knowledge obtained thereby is immediate, unlike the knowledge that results from inference, etc., which is mediate. The knowledge of the self that is said to liberate the soul from bondage is direct knowledge which is like unto perceptual knowledge. Only, even perceptual knowledge is not so immediate as self-knowledge. In sense-perception there is the intervention of a sense-organ between subject and object. Even in the case of internal perception there is the operation, according to one tradition (the Bhāmatī) in Advaita, of mind which is a sense-organ. The final release also is wrought by the mind which has taken on the mode of the impartite self (akhaṇḍākāra-vṛtti) as a result of continued meditation. But this mode subsides after having accomplished its end; and then the non-dual self alone remains.

The other Advaita tradition (the Vivaraṇa) holds that the mind is not a sense-organ, but an auxiliary to all types of knowledge. The final release, according to this view, is gained through the major texts of the Upaniṣads which teach non-difference of the so-called individual soul from the supreme self. It is not as if verbal testimony (śabda) cannot yield immediate knowledge. From verbal testimony one may gain mediate knowledge or immediate knowledge, depending on the nature of the object. If the object is remote, then one can have only mediate knowledge. If the object is immediate, then it is possible to obtain from verbal testimony an immediate knowledge thereof. Since there is nothing more intimate or immediate than the self, self-knowledge gained through the major texts like 'That thou art' can be immediate.

Other means of valid knowledge, such as inference, are useful in so far they can render intelligible the mediate knowledge of the self. The intuitive experience which is called self-realization is not infra-rational but supra-rational. Śaṅkara has pointed out in several places that reasoning is a necessary aid for understanding scripture. An unreasoned belief is no good at all. Hence, in the process of inquiry consisting of śravaṇa (study), manana (reflection), and nididhyāsana (meditation) rational reflection occupies a strategic place. Advaita does not advocate blind acceptance of authority; even scripture becomes authoritative only because its truth gets corroborated in one's own experience.

Swāmī Satprakāshānanda has expounded the epistemological position of Advaita in a clear and comprehensive manner. I have no doubt that this book will be well received by those who are interested in Advaita metaphysics and require a reliable modern introduction to the subject.

T. M. P. MAHADEVAN

Professor of Philosophy

University of Madras, India

PREFACE

In this book I have dwelt on the Vedāntic answer to the moot epistemological question 'How do we know?' In answering this question Advaita (Nondualistic) Vedānta has maintained six distinct methods of knowledge, called pramāṇas, that is, the means of valid cognition (pramā)—perceptual, non-perceptual, and transcendental —and has tackled various epistemological problems, such as—what is the nature of knowledge? what is its origin? how does it arise? what are its instruments? how is the sense-object related to the cognizer? what is the test of the validity of cognition? what causes illusion? how is non-existence known? what is the way to the knowledge of the ultimate Reality? To orient the general readers to the Advaita position I shall briefly state the cardinal epistemological truths that serve as the key to the solution of the problems of knowledge in this system. Being the essentials of cognition they have perennial value and can throw light on any investigation in the field.

Broadly speaking, Advaita philosophy views knowledge in its empirical and in its metaphysical aspect. Fundamentally, knowledge is Pure Consciousness beyond the relativity of the knower and the known. Consciousness is prior to every form of existence. But for this nothing can be affirmed or denied. It illuminates all objects. It has no illuminator. It is self-luminous and self-existent. It shines even when there is no object to illuminate. Non-relational, nondual Pure Consciousness is the ultimate Reality. Being is identical with Pure Consciousness. Relational knowledge is an expression of non-relational Pure Consciousness through a mental mode of the cognizer, the knowing self. It has varied forms according to the nature of the object. It may be either psychological or psychophysical. Internal cognition is psychological. Sense-perception is psychophysical. The same Pure Consciousness is individualized as the knowing self or the ego, being manifest through a particular mode of the mind characterized by 'I-ness'. So we see that in Advaita Vedānta epistemology is inseparable from metaphysics. The problems of knowledge are dwelt upon and solved with reference to its essential nature.

The essence of knowledge is self-shining consciousness. Self-revealing it reveals all objects. The luminosity of consciousness is contrary to that of physical light, which is unaware of itself and all else. Despite its radiance physical light is marked by nescience, so to speak. A non-luminous object cannot be seen without light. But light requires no other physical light to be seen. So physical light is apparently self-manifest. But actually it is not. That which is neither self-aware nor aware of anything else cannot make itself or any other thing known. Its manifestation depends on self-luminous consciousness, which alone makes it known. Physical processes can produce physical light, but not the light of consciousness, which is of opposite nature. This is a truth which some psychologists and philosophers are apt to overlook. Not even mental processes can bring forth consciousness, which inheres neither in the body nor in the mind, but in the luminous self, the cognizer of both. The point is, consciousness belongs to the cognizer as its essence and not to the cognized. Mental states are not conscious in themselves. They are illuminated by the radiance of the knowing self, which is ever the subject and never an object.

In all relational knowledge four distinct factors are involved—the knower, the object known, the process of knowledge, and the resultant knowledge. Among them the knower is primary. Process is the method that relates the knowing self with the object and brings about the knowledge. The knower and the object known are the two poles of knowledge, so to speak. As noted by George Hicks, 'Knowledge exhibits the two characteristic features—reference to a self that knows and reference to a reality other than self; and the former is no less a problem than the latter.'[1] The epistemological enquiry in the West, however, has been directed mainly towards the object.

Being of the nature of consciousness the self is ever manifest. Nobody doubts his own existence, because it is self-evident. The luminous self requires no proof. An individual's self-awareness is immediate and direct. No thinking process is involved in it. It is the irreducible epistemological fact. This is 'the given' in the true sense. Here is the foundation of human knowledge. From here all cognitive process starts. It is the radiance of consciousness proceeding from the luminous self that manifests all objects physical and psychical. As observed by Swāmī Vivekānanda, 'It is through the self that you know anything. . . . In and through the self all knowledge comes.'[2]

But the basis of each individual self is the omnipresent Supreme Self. One undivided, limitless Consciousness, all-pervading Brahman, being manifest through the psychophysical adjuncts of living creatures is apparently divided into numerous selves. So says Swāmī Vivekānanda: 'Whatever we know we have to know in and through Him. He is the essence of our own self. He is the essence of this ego, this "I", and we cannot know anything except in and through that "I". Therefore you have to know everything in and through Brahman.'[3]

It is said in the Mahābhārata that King Yudhiṣṭhira was once asked a number of significant questions. The first one was 'What

[1] 'Theory of Knowledge', Prof. George D. Hicks, University of London, *Enc. Brit.*, 1948, Vol. XIII, p. 449.

[2] CW II, p. 303. Advaita Ashrama, Mayavati, Almora, India, 1935.

[3] *Ibid.*, p. 133.

manifests the sun?' 'Brahman', answered the king. The point is that the sun, the illuminator of the entire solar universe, though apparently self-manifest, is actually not. In itself the sun is unaware and unknown. It is Brahman that makes it known or manifest.[4] Indeed, it is the radiance of Pure Consciousness called in Vedānta 'Brahman' that manifests all things at all times. As declared by the Kaṭha Upaniṣad, 'He shining all these shine. Through His radiance all these become manifest in various ways.'[5] This is the most profound of all epistemological truths, as far as I can see. It is Brahman that appears as the individual self in association with the finite mind. From the self the mind receives the radiance of consciousness and illuminates all things including light.

It is with the mind that a person knows all that he knows—from the lowest to the highest. In the attainment of any knowledge perceptual, non-perceptual, or transcendental—mind is the principal instrument. In every act of cognition there is a mental mode corresponding to the object. The more the mode corresponds with the object, the more correct and distinct is the knowledge. In indirect knowledge the mind has no contact with the object as in direct knowledge. In external as well as in internal perception the mental mode coincides with the object. In the Advaita view physical objects exist independently of the cognizer's mind. In this sense it is akin to the common sense realism. But it is vitally different from both Realism and Idealism.

Knowledge is revelatory. Its function is to manifest the object by removing from it the veil of unknown-ness, without affecting it in any way. It opens to view more or less what is hidden. It presents, but does not represent. Cogitation is not cognition. If knowledge is held to be constructive or interpretative by nature, then nothing can be known as it is; the fact underlying knowledge is bound to remain ever hidden. It is a wrong premise to start with. A wrong proposition is liable to create false problems and develop unfounded theories.

Each of the six methods of knowledge, e.g., perception, inference, comparison, postulation, non-apprehension, and verbal testimony, has its limitations. Each has its own way and sphere of operation. They do not contradict one another. Perception is the means of immediate cognition. It can be external and also internal—the experience of the physical objects and the experience of the mental states. Inference, comparison, and postulation, which are based on sense-perception, are the means of non-perceptual or indirect cognition. The non-existence of an object or an attribute is cognized neither by sense-perception nor by inference, but is known directly

[4] Cf. Tai. Br. III: 12.9.7. '[Brahman is] That Light by which illumined the sun shines (yena sūryastapati tejaseddhah).'

[5] II: 2.15.

by its non-apprehension or non-perception. Sense-perception and the three means of knowledge dependent on it can impart only the knowledge of the sensible facts, but not of the suprasensuous; whereas verbal testimony can convey the knowledge of both—the sensible and the suprasensible. Its own domain is the suprasensible. The direct perception or the immediate apprehension of the ultimate Reality is not considered a means of knowledge but its supreme end. The Vedic dictum declaring the identity of the individual self with the Supreme Self serves as a means to this achievement. In this transcendental experience, where Truth and Truth alone shines, is the culmination of all knowledge, is the final solution of all problems, is the cessation of all doubts, delusions, and darkness forever, and is the attainment of supreme blessedness.

The subject-matter of the book has been treated in two main parts. The first part dwells on the five of the six pramāṇas and is divided into seven chapters including one on 'Illusion; its Nature and Cause.' The second part deals with verbal testimony alone and contains five chapters. The theme of each chapter has been discussed under descriptive sub-headings. The second chapter of the second part of the book appeared under the caption 'The Vedic Testimony and its Speciality' in March and April issues of *Prabuddha Bhārata* (1962) published by Advaita Āshrama, Māyāvatī, Ālmōra, India.

As a background of Advaita philosophy I have provided in the Appendices a survey of the six Vedic systems of philosophy and their representative works (with available English translations), an outline of the sacred texts of the Vedas, and a short statement on the distinction of the Yōgic dualism from the Vedāntic nondualism, and on the Yōgic method of meditation leading to self-realization.

I acknowledge my obligation to Swāmī Mādhavānanda, whose English translation of Dharmarāja Adhvarīndra's *Vedānta-paribhāṣā* and of Śaṅkarācārya's commentary on the *Bṛhadāraṇyaka Upaniṣad* I have followed in certain cases while rendering into English the Sanskrit passages quoted from the said books.

It is my pleasant duty to acknowledge my indebtedness to all who have helped me in the production of this treatise. My special thanks are due to Dr T. M. P. Mahadevan, Professor of Philosophy, University of Madras, India, and Dr Huston Smith, Professor of Philosophy, M.I.T., for writing the Introduction and the Foreword. I am very grateful to Professor Huston Smith for reading the whole manuscript and for making amendments and comments and giving suggestions for improvement. I am also thankful to my brother-disciple Swāmī Prabhavānanda, who read parts of the manuscript while in St Louis on a visit, for his words of encouragement and the interest taken by him in the publication of the book.

I deeply appreciate the devoted service rendered by Mrs Virginia H. Ward in the preparation of the entire typescript, which required more than one revision. My thanks are also due to my other Vedānta students who have facilitated the work in different ways. Among them I should mention specifically Mrs Robert J. Gaddy for her assistance in preparing the Index.

I express my appreciation and gratitude to all authors and publishers from whose books I have quoted passages. Their names are recorded in the Bibliography. Reference to every passage is given in the footnote. Detailed reference is to be found in the footnote on the first passage quoted from each book. The publishers' kind permission for reprinting the material from their books has been secured in necessary cases.

SATPRAKĀSHĀNANDA

The Vedānta Society
St Louis, Missouri, U.S.A.
April 10, 1964

NOTE ON THE PRONUNCIATION OF TRANSLITERATED SANSKRIT ALPHABET

a	as in all
ā	as in far
i	as in tin
ī	as ee in deep
u	as in full
ū	as oo in loop
ō	as in note
ṛ	as ri in prick
ṁ	as ng in Hongkong
ḥ	as in oh!
g	hard as in good
n	as ng in king
c	as ch in church
ch	as chh in thatch-hut
jh	as geh in hedge-hog
ñ	n (palatal)
ṭ	as in tool
ṭh	as th in boat-house
ḍ	as in dog
ḍh	as in Godhood
ṇ	n (cerebral)
t	soft as in French
th	as in thin
d	as th in then
dh	as in Buddha
n	(dental) as in noun
ph	as in loophole
bh	as in abhor
v	as w
ś	as in short (palatal sibilant)
ṣ	(cerebral sibilant)

ABBREVIATIONS

AB	Ātma-bōdha
Ai. U.	Aitareya Upaniṣad
AS	Advaita-siddhi
ASS	Ānandāśrama Sanskrit Series, Poona.
AV	Ātmānātma-viveka
BG	Bhagavad-gītā
BP	Bhāṣā-pariccheda
BS	Brahma-sūtras
Br. U.	Bṛhadāraṇyaka Upaniṣad
Ch. U.	Chāndōgya Upaniṣad
Com.	Commentary
CSS	Chowkhamba Sanskrit Series, Varanasi
CW	Complete Works of Swāmī Vivekānanda
Is. U.	Īśa Upaniṣad
Ka.U.	Kaṭha Upaniṣad
Ken.U.	Kena Upaniṣad
LVV	Laghu-vākya-vṛtti
Ma.U.	Māṇḍūkya Upaniṣad
MK	Māṇḍūkya-Upaniṣad-Kārikā
Mn.U.	Mahānārāyaṇa Upaniṣad
MS	Manu-smṛti
Mu.U.	Muṇḍaka Upaniṣad
NPT U.	Nṛsiṁha-Pūrva-Tāpanīya Upaniṣad
NS	Naiṣkarmya-siddhi
NSP	Nirnaya Sagar Press, Bombay
PD	Pañcadaśī
PP	Pañca-pādikā
PPV	Pañca-pādikā-vivaraṇa
Pr. U.	Praśna Upaniṣad
PMS	Pūrva-Mīmāṁsā-sūtras
Rg.V.	Ṛg-Veda
SB	Srīmad-bhāgavata
Sat. Br.	Śatapatha Brāhmaṇa
S. com.	Śaṅkara's commentary
SD	Sāṁkhya-darśana
SDS	Sarva-darśana-saṁgraha
SK	Sāṁkhya-kārikā
SLS	Siddhānta-leśa-saṁgraha
SS	Saṁkṣepa-śārīraka
SV	Ślōka-vārttika
Sv. U.	Śvetāśvatara Upaniṣad
Tai. Ar.	Taittirīya Āraṇyaka
Tai. Br.	Taittirīya Brāhmaṇa
Tai. U.	Taittirīya Upaniṣad
Trans.	Translation
TS	Tarka-saṁgraha
US	Upadeśa-sāhasrī
VC	Viveka-cūḍāmaṇi
VP	Vedānta-paribhāṣā
VPS	Vivaraṇa-prameya-saṁgraha
VS	Vedānta-sāra
VV	Vākya-vṛtti
VVP	Vani Vilas Press, Sri Rangam, Madras
YS	Yōga-sūtras of Patañjali

SYNOPSES OF CHAPTERS

PART ONE

Perception, Three Means of Non-perceptual Knowledge, and the Way of Apprehending Non-existence

page

I. PERCEPTION; ITS SCOPE AND MEANS

1. The six methods of valid knowledge according to Advaita Vedānta 35
2. These methods are recognized by other Vedic schools in one form or another. A majority of them is admitted by a modern thinker 38
3. Internal perception is as valid as external 40
4. Is external perception possible without sense-object contact? 42
5. In the Vedāntic view mind cannot contact physical objects but through the sense-organs; the bodily organs are the outer stations of the real organs of sense, which are internal and subtle like mind and operate in what is called 'extra-sensory perception' 44
6. The luminous self, the knower within, causes the mind and the organs to move towards the objects. Reasons for distinguishing the mind 46
7. The sense-organs and the objects of perception 48
8. The sense-organs are composed of the same subtle and pure substance as the mind 50
9. The way the mind leads the organs 51
10. How the sense-organs come in contact with their respective objects 53
11. The difficulties the West is confronted with in accounting for sense-perception 55
12. Despite the different modern theories the problem of external perception remains unsolved 56

II. THE METAPHYSICAL BACKGROUND OF THE SENSIBLE UNIVERSE

1. The close relation between epistemology and metaphysics 61
2. The Advaita view of the sensible universe may be defined as metaphysical or absolute Idealism. It is neither objective realism nor subjective idealism 64
3. The Vedāntic position with regard to the world should not be misunderstood as illusionism or as pantheism 67
4. The Idealist's view that physical objects have no existence in themselves but are mere externalizations of mental ideas is not tenable 70
5. The theory of representationism, ancient or modern, is not consistent with the nature of sense-perception 72
6. The view that mind and sense-organs construct the diversified world on the ground of Reality is not admitted by Vedānta 73

page

7. The experiencer, the world of experience, and the all-knowing Īśvara, the Ruler of both, are co-existent. Their sole support is Brahman, the ground of all 75
8. It is Brahman that appears as the jīva (the individual being) 78
9. Consciousness is not a product nor a process 80
10. The fundamental reality underlying every phase of existence is Pure Consciousness 81

III. PERCEPTUAL KNOWLEDGE; ITS DISTINCTIVE CHARACTER AND PROCESS

1. Consciousness is all that is manifest 85
2. The nature of knowledge (jñāna) 88
3. Perceptual and non-perceptual knowledge. Their distinctive marks 90
4. The reason why internal cognition is invariably perceptual 92
5. Perception is wholly presentative. It is not representative. Nor can it be partly presentative and partly representative 94
6. The way the mental mode leads to external perception. Its twofold function 96
7. The cognitive process of external perception 98
8. The knower (pramātā), the object known (prameya), the knowledge (pramiti), and its means (pramāṇa) are the manifestations of the same underlying Consciousness 102
9. The perceptual method of *abhedābhivyakti* and its distinctiveness 104
10. Determinate and indeterminate perception 106
11. Recognition and recollection. The one is a case of perception; the other is not 107

IV. THE VALIDITY OF KNOWLEDGE

1. How is knowledge known? It is self-manifest. It is not known by another knowledge 110
2. The self-validity of knowledge 112
3. Criteria of knowledge 114
4. The Advaitin's test of valid knowledge 116
5. Psychologically, knowledge includes all forms of cognition, valid, non-valid, and invalid 119
6. Two main forms of cognition other than valid—error and doubt 120
7. Other forms of cognition that are not valid. Distinction of dream from memory and illusion 122

V. ILLUSION; ITS NATURE AND CAUSE

1. Illusion (adhyāsa) defined 124
2. The seven different theories of illusion (adhyāsa) 126
3. The distinctive character of the Advaita theory of anirvacanīya-khyāti (apprehension of the indefinable) 127

page

4. The nihilistic theory of asat-khyāti (apprehension of the non-existent) 127
5. The Idealistic theory of ātmakhyāti (apprehension of the subjective cognition) 129
6. The Mīmāṁsā theory of akhyāti (non-apprehension) 130
7. The Nyāya theory of anyathā-khyāti (misapprehension) 130
8. The Sāṁkhya theory of sadasat-khyāti (apprehension of the real-unreal) 131
9. The Viśiṣṭādvaita theory of sat-khyāti (apprehension of the real) 132
10. The Advaita view of the 'indefinability' of the illusory object explained 133
11. The process of illusory appearance 134
12. The objectivity of illusion testifies to its origin from ajñāna veiling the substratum 136
13. Illusion cannot be explained as a distortion of fact by the observer's mind 137
14. Man's egoism is a case of perennial illusion 138

VI. THREE MEANS OF NON-PERCEPTUAL KNOWLEDGE: INFERENCE, COMPARISON, AND POSTULATION

I. *Inference* (anumāna)

1. The core of inference (anumāna) is the knowledge of invariable concomitance (vyāpti) 142
2. The meaning of vyāpti (invariable concomitance). Its two different classifications 143
3. The syllogistic forms in Vedānta and the Western logic 144
4. The difference in the Advaita and the Nyāya syllogism 146
5. The distinctive character of the Indian method of inference. It is a combined deductive-inductive process of reasoning 147
6. How to ascertain the invariable concomitance (vyāpti) 148
7. The Advaitins do not accept the threefold classification of inference by Nyāya school. Why they do not 150
8. Inference as a means to suprasensuous knowledge 152

II. *Comparison* (upamāna)

1. Upamāna explained 153
2. Upamāna is neither a case of perception nor of inference. It is distinct from both 154
3. From the Advaita viewpoint upamāna cannot be regarded as a case of 'immediate inference' 155
4. The use of upamāna for the knowledge of the suprasensible 155

III. *Postulation* (arthāpatti)

1. Arthāpatti (postulation) defined 156
2. The varieties of arthāpatti (postulation) 156

page

3. Postulation is not a case of inference. It is not 'disjunctive reasoning' as the Sāṁkhya school maintains 158
4. The Naiyāyikas' attempt to reduce postulation to the form of inference from agreement in absence (vyatireka-vyāpti) is equally untenable 159
5. The distinction of postulation (arthāpatti) from hypothesis and deduction 160
6. Why God's existence and nature cannot be determined by arthāpatti 161

VII. NON-APPREHENSION: THE WAY OF APPREHENDING NON-EXISTENCE

1. Anupalabdhi (non-apprehension) is the only means to the valid knowledge of non-existence (abhāva) 163
2. Different views on existence and non-existence, which are both facts of cognition 164
3. The view of the Nyāya school that non-existence can be perceived is not tenable 166
4. Nor can non-existence be known by inference, as the Buddhist logicians maintain 167
5. Only *appropriate* non-apprehension causes valid cognition of non-existence 167
6. Four different kinds of non-existence; all cognizable by *appropriate* non-apprehension 168

PART TWO

Verbal Testimony

A Means of Valid Knowledge, Sensuous and Suprasensuous

VIII. VERBAL TESTIMONY, A UNIQUE METHOD OF VALID KNOWLEDGE

1. Śabda-pramāṇa (verbal testimony) defined 173
2. Verbal testimony is different from all other means of valid knowledge 175
3. Verbal knowledge is not a case of memory 177
4. The four conditions of verbal knowledge. Its process is different from that of perception or inference 178
5. The relation between a word and its meaning is natural and not conventional 181
6. Words refer directly to universals and indirectly to particulars 182
7. Primary and implied meanings of words and sentences 184
8. According to most Indian philosophers a word presents its meaning directly and not through sphōṭa (a latent unitary medium of expression), as the Grammarians hold 185
9. The distinctive character of verbal knowledge and its method 187

page

10. Knowledge gained from authority cannot be discounted as mere belief 189
11. Certain facts of everyday life are made known only by means of śabda (verbal testimony) 191
12. Śabda (verbal testimony) can even serve as a means of immediate knowledge (aparōkṣa-jñānam) 191

IX. VERBAL TESTIMONY AS THE MEANS OF SUPRASENSUOUS KNOWLEDGE. THE SPECIALITY OF THE VEDIC TESTIMONY

1. The twofold capacity of verbal testimony. It is the only vehicle of suprasensuous knowledge. It precedes intuitive perception 193
2. The Śruti is the only means to the knowledge of Nondual Brahman 196
3. It is by implication that the Śruti conveys the knowledge of Nondual Brahman that is beyond description 198
4. The identity of the individual self and the Supreme Self pointing to the sole reality of Nirguṇa Brahman is the Supreme Truth revealed by the Vedas 200
5. The knowledge of the identity of the jīva and Brahman is the only direct approach to ultimate Reality 201
6. The mahāvākya signifies a twofold approach to Nondual Brahman, the one is the direct, the other is the indirect 204
7. The universal sympathy and all-comprehensiveness of the Śruti. Its object is to lead men and women at all levels of life to the Highest Goal by providing methods suited to their individual capacities 205
8. Not only Brahman (the Supreme Being), but also dharma (moral ideal) is beyond the scope of normal experience and reason, being rooted in suprasensuous truth 207
9. The Vedic conception of Ṛta, the cosmic moral principle 209
10. Even the law of karma is disclosed by the Śruti. It cannot be determined by perception or inference 210
11. The supremacy of the Vedas is due to the fact that they are the only source of incontrovertible truths, the knowledge of which is the highest and most fruitful 212
12. Being the divine revelation of indisputable truths, the Vedas are intrinsically valid. They do not contradict perception or inference 215
13. From rational theology Medieval Scholasticism turned into dogmatic theology 216
14. The Vedas have no author. They are without beginning and without end. They are not produced, but revealed, by Īśvara in the beginning of each new cycle 216

X. SENSE-PERCEPTION, REASON, AND THE VEDIC TESTIMONY

1. There is no contradiction between the Śruti and sense-perception. The one deals with the suprasensible, the other with the sensible. They are valid in their respective spheres 219

page

2. Nor is there any contradiction between the Śruti and reason. The suprasensible is supra-rational, but not irrational 222

3. The allegiance to the Śruti has not militated against philosophic thought in India 224

4. Why reason independently of the Śruti cannot determine the nature of God. Neither syllogistic inference nor analogical argument is capable. The views of Sāṁkhya, Nyāya, and Vedānta 228

5. The empirical and the transcendental self. The Śruti as a means to the knowledge of the Self 230

6. An individual (the jīva) is, basically, the unchanging witness of all changes—psychical and physical 233

7. The real self (ātman) is the knower whose knowledge is intrinsic. It is its own proof. It needs no proof. The meaning of the Vedic testimony as the source of the knowledge of ātman 236

8. The process of reasoning in Vedānta to prove that the self is the light that never fails 239

9. Neither the ancient nor the modern view of the impermanence of the self is tenable 242

XI. 'THOU ART THAT', THE TRUTH OF TRUTHS

1. The dictum 'Thou art That' is the key to the realization of the ultimate Unity, which is the goal of human knowledge. It signifies the distinctive character of the Vedic monism 246

2. The beatific experience of Absolute Oneness as delineated in the Upaniṣads. Nirvikalpa and savikalpa samādhi. Śaṅkara's account of Nondual Brahman as perceived in samādhi 248

3. The immediate intuition of the all-transcendent Being cannot be characterized as ancient or modern, as Eastern or Western. The transcendental experiences of Plotinus and Śrī Rāmakṛṣṇa 251

4. To the seer who returns from nirvikalpa samādhi, Nondual Brahman shines in and through the manifold 254

5. The triple approach to Nondual Brahman—hearing the Vedic dictum, reasoning on it, and meditation 256

6. The different views of the Vācaspati and the Vivaraṇa school regarding the triple approach. The one holds 'meditation' and the other 'hearing' as the means to the direct knowledge of Brahman 258

7. Though holding different views as to the relative importance of the three methods, both schools recognize the necessity for the practice of all of them 261

8. Only the seeker of Liberation with the fourfold qualification is capable of following the triple approach. Other auxiliary virtues of the seeker 262

9. The imperative need of a competent teacher for the seeker of Liberation 264

10. The way the pupil should approach the teacher. The qualifications of each 266

page

11. The genial, intimate relation between the teacher and the pupil is a natural development of spiritual life 267

12. It is especially through the mahāvākya that the teacher imparts the knowledge of the Self to the pupil 269

13. The meaning of the *mahāvākya* 'Thou art That' 270

14. Being convinced of the true import of the *mahāvākya* through hearing and reasoning, the pupil has to practise intent meditation (nididhyāsana) for Self-realization 273

XII. 'THE KNOWER OF BRAHMAN ATTAINS THE HIGHEST'

1. Meditation on the Self is the direct approach to Brahman. Its culmination is immediate experience. Scriptural study, reasoning, and all other disciplines are subsidiary means 274

2. The way the seeker meditates on Nondual Brahman 277

3. The process of meditation that leads to the realization of Brahman in nirvikalpa samādhi 277

4. Rare individuals 'attain Brahman here' and live as free souls. A knower of Nirguṇa Brahman merges in Brahman at death 280

5. The illumined ones living as free souls demonstrate the truth, 'Thou art That' 283

6. A brilliant example of the attainment of nirvikalpa samādhi in the modern age is set by Śrī Rāmakṛṣṇa. Two eye-witnesses' report on his state of samādhi 284

7. The triple approach to Nirguṇa Brahman is meant for the specially qualified seekers. The difference between jñāna (knowledge) and dhyāna (meditation). Nididhyāsana is a special case of meditation that partakes of both 288

8. Dhyāna or upāsanā (meditation with the help of a symbol), which is distinct from nididhyāsana, is the way for the less qualified aspirants 290

9. The significance and efficacy of the symbol Ōm (aum) 291

10. Practice of meditation with the symbol Ōm 295

11. Gradation of spiritual disciplines to suit different types of individuals with the same ultimate Goal in view 297

12. What becomes of the seekers of Brahman at death? Some reach the Goal immediately, some gradually. But none suffers. No spiritual gain is ever lost 299

13. The Yōgic and the Nondualistic view of self-realization and its methods 301

14. The Vedas are of no use to a knower of Brahman 302

PART ONE

Perception, Three Means of Non-Perceptual Knowledge, and the Way of Apprehending Non-Existence

B

CHAPTER I

PERCEPTION; ITS SCOPE AND MEANS

1. *The six methods of valid knowledge according to Advaita Vedānta*

The Advaita school of Vedānta[1] admits six distinct means of valid knowledge: perception (pratyakṣa), inference (anumāna), verbal testimony (śabda or āgama), comparison (upamāna), postulation (arthāpatti), and non-apprehension (anupalabdhi). Each is called 'pramāṇa', the instrument (karaṇa) of valid knowledge (pramā).[2] By 'instrument (karaṇa)' is meant the special cause which, being operative, produces a specific effect. In visual knowledge, for instance, the organ of vision and the mind both are operative; as such both are its causes; but the organ of vision and its operation constitute the special cause (karaṇa). In audition the organ of hearing being operative produces the knowledge, so this is its special cause (karaṇa). In perceiving an object by a particular sense-organ the mind is not the special cause (karaṇa) of the knowledge, because its operation is common to all cases of external perception. Thus, pramāṇa is the special means by which some kind of right knowledge (pramā) is attained. The implication is that each pramāṇa has a characteristic way of conveying knowledge and presents a distinct type of knowledge; and it is not in the nature of one pramāṇa to contradict another.

Broadly speaking, perception (pratyakṣa)[3] is twofold: external and internal. Perception by any of the five sensory organs (of hearing, sight, touch, taste, and smell) is external. Mental perception (of pain

[1] See Appendix B, sec. 5.

[2] *Vide* VP I.

[3] The Sanskrit term 'pratyakṣa' etymologically means the function of any sense-organ with respect to its object (see Vātsāyana's commentary on *Nyāya-Sūtras* I: 1.3.). It refers to sense-perception as a means of direct or immediate knowledge of an object. In a wide sense, the word signifies any means of direct or immediate knowledge, not merely the process of sensory knowledge. Thus, as a substantive, pratyakṣa denotes a pramāṇa that leads to direct and valid knowledge. As an adjective the term can be applied to knowledge, the means of knowledge, and also the object of knowledge. For instance, 'pratyakṣa jñāna' means direct or immediate cognition, 'pratyakṣa pramāṇa', the method of such knowledge, and 'pratyakṣa viṣaya', the object of this knowledge.

or pleasure, of knowledge or ignorance, of love or hate, and so forth) is internal. Sense-perception is the natural and direct way of knowing external things. It leads to immediate cognition. In common with other living creatures man has the capacity for sensory experience. It is the principal means of his knowledge of the physical world.

Evidently, sense-perception is not the only way to immediate cognition. As stated in *Vedānta-paribhāṣā*: 'The immediacy of knowledge does not rest on its being caused by the sense-organs.'[4] According to Hobhouse, too, immediacy of cognition, and not sense-operation, is the intrinsic characteristic of perceptual knowledge. Says he: 'If we inquire into the common character uniting "ideas" of both kinds [simple ideas of sensation and reflection] we shall find it, not in their dependence on any sense-organ or any special kind of physiological stimulus, but in their immediate presence to consciousness.'[5] As defined by the Prabhākara school of Mīmāṁsā, Perception is immediate cognition (sākṣātpratītih pratyakṣam).'[6] Advaita Vedānta accepts this definition.

Another widely accepted but cultivated method of knowledge is inference (anumāna). Man alone is capable of this. Based on sensible facts, it goes beyond the reach of the senses. It explores the unseen. But whatever knowledge of the sensible universe or the beyond it may bring is invariably mediate. Perception acquaints us with the particulars of a thing (viśeṣāvadhāraṇa-pradhāna), and inference with its general nature (sāmānyāvadhāraṇa-pradhāna).[7]

A third and popular means of knowledge is verbal testimony, that is, authentic words, spoken or written. It adds vastly to our stock of knowledge. In fact, it is the principal medium of formal education. It communicates both sensuous and suprasensuous truths. But anything of this world or of the great beyond we cognize by this means is mediately known. Even the sacred texts, divine revelations though they may be, do not, as a rule, reveal spiritual facts to us. We do not perceive God or Soul only by reading or hearing about them. In the view of the Vivaraṇa school[8] of Advaita Vedānta authentic words can, in special cases, convey to the recipient the direct knowledge of the self, empirical or transcendental. We shall discuss this point in due course.

Of the three methods of knowledge—perception, inference, and verbal testimony, the third one is not as widely recognized as the

4 VP I.

5 L. T. Hobhouse, *The Theory of Knowledge*, p. 15, London, Methuen, 1905.

6 *Prakaraṇa-pañcikā* by Śālikanātha Miśra.

7 *Vide* YS I: 7, Vyāsa's com.

8 See chap. XI, footnote 46.

first two, but its efficacy as a distinct means of knowledge cannot be denied. A man's scope of perception is limited; the knowledge that he can gain from direct experience is inadequate. He must therefore draw from other sources. Verbal testimony (śabda or āgama) supplements perception (pratyakṣa)—external and internal—and inference (anumāna).

Most Indian philosophers recognize these three distinct ways of knowing, but Advaita Vedānta adds to them three more: comparison (upamāna), postulation (arthāpatti), and non-apprehension (anupalabdhi). All these are instrumental to valid knowledge when they are free from defects or deficiencies, for, as stated in *Vedānta-paribhāṣā*, 'the absence of defects is also admitted to be a cause'.[9] The Veda is included in verbal testimony (śabda or āgama) as the infallible authority in suprasensible matters. Verbal testimony has, therefore, two distinct phases: (1) relating to the sensible (laukika) and (2) relating to the suprasensible (vaidika).

As pointed out by Manu,[10] some orthodox thinkers reckon the last three methods of knowledge—comparison, postulation, and non-apprehension—with the method of inference; so they do not mention them separately.[11] But Advaita Vedānta sharply differentiates these three from inference and from one another. While inference (anumāna) is dependent on perception (pratyakṣa), verbal testimony (śabda) relating to the sensible is dependent on perception and inference as well. Perception is therefore the primary source of human knowledge. Every other means of knowledge except the Vedic testimony, which deals with the suprasensible, rests on this some way or other. As defined by Gaṅgeśa Upādhyāya, the founder of Neo-Nyāya school, 'Perceptual cognition is the knowledge to which no other knowledge is instrumental—jñānākaraṇakam jñānam [pratyakṣam]'.[12]

Perception is also defined by the Nyāya school as that knowledge which is caused by the contact of an organ (indriya) with its object and is infallible.[13] But Advaita Vedānta does not accept this definition, which does not include internal perception, unless mind (antaḥkaraṇa) is considered its instrument as an organ (indriya). In the Advaitin's view, as we shall see later, mind is not the instrument of internal perception as an organ (indriya), though the Nyāya school considers it such.

[9] VP VI, Non-apprehension.

[10] A well-known codifier of the Vedic rules of life; author of *Manu-Saṁhitā* (the Code of Manu or Institutes of Manu), an authoritative digest of Hindu laws and creeds.

[11] *Vide* MS XII: 105, Kullūka's com.

[12] *Vide Tattvacintāmaṇi.*

[13] *Vide* BP 52, *Siddhānta-muktāvalī*, and *Nyāya-Sūtras* I: 1.4.

2. *These six methods of knowledge are recognized by other Vedic schools in one form or another. A majority of them is admitted by a modern thinker.*

Indian philosophers differ in their opinion as to the methods of knowledge and their classification. The Cārvākas,[14] like the old materialists of the West, regard sense-perception as the only valid means of knowledge. They admit only four out of the five gross elements (mahābhūtas) that are recognized by other Indian systems. They reject the fifth element, ākāśa (ether, the finest and most pervasive of all material substances), on the ground that its existence cannot be perceived, but has to be inferred. Inference, they contend, is inconclusive, and therefore unreliable; verbal testimony, too, is not a sure means of knowledge, because it needs the support of inference. So they deny both.

The Vaiśeṣika school acknowledges two distinct sources of knowledge: perception and inference. It includes verbal testimony and the rest in inference.[15] The Non-Vedic Buddhists and the Jainas, too, accept only perception and inference. They do, however, depend on verbal testimony for empirical facts.

The Sāṁkhya and Yōga systems accept three pramāṇas: perception, inference, and authentic word (āpta-vacanam). According to Vācaspati, these three include all other pramāṇas.[16] By 'authentic word (āpta-vacanam)' they mean particularly the Vedic testimony, which conveys the knowledge of facts beyond the range of perception and inference, and, hence, constitutes an independent means of knowledge. The testimony of competent persons depends on perception and inference and is not, therefore, regarded as a separate pramāṇa.

The Naiyāyikas in general consider comparison (upamāna) as a separate source of knowledge. So they recognize four ways of knowing: perception, inference, comparison, and testimony.[17] They treat postulation (arthāpatti) as a form of inference.[18] Non-apprehension (anupalabdhi) is explained as a case of perception. The Nyāya school makes a keen investigation of the method of inference, and emphasizes its importance. The validity of every kind of knowledge has to be ascertained, according to this school, by inference.

The Prabhākara school of Pūrva-Mīmāṁsā (usually called

[14] The materialists of ancient India. Their view is called 'lōkāyatamata (common people's view)'.

[15] See *Vaiśeṣika-Sūtras* IX: 2.3 and Praśastapāda's com.

[16] *Vide* SK 4, 5 and com. *Tattvakaumudī*.

[17] *Vide* BP 52 and *Siddhānta-muktāvalī*. There is a class of the Naiyāyikas (the Ekadeśīs) who exclude comparison and acknowledge only three, perception, inference, and testimony.

[18] *Vide* BP 144.

Mīmāṁsā)[19] accepts five out of the six sources of knowledge. It does not treat non-apprehension (anupalabdhi) as a separate pramāṇa. But the Kumārila school of Mīmāṁsā acknowledges all six.

Thus, these six sources of knowledge (pramāṇas) are in one form or another recognized by other Vedic schools even when some are treated separately. Those which may appear to be excluded by a particular school are usually classified with one or another of those that are admitted by it. For example, the Nyāya school acknowledges comparison (upamāna) as a separate source of knowledge, while Vaiśeṣika and Sāṁkhya treat it as a form of inference.[20] The Buddhists consider comparison (upamāna) as a case of perception, the Jainas as a case of recognition (pratyabhijñā). Thus, Advaita Vedānta differs from other Vedic schools not in recognizing six modes of knowing but in the way it classifies and considers them.

On the same ground it can be held that most of these six sources of knowledge are in a way recognized by Western philosophers. A close examination of the six ways of knowing treated by Montague bears out this point. He has dealt with the following six: testimony, intuition, reason, sense-perception, practice, and doubt. One can see that the first four include five of the six Vedāntic sources of knowledge, such as perception, inference, verbal testimony, comparison, and postulation. Anupalabdhi (non-apprehension) has not been considered by Montague as a source of knowledge, while he has taken into account practice and doubt. As we shall see later, some Indian philosophers consider practical value as a *test* of knowledge; but it does not constitute knowledge. Doubt, in their view, does not convey knowledge; it is indecisive and, therefore, as cognition non-valid. It may, however, serve as an incentive to knowledge. Montague's concluding remarks on 'the six methods of logic' are pertinent:

'Treating logic, not in the restricted sense of a science consisting of rules for getting valid conclusions by deduction and induction from premises already accepted, but in the broader sense of a philosophical inquiry as to the sources of human belief and the consequent criteria for determining its truth, we outlined six distinct attitudes or theories which have been held with regard to the problem. These theories which we named authoritarianism, mysticism, rationalism, empiricism, pragmatism, and scepticism, were each of them based upon an attempt to extend a definitely given source of knowledge into a controlling method for the determination of truth. These definitely given sources from which the methods severally take their origin are ***testimony***, ***intuition***, ***reason***, ***sense-perception***, ***practice***, and

[19] For the two schools of Mīmāṁsā see chap. VI, footnote 1.

[20] Nyāya's interpretation of comparison (upamāna), however, differs from that of Mīmāṁsā and Advaita Vedānta.

doubt . . . we have endeavored to show, I. that, in spite of the divergencies of the various logical theories, they are nevertheless capable, with certain modifications, of being combined with one another in various fields of inquiry; and II. that the true solution of the methodological problem of logic consists in the federation of all six methods in a harmonious synthesis, in which each of the positive methods is assigned a pre-eminent, though not exclusive, role in a given domain of the objects of actual and possible philosophical inquiry.'[21]

3. *Internal perception is as valid as external*

A person concurrently observes two distinct orders of facts. On the one hand, he perceives external things and events, and, on the other, internal states and functions, such as pain and pleasure, love and hate, knowledge and ignorance, concentration and distraction, memory and loss of memory, and so on. It is true that external objects are observable by all, whereas the internal occurrences are subjective and private. Yet it cannot be denied that both are facts of normal experience. Just as sensible things are real, so are mental modes. Truly speaking, inner feelings, desires, cognitions, memories, imaginations, ideas, etc., dominate an individual's life even more than outer objects. Internal experience is no less valid than the external. Both have to be recognized as criteria of reality.

Perception is considered 'external' or 'internal' according as the object of cognition is external or internal. External objects are those that can be perceived by the sense-organs. In this sense respiratory and other organs within the body, including their functions, are external. A brain-surgeon can watch with his eyes a patient's cerebral movements, but not his mental operations. The former are, therefore, external, while the latter are internal. None of the sense-organs can perceive one's own mind or that of another. What is psychical and not perceptible to the senses can, thus, be distinguished from the physical objects and their properties as internal.

Philosophers and psychologists in general, with the exception of the radical Empiricists and Behaviourists, accept both these types of experience. 'Consciousness is the perception of what passes in a man's own mind', says John Locke.[22] Leibniz distinguishes between perception and apperception. As observed by a modern thinker, 'A percept is the result of the mind's direct mode of apprehending real things as distinct individuals. Hence a percept always refers to "this"

[21] William Pepperell Montague, *The Ways of Knowing*, Allen and Unwin, London, 1925, pp. 233–4.

[22] *An Essay Concerning Human Understanding*. Collated by Alexander C. Fraser, Vol. I, Book II, chap. 1, sec. 19. Oxford, The Clarendon Press, 1894.

or "that", some distinct individual thing having its own place in space or in time. Thus, I perceive, or have percepts of the objects in this room and of the tree which I see through the window. Similarly, one may perceive the particular states of consciousness in one's mind.'[23] According to Eddington, 'Mind is the first and most direct thing in our experience; all else is remote inference'.[24]

Most thinkers recognize that introspection is the direct approach to mental states, while the study of behaviour is an indirect method. An individual can observe his mental condition directly from inside, while others can know it indirectly through its physical expression. Indeed, the proof of such mental traits as joy, love, guiltiness, and so forth, is inner experience and not the outer behaviour, which may even belie the internal state. With no joy within one may appear to be joyous, with no love within one may appear to be loving, with the sense of guilt within one may appear to be innocent.

Internal perception is again twofold: (1) relative to the perceiving self and (2) relative to the states of the mind. In experiencing happiness, which is a state of the mind, a person is aware of himself as its experiencer, as is evident from such expressions as, 'I feel happy', 'I am happy'. But he ascribes to himself the mental state, although he is distinct from it as its experiencer. Every individual is more or less aware of himself as a doer and as an experiencer. But in his self-recognition no subject-object relation is involved. The self shines of itself and is not objectified. But like the vision of light obscured by mist a man's self-awareness is ordinarily hazy and faulty due to ignorance. Though a knower of the body, the organs, and the mind, he gets identified with the known, and realizes himself as a physical or a psychophysical being subject to growth and decay, hunger and thirst, weakness and strength, pain and pleasure. This means that he is aware of the empirical self, the ego, but not of the changeless luminous self ever distinct from the psychophysical adjunct as its witness.

It is the Upaniṣadic texts that convey the definite knowledge of the witness-self beyond the ego and its identity with the all-pervading Supreme Self. The realization of this identity leads to the immediate apprehension of the self as nondual, non-relational Consciousness that Brahman is. This is the culmination or the end of knowledge and not its means. So the intuitive perception of the self as Brahman beyond all distinction (aparōkṣa-Brahmānubhūti) is not counted in Vedānta as a pramāṇa.

In the Advaitin's view the mental states of pain, pleasure, fear,

[23] James Edwin Creighton, *An Introductory Logic*, New York, Macmillan, 1937, pp. 54, 55.

[24] Sir Arthur Stanley Eddington, *Science and the Unseen World*, London, Allen and Unwin, 1949, p. 24.

hope, love, hate, uncertainty, determination and so forth, are illuminated directly by the witness-self without any intermediary. So they are said to be 'manifested by the witness-self alone (kevala-sākṣi-bhāsya)', that is, unaided by any agency. The meaning is that in internal perception the mind and the sense-organs do not serve as instruments of knowledge as in the perception of the external objects; nor is any mental operation in the form of inference involved in it.[25] The mental states become known as soon as they arise. According to the sage Patañjali, the modifications of mind are invariably known because their master, the witness-self (puruṣa), is changeless.[26] Shining with constant effulgence the self is ever-present and illumines all external and internal objects of knowledge. The knower per se is self-manifest and is more than known, without being an object of knowledge. Thus, perceptual knowledge has three distinct phases: (1) regarding the physical objects, (2) regarding the mental states, and (3) regarding the knowing self.

4. *Is external perception possible without sense-object contact?*

Obviously, the sense-organs lead to perception when they are connected with their respective objects. The fact that we gain the direct knowledge of the physical things through their contact with the sense-organs is acknowledged by all. But although appropriate sense-object contact is admittedly the sure means to such knowledge, it is not viewed as the sole means by all schools of thought, ancient and modern. Some Western psychologists uphold 'extra-sensory perception', that is, perception by other means than the usual sense-object contact.[27] They have established their theories by experiments carried on in the psychological laboratory. These are also corroborated by the events of life.[28] In the words of J. B. Rhine:

'Clairvoyant perception is the awareness of objects or objective events without the use of the senses, whereas telepathy is the

[25] See VP I. According to the Nyāya school mind functions as the instrument of internal perception (antarindriya); so it is called 'the eleventh organ (indriya)'. But most Advaitins do not recognize it as an organ of internal perception, and refuse to call it 'indriya'. That the mind is the inner instrument (antaḥkarṇa) of external perception, of internal functions (such as cogitation, volition, determination), and of all mediate knowledge is recognized by all the six Vedic schools.

[26] YS IV: 18.

[27] The expression 'extra-sensory perception' includes telepathy and precognition other than clairvoyance.

[28] *Vide* J. B. Rhine, *New Frontiers of the Mind*, New York, Farrar Rhinehart, 1937; *Extra-sensory Perception after Sixty years* (in collaboration with others), New York, Henry Holt, 1940; also Swāmī Akhilānanda's *Hindu Psychology: Its Meaning for the West*, New York, Harper, 1946.

awareness of the thoughts of another person, similarly without sensory aid. The term "clairvoyance", although it literally means "clear seeing", in reality has nothing to do with vision. Clairvoyant impressions may be in the form of visual imagery, but they may also be of other types as well. Any direct apprehension of external objects is clairvoyance if the senses are not involved.'[29]

Most Indian schools of thought, including Non-Vedic Jainism, admit such extraordinary ways of perceiving things. Patañjali, the great exponent of the Yōga system, mentions that by a particular method of meditation on the effulgent light in the heart a person can gain knowledge of things that are very subtle, hidden, and remote.[30] According to the Sāṁkhya school the mind of the yōgī can come in contact with distant and hidden objects by virtue of a special power acquired by meditation. Evidently, the supernormal perception of the yōgī is effected by the mind unaided by the sense-organs.[31] To quote Swāmī Vivekānanda: 'All these extraordinary powers are in the mind of man. The individual mind is a part of the universal mind. Each mind is connected with every other mind. And each mind, wherever it is located, is in actual communication with the whole world.'[32] Of all the instruments of knowledge the mind is the supreme. The organs depend on the mind for cognition. From ancient times in most countries there have been seers reputed for the intuitive vision of the past, the present, and the future.

While maintaining sense-perception as the valid source of knowledge in the physical plane, Vedānta recognizes yōgic insight. It is said that Sañjaya, who related the entire message of the Bhagavad-gītā to the blind King Dhṛtarāṣṭra at Hastināpur, heard the dialogue between Śrī Kṛṣṇa and Arjuna directly, without being present in the battlefield of Kurukṣetra. He himself declares that he had been granted by the sage Vyāsa the supernal vision (divya-cakṣu) to see and hear from a long distance what happened there.[33] Vedānta also affirms the theistic view that Īśvara, though possessed of no sense-organ, has the direct knowledge of all things. 'Without eyes He sees. Without ears He hears.'[34]

The fact that mind is not a passive receptable of knowledge dependent on the sense-organs is being more and more recognized in modern times by, individual scientists, philosophers, and psychologists. As a result of their investigation into extra-sensory experi-

[29] J. B. Rhine, *The Reach of the Mind*, New York, William Sloane Associates, 1947, pp. 8–9.

[30] YS III: 25.

[31] SD I: 89–91, Vijñāna Bhikṣu's com.

[32] CW II, pp. 12, 13.

[33] *Vide* BG XVIII: 75, S. com.

[34] Sv. U. III: 19.

ences Professor J. B. Rhine and his co-workers have come to the conclusion that the mind is other than the physical body and has ways of its own and is not controlled by mechanical laws. As we have noted, Professor Rhine recognizes the special capacity of the mind to move out of the body and contact physical objects unaided by the sense-organs.[34a].

Many are the evidences that corroborate the view that mind can cognize external objects without sense-activity. An eye-witness reports that with the eyes closed a person could see what was in another room without having been there. Now the questions arise: Does mind actually perceive things and their properties in cases of clairvoyance? Does it see colour, hear sound, smell odour, taste flavour, tangibly feel heat and cold, when there is no evidence of sense-object contact? What distinguishes the perception of the physical objects from their mediate knowledge such as gained by inference or verbal testimony? That mind can imagine, recollect, infer, and dream of external objects and their qualities nobody can deny. But none of these mental operations can be regarded as a case of perception; because in none of them mind has actual contact with the outside world. And each of them is due to previous sensory experience. For instance, a person who has eaten cake before can know on seeing a cake that it is sweet without tasting it. Here the sight of the cake is perceptual knowledge, but the cognition of its sweetness is a case of inference based on memory. Unless mind can come in contact with the physical objects without the operation of the sense-organs there cannot be 'extra-sensory perception'. The point is that in perceptual knowledge the object of cognition must be presented to the cognizing agency.

5. *In the Vedāntic view mind cannot contact physical objects but through the sense-organs; the bodily organs are the outer stations of the real organs of sense, which are internal and subtle like mind and operate in what is called 'extra-sensory perception'*

According to Vedānta, clairvoyance is a case of perception, but it is not really 'extra-sensory'. It can be called 'extra-sensory' only in view of the fact that the outer organs of sense evidently take no part in it. It is to be noted that the Vedāntic conception of the sense-organs is different from the popular notion of them. The outer organs, such as the eyes, the ears, the nose, and the rest, located in the physical body and usually known as the sense-organs, are not the actual organs of sight, hearing, smell, etc. The real sense-organs (indriyas) are their subtle counterparts that belong to the subtle body, of which mind (antaḥkaraṇa) is the main component factor.

[34a] *Vide* J. B. Rhine, *New Frontiers of the Mind*, pp. 5, 6.

They are composed of the same type of subtle substance as mind is, and can expand and contract as freely as mind. In Vedānta the term 'indriya' strictly refers to them. The physical organs or the end-organs are their outer stations. Specifically, the five sense-organs are called 'buddhīndriyas' or 'jñānendriyas' (organs of perception) as distinct from the five motor-organs, which are called 'karmendriyas' (organs of action). The real organs of action, too, belong to the subtle body.[35] We shall use the expression 'sense-organ' for Vedāntic 'buddhi-indriya' (organ of perception), which includes the bodily organ or the end-organ as its apparatus in normal external perception.

In any external perception, normal or supernormal, mind is attended with one or more of the sense-organs according to the nature of the case. In all normal cases of external perception the bodily organs serve as vehicles or channels of the sense-organs and the mind. In extraordinary cases, such as clairvoyance, the sense-organs and the mind operate independently of the bodily organs. It is invariably through the sense-organs that mind comes in contact with the external world. In telepathy one mind communicates with another. Sense-organ is not indispensable to this. But the case of clairvoyance is different. Here mind has to contact the diversified physical order.[36] Sense-organs must be there to bring about the connection. All our contact with the external world is through the senses. As noted by Vidyāraṇya, mind cannot deal with the external objects unaided by the organs (indriyas).[37] Commenting on the Yōga aphorism relating to the extraordinary 'knowledge of things that are very subtle, hidden, and remote', which we have already referred to, Bhōjadeva remarks that this becomes possible through the development of superb power of mind (antaḥkaraṇa) as well as the sense-organs (indriyas).[38] Thus, according to Bhōjadeva, the sense-organs function in the extraordinary cases of external perception. Therefore, such cases are not actually extra-sensory, even though the bodily organs play no observable part in them. In this essay we are primarily

[35] It is to be noted that the conception of sense-organs differs among Indian philosophers. As held by Vedānta, the subtle body consists of five organs of perception, five organs of action, five vital forces (prāṇa), and mind (antaḥkaraṇa).

[36] Cf. J. B. Rhine, *The Reach of the Mind*, p. 32, 'Thought transference was more easily thought of as a step beyond physics. Its mind-to-mind relation seemed to transcend the mechanical principles which sensory communication involved. Clairvoyance, on the other hand, definitely involved interaction with matter. Some inter-operation of the mind with the object perceived had to be supposed to make phenomenon intelligible. Clairvoyance was more like an additional sense rather than a wholly non-sensory function, which telepathy appeared to be.'

[37] *Vide* PD II: 12.

[38] *Vide* YS III: 25, *Rāja-mārtaṇḍa*.

concerned with the normal way of knowing physical objects. We have dwelt on the extraordinary cases, which are unusual, in order to explain the normal process.

6. *The luminous self, the knower within, causes the mind and the organs to move towards the objects. Reasons for distinguishing the mind*

In any external perception four distinct factors are involved: the object, the cognate sense-organ, the mind (antaḥkaraṇa), and the knowing self. In the absence of any of these no perception is possible. Of these four the self alone is intrinsically luminous, being of the nature of consciousness; the rest are devoid of consciousness. It is the light of the self that manifests the object. So the self must be connected or related with the object. The mind conjoined with the sense-organ brings about this relation. The self is the perceiver, the knower *per se*. As such, it is distinct from the mind, which is knowable. Just as a person cognizes external things, so does he cognize his mental states. The cognizing self must be other than the cognizable. There is an essential difference between the cognizer and the cognizable. Consciousness is intrinsic in the cognizer, but not in the object cognized. The two are of contrary nature, like light and darkness. So the cognizer cannot be an object of cognition, nor can an object of cognition be the cognizer. As affirmed by Śaṅkara, 'The cognizer is invariably the cognizer; the cognizable is invariably the cognizable.'[39] Being cognizable, the mind can by no means be the cognizer, the knowing self.

In Western thought a clear-cut distinction between the mind and the knowing self is hardly noticeable; generally, mind is viewed as characterized by consciousness. But it is the consensus of Hindu philosophers that the self (ātman) and the mind (antahkaraṇa) are altogether different. Mind is an internal instrument of the knowing self; there is no consciousness inherent in it. The reason why mind cannot be the self (atman) is thus indicated by Patañjali: 'It [mind] is not self-luminous, because it is observable.'[40] Nor can mind be partly the knower and partly the known, that is, the subject and the object both, which are fundamentally different. Such a view has, however, been held by some ancient and modern psychologists. But this is not tenable. It is the luminous self that directs the mind and the organs to their respective functions. Being devoid of the light of consciousness they cannot move of themselves. The mover must be other than the moved. So the self is to be distinguished from all its limiting adjuncts, which are inert by nature. As declared by the Upaniṣad: 'The Ear of the ear, the Mind of the mind, the Speech of speech, the Life of life, and the Eye of the eye, is the Self. So a wise

[39] *Vide* BG XIII: 2, com.

[40] YS IV: 19.

man withdrawing from these [getting out of self-identification with mind, organs, etc.—the limiting adjuncts] and giving up all attachment becomes immortal.'[41]

That there is a mind distinct from the organs and the body one can know from actual experience in more ways than one. Without the use of any of the ten organs a person can inwardly think, feel, will, imagine, remember, rejoice, regret, and so forth. Thus, he knows that he has an inner instrument for these functions and this is called mind (antaḥkaraṇa). With closed eyes one can know whether one has joy or sorrow, love or hate, hope or fear, and so on. This inner experience must be due to mind. What is pleasing to the senses is often considered harmful by the mind. By losing any of the organs, such as the organ of vision, or the organ of hearing, or the organ of speech, a person does not lose his mind. So the mind must be different from the organs. In spite of physical suffering one can have a peaceful mind, and in spite of physical comforts one can have an uneasy mind; this shows that the mind is other than the body. Moreover, a person invariably distinguishes mental pain from physical pain. Frustration, depression, anxiety, and the like are mental ailments, while headache, stomach-ache, heart trouble, etc., are physical ailments. From the one a person seeks relief through psychiatry, from the other through medical treatment. If the body be out-of-order, the mind can take care of the body; but if the mind be out-of-order, the body cannot take care of the mind.

Yet many have doubts regarding the existence and the nature of the mind. So the Upaniṣad gives arguments to convince them: '[They say], "I was absent-minded, I did not see it", "I was absent-minded, I did not hear it". Obviously, through the mind one sees, through the mind one hears. Desire, deliberation, doubt, faith, want of faith, patience, impatience, shame, intelligence, and fear—all these are but [different modes of] the mind. Even if one is touched from behind, one knows it through the mind; therefore (the mind exists).'[42]

On the above text Śaṅkara remarks: 'Truly, there is a mind apart from the external organs such as the ear. Because it is a well-known fact that even when there is a connection between the external organ, the object, and the self, a person does not perceive the object present before him, and when asked, "Have you seen this form?" he says, "My mind was elsewhere—I was absent-minded, I did not see it." Similarly, when asked, "Have you heard what I have said?" a person says, "I was absent-minded, I could not hear, I have not heard it". Therefore, it is found that something else—the internal organ called mind, which joins with the objects of all the organs—exists, in the absence of which the eye and other organs, when con-

[41] Ken. U. I: 2. [42] Br. U. I: 5.3; S. com.

nected with their respective objects such as form and sound, fail to perceive them, although they have the capacity to do so, and in the presence of which they succeed. . . . After the existence of the mind has been proved, the text proceeds to describe its nature. . . . Another reason for the existence of the mind is being stated. Because even if one is touched by somebody from behind invisibly, one knows it distinctly, that this is a touch of the hand, or that this is a touch of the knee, therefore, the internal organ called mind exists. If there is no mind to distinguish, how can the skin alone do this? That which helps us to distinguish between perceptions is the mind.'

As pointed out by Vidyāraṇya, in perception it is the mind that judges merits and demerits of things and not the sense-organs.[43] Moreover, willing, feeling, deliberation, determination, memory, imagination all belong to mind. The sense-organ can deal with an object existing at the present time, but mind can deal with things belonging to the past, the present, and the future as well.

7. *The sense-organs and the objects of perception*

An individual has five organs of perception: the organ of hearing, the organ of sight, the organ of touch, the organ of taste, and the organ of smell.[44] Sensory experience is, accordingly, of five different types: auditory, visual, tactual, gustatory, and olfactory. Each organ has a particular location except the organ of touch which extends all over the body. Fundamentally, there are five objects of perception: sound, touch, sight (form and colour), taste, and smell. We perceive them as attributes of things or substances and as identified with them.[45] Size and shape belong to form. Weight of a thing is not

[43] *Vide* PD II: 13.

[44] These are the five sense-organs, buddhīndriyas or jñānendriyas (the organs of perception). Similarly, there are five motor-organs, karmendriyas (the organs of action), e.g., the organ of speech, the organ of grasping or giving, the organ of movement, the organ of evacuation, and the organ of generation. 'Indriya' is the general name of these organs. The term is also extended to mind, which is considered 'antarindriya' (the internal organ) by Hindu philosophers except some Advaitins, particularly, the authors of *Pañcapādikā-vivaraṇa* and *Vedānta-paribhāṣā*, who do not regard mind as an 'indriya (organ)'. The term 'antahkaraṇa' for mind is accepted by all. Among the Advaitins Vidyāraṇya refers to mind as an 'indriya'. (PD II: 18).

[45] According to all schools of Vedānta, attribute and substance are non-different. The relation between the two is the relation of identity (tādāmya-sambandha). So is the relation between universal and particular, between action and substance. The two are distinguishable in thought, but inseparable in fact. But Nyāya-Vaiśeṣika maintains a different relation between the two, called the relation of inherence (samavāya-sambandha). It is conceived as a category independent of the terms related (e.g., attribute and substance). Vedānta rejects the relation of inherence, since it involves *regressus ad infinitum* (*vide* BS II: 2.13, S. com.).

perceived, but inferred from the resistance it offers in lifting it; and so its movement is not perceived but inferred from the change of its position in relation to another thing. Time and space are perceived with the perception of the object, since everything is perceived as existing 'now' and as located 'here' or 'there'. In perceiving a particular object we perceive its individual characteristics and its generic attributes as well. While perceiving an individual cow, we also perceive cowness, that is, the essential characteristics common to all cows. In perceiving any fire, we perceive fireness as well. Its action, such as burning, too, is perceived. The relative position of things is also perceivable.[46]

It may be noted in this context that what is naturally incapable of being perceived by any of the sense-organs is not sensible. For example, the five subtle elements, the organs themselves, the mind, undifferentiated prakṛti, the self, are not perceivable by the sense-organs. The mental modifications are internally perceived, but not the mind as it is. The latent tendencies or the dormant impressions of past actions and experiences in the forms of merit (dharma) or demerit (adharma) that lie buried in the subsoil of the mind or in the causal body (ajñāna) are not perceivable. But no sooner do they arise in the mind as good or evil propensities or as virtues and vices than they become manifest to the witness-self.

As pointed out by Vidyāraṇya, the real organs—the instruments of perception and action termed 'indriyas'—are not the visible physical organs, such as the eye-ball, the ear-drum, etc., as the Buddhists hold, nor their special capacities, as held by the Mīmāṁsakas, but subtle material substances possessed of distinctive powers and dwelling in the physical organs.[47] The actual organs (indriyas) are imperceptible. We perceive or act through them, but we never perceive them. Their existence, however, is inferable. It is worthy of note that none of the ten organs operates on itself. Though members of the subtle body, the indriyas function through the corresponding physical organs including the brain centres. They are very fine and limited in size, but capable of quick expansion and contraction. An indriya does not function when its physiological apparatus is out of order.

Other Indian thinkers, however, do not subscribe to the Vedāntic view of the sense-organs. The Buddhists generally identify the sense-

[46] Cf. D. M. Datta, *The Six Ways of Knowing*, London, Allen and Unwin, 1932, pp. 117, 118. 'According to the Vedāntins a substance is perceived, and along with it and as inseparably identified with it are perceived universals (i.e. common attributes), relations (of the saṁyōga [conjunction] type), similarity (as possessed by the perceived object), and many other attributes of the substance which are ordinarily thought to be perceptible by other philosophers.

[47] *Vide* VPS Pt. III, p. 221, Ed. by Paṇḍit Pramathanātha Tarkabhūṣaṇa, Calcutta, Vasumatī Press, 1928.

organs with the physical organs, such as the globe of the eye, the globe of the ear, etc. Evidently, they represent the popular view. The Mīmāṁsakas maintain that the distinctive capacities of the bodily organs are the actual organs. Vedānta adduces reasons for not holding either of these views. There are instances of external perception without the usual sense-object contact. A hypnotized subject perceives things without the use of the external organs concerned. No physical ear is discernible in the serpents, yet they hear. The trees are said to have the power of perception, though no sense-organ is noticeable in them. Moreover, the differentiation of the organs from their physical apparatus or vehicles accounts for what is called 'extra-sensory perception', as we have explained above. Since the organs belong to the subtle body, a person does not lose them at death, which means the loss of the physical body. He is reborn with them. This is why some have such inborn capacities as taste for music, talent for painting, aptitude for dancing, and a gifted voice. Hereditary transmission or environment is not an adequate explanation of this fact. Geniuses are born of mediocre parents. Chill penury can hardly repress natural abilities. They shine under adverse conditions.

8. *The sense-organs are composed of the same subtle and pure substances as the mind*

Each sense-organ is produced by that very subtle element whose distinctive property it has the power to reveal. For instance, the organ of hearing is composed of the sattva aspect of subtle ākāśa (ether), whose specific property 'sound' is manifested by it. Similarly, the organ of touch is composed of the sattva aspect of subtle vāyu (air), whose specific property 'touch' is manifested by it; the organ of sight is composed of the sattva aspect of subtle tejas (light or fire), whose specific property 'colour' is manifested by it; the organ of taste is composed of the sattva aspect of subtle ap (water), whose specific property 'taste' is manifested by it; the organ of smell is composed of the sattva aspect of subtle kṣiti (earth), whose specific property 'smell' is manifested by it.[48]

[48] *Vide* Br. U. II: 4.11, S. com.; *Ātmānātma-viveka* 78–82. From the viewpoint of sense-perception the whole physical universe consists basically of five kinds of material substance: (1) audible, (2) tangible, (3) visible, (4) tastable, and (5) smellable. They have the following five forms: (1) etheric, (2) aerial, (3) fiery, (4) liquid, and (5) solid.

They are signified by the terms ākāśa (ether), vāyu (air), tejas (fire or light), ap (water) and pṛthivī (earth). These five gross elements (sthūla bhūtas) are all the ingredients of the sensible world. Ākāśa is the finest and pṛthivī the grossest of them all.

The sattva aspect of all the five subtle elements being combined produces mind (antaḥkaraṇa), which is therefore material and has constituent parts.[49] While sattva is predominant in it, rajas and tamas are overpowered. Basically constituted of the finest and purest essence of matter, mind (antaḥkaraṇa) has the special capacity to expand and contract and take the form of any object of knowledge, howsoever large or small, gross or fine, it may be. It can move instantaneously, so to speak. Though seated in the heart it pervades the whole body in the waking state. In dream state it recedes more or less to the subtle body. In deep sleep it is withdrawn to the causal body.

9. *The way the mind leads the organs*

According to the Nyāya school mind is infinitesimal (aṇu), partless (niravayava), and eternal (nitya). Since it is infinitesimal and partless, it cannot be connected with more than one organ at a time. So, in Nyāya view, an individual does not perceive more than one thing even when all the five sense-organs are connected with their respective objects; in such a case his mind may move so fast from one sense-organ to another that it will appear to him that he perceives by them simultaneously.

But according to Vedānta mind is finite, that is, of medium magnitude (madhyama parimāṇa). So it can be connected with one

The five gross elements are compounded of corresponding five subtle elements (sūkṣma bhūtas), which are rudimentary and imperceptible. While each gross element is a compound of all the five subtle elements, each subtle element is simple, that is, unmixed with any other subtle element. For instance, gross ākāśa consists of half subtle ākāśa and one-eighth of each of the four remaining subtle elements, but subtle ākāśa is pure and simple ākāśa. So the subtle element is also called 'tanmātrā' (lit. that alone). Each is composed of sattva, rajas, and tamas, which are the primal constituents of prakṛti, the origin of the entire objective universe, physical and psychical.

Sattva is the principle of serenity, conducive to purity, knowledge, and joy. Rajas is the principle of motivity leading to activity, desire, and restlessness or pain. Tamas is the principle of inertia resulting in inaction, dullness, and delusion. They are inseparable and form a triad, in which each has a tendency to overpower the two others. It is the preponderance of one or another of the three guṇas over two others in varying degrees that brings forth all varieties of objects in the universe.

[49] Similarly, the rajas aspect of the five subtle elements, being combined, generate prāṇa, the life-principle with its five main functions (biological processes). The rajas aspect of the five subtle elements severally produces the five organs of action in succession. Thus, the rajas aspect of ākāśa (ether) produces the organ of speech, of vāyu (air) the hands, the tejas (fire or light) the feet, and so on. Because of the prevalence of rajas, the five prāṇas and the five organs of action have motive force. The five subtle elements with tamas preponderant in each, being compounded by the process of quintuplication (pañcīkaraṇa) produce the five gross elements.

or more organs at the same time. Therefore a person can perceive different objects one after another or simultaneously. For instance, a student can listen to his teacher's words and see his face at the same time. Otherwise, he will miss his words while seeing him. Similarly, the five organs of action can operate one after another or simultaneously. Indeed, both types of organs can function together. For instance, an actor sees, speaks, and acts at the same time.

As held by the Sāṁkhya school mind is all-pervading (vibhu); but Vedānta distinguishes the individual mind from the cosmic mind, which belongs to Brahmā, the World-soul, who presides over the cosmos. According to both Sāṁkhya and Vedānta mind is a product and, therefore, not eternal.

Being composed of the subtlest and most transparent substance and closest to the self, mind (antaḥkaraṇa) receives the light of consciousness that belongs to the self and is illuminated by it. With no light of its own it appears luminous. It seems to cognize, though it is not a cognizer but only an instrument of cognition. A crystal looks bright because of the light it absorbs, an iron ball glows with fire that permeates it; similarly, mind shines with borrowed light of consciousness. Thus, it proves to be the most effective instrument of knowledge. From the grossest physical object to Brahman, the supreme Being, whatever a person knows he knows through the mind. There cannot be any knowledge unless there is a modification of mind corresponding to the object. Knowledge is but the manifestation of consciousness through an appropriate mental mode.

Mind is connected with the organs by means of the central nervous system, of which brain is a part. It is through the mind that the light of consciousness is transmitted to the sense-organs, which being made of sattva substance have the special power to receive the light. Thus they serve as the organs of *perception*. The light of consciousness radiating from the mind enables the motor-organs to function. All external perceptions, all actions, are due to the radiance of consciousness received by the organs from the luminous self (ātman) through the mind. In dream state when the radiance recedes from the body none of the ten organs can function, but the mind continues to operate. In deep sleep when the radiance recedes, even from the mind, all mental operations including egoism comes to a dead stop. Says Vidyāraṇya: 'Mind, the leader of the ten organs, is seated in the orb of the lotus of the heart. It is the inner instrument (antaḥkaraṇa), since it cannot by itself deal with external objects without the organs (indriyas).'[50]

Of the three aspects of mind (antaḥkaraṇa), cognitive, affective, and conative, the cognitive is basic. It underlies the other two. Feeling and willing are invariably associated with some kind of

[50] PD II: 12.

cognition. Vedānta stresses the cognitive mind and takes into account its four states or functions (vṛtti): deliberation (manas), determination (buddhi), egoism (ahaṅkāra), and recollection (citta). In every external perception these four are involved. On seeing a chair a person does not at once determine it as a chair. In the beginning he is vaguely aware of it as something. He is in an indecisive state. So he cogitates 'what is it?' 'what is it?' This function of deliberation is manas. Then he searches within and recalls some past impression akin to it. With this recollection he cognizes the object as 'this is a chair'. This function of determination is buddhi. The function of recollection is citta. With the knowledge 'This is a chair' arises the knowledge 'I know the chair'. This is the function of egoism. Because of the rapid succession of the four functions they seem to be instantaneous. The four functions represent four different states of the mind. Most Vedāntins recognize two main states of the mind (antaḥkaraṇa): deliberative (manas) and determinative (buddhi). *Vedānta-sāra* includes ahaṁkāra in manas and citta in buddhi.[51] Like 'antaḥkaraṇa' the term 'manas' is sometimes used for entire mind, and so is the term 'citta'.

10. *How the sense-organs come in contact with their respective objects*

The contact of the sense-organs (buddhi-indriyas) with their respective objects, which is essential to external perception, is effected, according to Vedānta, in two different ways. Two of the sense-organs stretch out of the bodily organs, their outer stations, to reach the objects; but the other three do not. While the organ of hearing and the organ of vision contact their respective objects by extending and meeting them where they are, the organs of touch, taste, and smell associate their respective objects abiding in their own sites.[52] It is to be noted that the organ of hearing and the organ of vision, being of the nature of ether (ākāśa) and light (tejas) respectively, can move instantly and freely. It may sound strange to many that two of the organs reach out to meet their respective objects, while the three others stay in their seats. But this difference in the behaviour of the organs is evidenced by some peculiarities of the sensory experiences due to them.

It is a common experience that we see things away from the eyes. The organ of vision invariably locates its object in space. When we hear some familiar sound, that of a kettle drum for instance, we can know the nature of the sound, even without seeing the sound-producing object. Apart from that, we can even determine what direction and what distance the sound comes from. It would have been impossible to locate the source of the sound externally in space,

[51] *Vide* VS sec. 13, Bombay, Nirnaya-sagar Press, 1925. [52] VP I.

if sound-vibrations had travelled and struck the ear in successive waves to produce the auditory-perception. In fact, we hear the sound coming from the distant kettle-drum and not from the region of the ear. It is too much to assume that such an experience as 'I have heard the sound of the far-off kettle-drum' is an illusion.[53] Vedānta rejects the view held by the Naiyāyikas that in auditory perception concentric sound-waves strike the ear-drum in succession. According to this school the visual organ moves out to its object, but the auditory organ does not.

It is obvious that, unlike the organ of vision and the organ of hearing, the organ of touch and the organ of taste perceive their objects in actual contact with them. The organ of smell does also. We smell the flower on the altar (for instance) when its fragrance reaches the nose. We do not smell the flower right there on the altar where we see it. We see it there, but we smell it where we are. In the case of sound we can locate its source without seeing it. In the case of smell we cannot locate the source in the same way. When we smell some odour, say of undressed hide, we can determine its cause, though not open to vision, but we cannot locate its source in the way we can locate the source of sound.

The Buddhists who identify sense-organs with bodily organs (the globe of the ear, the globe of the eye) hold that the auditory and the visual organs apprehend their objects at a distance even without coming in contact with them. Were this so it would be possible to hear a sound or see a sight at any distance. So Vedānta rejects the view as untenable. In fact, none of the organs can perceive their objects without coming into contact with them.

United with the sense-organs the mind (antaḥkaraṇa) contacts the objects. There cannot be any perception unless the mind is connected with the objects as well as the organs. The outgoing sense-organs, the auditory and the visual, serve as the vehicles by which the mind reaches its objects. The mind leads these organs. The visual organ needs light and the auditory organ air or some other elastic medium to get to their objects. These serve as means of communication. One may believe in the instantaneous movement of the mind, such as thought-transferance, though not of the sense-organs. But it is to be noted that in the Vedāntic view the sense-organs are composed of the same type of subtle and pure substance as the mind is. As we have stated above the sattva aspect of each of the five subtle elements, (ether, air, fire, water, earth) jointly produce the mind, and severally the five organs of perception (the organs of hearing, touch, sight, taste, and smell) in succession. Each sense-organ tends naturally to manifest its own object. The organ of hearing is adapted to sound, being composed of the sāttvic aspect of ether, whose special

[53] VP I.

property is sound. The organ of vision is adapted to sight, being composed of the sāttvic aspect of tejas, whose special property is sight (visibility); and so on.

It is the direct contact with the sense-objects that leads to such direct cognition as, 'I hear the dog barking in the street', 'I see the apple tree standing in the yard'. Sensory experience is definite and assuring, because the object is directly presented to the knowing self by the agency of the sense-organ and the mind. Perception means, as we have noted above, immediate apprehension of an object. Without actual contact of the sense-organ and the mind with the object this is not possible. We shall explain later how such contact leads to direct knowledge of the object. Meanwhile, we shall dwell on the interpretation of the perceptual process by some Western thinkers. According to them the mind and the sense-organ remain passive, while the object acts on them and stimulates the sensory operation. But it seems more natural for the mobile mind and the sense-organ to approach the inert object than for the inert object to approach them.

11. *The difficulties the West is confronted with in accounting for sense-perception*

In the Western view the organ of sight is stationary. It does not come into direct contact with the object. It reacts to the light stimuli received from the object, which takes the initiative, so to speak. The influence of light on the visual organ initiates a physiological process resulting in the perception of the object, as described below:

'The sense of vision is excited by the influence of light on the retina, the special terminal organ connected with the optic nerve. By excitation of the retina, a change is induced in the optic nerve fibres, and is conveyed by these to the brain, the result being a luminous perception, or what we call a sensation of light or colour. If light were to act uniformly over the retina, there would be no image of the source of the light formed on that structure, and consequently there would be only a general consciousness of light, without reference to any particular object. One of the first conditions, therefore, of vision for useful purposes is the formation of an image on the retina.'[54]

Visual perception is interpreted above, as far as we can see, wholly as a physiological function. In viewing the perceptual process as a mere physiological operation one is confronted at the outset with an

[54] *Encyclopaedia Britannica*, 1948, 'Vision or Sight' by Charles Bernard Goulden, M.D., Specialist in Ophthalmology.

insoluble problem. The question arises: How can purely physical actions give rise to 'luminous perception' called 'sensation', which means the awareness of sense-data, such as colour, form, size, and so forth? There is a vital difference between physical light and the light of consciousness. Despite its luminosity physical light is stark blind. It is neither aware of itself nor of anything else. On the contrary, the light of consciousness is self-aware, and also aware of whatever else comes in its way. Physical means can produce physical light, which is similar to it in nature, but not the light of consciousness, which is of contrary character. Like any other material object physical light is invariably an object of cognition. But consciousness is never cognized. It is self-manifest and manifests all else including light. Consequently, physiological process cannot lead to perception. It cannot even generate 'sensation', that is, the awareness of sense-datum.

Many realistic thinkers have tried to obviate this difficulty by recognizing the existence of mind or consciousness in some form or other. They explain the perceptual process as psychophysical. But hardly do they maintain that the object perceived is directly apprehended either by the sense-organ or the mind. In cognizing an object all that is directly known by the senses is its qualities, such as colour, sound, touch, taste, smell. Since they are immediately presented to the senses, Bertrand Russell and many other philosophers call them 'sense-data'. Sensations mean the awareness of sense-data. They are the 'elements' of sense-knowledge. According to most Western thinkers, both realistic and idealistic, sensations are the only direct experience that man has in the cognition of an object. Some have gone so far as to maintain that the existence of the objects of perception is inferred from present sensations or awareness of sense-data. The Neo-realists, however, maintain that the objects are directly presented to the senses. The phenomenalists hold that what we call a physical object, a flower for instance, is only a collection of sense-data, such as colour, size, shape, softness, fragrance, and so forth. A red flower is but a group of sense-data inclusive of redness, appearing as such.

12. *Despite the different modern theories the problem of external perception remains unsolved*

But the fact is that in every act of perception what we actually experience is not just a sense-datum, or a combination of sense-data, but a concrete object to which these belong as attributes or are related somehow. In perceiving colour we perceive something of which colour is a quality. In perceiving sound we perceive something as its medium. In feeling heat we contact something which is hot, it may be air or some other substance. In tasting sweetness we taste something that is sweet. In smelling fragrance we smell something which is fragrant or the air that transmits fragrance. Indeed, a sense-object is something more than a sense-datum or an aggregate of sense-data. It is an entity that holds them as its qualities. Dr Chatterjee rightly observes:

'The perceptions arise along with the sensations. To see the color of a tree is to perceive the tree at the same time. Hence to say that the one is perceived and the other is only inferred or imagined is to evade the real problem of perception. What we ought to do is not to reduce perception to sensation, but to explain how along with the sensation we have the perception of an object.'[55] This is the problem which has not been tackled successfully by Western thinkers, as far as we can see.

Professor D. M. Datta has made explicit remarks on the nature of the problem:

'The general Western view is that in perception, mind does not go out to the object, but only receives the stimuli coming from the object. It seems strange that even thoroughgoing realists do not challenge this customary analysis, in consistency with which our knowledge of the external world can at best be an inference; representationism being the only logical conclusion of such a theory of perception. But without direct contact with the external world we could hardly have even an inference about it from its supposed physiological effect. To take the case of visual perception, it is extremely doubtful whether from the retinal pictures of external objects we could construct the external world of three dimensions as we have it now. Some Western psychologists make elaborate efforts to explain how from the distribution of light and shade in the retinal pictures we obtain, through inference, the world of three dimensions. What we should like to emphasize, as regards such an account, is that without previous knowledge of the external, the mere distribution of light and shade or other local signs would remain mere qualities of pictures painted on a level screen. No herculean effort of inference could make us project our internal percepts into external space and see them in their real order, magnitude and dimensions. . . . According to the commonly accepted Western theory, when an object, say a tree, is perceived, different parts of the tree send their respective stimuli, and thus different sensations are obtained. The difficulty therefore arises as to how, from these different unitary

55 *Vide* Satischandra Chatterjee, M.A., Ph.D., *The Problems of Philosophy*, Calcutta, Das Gupta, 1949, p. 108.

sensations, we acquire the knowledge of the object as a whole in all its form and dimensions.'[56]

According to Hobhouse, nothing external can be directly known. Perception is wholly psychical in character. Only the sensations are immediately apprehended, not even the sense-data. Says he: 'How is it psychologically or metaphysically possible that we should get to know anything of an order of things independent of the mind? The primary fact of perception is that which is present to our consciousness, and surely that which is present to is also "in" our consciousness, in the sense of being some one of its states, modes, or manifestations. Granting this, can we ever arrive at a knowledge of external things? I should answer, certainly not.'[57]

James Ward, as a psychologist, is confronted with the same problem. The fact that perception involves 'objective reference' is recognized by him:

'We may perceive a sound or a light without any presentation of that which sounds or shines; but none the less we regard such sound or light as the quality or change or state of a *something* that is distinct not only from the subject attending but from all the impressions to which he is attending. Here again actual separation is impossible, because this "objective reference" has been so intertwined throughout our mental development with the other two. Still a careful psychological analysis will show that such "reification", as we might almost call it, has depended on special circumstances, which we can at any rate conceive absent. These special circumstances are briefly the constant conjunctions and successions of impressions, for which psychology can give no reason, and the constant movements to which they prompt. Thus we receive together, e.g., those impressions we now recognize as severally the scent, colour, and "feel" of the rose we pluck and handle. We might call each a "percept", and the whole a "complex percept". But there is more in such a complex than a sum of partial percepts; there is the apprehension or intuition* of the rose as a thing having this scent, colour, and texture. We have,

(* Intuition is used here to denote a complex of simple percepts synthesized as a unity in space and time. But to speak instead of a complex or of an acquired percept does not adequately indicate either the unity or the 'ideal construction' that 'thinghood' implies. The German *Anschauung* is frequently used in a like sense.)

---

56 *The Six Ways of Knowing*, p. 65.

57 L. T. Hobhouse, *The Theory of Knowledge*, p. 531.

then, under perception to consider (*a*) the recognition and (*b*) the localization, of impressions, and (*c*) the "intuition" of things.'[58]

Various theories have been propounded to solve the problem of external perception, but no satisfactory answer has yet been found. Bertrand Russell aptly remarks: 'Empiricism and idealism alike are faced with a problem to which, so far, philosophy has found no satisfactory solution. This is the problem of showing how we have knowledge of other things than ourself and the operations of our own mind.'[59] It is evident from the foregoing discussion that Vedānta has averted this problem by recognizing the special capacity of the mind, and the organs of audition and vision to reach their objects far away though they may be. For the root of the problem is the conception that the mind and the senses are confined to the psycho-physical system and serve as passive instruments of external perception.

In his concluding remarks on the contemporary theories of perception Thomas Hill brings out the problem:

'In our review of idealist, realist, and mediating theories, this central problem [the problem of the relation between cognitive experiences and their objects] has turned out to include three major issues, first that between idealists and realists concerning whether the objects of knowledge are experiential or independent of experience; second that between idealists and monistic realists, on the one hand, and dualistic realists on the other, concerning whether or not apprehending experiences are to be regarded as distinct from objects apprehended; finally the issue that emerges from the discussion of the other two, concerning how independent objects can be apprehended through experiences that are distinct from them.'[60]

Finally, he observes:

'In concluding the discussion of theories of knowledge that focus upon the problem of the relation between cognitive experiences and their objects, one seems obliged to accept the current view that while these theories yield many interesting and illuminating suggestions, they have by no means resolved the problem or produced a pattern of ideas from which a solution can be drawn.'[61]

[58] James Ward, *Psychological Principles*, Cambridge, University Press, 1933, p. 142.

[59] Bertrand Russell, *A History of Western Philosophy*, London, Allen and Unwin:,New York, Simon and Schuster, 1946, p. 611.

[60] Thomas English Hill, *Contemporary Theories of Knowledge*, New York, Ronald Press Company, 1964, pp. 284–5.

[61] *Ibid.* p. 290.

But the crux of the problem of sense-perception, as far as we can see, is not how it is possible for a person to perceive things that are evidently beyond the reach of his mind and the senses, being apart from him, or whether the objects perceived are actually independent of him or not, but what manifests the objects and how they become manifest. In the Vedāntic view none of the organs, nor the mind, nor their conjunction can bring about cognition, there being no light of consciousness in any of these. Indeed, the problem of perception cannot be solved either on the psychological or the psychophysical level. It has its root in the metaphysical basis of the psychophysical realm. Radiance of consciousness underlies all perceptions, external as well as internal. It belongs neither to the body, nor to the organs, not even to the mind. Unmanifest themselves they cannot manifest anything whatsoever.

As pointed out by the sage Patañjali, even the mind is not self-luminous because it is observable.[62] Consciousness is intrinsic in the knowing self, the subject *per se*, which illumines the mind and the senses and manifests the objects perceived. It is all-pervading Pure Consciousness, the fundamental reality, that shines as man's inmost self, which is ever the knower and is never known, that is to say, objectified. Other than the knowing self the rest are blind, being devoid of the power of vision or awareness. Try howsoever they may, any number of blind persons gathering together can have no sight, not even a single glimpse of light.

[62] YS IV: 19.

CHAPTER II

THE METAPHYSICAL BACKGROUND OF THE SENSIBLE UNIVERSE

1. *The close relation between epistemology and metaphysics*

The whole perceptual process delineated by Vedānta is based on its metaphysics rather than on its psychology and physiology.[1] Even the rudimentary experience of sensations cannot be explained as a mere physiological operation. The question—how mechanical brain-processes turn into psychical functions—remains unanswered. Nor can perceptual knowledge result wholly from purely mental operations; because consciousness is not inherent in mind. A thoroughgoing study of sense-perception has to take into account not only the physical and the psychical factors involved, but also the fundamental reality underlying them, which alone is self-existent and self-luminous. Brahman, the Supreme Being, is Pure Consciousness. It is the Light of lights, the One source of all knowledge. It underlies

[1] Cf. Dr Paul Deussen, *The System of the Vedānta* (Authorized Translation by Charles Johnston), LaSalle, Open Court Publishing Co., 1912, pp. 47, 48. 'The thought that the empirical view of nature is not able to lead us to a final solution of the being of things, meets us not only among the Indians but also in many forms in the philosophy of the West. More closely examined this thought is even the root of all metaphysics, so far as without it no metaphysics can come into being or exist. For if empirical or physical investigation were able to throw open to us the true and innermost being of nature, we should only have to continue along this path in order to come at last to an understanding of all truth; the final result would be Physics (in the broader sense, as the teaching of nature) and there would be no ground or justification for METAPHYSICS. If, therefore, the metaphysicians of ancient and modern times, dissatisfied with empirical knowledge, went on to metaphysics, this step is only to be explained by a more or less clear consciousness that all empirical investigation and knowledge amounts in the end only to a great deception grounded in the nature of our knowing faculties, to open our eyes to which is the task of metaphysics.

Thrice, so far as we know, has this knowledge reached conviction among mankind, and each time, as it appears, by a different way, according to conditions of time, national and individual character; once among the Indian . . . again in Greek philosophy through Parmenides, and the third time in the modern philosophy through Kant.'

the subject and the object both. It is manifest in the subject as the inmost self, but veiled in the object. While the subject is self-luminous, the object is stark-blind and wrapped in darkness. The light of consciousness proceeding from the knowing self unveils the object. Anything known, or we may say, every form of existence, presupposes the knowing self or the light of consciousness that the self is.

The whole world of phenomena is grounded on Pure Consciousness, which is identical with Pure Being. Brahman is Being-Consciousness-Bliss. It is the sole entity, the thing-in-itself.[2] The individual self is essentially That. Consciousness is not a quality of the self, but its essence. The self is consciousness pure and simple. It is immediate awareness. Brahman is immediate and direct as the self within.[3] Nor is consciousness a mental process or state. What is regarded as conscious state or process is but an expression of Pure Consciousness through a certain modification of the mind. Through each and every function of the mind the light of consciousness shines. There cannot be any feeling, willing, thinking, imagination, or memory without the light of consciousness, howsoever dim it may appear to be. It underlies the psychical processes and is not their product. The self is aware of all mental modifications. They are objects of consciousness. Not even the ego-idea or I-ness is the origin of consciousness. Ego-consciousness is but the manifestation of the supreme Consciousness through a mental modification characterized by 'I-ness'. In dreamless sleep when the ego-idea subsides, and with it all mental operations cease, the light of consciousness endures and manifests the utter passivity of mind shrouded in darkness. The luminous self beyond the ego witnesses sleep, a state of complete ignorance and restfulness. It shines when all other lights fail.

The central principle in all knowledge is consciousness, the light that reveals the object. According to Hamilton consciousness lies at the root of all knowledge. 'It constitutes the fundamental form of every act of knowledge', says he.[4] Knowledge is revelatory, being the manifestation of Consciousness through a mode of the mind corresponding to the object. It does not derive from any physiological or psychological or biological or psychophysical process. Each and every act of cognition is but an expression of Pure Consciousness through a mental mode (antaḥkaraṇa-vṛtti). As stated in *Vedānta-paribhāṣā*, 'Perceptual knowledge, according to Vedānta, is nothing but Pure Consciousness.'[5]

Thus valid knowledge (pramā) is viewed in Advaita Vedānta in

[2] *Vide* VS, sec. 6, 'Vastu Saccidānandādvayam Brahma.

[3] *Vide* Br. U. III: 4.2.

[4] Sir William Hamilton, *Lectures on Metaphysics*, XV, Boston, Gould and Lincoln, 1859, p. 183.

[5] VP I, Perception.

two main aspects: as Pure Consciousness (śuddha caitanya) and as modal consciousness (vṛtti-caitanya). Pure Consciousness is beyond the subject-object relation. Even the distinction of substance and attribute does not obtain there, so it is called 'Pure'. It is nondual, non-relational, limitless, unvaried, self-shining Reality. The Absolute, as conceived by Hegel, is the subject conscious of himself as the object. But in Advaita Vedānta the Absolute is neither the subject nor the object. It is beyond the subject-object relation, being the ultimate ground of all relations. Every relation signifies dependency. 'A relation is a sort of dependence,' says St Thomas.[6] Modal consciousness finds expression through the subject-object relation. It is relational, finite, varied in kind, and marked by degrees of manifestation.

Pure Being and Pure Consciousness are inseparable. The self-existent cannot but be self-luminous. It must be Its own proof. Similarly, what is self-luminous must be real by Itself. Neither Being nor Consciousness can be studied without reference to the other. The close relation between epistemology and metaphysics cannot be denied. No thoroughgoing enquiry into the origin and the nature of knowledge and the ways of knowing is possible without reference to fundamental reality. Then again metaphysical investigation into the nature of Being or Reality cannot attain its goal unless consistent with sound epistemological principles.

The relative priority of epistemology and metaphysics (ontology) has been a moot point in Western philosophy. On the one hand, philosophers like Descartes, Locke, and Kant have based their metaphysical speculations on their epistemological findings; on the other hand, metaphysical thinkers like Spinoza, Hegel, and A. N. Whitehead have based their epistemological enquiry on their metaphysical concepts. Unlike the Kantian school, Vedānta in its epistemological enquiry has given priority to the metaphysical truths revealed by the Śruti and experienced by the seers. This has been necessary for the orientation of its epistemological study, since in the Vedāntic view Pure Being is identical with Pure Consciousness, the One ground of all knowledge. As observed by D. M. Datta:

'The Vedāntins freely draw upon their metaphysical theories in order to explain many of the problems of perception. To a modern student of philosophy this method would appear to be dogmatic. The theories of perceptual knowledge would be regarded as vitiated by gratuitous metaphysical assumptions and consequently little or no value would be attached to the Vedāntic conclusions. But if we

[6] Saint Thomas Aquinas, 'Summa de Veritate', qu. 21. Eng. Trans. by Robert W. Schmidt, S.J., *Truth*, Vol. III (qu. XXI–XXIX), Chicago, Regnery, 1954, p. 6.

closely examine the modern epistemological theories of perception, it will not be diffcult to find that in spite of their loud protests against metaphysics, epistemologists have tacitly assumed without criticism certain theories of reality on the truth of which alone their epistemological conclusions can stand. If so, is it not far better to express the metaphysical grounds, and confess plainly and honestly that the final guarantee of these epistemological theories would come from the truth of the metaphysical assumptions? In such cases metaphysics and epistemology have to be considered in relation to each other.

For Vedāntins, however, the inclusion of metaphysical considerations is doubly necessary. It is needed primarily as a necessary explanation that Vedāntic metaphysics owes to the problems of perception. Vedānta has to show that the problems of perception can be satisfactorily accounted for consistently with its metaphysics.

The second necessity of including metaphysics is to impart a thoroughness to the epistemological conclusion itself, which would otherwise remain vague, as depending on uncriticized and unacknowledged grounds.'[7]

2. *The Advaita view of the sensible universe may be defined as metaphysical or absolute Idealism. It is neither objective realism nor subjective idealism*

It may appear to some from the foregoing discussion on sense-perception that the Vedāntic view of the physical world resembles naïve realism, which is also called common sense, natural, or intuitive realism. But the similarity is on the surface. Underneath, there is an immense gulf of difference between the two. According to both, the physical objects exist independently of the individual mind and the senses, which apprehend them directly as they are. Besides this, there is little in common between Realism and Vedānta. Realism upholds the primacy of the material existence; whereas Vedānta upholds the primacy of the spiritual reality, self-luminous Consciousness. The realists maintain that matter can exist as ultimate reality without mind or consciousness, these being derived from it. In fact, some Neo-realists deny the very existence of mind or consciousness. In the Vedāntic view the mind is as devoid of consciousness as any external material thing, but, being composed of sattva, has the transparency to receive and transmit the light of Pure Consciousness. The physical and the mental endure as distinct entities on the relative plane. Both are empirically real; but neither is self-existent. They exist because of the underlying immutable Self, their witness. Brahman, the all-pervading Pure Consciousness, is the fundamental reality. This alone exists in the absolute sense. The relative order has

[7] D. M. Datta, *The Six Ways of Knowing*, pp. 32, 33.

an apparent existence superimposed on it. This imposition endures until Brahman is realized.

The truth is that Vedānta views the manifold as a coherent whole. It takes into account all three types of human experience, which reveal the three levels of existence—physical, mental, and spiritual—that constitute the cosmos. Sense-perception is the key to the physical order. It does not reveal the psychical, which is directly known by introspection. While acknowledging the facts of sense-experience, Vedānta does not deny the facts of introspection, as the Naturalists generally do. Internal perception, as we have stated, is again twofold. (See chap. 1, sec. 3). While a person observes his mental life, he is also aware of himself as an observer. He has self-experience. He can also apprehend himself as a knower distinct from the known. This inner perception reveals his true being as immutable consciousness, self-existent and self-manifest, invariable in the midst of the variable. Indeed, the luminous self persists as the experiencer in waking state, in dream, and in deep sleep. As a person develops this insight, the self within is found to be essentially one with the all-pervading Supreme Self. The knower, which is self-manifest and precedes every fact of experience, cannot be different from the fundamental reality. Finally, the self is realized as Nondual Brahman, Pure Being-Consciousness-Bliss beyond the distinction of the subject and the object.

Vedānta has due regard for the evidence of the senses so far as the external world is concerned. Sense-perception is the foundation of our knowledge of the physical world. Hence Vedānta stresses the point that our view of physical objects must be determined by the nature of sense-perception, and not *vice versa*. We should not explain sense-perception by preconceived ideas of the physical world. It is the universal character of sense-perception that we apprehend the objects as concrete entities existing in space and time independently of the senses and the mind. Our determination of existence and non-existence of things must rest on this indubitable fact. We cannot alter fact, nor should we deny it. All that we have to do is to explain it. As stated in the *Brahma-sūtras*, 'Non-existence [of external objects] is not true, because they are experienced.'[8] Had they been non-existent like the horns of a hare they could not be perceived by the senses. Vedānta refutes subjective idealism and epistemic dualism mainly on the ground that neither is true to the nature of sense-perception. We shall dwell on this point later

It is true that sense-perception is not always reliable. It is often found to be deceptive. The sun appears different from what it is. A stick thrust into water looks bent. Yet reason has to work on the observed facts. It can differentiate perception from hallucination,

[8] BS II: 2. 28.

and valid cognition from illusion. When one experience is wrong, another experience contradicts it, as in the case of mirage or dream. That which is uncontradicted must be acknowledged as real, as far as the domain of experience goes. Vedānta accepts sense-perception as the authentic source of knowledge in the empirical realm, just as it accepts the authority of the Śruti with regard to the knowledge of transcendent reality. Each is valid in its own sphere. Sense-perception is not veridical, unless certain conditions are fulfilled. It has to be properly regulated and logically tested. Its falsity, when there is any, is due to adventitious causes. Because of defect in the visual organ or insufficient light something may appear different from what it is. Such cases of illusion do not invalidate perception as a source of knowledge, just as erroneous conclusions due to wrong premises or fallacious arguments do not invalidate inference as a source of knowledge.

According to Vedānta the difference between the subjective and the objective is quite valid on the relative plane. One cannot be reduced to the other. Vedānta recognizes the empirical reality of individual selves, internal ideas, and external objects. These three orders of existence are distinct from one another as facts of experience and are interrelated. They form a triple existence. To deny any one of the three, or to identify one with another, is not right. None of them, as such, is ultimately real. From the absolute standpoint all the three are non-existent. Nondual Brahman or Pure Consciousness being the sole reality. Vedānta may be characterized as metaphysical or absolute Idealism, inasmuch as it maintains the ultimate reality of one undifferentiated supreme Consciousness and views everything as identical with It in essence. But the point is that its world-view differs fundamentally from subjective Idealism on the one hand and objective Realism on the other. As observed by Professor Radhakrishnan, 'The essential correlativity of subject and object, which is the central truth of all idealism, is accepted by Śaṅkara, who sets aside both mentalism and realism as inadequate to the facts of experience.'[9] Mental ideas and physical objects are both appearances from the standpoint of fundamental reality. But so far as the phenomenal order is concerned, they endure as distinct entities. In the words of Swāmī Vivekānanda:

'Without the "I" there can be no "you" outside. From this some philosophers came to the conclusion that the external world did not exist save in the subject; that the "you" existed only in the "I". Others have argued that the "I" can only be known through the "you" and with equal logic. These two views are partial truths, each

[9] S. Radhakrishnan, *Indian Philosophy*, Vol. II, Second Edition, London, Allen and Unwin, 1931, p. 498.

wrong in part and each right in part. Thought is as much material and as much in nature as body is. Both matter and mind exist in a third, a unity which divides itself into the two. This unity is the Ātman, the real Self.'[10]

3. *The Vedāntic position with regard to the world should not be misunderstood as illusionism or as pantheism*

It is true that, according to Advaita Vedānta, Brahman alone is real and the world is unreal. But the unreality of the world does not mean, as is often misunderstood, that the world is a mere shadow without substance, a pure illusion, or a void. The world *as it appears to us* is unreal because it has no absolute existence; but *in its essential nature*, as Brahman, the world is absolutely real, for it is Brahman that appears in this form, without undergoing any change whatsoever. So says Śaṅkara, 'Brahman, the Cause, does not lack existence at any of the three periods of time, neither does the world, its effect. Since there is only one Existence pure and simple, the effect is non-different from the cause.'[11] All effects with different names and forms are real only as Pure Existence but unreal in themselves. Just as a clay pot has no existence apart from clay so the manifold has no existence apart from Brahman, its cause. In itself it is a conglomeration of names and forms. It should not be regarded as a self-subsistent entity. As identical in essence with Brahman it is real.[12]

There are three orders of existence according to Advaita Vedānta (1) absolute existence (pāramārthika sattvam), (2) empirical existence (vyavahārika sattvam), and (3) illusory existence (prātibhāsika sattvam).[13] Neither the empirical nor the illusory is non-existent as a barren woman's son, which is entirely false (tuccha, alīka). Then again, the empirical is not unreal in the same way as the illusory. As stated by Śaṅkara, 'Relative to the illusory objects, such as mirage, actual water and the like are real'.[14] While the illusory appear and disappear, the empirical existence of cause and effect persists till the direct knowledge of Brahman is attained, which is a rare achievement for the jīva (individual soul).

As long as a person cannot realize Brahman all differences of kind, quality, and quantity in the relative plane are facts for him. He cannot ignore the distinction between virtue and vice, happiness and misery, knowledge and ignorance, the saint and the sinner, the living and the non-living, the action and the result, the fine and the gross, the great and the small. It is through the observance of these distinctions that he can go beyond them and reach the Nondual Brahman.

[10] CW VII, p. 99. [11] BS II: 1.16, com. [12] *Vide* Ch. U. VI: 2.1, 2; com.
[13] *Vide* VP II. [14] Tai. U. II: 6, com.

The dream-objects are quite real to the dreamer until he wakes up. Day and night exist for him who sees the sun rise and set, even though they are non-existent from the viewpoint of the sun.[15] True, all are in essence Brahman, yet there is difference in their manifestations in the relative plane. A sentient being is a higher manifestation of Brahman than is an inanimate thing. Virtue is a higher manifestation of Brahman than vice. So he has to rise from the lower to the higher and from the higher to the still higher in order to attain Brahman, which transcends all relativity.

The external world can be said to be unreal in two different senses: either it is altogether non-existent, or it is a mere form of inner consciousness appearing as something outside as in dream. Subjective Idealism (Vijñānavāda) maintains the second position. But Vedānta holds neither of these two views. Had the external things been non-existent like the horns of a hare, they could not be perceived by the senses. Since they are objects of perception, their existence cannot be denied. Nor can they be reduced to mere forms of internal cognition, as subjectivism assumes. In the perception of an object we are conscious not only of cognition itself but also of the object as distinct from and external to it. Nobody perceives the object as identical with cognition itself. The object and its cognition are two distinct facts of experience. While one is external, the other is internal. Since the object is perceived as external to and distinct from the act of cognition its separate existence should be acknowledged. Thus argues Śaṅkara while refuting the subjective idealism of the Yōgācāra School.[16] Says he: 'Nobody perceives cognition itself as a pillar, as a wall, and so forth, but everybody perceives them as objects of cognition.'[17]

The same argument applies to subjective idealism of modern times. The idealism of George Berkeley is not wholly subjective.[18] He acknowledges the existence of the self and of God independently of the mind. But in his view, too, physical objects do not exist apart from

[15] *Vide* MK III: 36, Ānandagiri.

[16] The Yōgācāra is one of the four principal speculative systems of Buddhism. Two of them, the Vaibhāṣika and the Sautrāntika schools, are realists. They belong to the Hīnayāna branch of Buddhism. The two other, the Yōgācāras and the Mādhymikas, belong to the Mahāyāna branch. The Yōgācāras are idealists. The Mādhyamikas are called nihilists; they deny the reality of all but the absolute.

[17] BS II: 2.28, com.

[18] The distinction is thus noted by Dr Chatterjee, *The Problems of Philosophy*, p. 309, 'Berkeley's idealism is not subjective in the strict sense for he admits the reality of the self and of God, although we have no perceptions or ideas of them. According to him, we have not any idea but a *notion* of the self and we know God as the cause or source from which ideas of objects are transmitted to our mind. He seems, therefore, not to reduce everything or all reality to subjective ideas or experiences of the mind.'

their perceptions. He admits the perceptibility of things, but identifies them with perceptions. As stated by him:

'That the things I see with my eyes and touch with my hands do exist, really exist, I make not the least question. The only thing whose existence we deny is that which *philosophers* call Matter or corporeal substance.'
'. . . we eat and drink and are clad with the immediate objects of sense, which cannot exist unperceived or without the mind. . . .'
'Ideas imprinted on the senses are real things, or do really exist, this we do not deny, but we deny they can subsist without the minds which perceive them, or that they are resemblances of any archetypes existing without the mind, since the very being of a sensation or idea consists in being perceived, and an idea can be like nothing but an ideal.'[19]

But, according to Śaṅkara, the existences of sensible objects do not depend on their perceptions; perceived or unperceived they exist as such. Jadunath Sinha aptly observes: 'Berkeley argues that the existence of a sensible object consists in being perceived—*esse* is *percipi*—and therefore it is an idea of the mind. Śaṅkara, on the other hand, argues that an object is perceived because it actually *exists* external to the mind; an object is distinctly perceived as existing independent of the act of perception. No one can argue a fact of experience out of existence.'[20]

The Advaitin's view of the world is misunderstood by some as illusionism and, contrarily, by others as pantheism. It is true that the Upaniṣad declares: 'All this is verily Brahman.'[21] But this does not mean that Brahman has turned into this diversified sensible universe. It only means that Brahman appears as such. Vedānta maintains both immanence and transcendence of Brahman with regard to the manifold. Pervading the whole world of multiplicity as pure spirit, that is, as the luminous Self (ātman) of all, and existing far beyond, Brahman is unaffected by any distinction whatsoever that belongs to it. This idea is expressed throughout the Vedāntic literature. We quote a few passages:

'The whole universe is His glory. He (the cosmic Being) is, indeed, greater than His glory. All beings existing in the past, the present,

[19] George Berkeley, *The Principles of Human Knowledge*, LaSalle, Open Court Publishing Co., 1920, sec. 35, 38, 90.
[20] Jadunath Sinha, *Indian Realism*, London, Kegan Paul, Trench, Trubner, 1938, p. 231.
[21] Ch. U. III: 14.1.

and the future form only a quarter of Him. The other three quarters remain in the immutable and luminous state.'[22]

'One effulgent Being is hidden in all creatures. He is all-pervasive and is the innermost Self of all. He presides over the law of karma and all beings reside in Him. He is the Witness and He is Pure Consciousness, transcendent and free from relativity.'[23]

'Just as the sun which helps all eyes to see is not tainted by the defects of the eyes or the external objects revealed by it, even so the same undiversified innermost Self is not contaminated by the misery of the world, being beyond it.'[24]

The following remarks of Professor Hiriyanna are pertinent: 'It is now usual to represent the monism of the later Mantras and the Brāhmaṇas as pantheistic; but it is not correct to do so, since the term as applicable to this teaching connotes the idea not merely of immanence but also of transcendence.'[25] In the words of Radhakrishnan: 'Pantheism is the view that identifies God with the sum of things and denies transcendence. If the nature of the absolute is exhausted completely by the course of the world, if the two become one, then we have pantheism. In the Upaniṣads we come across passages which declare that the nature of reality is not exhausted by the world-process. The existence of the world does not take away from the perfection of the absolute.'[26] To quote Swāmī Vivekānanda: 'The Vedāntist [Advaitin] says, "The universe is not real, it is only apparent. Nature is God seen through nescience [ajñāna]". The Pantheists say, "God has become nature or this world." The Vedāntists affirm that God is appearing as this world, but He is not this world.'[27]

4. *The Idealist's view that physical objects have no existence in themselves but are mere externalizations of mental ideas is not tenable*

There is a vital difference between a thing cognized, a tree for instance, and its idea. The one cannot be the objectification of the other. The idea of the tree is invariably cognized as something internal and non-material, whereas the tree is cognized as something concrete

[22] Rg.V. X: 90, *Puruṣa Sūktam*; see also Ch. U. III: 12.6.

[23] Sv. U. VI: 11.

[24] Ka. U. II: 2.11.

[25] M. Hiriyanna, *The Essentials of Indian Philosophy*, London, Allen and Unwin, 1949, p. 16.

[26] S. Radhakrishnan, *Indian Philosophy*, vol. I, p. 202.

[27] CW VII, *The Inspired Talks*, p. 48. Ajñāna is not the absence of knowledge but the reverse of knowledge, antiknowledge.

and external. In actual experience the perception of the tree precedes the idea of the tree, and not *vice versa*. We get the idea of the tree from its perception and not the perception of the tree from its idea. Moreover, unlike the idea, the perception of the tree is spatially and temporally determined. The idea of the tree we can carry within us wherever we go, but the perception of the tree we cannot. We can recall the idea of the tree at will, but not its percept. Had the perception of the tree been nothing more than the externalization of the internal idea, then a person could have the experience of the tree anywhere without sharing it with others. But this never happens except in hallucination. A tree that is perceived by one person is perceived by others as well at the same time and at the same place. And the perception can be repeated exactly in the same way. Any sense-object is universally observable. All these point to the fact that a physical object exists independently of the percipient's mind and the sense-organ concerned, even though it cannot be perceived without them.

An external object cannot be identified with its idea. Though closely related they are separate existences. The one belongs to the realm of the senses, the other to the realm of the mind. The physical and the mental co-exist in the relative as distinct entities, but are not ultimately real as such. That a concrete object is not the same as the apprehending idea, that *esse* is not *percipi*, is also evident from the fact that every idea does not present itself in a corresponding material form. The idea of love, of pain, of fear, and so forth, we do not find in specific concrete images like the idea of tree, of dog, of book, etc. One may ask 'Why does not the idea of love externalize itself in the way the idea of a tree does?' The reply may be: 'All ideas are not of the same class; some externalize themselves as sense-objects, others do not.' Truly, in Locke's view there is a distinction between ideas of sensation and ideas of reflection, which George Berkeley acknowledges. But Locke holds that ideas of sensation are derived mainly from the knowledge of external objects and ideas of reflection mainly from the knowledge of internal facts.[28]

We have noted how Śaṅkara refutes the Idealistic position, particularly, that of the Yōgācāra school of Buddhism, which identifies the material objects with the ideas of the human minds. In George Berkeley's view what we perceive as external objects exist in God's mind as ideas. Even so, the difference between physical objects and mental ideas is a fact for human beings. The two are not identical. The point is this. In sense-perception we are not concerned with the fundamental nature of things, but with their present status. To give an illustration. Ice and steam, though originating from the

[28] *Vide* John Locke's *An Essay Concerning Human Understanding*, Bk. II, chap. I–VII.

same substance water, are perceived differently and serve different purposes. Their difference as objects of experience cannot be denied or ignored. The sensible universe may be fundamentally God's ideas. But the objects of sense, as manifest to us, belong to an order different from that of internal ideas, which are not perceptible by the senses nor universally observable. Advaita Vedānta explains the manifold as the manifestation of Brahman, yet in the empirical order it recognizes the difference between external objects and internal ideas and affirms that things perceived are independent of their perceptions.

5. *The theory of representationism, ancient or modern, is not consistent with the nature of sense-perception*

Long before John Locke (1632–1704) a theory of knowledge similar to epistemic dualism or representative realism was maintained by the Sautrāntika Buddhists, who arose in all probability in the first century, BC, about four hundred years after Buddha's death (Parinirvāṇa).[28a] Unlike the Idealists of the Yōgācāra school, the Sautrāntikas recognize the difference between the mental idea and the concrete object apprehended by it. So in their view the external world exists independently of the mind. The physical and the mental both are real. Neither is a form of the other. But they hold that the mental states and ideas are directly perceived, whereas the external objects are indirectly known through the images they produce on the mind, just as things can be known, through their reflections on a mirror. So they propound the theory of the inferability of the external objects (bāhyānumeya-vāda).

The modern theory of representationism is similar to this. According to the modern theory, when we cognize an object, a tree for instance, we do not directly apprehend it, but infer its existence from the mental image or idea caused by it, that is, from its representation to the mind. Thus, it is assumed that in sense-perception there is no direct presentation of the external objects to the percipient mind, but only their representation through the images and the ideas created by them. The view that the existence of an external object of perception is inferred from the sensations, that is, from the apprehension of its sense qualities is prevalent among the Idealists and the Realists as well.

That such a view overlooks the distinctive character of sense-perception is not difficult to see. It is evident that no mental process of inference is involved in such cases of perception, as 'This is a chair', 'I see the tree', 'I hear the sound', 'I smell a sweet fragrance', and so on. In each of these instances there is a directness of appre-

[28a] Final entry into nirvāṇa or bōdhi (Illumination). It occurred in 544 BC according to Theravada Buddhism.

hension which inferential knowledge does not have. To experience a fire and to infer its existence on seeing smoke are two different types of cognition. Perceptual knowledge is invariably marked by immediacy and certitude, whereas inferential knowledge is by nature indirect and indefinite. The one must not be identified with the other. In every case of sense-perception there is a direct or immediate apprehension of the object present. This is what distinguishes perceptual knowledge from inference, memory, conception, imagination, and other forms of mediate knowledge.

According to Hobhouse 'an external order of things independent of the mind' cannot be directly known. 'The perception is undoubtedly *qua* perceptive act the mind's own creation. It is thoroughly psychical in character',[29] he holds. He refutes even the inferrability of the external objects from the internal ideas. Says he, 'We must accordingly give up the notion that a world external to mind can be known by inference alone, while direct perception is confined to the mind's inward states'.[30]

6. *The view that mind and sense-organs construct the diversified world on the ground of Reality is not admitted by Vedānta*

Most scientists and philosophers, while they disagree as to the fundamental nature of things, agree on the point that the sense-organs perceive their objects not in their intrinsic character but in their present extrinsic forms. Likewise, Vedānta holds that we perceive things in their empirical aspects and not in their essential nature. Brahman, Pure Being-Consciousness-Bliss, is the ultimate Reality underlying all our experiences. Any kind of existence is essentially Brahman. The manifold is the manifestation of Brahman through cosmic māyā, the principle of becoming that apparently diversifies the undiversified One. The multiple concrete universe subsists in the all-pervading Self that holds and controls māyā as the Supreme Lord (Īśvara). The sensible world is not the projection of the finite mind. The human mind and the sense-organs are revelatory or interpretative rather than creative. Truly speaking, man's originality of construction, where there is any, means the rearrangement of the materials existing in nature and not their origination. An individual perceives diverse objects in their existing forms without knowing their ultimate nature. He views things, of course, according to his view-point. They appear to him in the way his sense-organs meet them. At no time does he perceive a thing in its entirety. A house looks different from different angles. The sun appears small and flat from the earth. Then again, human minds react differently to the same thing. As stated in the *Pañcadaśī*:

[29] L. T. Hobhouse, *The Theory of Knowledge*, p. 531. [30] *Ibid*, p. 532.

'The will of the Lord, which is a mode of māyā, is instrumental in the act of creation; the will of the jīva, which is a mode of his mind, is instrumental in the act of experience.

While the thing created by Īśvara, such as a gem, remains identical; its experience varies because of differences in the mental states of the experiencers.

One may rejoice on getting the gem, another may grieve for not getting it; while a third who is indifferent to it sees it without joy or grief.

The three feelings of joy, grief, and indifference in relation to the gem are created by the jīva; whereas the gem that is common to them is created by Īśvara.'[31]

The mind and the sense-organs do not construct, but cognize things. Whatever powers of construction an individual has belong to his organs of action (karmendriyas) and not to the organs of perception (buddhi-indriyas). The mind is, of course, common to both. Neither the mind nor the sense-organs, singly or jointly, can convert a tree into timber or a chair. They cognize things as they exist in their present forms. In perceiving an object they do not produce it out of its original nature. They do not create diversities on the ground of reality, which is beyond their ken. A horse appears as a horse, and a dog as a dog to all, because they exist as such. Hardly does an individual mistake the one for the other. Sugar tastes sweet because the quality of sweetness is in the substance called sugar. Salt tastes salty because the quality of saltiness is in the substance called salt. This is why sugar is sugar everywhere, and salt is salt everywhere. Nobody uses salt to sweeten his food or drink, except by mistake. The sensible world is coexistent with the psycho-physical organism, which cannot exist without it. The one cannot possibly be a construction by the other. Even the physical body of an individual, where the organs are located, is a part and parcel of the sensible universe. From the same material elements arise the physical body, the end organs, and their objects, in concrete forms, including food, drink, habitat, etc. As stated by Śaṅkara, mind and the senses perceive objects as they exist: 'Truly in every act of perception we apprehend the external objects, such as a pillar, a wall, a jar, and a cloth.'[32]

So the view that the sensible objects are the constructions of the knowing subject, as stated by Dr Chatterjee, is not consistent with the Vedāntic position, as far as we can see. In his words:

'The objects of knowledge are the stable constructions that we make

[31] PD IV: 19–22.

[32] BS II: 2.28, com.

of the real through certain instinctive modes of thought and speech, and they are the same for us in so far as they serve the same needs of our practical life.'

Further,

'So we may say that existence is the pure datum of sensation. Now the specification of this datum as a particular existent like color, smell, etc., and the farther specification of it as *something* colored, smelling, etc., is due to our mind-body or the animate organism. It is the body with the sense-organs that manifests colors, sounds, smells, etc., when it specifically responds to the influences of a reality existing outside. And it is our mind, or more especially our understanding that presents these colors, sounds, etc., as the qualities of individual objects like a chair, a table, a tree. Thus it comes about that we have the perception of objects when we receive certain influences from an environing existence or being *as such.*'

He adds:

'Therefore, objects are, in a sense, constructed by our mind-body. But since the synthesis of sense-data is not a matter of choice for us, but is due to the constitution of our mind-body, and also because there is in us neither an effort of will for nor any consciousness of the synthesis, it is, for all practical purposes, a standing fact, a sort of standing awareness of objects. And this standing awareness is the perception of objects.'[33]

Perception means presentation of the object perceived. It is neither representation, nor construction. This intrinsic character of perception is too vital to be ignored.

7. *The experiencer, the world of experience, and the all-knowing Īśvara, the Ruler of both, are co-existent. Their sole support is Brahman, the ground of all*

In the Vedāntic view the entire relative order is a triple existence consisting of individuals (the jīvas), the objective universe (jagat), and their supreme Ruler (Īśvara). These three are interrelated and without beginning. The existence of one implies the existence of two others. Neither the living nor the non-living are self-sustaining. Their existence as an ordered whole could not be possible without an all-knowing and all-powerful Being. Then again, had there been no such world to rule over the existence of the supreme Ruler would

[33] Satischandra Chatterjee, *The Problems of Philosophy*, pp. 102, 145, 146.

have no meaning. Manifest or unmanifest, the world ever is, and its sole Ruler is God (Īśvara). It rotates from one state to the other. Its projection, preservation, and dissolution continue endlessly in cyclic order under the guidance of the one supreme Ruler (Īśvara). We cannot trace its origin beyond the causal state, the undifferentiated prakṛti or māyā, which He holds as His creative energy. We cannot trace the origin of the tree beyond the seed-form. The world comprising the living and the non-living cannot come out of nothing, nor can it come out of God Himself. Both the positions are untenable, as explained by Śaṅkara in his commentary on the *Brahma-sūtras*, which states: 'That the world is without beginning is supported by reason and is also known from the scriptures.'[34] As declared by the Upaniṣad, the animate being and the inanimate nature both are unborn.[35] The creative process is intended for the experience and the liberation of the individual souls.

Brahman the Absolute underlies the triple existence. Immutable and non-relational though It be, It sustains the relative order. In that secure foundation exists the triad—the individuals, the objective universe, and the supreme Lord.[36] Brahman is their very being. In fact, they are the threefold manifestation of Brahman through māyā, the matrix of all names and forms, the superimposition of which makes the undiversified One apparently diversified. 'When the experiencer knows all these three to be Brahman, then he is freed from fetters,' declares the Upaniṣad.[37]

Īśvara is the highest manifestation of Brahman in the relative order.[38] He is associated with māyā as His limiting adjunct (upādhi), but is not affected by its faculty of superimposition. He controls māyā and holds it as His manifold power to rule over the cosmic process. In Him Brahman is manifest as cosmic and acosmic Consciousness. He has the knowledge of the manifold with full Self-awareness as Nondual Brahman. Māyā has countless facets as finite or individual māyā, which is usually termed 'avidyā' or 'ajñāna'. Thus, māyā has two main aspects: cosmic (samaṣṭi) and individual (vyaṣṭi).[39] Cosmic māyā is the limiting adjunct of Īśvara, individual māyā (called ajñāna or avidyā) is the limiting adjunct of the jīva (the individual being). Being of pure sattva, by which rajas and tamas are completely overpowered, cosmic māyā does not limit Īśvara's knowledge, power, or freedom.

In the jīva (the individual being) Brahman is manifest as finite consciousness. Being associated with individual māyā as his limiting

[34] BS II: 1.36, com. [35] *Vide* Sv. U. I: 9, IV: 5.

[36] *Vide* Sv. U. I: 7, com. [37] Sv. U. I: 9.

[38] *Vide* the author's article, 'Īśvara and His Māyā,' *Prabuddha Bharata*, July and August issues, 1960.

[39] *Vide*, VS, sec. 7.

adjunct (upādhi), in which rajas and tamas are preponderant, the jīva is subject to its binding capacity—its twofold power of concealment and projection. Brahman, as the controller of māyā, is Īśvara; Brahman as controlled by māyā is the jīva. Īśvara is one, whereas the jīvas are many. The creation of the universe, physical and psychical, is due to cosmic māyā. The individual ajñāna is particularly responsible for the jīva's lack of discrimination between the self and the not-self.

The phenomenal world is a fact from the jīva's position. But its existence is not due to his ajñāna. With individual ajñāna there is cosmic māyā. The one betokens the other, just as the fruit betokens the tree. The jīvahood is invariably linked with Īśvarahood. The one cannot exist without the other. The jīvas are born and reborn under the rulership of Īśvara, who is beyond birth and death. He guides the cosmic process eternally throughout its projection, preservation, and dissolution. It is true that when an individual realizes Brahman, all distinctions and differences vanish; undivided, limitless Consciousness alone shines; freed from all limiting adjuncts, including their root-cause, ajñāna, he becomes identified with Brahman as he attains final Liberation. But the universe continues to exist as a fact of experience of countless other jīvas.[40]

In inanimate nature Brahman is manifest as being or existence; consciousness is hidden. All variations are due to the superimposition of names and forms by māyā on immutable Brahman. Every object is a form of existence. When its form (as the chair, for instance) changes, existence appears in another form (perhaps as wood). We never perceive existence without form. Consequently, we do not know the fundamental nature of anything. It is always hidden in some extrinsic form or other. Each and every transitory form has the Absolute as its content. This is why not a thing can go out of existence. Not a grain of sand can be annihilated. The whole world of objects is a mass of multiple forms screening Reality. It is an appearance. It exists because of Brahman. It is not real in itself. Yet it is not unreal like the horn of a hare; because it is perceived. Essentially, it is not different from Brahman, its basis and being.[41] As an appearance, it is neither real nor unreal; neither different nor non-different from Brahman. So says Gauḍapāda: 'This manifold does not exist as identical with the Self, nor does it stand by itself independent of the Self. They are neither different nor identical; this is what the seers see.'[42]

[40] *Vide* YS II: 22, com. *Tattvavaiśāradī*; VP VII, Liberation. According to the theory of multiple jīvas, Liberation of one does not lead to the Liberation of all. Even according to the view that avidyā (nescience) is one, the simultaneous Liberation for all is not possible.

[41] *Vide* BS II: 1.14. [42] MK II: 34.

In their essential nature as Brahman there is no difference between the jīva and Īśvara; the two are identical. But there is an immense gulf of difference between them in the manifest state. The one is bound, while the other is the Liberator of souls. The jīva can by no means attain Īśvarahood, the lordship of the universe.[43] He is to worship Īśvara for liberation. Finally, he can realize his identity with Īśvara as Brahman, the innermost Self of one and all. Being immanent in the universe as the all-pervading Self, Brahman is its Internal Ruler and the jīva's immortal Self. As declared by the Upaniṣad:

'He who inhabits the earth but is within it, whom the earth does not know, whose body is the earth, and who controls the earth from within, is the Internal Ruler. He is your immortal Self.'

'He who inhabits the sky but is within it, whom the sky does not know, whose body is the sky, and who controls the sky from within, is the Internal Ruler. He is your immortal Self.'

'He who inhabits darkness but is within it, whom darkness does not know, whose body is darkness, and who controls darkness from within, is the Internal Ruler. He is your immortal Self.'

'He who inhabits light but is within it, whom light does not know, whose body is light, and who controls light from within, is the Internal Ruler. He is your immortal Self.'

'He who inhabits all beings but is within them, whom none of the beings knows, whose body is all beings, and who controls all beings from within, is the Internal Ruler. He is your immortal Self.'

'He who inhabits the eye but is within it, whom the eye does not know, whose body is the eye, and who controls the eye from within, is the Internal Ruler. He is your immortal Self.'

'He who inhabits the mind but is within it, whom the mind does not know, whose body is the mind, and who controls the mind from within, is the Internal Ruler. He is your immortal Self.'

He is never seen, but is the Witness; He is never heard but is the Hearer; He is never thought but is the Thinker; He is never known, but is the Knower. There is no other witness but Him, no other hearer but Him, no other thinker but Him, no other knower but Him. This Internal Ruler is your immortal Self. Everything else but Him is mortal.'[44]

8. *It is Brahman that appears as the jīva (the individual being)*

As one and the same radiant sun being reflected in many water-vessels appears to be many suns, even so resplendent Brahman, though One without a second, being reflected in countless facets of māyā, that is, innumerable individual ajñāna or avidyā, is individual-

[43] *Vide* BS IV: 4.17. [44] Br. U. III: 7.3, 6, 13–15, 18, 20, 23.

ized as countless souls.[45] Ajñāna is the causal body of an individual. Under its spell the finite soul gets identified with mind (antaḥkaraṇa, which belongs to the subtle body) and appears as the ego. Being further identified with the gross body and the organs, it becomes a distinct individual. The reflection of the sun is but the sun appearing as such. It is the apparent sun. It has no existence apart from the real sun. Similarly, the individual soul is but Brahman appearing as such. Behind the ever-changing ego Brahman shines as the immutable self (kūṭastha). While the individual soul functions as the experiencer (bhōktā) and as the doer (kartā), the immutable self (kūṭastha) stays behind as the witness (sākṣī) of all cognitions and actions. In deep sleep when all mental operations cease and even ego-consciousness subsides, the self endures as the witness of complete inapprehension and restfulness of the mind in the causal state. This is the light that shines in darkness. It manifests ajñāna, the causal body.

Though Brahman is intrinsically unvaried and immutable, yet dwelling within the limiting adjuncts of the body, the organs, mind, etc., it appears to undergo such changing conditions as growth and decay, hunger and thirst, which are the properties of the limiting adjuncts, but are wrongly ascribed to the indwelling self through ajñāna.[46] When the reflection of the sun quivers because of the quivering of the water-vessel, the sun does not quiver. Similarly, when the individual soul with its limiting adjuncts suffers, Brahman that holds it does not suffer. All miseries of the jīva are owing to ajñāna.[47]

When a person overcomes ajñāna by the cultivation of the knowledge of the true nature of the self, then he goes beyond all limitations. The knower of Brahman verily becomes Brahman. So it is said:

'Having realized this [the supreme Self] the seers become fully satisfied with that knowledge. With their souls established in the supreme Self they become free from all attachment and peaceful. Such contemplative persons whose minds are ever united with the supreme Self perceive everywhere the all-pervading One [as long as they live] and [at death] enter into That which is all this [Nondual Brahman].

Having been convinced of the truth, the end of Vedāntic know-

[45] *Vide* BS III: 2.18, S. com. Another illustration has been given in the *Brahma-bindu Upaniṣad* (12): 'Like the moon reflected in ripples of water, one and the same all-pervading Self dwelling within each and every individual appears to be many selves that are similar and various.' Cf. SB XI: 18.32, 'The One Supreme Self alone dwells in the bodies of all beings and in one's own body like the moon reflected in many vessels of water.'

[46] *Vide* BS III: 2.20, S. com.

[47] *Vide* BS II: 3.46, S. com.

ledge, the earnest seekers, with their minds purified by the practice of renunciation, become united with Brahman and experience supreme immortality [while living] and, at the end, being free from death once for all, they attain complete freedom.'[48]

9. *Consciousness is not a product nor a process*

Consciousness is at the root of life. The materialistic view that consciousness originates from the bodily processes is not tenable. It leaves the fundamental question regarding the origin and development of a living organism unanswered. The point is this. What is it that unites the physical elements into a coherent system so as to make it live and grow according to a certain pattern? It is certain that inert material elements cannot join together for concerted action. Dull, insentient physical objects cannot have any plan or purpose of their own. Purposiveness implies consciousness. Life is ever associated with a central principle of sentiency. No living organism can function without being animated by it. The very existence of a living organism signifies consciousness as its guiding force, implicit though it may be in some cases. That which fashions the material form, develops, animates, and cognizes it, must be something other than the form itself. It is the non-physical luminous self, whose substance is consciousness. As stated in Sāṁkhya philosophy, 'The building of the body, the seat of experience, is due to the presence of the indwelling experiencer; otherwise, its decomposition would result.'[49]

Consciousness precedes all mental operations. Manifest or latent, it is there. Unconscious will is a misnomer. Will implies self-determination, which is not possible without well-developed consciousness. Instinct is dormant intelligence. Instinctive behaviour is purposive and, therefore, different from mechanical or reflex action. To quote Dr McDougall:

'A common view represents instinctive behavior as "unconscious" and intelligent behavior as "conscious" and raises the question—at what stage of evolution did Intelligence or "Consciousness" begin to supplant or modify unconscious Instinct . . . I have tried to show my readers that the rudiments of Mind are implied by the behavior of the most lowly animals, and that we cannot hope to trace the genesis of purposive behavior out of mechanical processes; because the two conceptions are radically different. Eventually it may be shown that all processes are of one type; but it seems more likely that the processes of inorganic nature may ultimately be shown to be pur-

[48] Mu. U. III: 2.5, 6.

[49] SD V: 114.

posive than that the behavior of animals will be shown to be purely mechanical.'[50]

Consciousness does not originate from mechanical processes. It is at their start. No human ingenuity can invent a machine that can think or feel. A robot can have technical skill, but not the power of cognition. A material object cannot even move of itself.[51] It is characteristically inert. It needs a conscious agent to move it. Only a sentient being is found to be self-acting in the true sense. An insentient thing is impelled to act. An automaton lacks initiative. It is set to function in a certain way. Whatever is devoid of consciousness, be it solid matter, or energy, or mind, moves because of its contact, direct or indirect, with conscious spirit. Inanimate nature does not beget consciousness. All its movements are due to some self-intelligent Power.

Thus, Vedānta declares intangible Consciousness, the subtlest of all existents, to be reality itself. It reverts the materialistic position that tangible, solid matter is real in itself and that consciousness is but a mere process. Pure Consciousness (śuddha caitanya, cinmātra) is the basis and being of the variegated universe. All variations are due to the superimposition of names and forms by māyā, the principle of appearance, which is neither real nor unreal. One self-effulgent Being underlies the manifold. Its manifestation as finite centres of consciousness is noticeable only in living organisms; while in the non-living it is hidden. One indivisible, limitless Consciousness is seemingly divided into myriad souls, being apparently limited by countless finite minds dwelling in countless physical structures of various orders of life from the lowest to the highest. In a human being Consciousness is manifest as a distinct individual self. Man's self-awareness is well defined, wrong though it may be.

10. *The fundamental reality underlying every phase of existence is Pure Consciousness*

One and the same reality underlies the world of phenomena external and internal. This is the fundamental principle of Consciousness that is manifest within each individual as the inmost self (ātman). What is innermost in the universe must be innermost in every individual being. A man discovers the Self of the universe by knowing the self within. It is this inner light that manifests to him all objects external and internal. It reveals his knowledge and ignorance as well. It is because of the luminous self that an individual knows what he knows

[50] William McDougall, *Outline of Psychology*, New York, Scribner, 1924, p 203.

[51] *Vide* BS III: 2.38, S. com.

and what he does not know. The witness-self (sākṣī) that transcends the ego illuminates all that is known and unknown to him.[52]

The transcendental self has no limit. It is not confined within the psychophysical system. Basically, it is the same as the all-pervading Self. But as related to each individual it is apparently different, so it is called the 'jīva-sākṣī (the individual witness-self).' To give an illustration, though the sky is one and the same and without limit, still it appears different and limited from each window.

The subject and the object, though related, are not interdependent. Both are not real in the same sense. It is the object that changes, but not the subject, the knowing self. The objects depend on the subject for their manifestation; but the subject is self-luminous. It is the ground of all cognition and is never cognized. It is not a thing among other things. It is beyond the category of objects and stands by itself as contentless consciousness. Its relation with objects is only apparent. It is invariable in the midst of the variable, changeless in the midst of the changeful, conscious in the midst of the non-conscious. In waking, dream, and dreamless sleep the knower is the same. So a person says, 'I dream', 'I sleep', 'I wake up'. As the witness of all changes, physical and psychical, the self is immutable. Changes imply an unchanging observer that relates the succeeding to the preceding condition or event.

What is generally called 'the waking' or 'the conscious' state is actually the domain of ego-consciousness. Its scope is very much limited. We may say that the subconscious or the unconscious level of mind is below ego-consciousness, whereas the super-conscious state is above it. The immutable self beyond the ego covers all the three levels. According to Patañjali, by the practice of concentration on the mind (antaḥkaraṇa) in the lotus of the heart one can gain the knowledge of its contents, that is, the latent tendencies, desires, etc., imbedded in the subsoil of the mind; by the practice of concentration on the self distinct from the mind one can get free from egoism and gain the knowledge of the luminous self.[53]

Consciousness is not an attribute or characteristic of the self, but its very essence or substance. It is prior to everything. Each and every form of existence presupposes consciousness by which it is illuminated. But for this nothing could appear to exist. With existence everywhere Brahman shines, howsoever vaguely, as the consciousness that manifests it.[54] It is consciousness dwelling in man that determines the nature of the things he perceives, their existence and non-existence, action and inaction, origination and dissolution, and so forth. Consciousness has neither beginning nor end. Its

[52] *Vide* PPV, 'Sarvam vastu jñātatayā vā ajñātatayā vā sākṣicaitanyasya viṣaya eva.'

[53] *Vide* YS III: 34, 35.

[54] *Vide* BS II: 1.6.

beginning or end cannot be established without positing consciousness as a witness.[55] It is the datum, the starting-point of all experience. It is self-existent as well as self-luminous.

Consciousness being its very essence, man's inmost self shines of itself. It is awareness, immediate and direct. It becomes more or less manifest through the mind (antaḥkaraṇa), the main limiting adjunct (upādhi) of an individual. It invariably finds expression through the ego-idea, a mode of the mind. This is why a person, though lacking in the knowledge of the true nature of the self, is spontaneously aware of his own existence as 'I am'. This is the first expression of a man's knowledge, vague though it may be in the beginning. From this arise all his cognitions. Every individual, cultured or uncultured, mature or immature, intuitively knows that he is. His existence is self-evident. He invariably accepts this as an established fact. None in the world is able to controvert it. This is the only self-authenticated knowledge that every human being has as innate in him. It awaits no verification or confirmation. No reasoning process, no 'cartesian doubt', is involved in it. 'I am, therefore I think', and not 'I think, therefore I am (*cogito ergo sum*)'. All cognitive processes proceed from this central fact of man's self-awareness. Since man's awareness, vague though it be, is valid in itself, how can it be otherwise when it is fully manifest? No wonder that the seer's experience of the self as Pure Consciousness, beyond all relativity, proves to be its own evidence (svasaṁvedya).

An individual self (jīvātmā) has two main aspects: empirical (vyavahārika) and transcendental (pāramārthika). Consciousness as reflected in finite ajñāna and identified with mind is the empirical self, the ego, jīva-caitanya, the doer of actions and experiencer of their fruits (kartā-bhōktā). This functions as the cognizer (pramātā). Being subject to ajñāna, it ascribes to itself various psychical and physical conditions. It is also called 'cidābhāsa (the reflected self).'

Consciousness associated with finite ajñāna and the mind as their spectator and distinct from them is the witness-self (sākṣi-caitanya). It is not affected by ajñāna, of which it is the witness. All mental modifications are revealed to it. Unchanging it witnesses all changes —psychical and physical. So it is called 'kūṭastha', lit. *firm as an anvil*, that is, immutable. Just as the sun remains the same while its reflection in water varies, so does the witness-self (sākṣi-caitanya) remain the same while the reflected self varies. It is the immutable self that holds the reflected self, the ego, with all its limiting adjuncts. In fact, the reflected self is no other than the immutable self appearing as such, just as the sun's reflection is but the sun appearing as such.

Pure Consciousness is all that exists. It appears to be many. All

[55] *Vide* PD I: 7, Rāmakṛṣṇa's com.

differentiations are apparent. Anything we perceive is but a form appearing as an entity because of the underlying Reality. Indeed, we do not cognize the essential nature of any object of knowledge. This Vedānta declares to be Pure Consciousness. It is the sole entity, all else is mere form. What we perceive as a chair is Pure Consciousness apparently limited by the 'chair' form. Fire is Pure Consciousness apparently limited by the 'fire' form. Heat is Pure Consciousness apparently limited by the 'heat' form. Sound is Pure Consciousness apparently limited by the 'sound' form. A sense organ, ear, for instance, is Pure Consciousness apparently limited by the 'ear' form. A mental modification is Pure Consciousness apparently limited by that particular mental mode. Happiness is Pure Consciousness apparently limited by the mental mode of happiness. Mind (antaḥkaraṇa) is Pure Consciousness apparently limited by the 'mind' form. Cognition is Pure Consciousness apparently limited by the cognitive mode of mind. Cognizer (pramātā), cognition (pramiti), and the object of cognition (prameya) are but variants of Pure Consciousness. The limiting forms are mere superimpositions. They have no existence apart from Pure Consciousness.

There are differences in the manifestation of Consciousness in these various forms. But the only direct manifestation of consciousness to an individual is the witness-self (sākṣī-caitanya). It is the knower that is never known. It is not an object of knowledge, but the basis of all knowledge. All ontological and epistemological enquiry rests on this. It is the fountain-head of all cognitive processes. All methods of knowledge issue from this. The witness-self manifests the cognizer (pramātā, the percipient ego), cognition (pramiti), and the object of cognition (prameya). It reveals both knowledge and ignorance. It is the light that manifests darkness. Receiving this light mind gains the capacity to unveil things.A mental mode corresponding to the object is indispensable to any knowledge. Being made of sattva, mind and sense-organs reflect the light of the self more or less and prove instrumental in the perception of external objects.

CHAPTER III

PERCEPTUAL KNOWLEDGE; ITS DISTINCTIVE CHARACTER AND PROCESS

1. *Consciousness is all that is manifest*

Things appear to exist because of the radiance of underlying Consciousness. But for it, nothing can be manifest. This alone shines in and through everything. Bereft of the luster of Consciousness all objects, physical and psychical, merge in the darkness of ajñāna (antiknowledge). The following illustration will elucidate the point. As the morning sun lights up the stained glass of a memorial window, the multicoloured paintings that never appear in the darkness of night, immediately become vivid. The various forms and figures in different hues seem to be aglow. The blue sky, the fleecy clouds, the grey mountains, the trees and shrubs with green foliage, the sparkling streams, the grassy meadows, the dusky cottages, the yellow and red robed human forms—all come into full view. Each and every painted object appears distinct and manifest in its own way. But, as a matter-of-fact, in and through the entire picture all that is manifest is the light of the sun. That shining, all else appears to shine. As the sunlight gets dim, the whole painting gets dim. With the disappearance of the sunlight the painting vanishes. The very window is hardly noticeable in the absence of light. Similarly, whatever is manifest in the universe is manifest through the light of Consciousness. 'Through Its radiance all this shines', declare the Upaniṣads.[1]

It is through Consciousness that the subject knows and the object becomes known to him. Both are manifest through Its radiance. It is not physical light that makes things visible, but the light of Consciousness. Nothing else is self-manifest. Nothing else has light of its own. Where there is no expression of Consciousness as self-awareness, vague though it may be, there is no manifestation, that is to say, no cognition of any kind. The knower, knowledge, and the known—all come to light through the light of Consciousness. This is what manifests all variations of existence, including darkness. The world appears only to a conscious being. To an insentient thing, say

[1] Ka. U. II: 2.15; Mu. U. II: 2.10; Sv. U. VI: 14.

a mountain, nothing is revealed. Nor does the mighty mountain unveil itself. Even the resplendent sun, the sole illuminator of the solar universe, is unaware of its own existence and of all that is illuminated by it. It is the light of Consciousness shining within sentient beings that manifests all objects. Through each and every thing, that alone shines. Illuminated by the light of Consciousness all things and beings, whatsoever they may be, appear to exist. With all its luminaries the entire physical universe of variegated forms, colours, tactilities, tastes, and odours, would be reduced to a homogeneous mass of darkness but for the light of Consciousness.

In the sensible universe physical light appears to be self-manifest. Everything else seems to be manifest through it. Nothing is manifest where there is no light. When light goes out nothing appears. It shines through all that appears. But the Light of lights is Consciousness. Physical light cannot help where there is no manifestation of Consciousness. It is true that nothing can be seen without external light. But external light helps the eyes only when they are associated with Consciousness. This is why even in broad daylight a person cannot see what is in front of him when he is absent-minded or happens to be asleep with the eyes open. The inner light of Consciousness conveyed by the mind (antaḥkaraṇa) through the organ of vision first illuminates external light. When illuminated by the light of Consciousness external light unveils things. Just as the lantern which a person carries with him through the darkness reveals what is in front of him, similarly, the consciousness which is carried by the mind illuminates things (including light) as it approaches them through the vehicles of the sense-organs.

Indeed, the manifestation of things is not due to physical light nor to the organ of vision. For visual perception light is no doubt necessary. It is an indispensable aid to the organ of vision. Both are responsible for the specific character of perception as visual, but not for perception itself. Similarly, other sense-organs characterize perception, each in its own way, but do not generate it. It is the light of the ever-luminous self (ātman) that is responsible for all perceptions, internal and external. In the absence of physical light, all perceptions save the visual are possible. One can hear, touch, taste, and smell in complete darkness. When none of the sense-organs function, there is no cessation of cognition; one can think, feel, will, imagine, recollect, and reflect upon one's mental modifications. The mind causes variations in cognition, but is not responsible for cognition itself. In deep sleep when all mental operations cease, the self endures as the observer or the witness of that passive state of complete inapprehension.

The luminous self manifest within is not limited to the psychophysical system. As Pure Consciousness it is all-pervading. So says

Śaṅkara: 'This is the all-pervading Being, whose self-effulgence is utmost, because He is the illuminator of everything and not illumined by anything else.'[2] The Self-effulgent, Omnipresent Brahman is the Light of all lights. How can any light, whose luminosity is not intrinsic, manifest That? So the Upaniṣads affirm: 'There the sun does not shine, nor the moon, nor any of the stars. Nor do these lightnings flash there, to say nothing of this [terrestrial] fire? He shining, everything shines after Him. Through His radiance all these are manifest.'[3]

The Upaniṣad demonstrates the self-luminosity of Ātman by the following dialogue between Janaka, the Emperor of Videha, and the sage Yājñavalkya.[4]

Janaka: 'Yājñavalkya, what serves as the light for a man?'

Yājñavalkya: 'The light of the sun, O Emperor. It is through the light of the sun that he sits, goes out, works, and returns.'

Janaka: 'Just so, Yājñavalkya. When the sun has set, Yājñavalkya, what serves as the light for a man?'

Yājñavalkya: 'The moon serves as his light. It is through the light of the moon that he sits, goes out, works, and returns.'

Janaka: 'Just so, Yājñavalkya. When the sun and the moon have both set, Yājñavalkya, what serves as the light for a man?'

Yājñavalkya: 'The fire serves as his light. It is by means of fire that he sits, goes out, works, and returns.'

Janaka: 'Just so, Yājñavalkya. When the sun and the moon have both set, and the fire has gone out, Yājñavalkya, what serves as the light for a man?'

Yājñavalkya: 'Speech [sound] serves as the light. It is through the light of speech that he sits, goes out, works, and returns. Therefore, O Emperor, even when one's own hand is not clearly visible, if a sound is uttered, one manages to go there.'

[Śaṅkara comments: 'How can speech be called a light, for it is not known to be such? . . . Even when as in the rainy season, owing to the darkness created by the clouds frequently blotting out all light, one's own hand is not visible—though every activity is then stopped owing to the want of external light—if a sound is uttered, as, for instance, a dog barks or an ass brays, one manages to go there. That sound acts as a light and connects the ear with the mind: thus speech (sound) does the function of a light there. With the help of that sound serving as a light, the man actually goes there, works at that place and returns. The mention of the light of speech include smell, touch, and taste.']

[2] Br. U. IV: 3.7, com. [3] Ka. U. II: 2.15; Mu. U. II: 2.10; Sv. U. VI: 14.
[4] Br. U. IV: 3.1–7.

Janaka: 'Just so, Yājñavalkya. When the sun and the moon have both set, the fire has gone out, and speech has stopped, Yājñavalkya, what serves as the light for a man?'

[During dream and deep sleep when external lights do not help and the organs do not function, there must be some light for a man's experiences in those states. He sees, moves, meets people in dream. He awakes from deep sleep with the remembrance that he slept happily and knew nothing.]

Yājñavalkya: 'The self serves as his light. It is through the light of the self that he sits, goes out, works, and returns.'

[Śaṅkara comments: 'By the word "self" is meant that light which is different from one's body and the organs, and illumines them like the external lights such as the sun, but is itself not illumined by anything else.']

Janaka: 'Just so, Yājñavalkya. Which is the self?'
Yājñavalkya: 'This all-pervading Being that is identified with the cognitive mind and is in the midst of the organs, the self-effulgent light within the heart [the seat of Consciousness].'

It is through the unvarying light of the immutable self, ever-shining Consciousness, that we know all that we know and all that we do not know. It manifests darkness as well as light.

2. *The nature of knowledge (jñāna)*

Knowledge arises when there is a modification (vṛtti) of mind (antaḥkaraṇa) in the form of the object. It is an expression of Pure Consciousness through the mental mode (antaḥkaraṇa-vṛtti) corresponding to the object. Being thus illumined, the mental mode manifests the object to the self. Primarily, knowledge is Pure Consciousness. Its expression through the mental mode is secondarily called knowledge. It is in the sense of this modal consciousness (vṛtti-caitanya or vṛttijñāna) that the term knowledge (jñāna) is generally used. The same basic consciousness assumes various forms through different mental modes corresponding to different objects. Thus, a person has knowledge in many forms: knowledge of a thing, e.g., tree, house, horse; knowledge of an attribute, e.g., redness, beauty, roundness; knowledge of an action, e.g., flow, flight, blow. Like the varied knowledge of external objects there is also varied knowledge of mental states, such as happiness, fear, love, imagination, memory.

By taking the forms of diverse objects, mind causes variations in knowledge or consciousness, but does not generate it.

Vedānta rejects the Nyāya theory that knowledge is a product, that it arises from the contact of the self with the mind, or from the connection of the self, the mind, the sense-organ, and the object. D. M. Datta aptly remarks: 'In the Vedāntic theory knowledge or consciousness is not a product. The antaḥkaraṇa [mind] can thus be regarded only as a factor in the modification of the already existing consciousness, and not as an instrument in the generation of knowledge as the Naiyāyikas and others suppose it to be.'[5]

As the manifestation of Consciousness through a mental mode corresponding to the object, knowledge is varied and has a beginning and an end. It lasts as long as the mental mode lasts. It can be valid (pramā) or invalid (apramā).[6] It is continuous and not successive. It is not a series of momentary points of consciousness. Since the mental mode (antaḥkaraṇa-vṛtti) determines the form of cognition in each case, it is figuratively designated as knowledge.[7] It is to be noted that any determination or limitation of knowledge is apparent. Knowledge in itself (svarūpa-jñāna), that is, as Pure Consciousness is unvaried, without beginning and end, and self-established (svayaṁsiddha). There cannot be any question of validity or invalidity with regard to this. It is the ultimate presupposition of all means of knowledge. Thus, according to Nondualistic Vedānta, knowledge has two main aspects: metaphysical and empirical.

Knowledge, according to the Rāmānuja school of Viśiṣṭādvaita (qualified monism) is an intrinsic quality of the self (ātman). But according to Advaita Vedānta, knowledge as self-shining Consciousness is the very essence or substance of the self (ātman) and not its attribute. Knowledge, as it is, cannot be regarded as a quality inherent in mind, for mind is by nature devoid of consciousness, as we have noted above (chap. 1, sec. 6). Nor can knowledge in itself be characterized as a mental state or function, which is an object of cognition. Mental states and functions are not conscious in themselves. They are illuminated by the witness-self (sākṣi-caitanya). Knowledge as Pure Consciousness cannot be defined as subject-object relation, which is manifested by it. It precedes all relations. As observed by Reid: 'That knowledge is not itself a relation, but an apprehension of relations seems to be as clear to me as midday sunshine.'[8]

[5] D. M. Datta, *The Six Ways of Knowing*, p. 58.

[6] The English word 'knowledge' strictly means 'knowledge of truth' or 'true knowledge', that is, valid cognition (pramā), but we have used the word in a wide sense as synonymous with the Sanskrit term 'jñānam', which includes both valid and invalid cognition.

[7] *Vide* VP I.

[8] Louis Arnaud Reid, *Knowledge and Truth* (An Epistemological Essay), London, Macmillan, 1923, p. 139.

Of the threefold modification of mind, cognition, emotion, and volition, cognition is basic. There can be cognition without emotion and volition, though there cannot be emotion and volition without cognition. A person can cognize an object without any agreeable or disagreeable feeling with regard to it and without any will to gain or shun it. But one cannot have any feeling of pleasure or pain with regard to an object without cognizing it directly or indirectly. Nor can one have a will to secure or discard an object without knowing it. Thus, emotion and volition are invariably associated with cognition, but cognition may or may not be associated with either of the two.

Knowledge is simple awareness of an object. It is not an action directed to the object. Among the Indian philosophers the Mīmāṁsakas and the Buddhists conceive knowledge as an activity of mind with regard to an object. Some modern philosophers and psychologists hold a similar view. Śaṅkara refutes this idea.[9] Unlike knowledge, contemplation and meditation are mental acts with regard to an object. They do not necessarily correspond with the object. For example, one can meditate on an image of Viṣṇu as Viṣṇu. But knowledge must conform to its object. As the object is, so is its cognition. Knowledge does not act upon an object, but reveals it, whereas an action affects or tends to affect the object. Moreover, an action, mental or physical, depends upon the will of the agent. He may or may not act in a certain way, or he may act differently. In contrast, the manifestation of knowledge depends not upon the cognizer's option, but upon the right means of cognition. Knowledge spontaneously arises when the object and the appropriate means of knowing it are present. It does not rest on the cognizer's choice to know, or not to know, or to know otherwise. For example: if some words are spoken into one's ears, one will hear them whether one wants to or not; if one's eyes fall upon an image, one will see it as it is whether one likes to or not. The point is this. Knowledge is revelatory. It discovers, it does not create; it apprehends an object as it is, it does not construct or transform. Its sole purpose is to unveil what is.

3. *Perceptual and non-perceptual knowledge. Their distinctive marks*

Perceptual knowledge is direct cognition or immediate apprehension. Essentially, it is awareness pure and simple. The only direct cognition, in the strict sense, is Pure Consciousness manifest within each and every individual as the luminous self. It is the ground of subject-object relation. It shines of itself without objective content. It is manifest even when it has nothing to manifest. As pointed out by *Vedānta-paribhāṣā*, the valid perceptual knowledge, according to Vedānta, is nothing but Pure Consciousness.[10] This the Upaniṣad

[9] *Vide* BS I: 1.4, com.

[10] VP I.

declares as 'Brahman that is direct and immediate.'[11] Brahman is manifest in every human being as self-awareness that is direct and intuitive. This is immutable Consciousness (kūṭastha) ever present as the witness-self (sākṣī). It illumines the mental states: pleasure, pain, hope, fear, knowledge, ignorance, love, hate, memory, loss of memory, and so forth. The mental states are immediately cognized because of their presence to the witness-self. It is the immediacy of self-awareness that makes an object immediately known. To be directly cognized an object must be allied with the luminous self. Knowledge is direct, that is, perceptual, when the object is known directly.

The immutable consciousness that the witness-self is, being reflected in the mind and apparently limited by it, appears as the ego, the empirical self, which functions as the percipient (pramātā). So the percipient is inseparable from the witness-self, its basis. In perceiving an external object its alliance with the percipient is brought about by the outgoing mind (antaḥkaraṇa). In visual perception, for instance, the mind reaches out in the wake of the organ of vision to the object, becomes unified with it and assumes its form. This mental modification unveils the object, unites it with the percipient and leads to its immediate cognition. We shall dwell on this process later. Thus, in external perception the mental mode, 'antaḥkaraṇa-vṛtti', plays a vital role and serves as its direct cause. It is to be noted that in Advaita Vedānta the term 'antaḥkaraṇa-vṛtti' usually refers to the cognitive mode of mind. The term 'antaḥkaraṇa-pariṇāma' is generally used with reference to all the three modifications of mind—cognitive, affective, and conative.

Perceptual knowledge can be valid or invalid. When a rope is mistaken for a snake, it is a case of illusory perception. Mirage is an optical illusion. The blue vault of heaven is an illusory appearance common to all human beings. So are the rising and the setting sun. An erroneous perception is of two kinds: (1) perceiving one thing as another, e.g., mistaking an oyster for silver, or mistaking a pillar for a policeman; (2) perceiving a thing as different from what it is, e.g., seeing a white conch as yellow, or tasting a sweet fruit as bitter.

A valid cognition, direct or indirect, is a mode of the mind corresponding to the object. It is, of course, an expression of Pure Consciousness through the mental mode. As a mental modification knowledge is directly cognized by the witness-self. So, when a person knows something, say, a lotus, he at the same time knows that he has the knowledge of the lotus. Knowledge is intermediate between the witness-self and the object known. With reference to the witness-self, it is invariably a direct cognition. But with reference to the object, it can be either direct or indirect. In case the object is

[11] Br. U. III: 4.1.

indirectly known, the knowledge is indirect. Thus, the immediacy or the mediacy of knowledge depends on its relation with the object. When a person infers the existence of fire on a hill on seeing smoke arising from it, he gains the knowledge, 'The hill has fire'. Here the knowledge is direct, so far as the hill is concerned, but it is indirect with regard to fire. So one has the inner cognition in such form as 'I see the hill and I infer the fire'.[12] An external object is directly known when it is presented to the cognate sense-organ and is unified with the mental mode, which again unites it with the knowing self. It is to be noted that all knowledge, mediate or immediate, is due to the modification of mind. The mind, as it is, does not convey any knowledge. Even the percipient ego-consciousness becomes manifest through a mode of the mind, such as 'I (aham)'.

Perceptual knowledge rests on the very object known here and now. It is marked by immediacy. It does not follow from the knowledge of something else. The knowledge of fire on the hill in the foregoing example proceeds from the knowledge of smoke and its invariable concomitance with fire. Thus, the knowledge gained by inference (anumāna) is necessarily mediate, that is, non-perceptual. While the object perceived (hill in the above example) is manifest to the knower, the object inferred (fire in the same example) is not. Similarly, the knowledge gained by comparison (upamāna) proceeds from the knowledge of something other than the object known and is, therefore, mediate or non-perceptual. The knowledge gained by postulation (arthāpatti) is likewise non-perceptual. We shall dwell on these three methods of non-perceptual knowledge in a separate chapter. Broadly speaking, non-perceptual knowledge lacks the definiteness of perceptual knowledge. As we have noted above (chap. 1, sec. 1), the one is more or less general, the other is specific.

4. *The reason why internal cognition is invariably perceptual*

The coincidence of the mental mode (antaḥkaraṇa-vṛtti) with the object of cognition is essential to perceptual knowledge. In internal perception this inevitably occurs and is its only requisite. For, the objects of internal perception are the states of mind. The cognitive mode of mind naturally coincides with them. The mind has not, therefore, to go out to unite with the object, as in the case of external perception. The mental state of happiness, for instance, is not cognition itself. But as it arises it is revealed by the witness-self, so the percipient has the direct knowledge 'I am happy'. The cognition of happiness is a mode of the mind. It is perceptual knowledge because the cognitive mode invariably coincides with the object, the state of happiness. The presence of the cognitive modes in the

[12] *Vide* VP I.

perception of the mental states is recognized by *Vedānta-paribhāṣā*: 'Being cognized by the witness-self alone does not mean that the mental states are the objects of the witness-self without the presence of the mental modes [corresponding to them], but that they are the objects of the witness-self without the activity of the means of knowledge, such as the organs and inference.'[13] The mental states are known to the witness-self directly without any cognizing agency. So they are said to be 'manifested by the witness-self alone [that is, unaided by any means]'.

With the rise of the affective state arises the cognitive mode coincident with it. Owing to his identification with the mind, the percipient ascribes the mental mode to himself and says, 'I am happy'. This is an expression of the direct experience of the state of happiness due to the coincidence of the mental mode with it. The coincidence of the affective and the cognitive mode means the coincidence of the Consciousness underlying each. And this is the criterion of the perceptuality of internal cognition, according to *Vedānta-paribhāṣā*. We have mentioned above (chap. II, sec. 10) that everything finite is but an apparent form of Pure Consciousness, the fundamental reality. To quote *Vedānta-paribhāṣā*: 'Since the Consciousness limited by the state of happiness and the Consciousness limited by the [cognitive] mode relating to this are invariably limited by the two limiting adjuncts that coincide, the knowledge 'I am happy' is invariably a perception.'[14] Most philosophers, Eastern and Western, agree on the point that mental states are directly cognized.

The mental modifications (pariṇāma)—cognitive, affective, or conative—are invariably revealed by the witness-self as soon as they arise. So there cannot be an unknown mental modification. In the words of Patañjali: 'Because the self-intelligent ātman (puruṣa), the Lord of the mind, is immutable, the modifications of the mind (citta-vṛtti) are invariably known to it.'[15] The recognition of changes is due to an unchanging observer. It is not that the mind apprehends its own inner states, as Leibniz and many other Western philosophers maintain, but rather that the changeless luminous self beyond the mind apprehends its modifications. Patañjali has used the term 'citta-vṛtti' with regard to mental modifications in general. The term 'citta' is synonymous with 'antaḥkaraṇa' in this context. An external object may be either known or unknown, but not the mental mode. As pointed out by Vidyāraṇya: 'The states of being known or unknown do not hold good with regard to the mental modes (vṛttis) as in the case of external objects.'[16] Being revealed by the witness-self,

[13] VP I, Perception. [14] *Ibid.* [15] YS IV: 18.
[16] *Vide* PD VIII: 23.

they are invariably known. Only mind in itself is not perceivable, despite the fact that its modifications are invariably known.

Each cognition lasts as long as the corresponding mental mode lasts. When the mode disappears it leaves an impression (saṁskāra) on the mind. The memory of the cognition is due to this. A cognitive mode does not require any other cognitive mode for its manifestation, so it is said to be self-manifest. It is not an object of cognition like other mental modes, inasmuch as it is directly manifest by the witness-self.

5. *Perception is wholly presentative. It is not representative. Nor can it be partly presentative and partly representative*

According to Advaita Vedānta there cannot be any perception of unpresented objects. Nor can there be a conjunction of presented and unpresented elements in perceptual knowledge. In sense-perception the object of cognition must be present to the cognate sense-organ and directly known by the subject. There must be an actual contact between the cognizer and the thing cognized. The fundamental difference between perceptual and non-perceptual knowledge is this: in the one the object is manifest to the subject through the relevant sense-organ, in the other it is not. We have already explained (chap. 2, sec. 5) why Advaita Vedānta rejects the representative theory of perception. It also rejects the view that perception can be partly presentative and partly representative. Immediacy is the characteristic mark of perception. It can by no means be mediate.

Such instances of complex cognition as, 'I see there a piece of fragrant sandalwood', 'Ice appears cold', 'The orange looks sweet', are explained by Advaita Vedānta as cases involving coordination of perceptual and non-perceptual modes. Each is a composite of two distinct cognitions, one immediate, the other mediate. None of the instances can be regarded as a single act of perception partly presentative and partly representative. Let us elucidate the point with reference to the first example.[17] The piece of sandalwood is evidently present to the organ of vision, which cannot perceive fragrance. The organ of smell alone can apprehend fragrance, but it has no contact with its object because removed by distance. The size, shape, and colour of the sandalwood are perceived directly, but its fragrance is not; it is surmised through either recollection or inference. If the piece of sandalwood has been smelt before, the cognition of fragrance arises from memory; if it has not been smelt before,. it arises through inference from previous experience of the fact that sandalwood is inherently fragrant.

Jadunath Sinha thus explains the Advaita position in this context:

[17] *Vide* VP I.

'In the visual perception of fragrant sandal is the apprehension of sandal presentative or non-presentative? . . . It cannot be presentative because here the apprehending mental mode does not take the form of fragrance and identify itself with it, which is a condition of perception, according to the Śaṁkarite . . . the apprehension of fragrance must be non-presentative; for if the fragrance of this piece of sandal were already perceived, then the apprehension of fragrance in this case would be a recollection (smṛti), and if it were not already perceived then the apprehension of fragrance in this case would be inferential. It can never be presentative because fragrance is not an object of visual perception. Thus, according to the Śaṁkarite the visual perception of fragrant sandal is a mixed consciousness made up of presentative element and representative element. It is a compound perception or tied perception in which an idea is tied to a percept. It is a presentative-representative complex.'[18]

The Advaitins do not accept the Naiyāyikas' interpretation of this type of complex cognition as an integral visual perception of the fragrant sandalwood piece. According to the Naiyāyika school, with the sight of the piece of sandalwood its fragrance is also perceived by the eyes due to the past experience that sandalwood is fragrant. Although the organ of vision has no normal connection with fragrance, which is not its object, yet a supernormal connection (alaukika jñāna-lakṣaṇa sannikarṣa) is formed between the two in this case as a result of previous knowledge.[19] A person who has seen sandalwood and smelt its fragrance before has the two cognitions so closely associated in his consciousness that on seeing sandalwood he immediately perceives its fragrance. As stated by Jadunath Sinha: 'The visual perception of the sandal brings to consciousness the idea of fragrance by association, which serves as the extraordinary intercourse in the visual perception of the fragrant sandal.'[20]

Some modern psychologists interpret such cases (e.g., the orange looks sweet, ice appears cold) in a way similar to the Naiyāyikas. According to James Ward these are cases of complex *perception* partly presentative and partly representative. Says he: 'When we actually perceive an orange by sight we may say that its taste or feel is represented, when we perceive it by touch or taste we may in like manner say that its color is represented.'[21] There is in these

[18] Jadunath Sinha, *Indian Psychology—Perception*, p. 88, Kegan Paul, Trench, Trubner and Co. Ltd., London, 1934. In the next to the last sentence of this passage, the term 'perception', which occurs twice, does not seem to be a happy one. We would prefer the term 'cognition'. It is a case of complex *cognition*, but not of complex *perception*. This is what Prof. Sinha evidently means.

[19] *Vide* BP 63, 64, *Siddhānta-muktāvalī*.

[20] Jadunath Sinha, *Indian Psychology—Perception*, p. 81.

[21] James Ward, *Psychological Principles*, p. 168.

instances, in their view, 'not a mere revival of past ideas, as in memory, but a consequent *perception* of the unpresented elements.'[22] Such a view is not consistent with the intrinsic character of perception, in which the object must be presented to the subject. Otherwise, there cannot be direct cognition. Moreover, had the cognition of the unpresented element, e.g., the sweetness of an orange been a perception, that is, a gustatory experience, then a person could rest satisfied even with the sight of an orange without tasting it with the palate. According to Advaita Vedānta, the cognition of the sight of the orange is a case of perception, while the cognition of its sweetness is a case of memory or inference.

An ocular perception of fragrance or sweetness is inconceivable. It is contrary to the nature of the sense-organs. It is worthy of note that each sense-organ has the inherent tendency to keep to its own place. It does not encroach on another's sphere. The sense-organs coordinate, but do not conjoin. Consequently, in spite of their close association, no 'complication' of sense-perceptions is possible. It is true that the sense-qualities of an object, such as colour, fragrance, sweetness, softness or hardness, are inseparable. But the senses adroitly separate them. Each organ apprehends exclusively its own object. If a flower is presented to a person his eyes will receive only its sight (colour, shape, size), the olfactory organ mere fragrance, the organ of touch mere softness. Each sense-organ fulfils its particular function independently of the rest. So the perceptions are discrete. A person can only see, or only touch, or only smell, or only taste an orange through the appropriate sense-organ. Or he can see, touch, smell, and taste the orange at the same time by the different sense-organs carrying on their respective functions.

So the process of 'complication' by which the psychologists like Ward and Stout explain such cases of complex cognition, as—the orange looks sweet, ice appears cold, I see a fragrant flower, is not tenable. It is 'a process by which sensations or perceptions of different senses become so closely associated as to become integral parts of a single perception'.[23] The cognitions of presented and unpresented elements, howsoever closely associated they may be, cannot form integral parts of a single perception.

6. *The way the mental mode leads to external perception. Its twofold function*

The Advaitins hold that the mind must be united with the object in external perception as in the internal. This is what distinguishes

[22] D. M. Datta, *The Six Ways of Knowing*, p. 126.

[23] Satischandra Chatterjee, M.A., Ph.D. and Dhirendramohan Datta, M.A., Ph.D., *An Introduction to Indian Philosophy*, University of Calcutta, India, 1950, p. 179.

perceptual knowledge from the non-perceptual. In inferential knowledge, for instance, the mental mode (antaḥkaraṇa-vṛtti) corresponds to the object, but there is no contact between the two. In internal perception the mental mode is invariably united with the object, which is a state of the mind. In visual and auditory perception as well, the mind conjoined with the organ concerned, reaches out to the object and becomes unified with it in whatever aspect it is perceived. But in either case neither the mind nor the organ leave the body altogether. Obviously, in tactile and gustatory experience the mind as well as the organ stay in the body. As we have noted above (chap. 1, sec. 10), the olfactory organ also, in association with the mind, contacts the object while remaining in its own location.

Of the five types of sensible objects, the visual are the most conspicuous. As a consequence, in enquiries into sensory experience visual perception naturally has engaged the special attention of philosophers in East and West. There are differences of opinion among the Advaitins as to the exact way an object becomes manifest to a subject. These differences are due primarily to the differences in their conceptions of the knowing self and its relation to the objective world. Broadly speaking, there are in Advaita Vedānta three different views as to how the mental mode (antaḥkaraṇa-vṛtti), united with the external object, leads to its perception.[24] These three ways are known as:

(1) Ciduparāga, tinging the subject-consciousness (with the object).
(2) Āvaraṇa-bhaṅga or āvaraṇābhibhava, the removal of the veil (of ignorance that hides the object from the subject).
(3) Abhedābhivyakti, manifestation of the oneness (of the consciousness underlying the object with the consciousness underlying the subject).

Instead of going into the details of each method, which is related to a particular Advaita view of the jīva (the individual self), we shall delineate the main features of the perceptual process on which most Advaitins agree. The followers of Padmapāda and Sureśvarācārya, two great exponents of Advaita Vedānta among the disciples of Śaṅkarācārya, generally recognize a twofold function of the mental mode (antaḥkaraṇa-vṛtti) in external perception, viz. (1) removing the veil that hides the object from the subject and (2) associating the object with the subject-consciousness. In fact, this dual course comprises the first two of the three aforesaid ways.

[24] *Vide* AS, chap. 1, sec. 30, 'Pratikarma-vyavasthā', Bombay, Nirnayasagar Press, 1937, p. 479; *Siddhānta-bindu* on *Nirvāṇa-daśakam*, St. I, sec. 138; SLS, chap. 1, sec. 10, 11, Acyuta-granthamala, Banaras, India.

As pointed out by Madhusūdana Sarasvatī, the twofold function of the mental mode, namely, (1) āvaraṇabhaṅga (the removal of the veil of ajñāna that hides the object from the subject) and (2) ciduparāga (tinging the subject-consciousness with the object) is acknowledged by the Advaitins who conceive the individual soul as a finite being apparently limited by the mind (antaḥkaraṇa), and also by those who conceive the individual soul as consciousness reflected in avidyā and all-pervasive and detached.[25] It may be contended that in case the individual soul is held to be all-pervasive, then it must have contact with all objects at all times, and there cannot be any need of the mental mode for cognizing them. The point is this. The individual soul, all-pervasive as Consciousness reflected in avidyā though it be, functions as the percipient (pramātā) through the limiting adjunct of the mind (antaḥkaraṇa) located in the body. Consequently, such a case does not preclude the twofold purpose of the mental mode.

The Advaitins who regard the individual soul as finite and limited generally uphold the method of abhedābhivyakti, manifestation of the oneness of the consciousness underlying the object with the consciousness underlying the subject. It has been especially dwelt on by the author of *Vedānta-paribhāṣā*. We shall discuss this method also.

7. *The cognitive process of external perception*

Perception of an object means its manifestation to the subject-consciousness. When a person infers or remembers an external object, the mental mode corresponding to it becomes manifest to his inner consciousness, but not the object itself. We have noted above (chap. 2, sec. 10) that consciousness is immanent in every phase of existence. While it is hidden in all physical objects, it is manifest more or less in every sentient being. In a human individual it finds expression as distinct self-awareness, which is the only immediate and direct cognition in the strict sense. An object becomes directly known through its association with the immediacy of subject-consciousness. The mental mode brings about the association.

An object becomes manifest through the manifestation of the consciousness underlying it. Just as in the absence of light no physical object is visible, similarly, without the manifestation of consciousness underlying it no object (including light) is cognizable. As we have explained above (chap. 2, sec. 7), all objects of external and internal cognition as well, are but transformations of māyā or ajñāna (lit. antiknowledge, the matrix of the phenomenal world)

[25] *Vide Siddhānta-bindu* I, sec. 138.

and have no light of their own.[26] They are by nature shrouded in darkness, so to speak, being characterized by non-consciousness. Just as the visibility of an object means the visibility of the light associated with it, similarly the manifestation of an object (including light) means the manifestation of consciousness underlying it. Nothing but Pure Consciousness is self-manifest. It alone is responsible for the manifestation of all objects (including light).

When a person sees a red glass-pane he actually sees the light transmitted through it; neither the glass-pane nor its redness is noticeable in the absence of light. Or, when the glass is covered with soot or dirt and light does not get through it, then also he cannot see it. Similarly, no object can be perceived until the veil of ajñāna, that is, the darkness of non-consciousness that shrouds it and hides it from the percipient, is withdrawn and the underlying consciousness becomes manifest. Before a person cognizes an object, a jar for instance, as 'this is a jar,' it is unperceived by him, that is to say, hidden from him by a veil of ajñāna (the darkness of non-consciousness). It is on the removal of this veil and the consequent manifestation of the underlying consciousness through the operation of the mental mode that the object becomes known as 'this is a jar'. This veil of non-consciousness that hides the object before its perception is subsidiary or minor (tula) ajñāna. It is but a phase of the primal (mūla) ajñāna, of which the entire cosmos is a product. While primal ajñāna conceals Brahman, subsidiary (tula) ajñāna conceals or envelops all its products. The withdrawal or removal of subsidiary ajñāna means only the temporary uncovering of what is perceived by an individual. This is why the removal or the withdrawal of the veil (āvaraṇa-bhaṅga or āvaraṇa-abhibhava) is necessary each time a person perceives something.

Anything perceived is revealed by percipient-consciousness (pramātṛ-caitanya). When there is no contact with the perceiving self things lie hidden by ajñāna or non-consciousness. That this is a fact, as held by Advaita Vedānta, I shall try to substantiate by an illustration. Suppose in a well-lighted lecture hall, the speaker and the audience all fall asleep. What will happen then? Assuredly, there will be no knower and nothing known inside the room. This means that no manifestation of any kind will be there in spite of the illumination. Even light, apparently the manifester of things, will not be manifest as when perceived. The human individuals will be unaware of themselves and all else. All inanimate objects, including the shining lights,

[26] The terms 'māyā', 'prakṛti', 'ajñāna', 'avidyā', 'avyākṛta', though etymologically different, are often synonymously used. 'Ajñāna' is not absence of knowledge, but antiknowledge. It is *contradictory* to knowledge, being eradicated by the direct experience of Brahman. But it is *contrary* to Pure Consciousness, Brahman, its locus.

will be likewise unknown and unknowing. The darkness of ajñāna or non-consciousness in its two aspects of unknowingness and unknownness will envelope all things, living and non-living, luminous and non-luminous. This shows that in the absence of any contact with a perceiver physical objects remain enveloped by ajñāna in the form of unknownness. There cannot be any question with regard to their unknowingness. Anything unperceived is veiled by ajñāna.

An object is perceived in that aspect or form with which the mental mode coincides. In each case this removes the partitioning veil of ajñāna with respect to the perceiver alone. The mental mode conforms to its object in the way the sense-organ does. In the visual perception of a flower, for instance, the perceiver's mind, proceeding with the organ of sight, coincides with the object in its visual phase presented by the organ and characterized by such qualities as colour, shape, size, location, etc. In this case the mental mode removes the ajñāna that hides the visual phase from the perceiver concerned.[27] When a person smells the same flower the mental mode conjoined with the olfactory organ coincides with the fragrance emitted by it and removes the corresponding veil of ajñāna. As noted above (chap. 1, sec. 10), the organ of smell does not leave its location.

Impelled by its outgoing tendencies consequent upon the impressions of past karma, the mind runs after sense-objects. The sense-organs are also naturally inclined to their respective objects. It is with the aid of the organ concerned that the mind contacts anything physical. This is why no perception is possible in case the bodily organ is defective, or where there is lack of facilities for the sense-organ to reach its object. If the object is too near or too far, or if there is no medium of communication between it and the organ, or in case the object is incapable of being perceived by the senses, there cannot be any perception. In visual and auditory perception the mind conveyed by the relative organ swiftly flows to the object far though it may be. Light is the usual channel of communication for the first and air space for the second. Vision is affected by the conditions of light and even more is hearing by the atmospheric conditions. The mind and the organ conjointly serve as the connective between the percipient and the object perceived.[28]

[27] *Vide* AS, chap. 1, sec. 30, 'Pratikarma-vyavasthā'.

[28] Being composed of a very pure and fine substance (sattva aspect of subtle tejas; see chap. 1, sec. 8), the organ of sight has the capacity to move many times faster than physical light, which is after all a gross element. On a clear night a person can see a distant star as soon as his eyes turn towards it, since his mind conveyed by the organ of vision instantly reaches the luminary speeding through its light that has previously arrived where he is. When there is a flash of lightning the observer does not see it immediately. His organ of vision darts to the outburst of flame as its light impinges on his eyes. (The velocity of light is reckoned to be 186,000 miles per second.) He hears the peal

The mind (antaḥkaraṇa) being transparent and closest to the luminous self receives the reflection of its radiance. The mental mode is instrumental to perception more than anything else, because it conveys the reflected light of consciousness. Says Śaṅkara: 'Buddhi [the cognitive mind] is the instrument for the perception of all objects like a lamp placed in front amid darkness. It has been said, "It is through the mind that one sees, that one hears". Indeed, everything is perceived on being invested with the light of buddhi [the cognitive mind] like an object in the dark illumined by a lamp placed in front. The other organs are but the channels of buddhi.'[28a] Without external light nothing can be seen; but external light helps to manifest things illumined by the light of consciousness reflected in buddhi.

As the mental mode shining with the reflected light of consciousness coincides with the object, the veil of ajñāna that hides it from the percipient is withdrawn. Then the consciousness underlying the object, being manifest through the mental mode that is transparent, illumines the object. It is to be noted that the consciousness underlying the object is identical with the consciousness underlying the mental mode which is coincident with it. Just as something existing in darkness is seen by an observer when illuminated by light, similarly, an object being illumined by the underlying consciousness and associated with the subject-consciousness is directly cognized.

Evidently, the part of the mind (antaḥkaraṇa) that extends from the percipient's body to the object connects the object-consciousness with the subject-consciousness. The mental mode (antaḥkaraṇa-vṛtti) that brings about the perception of the object includes this part and also the part of the mind that coincides with the object. The following remark of Madhusūdana in his *Advaita-siddhi* sums up the cognitive process of external perception: 'It is the conscious-

of thunder after seeing the flash of lightning. Probably the peal follows the flash; they do not synchronize.

Even without seeing the lightning a person realizes on hearing the thunderpeal what direction and what distance it comes from. It is because the auditory organ rushing through the air space perceives the sound where it is produced. Very much restricted by the atmospheric conditions the sound waves have far less speed than light. No sooner do they strike the ear than the auditory organ proceeds toward their source. This is perhaps the main reason why one hears the peal after seeing the flash. It is a commonplace observation that the range of audition is very much limited compared with the range of vision.

When a person listens to a telephone call, say a long distance one, he hears the speaker's words as reproduced on the receiver. His organ of hearing does not travel to the other end of the line to receive the message. Consequently, on hearing the voice he cannot know (except by guessing) where it comes from. In case the sensation of sound by the auditory nerve generated its perception, the hearer could not locate its source instantaneously.

[28a] Br. U. IV: 3.7, com.

ness underlying the object which being manifest and related to the jīva (the percipient) by the mental mode manifests the object to him.'[29]

8. *The knower (pramātā), the object known (prameya), the knowledge (pramiti), and its means (pramāṇa) are the manifestations of the same underlying Consciousness*

Thus the whole process of visual perception consists of the following steps:

(1) The mind conjoined with the organ of vision reaches out to the object and coincides with it.
(2) The mental mode removes the veil (the darkness of ajñāna) that hides the object from the percipient.
(3) Consciousness underlying the object, being manifest through the mental mode, illumines the object.
(4) The mental mode associates the object-consciousness with the subject-consciousness.
(5) The subject perceives the object.

Consciousness manifest through the mental mode coincident with the object serves as the knowledge of the object. This is called in Advaita Vedānta 'phala (fruit)' being the resultant knowledge.

The mind (antaḥkaraṇa) has three main divisions in perception: (1) the part that stays in the body, (2) the part that extends from the body to the object, and (3) the part that coincides with the object. Because of the transparency of the mind consciousness underlying it, though one and the same, finds expression through the three parts in three different ways. Consciousness manifest in the part within the body functions as the percipient (pramātā). Consciousness manifest in the part intervening between the body and the object serves as the perceptive means (pramāṇa). Consciousness manifest in the part coincident with the object serves as the percept (pramiti).[30]

The object perceived is but the underlying consciousness manifest or appearing as such. It has no existence apart from the all-pervading Consciousness. That all-pervading Consciousness (Brahma-caitanya) which underlies the object unknown, that is to say, to be known, becomes manifest as the object known. So says Madhusūdana in *Siddhānta-bindu*: 'The object to be perceived (prameya) is but the all-pervading Consciousness (Brahma-caitanya) under-

[29] Quoted by Brahmānanda Sarasvatī in his com. *Nyāya-ratnāvalī*, on Madhusūdana Sarasvatī's *Siddhānta-bindu*, an elaborate exposition of Śaṅkarācārya's *Ten Stanzas on Nirvāṇa*, St. I, sec. 138, The Works of Śaṅkara, Pt. I, Beng. edn. by Rajendranath Ghose, Calcutta, 1927.

[30] *Vide* VPS Pt. II, p. 118, and *Siddhānta-bindu*, St. I, sec. 135–137.

lying it and unknown. The same is known as the object perceived.'[31] Further, in *Advaita-siddhi*: 'That Brahmacaitanya which is the object of knowledge being unknown is the knowledge of the object, when known.'[32] The Vedāntic term for the resultant knowledge is 'phala (fruit)' since it is the fruition of the perceptual process (pramāṇa-phalam). It signifies the cognition of the object perceived. Madhusūdana evidently follows Sureśvarācārya, who says: 'That Pure Consciousness (samvit) recognized as the resultant knowledge in the external objects of knowledge is the end of knowledge in Vedānta by such valid means as the Śruti texts.'[33]

While Madhusūdana declares Brahma-caitanya to be the resultant knowledge (phala-caitanya), Vidyāraṇya affirms the reflection of Consciousness (cidābhāsa) as the resultant knowledge. Says he in his *Pañcadaśī*: 'The cognition of a jar means the knowledge resulting from the reflection of Consciousness [in the mental mode coincident with the jar]. The resultant knowledge is not Brahma-caitanya, which is prior to perception.'[34] Evidently, Madhusūdana contradicts Vidyāraṇya. But the contradiction is only apparent. In declaring Brahma-caitanya to be the resultant knowledge, Madhusūdana does not mean Brahma-caitanya as It is, but as reflected in the mental mode coincident with the object. Vidyāraṇya also quotes Sureśvarācārya's verse mentioned above and explains it in support of his view: 'Here the author of the Vārttikam [*Bṛhadāraṇyaka-Upaniṣad-bhāṣya-vārttikam*] means that the reflection of consciousness, which is similar to Brahma-caitanya, is the resultant knowledge. For the difference between Brahma-caitanya and the resultant knowledge is known from *Upadeśasāhasrī* [*A Thousand Teachings* by Śaṅkarācārya].'[35]

As pointed out by Vidyāraṇya, the distinction between Brahma-caitanya and Its reflection on the mental mode is noticeable from the following fact: 'The consciousness reflected in the mental mode coincident with the jar manifests simply the jar. The fact that the jar is known is manifested by Brahma-caitanya.'[36] Again, 'The statement, "This is a jar" is due to the favor of the reflection. The statement, "The jar is known", is due to the favor of Brahma-caitanya [the underlying Consciousness].'[37] Brahma-caitanya and

31 *Siddhānta-bindu*, St. I, sec. 137.

32 'Ajñātatvena yat Brahma-caitanyam viṣayah tadeva jñātam sat phalam.

33 Quoted by Vidyāraṇya in *Pañcadaśī* (VIII, 11) and also by Madhusūdana in *Advaita-siddhi*.

34 PD VIII: 10. As defined by Rāmākṛṣṇa in his commentary on PD VII: 90, the resultant knowledge is consciousness reflected in the mental mode (coincident with the object). 'Phalam vṛtti-prativimbita cidābhāsah.'

35 PD VIII: 12.

36 *Ibid.* 4.

37 *Ibid.* 16.

Its reflection shine together in external perception. The jar and its knownness become manifest simultaneously.

It is because of self-luminous Pure Consciousness that the subject knows and the object is known. While in the subject Its manifestation is constant, though imperfect, in the object Its manifestation is inconstant and imperfect as well. The mind functions as the instrument of knowledge because of the Pure Consciousness transmitted by it. Being made of the same subtle sattva element as the mind, the sense-organs receive its radiance of reflected consciousness and serve as the instruments of perception. Indeed, the same unvaried all-pervading Consciousness shines through the knower (pramātā), the object known (prameya), the knowledge (pramiti), and the instrument of knowledge (pramāṇa). Its varied manifestations are due to the variations of the mental modes through which It finds expression.

9. *The perceptual method of abhedābhivyakti and its distinctiveness*

The fundamental note in the Advaitins' interpretation of the process of sense-perception is that an object is directly known by being linked with the perceiver's self-awareness which is spontaneous and immediate. We have explained above how the mental modification (äntaḥkaraṇa-vṛtti) leads to perception by connecting the consciousness underlying the sense-object with the subject-consciousness. In this process the two forms of consciousness are inter-connected, but do not coincide. The intervening mental modification extending from the perceiver to the object serves as the connecting link. The limiting adjunct of the percipient-consciousness is the mind inhabiting the body. The perceiver dwells in the body apart from the object.[38]

The perceptual method of 'abhedābhivyakti' (the manifestation of the object as non-different from the consciousness underlying the subject), which we have mentioned already, is different from the method described by us. In this the object-consciousness (prameya-caitanya) and the subject-consciousness (pramātṛ-caitanya) coincide. Thus, there is direct contact between the two. Dharmarāja Adhvarīndra has explained the process in his *Vedānta paribhāṣā*. The upholders of this method conceive the subject to be co-extensive with the mind, its limiting adjunct. With the mental mode the subject extends to the object and coincides with it. Thus, the consciousness limited by the mind, that is, the subject-consciousness (pramātṛ-caitanya), the consciousness limited by the mental mode (pramāṇa-caitanya), and the consciousness limited by the object (prameya-caitanya) become united.[39] This unity does not mean their identity, but coincidence,

[38] *Vide Siddhānta-bindu* I, sec. 136, 137, com. *Nyāya-ratnāvalī*.
[39] *Vide* VP I, Perception, its criterion.

inasmuch as the limiting adjunct of each endures. To illustrate: the all-pervading ākāśa (the finest and the most pervasive of all material substances) within a jar coincides with the ākāśa within the water and the ākāśa within the air inside the jar, without being identical. As a result of this unity or coincidence of the three forms of consciousness, the object becomes manifest to the subject, being unveiled and illuminated by the mental mode, the transparent transmitter of the light of consciousness.

To quote *Vedānta-paribhāṣā*:

'The perceptuality of objects, such as a jar, consists in their being not different from the subject [percipient-consciousness].'

'The absence of difference from the subject does not indeed mean identity; it means having no existence apart from that of the subject. To be explicit, since a jar, etc., are superimposed on the Consciousness limited by them, their existence is but the existence of the Consciousness associated with the object, for the existence of what is superimposed is not admitted to be something over and above that of its substratum. And since the Consciousness associated with the object is but the Consciousness associated with the subject, the latter Consciousness alone is the substratum of a jar, etc., and hence their existence is but that of the subject, and not something else. So the immediacy of a jar, etc., [in knowledge] is proved.'

'An object is said to be cognized by perception when it is capable [of being perceived] and is devoid of any existence apart from that of the Consciousness associated with the subject, on which [Consciousness] is superimposed a mental modification in the form of the object.'[40]

This method of abhedābhivyakti is open to a serious objection. One may say, 'Since the object, a jar for instance, is perceived as non-different from the subject-consciousness, why does not the perceiver have such experience as "I am a jar" or "In me is a jar" instead of "there is a jar"? Our answer is this: the nature of perception, as we have already explained, is determined by the nature of the mental mode that coincides with the object. In the visual perception of a jar the mental mode is qualified by its colour, size, shape, and also its location as presented by the attendant organ of sight. Further, though the subject-consciousness is associated with the entire mind, its limiting adjunct, it finds expression as the perceiver through the mental modification of 'I-ness' (aham-vṛtti), which is inevitably associated with the physical body in the waking state. So the perceiver of sense-objects invariably identifies himself with the body and does not extend with the mind. Consequently, he cognizes the jar where it is, located away from himself.

[40] VP I, Perception defined.

10. *Determinate and indeterminate perception*

Besides the two main divisions or types of perceptual knowledge—external and internal, Advaita Vedānta recognizes its two distinct forms or patterns, e.g., determinate (savikalpaka) and indeterminate (nirvikalpaka).[41] The determinate knowledge is relational. It is that which grasps the relatedness of the substantive and the qualifying attribute. The knowledge 'This is a jar' is determinate, because it apprehends the jar and its generic attribute 'jarhood' as related to each other. Similarly, the knowledge 'there is a bird on the tree' is determinate, because its object is the bird as related to the tree. So is the knowledge 'John has the book' is determinate, its object being the book as related to John. Generally, knowledge is relational and therefore determinate.

Indeterminate perception is non-relational and far less common than the determinate. It does not apprehend the relatedness of the substantive and its attribute. For example, the knowledge 'This is that man' is indeterminate, because the expression points to the man divested of the qualifying attributes 'this' and 'that'. Similarly, the knowledge imparted by the supreme Vedic teaching (mahāvākya), 'Thou art That', is indeterminate. By declaring the identity of the individual self (jīva) and the Self of the universe (Īśvara), the dictum points to Indivisible Pure Consciousness, the Nondual Reality underlying them, while dismissing from the seeker's mind their limiting adjuncts, the superimposed differentiating factors. Later on we shall dwell at length on the intended meaning of the great saying (mahāvākya) and its immediate apprehension.

Thus, in Advaita Vedānta the determinate and the indeterminate cognition mean two distinct forms or patterns of perceptual knowledge. But in Nyāya-Vaiśeṣika,[42] Mīmāṁsā, and Sāṁkhya systems,[43] they represent two distinct stages of development in the perception of a sense-object. According to these schools the indeterminate is the primary or the undeveloped state of perceptual knowledge. It is the immediate apprehension of the bare existence of an object at the first contact with the sense-organ. It does not comprehend the object as related to its kind or quality. Before the determinate knowledge of a jar, for instance, there arises a knowledge which does not comprehend the relation between the substantive jar and jarhood. This is indeterminate knowledge. The indeterminate state is implicit in perception and known only by inference. 'The knowledge that is called indeterminate is considered to be beyond the senses', says Viśvanātha of Navya-Nyāya (Neo-logic) school.[44] Further, 'Indeterminate knowledge is neither valid knowledge nor error. For it is

[41] *Vide* VP I, Perception.
[42] *Vide* BP 58, 135, 136; TS 46.
[43] *Vide* SK 27, com. *Tattvakaumudī*.
[44] BP 58.

devoid of reference to an adjectival feature, etc., and does not concern itself with relations.'[45]

As defined by Kumārila Bhaṭṭa (an eminent exponent of the Mīmāṁsā system and the founder of one of its two schools):

'There is the primary state of perception, vague awareness of something (ālōcana-jñānam) which is indeterminate, which arises from the object pure and simple, in which its generic and specific attributes are not comprehended but only its existence as a single thing, and which is like the knowledge of the infant and the dumb (and therefore inexpressible).'[46]

The determinate perception, on the other hand, is the distinct apprehension of an object with its generic and specific attributes. It means the cognition of a white horse not as a vague something but as an animal belonging to the species 'horse' and white in colour. It is invariably relational. It grasps an object in relation to its qualities, in relation to the subject, and in relation to other objects associated with it. For example, 'This is the largest fig tree in our orchard', 'I see a royal mansion on the river', 'John is riding a white horse', and so on. Each sentence sets forth the relation between the subject (uddeśya) and the predicate (vidheya).

It is to be noted that indeterminate knowledge is not recognized by monotheistic Vedānta comprising the five schools of Vaiṣṇavism,[47] which uphold Brahman with attributes (saguṇa) as the ultimate Reality. According to the Grammarian philosopher Bhartṛhari also, all knowledge is determinate, being relational. In his view each cognition is penetrated by a word signifying the object cognized; there cannot be any knowledge without apprehending the relation between the word and the object signified.[48]

11. *Recognition and recollection. The one is a case of perception; the other is not*

Recognition (pratyabhijñā) is the perception of something as identical with something previously known. It is experience associated with memory.[49] This relates the present context of the object

[45] BP 135, 136.

[46] *Ślōka-vārttika*, Pratyakṣa-sūtra, 112, 113. See footnote 1, chap. VI.

[47] These are (1) the Viśiṣṭādvaita of Rāmānuja, (2) the Dvaitādvaita of Nimbārka, (3) the Śuddhādvaita of Vallabha, (4) Dvaita of Madhva, and (5) Acintyabhedābheda of Baladeva Vidyābhūṣaṇa (a follower of Jīva Gosvāmī). See Appendix B, sec. 8–12.

[48] *Vide* Bhartṛhari's *Vākyapadīyam*, Brahma-kāṇḍam, 123, The Kashi Sanskrit Series, Banaras, India.

[49] Cf. Jadunath Sinha, *Indian Psychology—Perception*, p. 98, 'According to the Vedāntist, recognition is a single complex psychosis containing presentative and representative elements—it is a presentative–representative process.'

perceived with the context in which it was previously known and differentiates it from both. Such cognition as 'This is the man I saw yesterday,' is perception as far as the present experience of the man is concerned. It identifies the man perceived with the man recalled by apprehending him as distinct from the time and the space elements that qualify the present and the past experience. Recognition is not a repetition of past experience. It is a new apprehension of the object in a different context. As such, it is valid knowledge (pramā), which is defined in *Vedānta-paribhāṣā* as 'that knowledge which has for its object something that is not already cognized and is uncontradicted.'[50] Even when we perceive the same thing in the same place a second time it is a novel experience being distinguished from the past by the time factor.

There can also be recognition of something previously heard, read, or thought about, such as 'This is the house you told me about', 'I see the python I read about', 'The design of the arch is the same as I thought about'.

Indian philosophers, including the Advaitins, are divided in their opinion as to whether recollection (smṛti) should be regarded as valid knowledge (pramā) or not. According to most of them recollection or memory is a form of cognition (buddhi) distinct from feeling and volition, but not valid knowledge (pramā). Nyāya-Vaiśeṣika classifies cognition (buddhi) under two distinct heads: knowledge (anubhūti) and memory (smṛti). Knowledge again has four distinct forms according to its source—perception, inference, comparison, and verbal testimony.[51] Recollection or memory is caused by the impressions due to previous knowledge of any of the four kinds.[52] It can be true or false according as it agrees with the past knowledge that is recalled. Even right recollection is not considered valid knowledge (pramā) by most Indian philosophers, because it is a reproduction of a past knowledge and not a new apprehension of an object.[53]

Recollection or memory of a past experience cannot be treated as a case of perception, for what is recalled is not presented, but represented to consciousness. It is the revival of the sub-conscious impression of the past experience by association. We have in this case a mental image of a known object (visual, auditory, or otherwise) or an incident with a setting or background. The mind has no direct contact with the experienced fact, which is a prerequisite of perception. For the same reason, the recollection of an inner experience, such as 'I was happy before' is not a perception so far as the past happiness is concerned. The mental mode of recollection is not united with the happiness previously experienced.

[50] *Vide* VP I, and com. *Śikhāmaṇi*.
[51] *Vide* BP 51, 52.
[52] *Vide* TS 35, 36.
[53] *Vide* VP I, definition of valid knowledge.

As stated in *Vedānta-paribhāṣā*:

'The happiness that is recollected being a past event, and the mental state in the form of recollection being a present event, the two limiting adjuncts in the mind belong to different times, and hence the consciousness limited by each is different; for the criterion of the unity of the underlying consciousness is that the limiting adjuncts must occupy the same space at the same time.'[54]

It is to be noted that the prerequisite of internal perception, such as that of happiness, is the unity of the consciousness reflected in the cognitive mode (the means of knowledge) and the consciousness limited by the mental state of happiness (the object of knowledge). This unity is not possible unless the means of knowledge coincide with the object of knowledge.

There is a vital difference between perceptual and non-perceptual knowledge. The one is immediate, the other is mediate. The one manifests the object to us, the other does not. While immediate knowledge is definite and assured, mediate knowledge is indefinite and indecisive. The veil of ajñāna, according to Advaita Vedānta, is twofold: (1) veiling the existence of the object (asattvāpādaka) and (2) veiling its manifestation (abhāṇāpādaka). Mediate knowledge removes the first veil. As a result, we can know that the object exists but cannot know its nature because of the second veil. The object is presented, but with a covering, so to speak. The immediate knowledge unveils it completely. As a result, we know the object definitely as it is. It is mediate knowledge that sets man in search for God. There cannot be any search for that the very existence of which is unknown. Nor can there be any search for that which is manifest or revealed. The affirmation that God is 'unknown and unknowable' testifies to the agnostic's mediate knowledge of Him. There cannot be any avowal or disavowal of what is absolutely unknown.

[54] VP I, Subjective Perception.

CHAPTER IV

THE VALIDITY OF KNOWLEDGE

1. *How is knowledge known? It is self-manifest. It is not known by another knowledge*

When a person knows something, say a camel, he also knows that he has the knowledge of the camel. How does he know this knowledge? Philosophers agree that knowledge manifests things, but they disagree as to what manifests knowledge. According to Advaita Vedānta knowledge is self-manifest (svataḥ-prakāśa). It requires no other knowledge to know it. When an object is known, its knowledge also becomes manifest to the knower at the same time. It is the very nature of knowledge to reveal its object and also itself. But this does not mean that knowledge apprehends itself. It only means that knowledge is self-revealing and that its manifestation is not due to any other knowledge. Knowledge neither apprehends itself, nor is apprehended by another knowledge. Like sunlight it shines *of* itself and does not require any other light for its manifestation while manifesting other things. It is in this sense that Vedānta maintains the theory of the self-luminosity or self-manifestedness of knowledge.

As defined by Citsukhācārya, 'The self-luminosity of knowledge means its competence of being treated as immediately apprehended without being objectified'.[1] In the case of a jar its perception is dependent on its objectification, since it is not self-manifest. But not so in the case of knowledge. Along with the knowledge, 'This is a jar', one has the knowledge, 'I know the jar'. Evidently, the jar and its cognition both are known simultaneously.

While the percipient cognizes the jar as 'This is a jar', the witness-self (sākṣī) manifests the cognition 'I know the jar'. We have mentioned above that Pure Consciousness dwelling within man as the unchanging spectator of all mental modifications and aloof from them is the witness-self (sākṣī). The same Consciousness reflected on the mind (antaḥkaraṇa) and identified with it proves to be the individual self, the jīva. It is also known in Vedānta as the reflected self (cidābhāsa, lit. reflected consciousness). This functions as the percipient (pramātā). It finds expression as the ego through a

[1] *Tattva-pradīpikā* (also called 'Citsukhī'), p. 9. Nirnaya-sagar Press, Bombay. See Appendix B, sec. 7.

particular mode of the mind characterized by "I-ness". In each individual Pure Consciousness dwells as the witness-self (sākṣī) and also as the reflected self (cidābhāsa). The one is the basis and being of the other. The one can be regarded as the transcendental or real self and the other as the empirical or apparent self. The individual consciousness has these two facets, so to speak.

The cognizer (pramātā), the object cognized (prameya), and the cognition (pramiti)—all the three are revealed simultaneously by the witness-self (sākṣī). The same unvarying light of Pure Consciousness that the witness-self is, illumines the mental mode of cognition (buddhi-vṛtti, or bōdhākarā antaḥkaraṇa-vṛtti), whether perceptual, inferential, or verbal. In each case the cognitive mode (buddhi-vṛtti) conforms to the object cognized and manifests it to the cognizer directly or indirectly. In perception, external as well as internal, the cognitive mode coincides with the object perceived. Being illuminated by the light of the witness-self the cognitive mode manifests the object of knowledge, such as the jar, but does not require any other cognitive mode for its own manifestation. Without being objectified like a jar it becomes manifest as soon as it originates, since it is revealed directly by the witness-self. This is what the self-manifestedness of knowledge actually means, as defined by Citsukhācārya. Knowledge is self-manifest not only in itself, that is, as Pure Consciousness, but also as modal consciousness, that is, as the cognitive mode of the mind that corresponds with the object of cognition and manifests it to the cognizer.

The immutable consciousness (kūṭastha caitanya) that the witness-self is shines of itself. Strictly speaking, this alone is self-luminous. As pointed out by Sureśvarācārya, none of the triad—the cognizer, the object cognized, and the cognition—has light of its own. They cannot know themselves nor can they be known by one another.[2] They are revealed by the witness-self that shines with constant effulgence in waking, dream, and dreamless sleep.

The theory of the self-manifestedness of knowledge (svataḥ-prakāśa-vāda) is also maintained by the Sāṁkhya system and the Prabhākara school of Mīmāṁsā in different ways. According to Sāṁkhya system, valid knowledge (pramā) is the reflection of the self-intelligent puruṣa (conscious self) in the mental mode (buddhi-vṛtti) corresponding to the object and, therefore, self-manifest.[3] In the view of Prabhākara school of Mīmāṁsā knowledge is ever related to the knower and the object known. Accordingly, there cannot be any knowledge without the correlation of these three factors (tripuṭa). To manifest the object to the subject is the function of knowledge. The three become known simultaneously. Conjointly they manifest knowledge and its validity.

[2] *Vide* NS II: 106. [3] *Vide* SK 4; YS I: 6; and commentaries.

The Kumārila school of Mīmāṁsā and the Nyāya school hold a contrary theory of knowledge (parataḥ-prakāśa–vāda), according to which the manifestation of a particular knowledge does not rest on itself but on another knowledge. They differ however in their interpretations of the theory. According to Nyāya, the cognition 'This is a jar' is manifested by a subsequent reflective knowledge (anuvyavasāya) in the form of 'I have the knowledge of the jar'. But, according to Kumārila Bhaṭṭa, the knowledge of the jar is known by inference. When the jar is known it acquires the quality of 'knownness (jñātatā)', which is observable. By perceiving this mark of 'knownness' in the jar one infers one's antecedent knowledge of the jar. Thus, while the jar is known directly, its knowledge is known indirectly, by inference.

Vedānta refutes both these views. It points out that knowledge that is unmanifest cannot manifest its object. Only what is luminous can reveal what is non-luminous. Moreover, if knowledge is not self-manifest, if one knowledge depends on another for its manifestation, then the second would depend on a third, and the third on a fourth, and so on *ad infinitum*.

2. *The self-validity of knowledge*

Vedānta maintains the theory of self-validity of knowledge (svataḥ-prāmāṇya-vāda).[4] It is a dual proposition. Its two parts are: (1) that the validity of knowledge is intrinsic (svataḥ-siddha), and (2) that the validity of knowledge is self-evident (svataḥ-prakāśa). The first part means that the validity of knowledge results from the totality of those very causes that produce knowledge (pramā). Whenever all the conditions necessary for the generation of a specific knowledge are fulfilled there must be that knowledge and it must be valid. Thus the validity of knowledge (pramā) is spontaneous and inherent in it. This is not imparted to it by anything other than the actual causes. With the origination of knowledge (pramā) from any of the six sources (perception, inference, verbal testimony, comparison, postulation, and non-apprehension) that is free from deficiencies, its validity arises as a matter-of-course.

When knowledge proves to be invalid, its invalidity is due not to the causal factors themselves, but to the presence of adventitious defects in them. Thus, while the validity of knowledge is intrinsic, its invalidity is extrinsic. Strictly speaking, invalid knowledge cannot be counted as knowledge. Indeed, in Western philosophy the word 'knowledge' signifies valid knowledge, the Sanskrit equivalent of which is 'pramā'. The term 'jñānam' in Sanskrit refers to both valid

[4] *Vide* VP VI, chap. on Non-apprehension.

and invalid knowledge. We have generally used the word 'knowledge' as synonymous with 'jñānam'.

The second part of the theory—that the validity of knowledge is self-evident—means that with the apprehension of knowledge its validity is spontaneously apprehended. Those very agencies that cause the apprehension of knowledge also cause the apprehension of its validity.[5] Along with the manifestation of knowledge by the witness-self there is the manifestation of its validity. Any knowledge that arises in the human mind is invariably apprehended as valid. Its validity is questioned only when some deficiency is noticeable in the causes of knowledge, such as the defect of the eyesight or the insufficiency of light in the case of visual perception, and erroneous reasoning in the case of inferential knowledge. The invalidity of knowledge, wherever there is any, is not apprehended with the apprehension of knowledge. It is determined by inference. For instance, the falsity of the perception of silver in nacre is known from the unsuccessful effort to gain silver. Until then the perception is apprehended as real. 'Thus, the invalidity of knowledge arises from, and is apprehended by, extraneous agencies alone.'[6]

Unlike Vedānta the Nyāya school maintains the theory of the extrinsic validity of knowledge (parataḥ-prāmāṇya-vāda). According to this theory, the validity of knowledge and the apprehension of its validity are due not to the causes of knowledge themselves but to conditions and agencies external to them. Similarly, the invalidity of knowledge, and the apprehension of its invalidity are due to extraneous conditions and agencies. On the latter point, of course, there is agreement between Nyāya and Vedānta.

As regards the validity of knowledge, Nyāya contends that this rests on something other than the causes of knowledge, that is, on additional conditions, such as the soundness of the organ of vision, the sufficiency of light, in the case of visual perception. This argument is refuted by Vedānta on the ground that all these conditions are integral parts of the causes themselves; otherwise there would be no knowledge. As to the apprehension of the validity of knowledge, Nyāya maintains that it does not arise spontaneously from the apprehension of knowledge, but is determined by another through inference. This position, too, is untenable, for it undermines the validity of the second knowledge as well, requiring a third knowledge to substantiate it. Thus, this view leads to a *regressus ad infinitum* and renders knowledge impossible.

Except Nyāya-Vaiśeṣika, all the other Vedic systems—Kumārila and Prabhākara schools of Mīmāṁsā, Sāṁkhya-Yōga, and Vedānta—maintain the theory of the self-validity of knowledge. In their

[5] *Vide Tattva-pradīpikā* by Citsukhācārya, p. 124. (See Appendix B, sec. 7.)
[6] *Vide* VP VI.

view, the validity of knowledge arises from the very causal conditions that produce the knowledge and is, therefore, intrinsic; with the apprehension of knowledge there is the apprehension of its validity. They also agree that the invalidity of knowledge, wherever there is any, is due to elements extraneous to the causes, and is apprehended by means other than what manifests knowledge.

As we have noted above, the Kumārila school of Mīmāṁsā does not uphold the theory of the self-manifestedness of knowledge, though it upholds the theory of the self-validity of knowledge. Thus we find that, according to the Prabhākara school of Mīmāṁsā, Sāṁkhya-Yōga, and Vedānta, it is the very nature of knowledge to reveal itself, its knower, and its validity, while revealing the object. All these become simultaneously manifest. Truly speaking, it is the ever-shining witness-self that manifests them all.

3. *Criteria of knowledge*

Valid cognition, that is knowledge as the apprehension of truth or fact, naturally arises when all the necessary conditions are fulfilled. Otherwise, invalid cognition in the form of error, doubt, or disbelief results. For correct vision the eyes must be free from defects, there must not be any obstruction between the organs and the object, light should be adequate for the purpose, and so forth. Wrong premises or unsound arguments lead to faulty conclusions. Ambiguous words or expressions create confusion or misconceptions. Thus, wrong knowledge invariably proceeds from defective causal conditions. Consequently, it becomes necessary to distinguish true knowledge from error.

We have noted above that according to Vedānta, it is the validity of knowledge that is apprehended with the apprehension of knowledge, but not its invalidity where there is any. Since the invalidity of knowledge is due to extraneous elements associated with the factors contributory to true knowledge, it has to be ascertained through the detection of those extraneous elements. Invalid cognition is apprehended as valid by the cognizer until he has reason to doubt its validity. Dream-experience is valid to the dreamer. The appearance of the sky as a blue canopy and of the sun moving around the earth are accepted as valid experiences by most human beings. Thus arises the question of the verification of the truth of knowledge. It is to be noted that the method of verification only tests the validity or the invalidity of knowledge that is already there, but does not cause either.

Indian philosophers, like the philosophers of the West, hold different views regarding the criterion of true knowledge. In some cases there is striking similarity between the Eastern and the Western views. According to Nyāya-Vaiśeṣika, the validity of knowledge consists in its conformity (sārūpya) with its object. To cognize something as possessed of what attributes it actually has is true knowledge and this is called pramā.[7] To know a white conch as it is means true knowledge; to know it as yellow, or as something else, or as differently located, means wrong knowledge or error. Thus, the truth of knowledge can be known by knowing its correspondence with the object. The Kumārila school of Mīmāṁsā holds a similar view. This resembles the correspondence theory of the Realistic school of the West. But the correspondence of knowledge with its object has to be tested by its practical effect or its coherence with the facts of general experience.

According to Nyāya-Vaiśeṣika, a true experience has the competence to lead to fruitful effort (samartha-pravṛtti-janakatva). A piece of shell mistaken for silver cannot serve the purpose of silver. Mirage is an optical illusion, since it cannot quench the thirst of the perceiver, nor can it moisten a grain of sand in the desert. Some Buddhist logicians, too, hold that the validity of knowledge can be determined by its practical value. According to Dharmakīrti: 'That is valid knowledge which reveals an object capable of producing the desired effect.' Or: 'That is valid knowledge through which the purpose of the object is fulfilled.'[8] According to the Prabhākara school of Mīmāṁsā, true knowledge must be an incentive to action that fulfills a practical need (artha-kriyā-kāritva), otherwise it is erroneous.

The above method of verification resembles the modern pragmatic test of knowledge with an important difference. Professor Hiriyanna aptly remarks: 'It should however be carefully noted that this pragmatic criterion is here only a test of truth and does not, as in modern pragmatism, constitute its nature.'[9] So says Dr Chatterjee: 'But we are to point out that verification by different kinds of experiences is a *test* of truth and that it does not make or constitute truth.'[10]

Evidently, the above statements have reference to William James' pragmatic theory of knowledge. As expressed by him: 'The truth of an idea is not a stagnant property inherent in it. Truth *happens* to an idea. It *becomes* true, is *made* true by events. Its verity *is* in fact an event, a process: the process namely of its verifying itself, its veri-*fication*. Its validity is the process of valid-*ation*.'[11] Joachim, on the contrary, observes: 'Truth is discovered, and not invented; and

[7] *Vide* TS 37 and BP 135, com. *Siddhānta-muktāvalī*.
[8] *Nyāya-bindu*, I. 1, and *Nyāyabindu-ṭīkā* by Dharmōttara.
[9] M. Hiriyanna, *The Essentials of Indian Philosophy*, p. 99.
[10] Satischandra Chatterjee, *The Problems of Philosophy*, p. 176.
[11] William James, *Pragmatism*, New York, Longmans, Green, 1949, p. 201.

its nature is unaffected by the time and process of discovery, and careless of the personality of the discoverer. It is to this independent entity that the judgement of this or that person must conform if *he* is to attain truth. Correspondence of *his* thinking with this "reality" is truth *for him*; but such correspondence requires an independent truth as one of its factors and is not itself the essence of truth.'[12] We have already explained (chap. 3, sec. 2) that knowledge is revelatory, that it discovers, it does not create.

Philosophers of East and West admit that the essential condition of a true proposition is self-consistency. It must not contradict itself. Self-contradictory statements, such as 'I can neither write nor speak', 'I am silent', 'I know I know nothing', 'The barren queen has at last borne a child, the king's sole successor', are unacceptable. A self-consistent proposition may or may not be true, but a true proposition must be self-consistent.

Indian philosophers also hold the view that besides being self-consistent a true proposition must be in accord with other known facts or truths. The statements 'The hare's horns are broken', 'The lake has fire in it', are false, since they are contrary to general human experience. No one has ever seen a hare with horns or a lake of fire. True knowledge must be in conformity with (samvādi) established facts and not contradict them. This view is similar to the Western coherence theory. 'The coherence criterion', says Brightman, 'looks beyond the mere self-consistency of propositions to a comprehensive, synoptic view of all experience. It takes into account all our propositions as a connected "sticking together" whole. The coherence theory would then offer the following criterion. Any proposition is true, if it is both self-consistent and coherently connected with our system of propositions as a whole.'[13] This means that a proposition is valid if it does not contradict itself nor is contradicted by any proposition in the system with which it is associated.

4. *The Advaitin's test of valid knowledge*

All these three criteria of true knowledge, viz., correspondence, practical efficacy, coherence, have, according to Advaita Vedānta, limited spheres. Each has relative validity and holds good in the realm of diversity under certain conditions. None of them can be regarded as a universal or ultimate test of truth. None can be applied to the knowledge of the Absolute. The crucial test of truth, according to Vedānta, is its non-contradictedness, 'satyatvam bādharāhit-

[12] Harold H. Joachim, *The Nature of Truth*, Oxford, The Clarendon Press, 1906, p. 20.

[13] Edgar Sheffield Brightman, *An Introduction to Philosophy*, New York, Holt, Rinehart and Winston, 1953, p. 69.

yam.'[14] As defined by *Vedānta-paribhāṣā*, 'That knowledge is valid which has for its object something that is uncontradicted'.[15] All other tests of knowledge conform to this. To cognize a rope as rope is valid knowledge, since the object of this knowledge is not contradicted. But to cognize a rope as a snake is not valid knowledge, because the object of this knowledge, the snake, is contradicted by the knowledge of the rope. Any erroneous experience or invalid proposition can be refuted on the ground of being contradicted. The knowledge that is not contradicted is generally accepted as true. The sun moving around the earth was acknowledged as a fact until Copernicus established the contrary theory.

The reason why Advaitins disregard the other tests of knowledge and hold to non-contradictedness as its sole criterion is clearly stated by D. M. Datta:

'The Advaita school of Vedānta, however, favors a fourth view according to which the truth of knowledge consists in its non-contradictedness (abādhitatvam). The correspondence view of truth cannot directly prove itself. The only way to prove correspondence is to fall back on the foreign method of consilience or coherence (samvāda)—that is to infer the existence of a real correspondence between knowledge and reality from the facts of the harmony of experience. But all that we can legitimately infer from the harmony of knowledge with the rest of our experience up to that time, is not that the knowledge is absolutely free from error, but that it is not yet contradicted. For we do not know that we shall not have in future any experience that can falsify our present knowledge. As regards the pragmatic test of causal efficiency (artha-kriyā-kāritva), the Advaitins argue that even a false cognition may, and sometimes does, lead to the fulfilment of a purpose. One of the examples[16] they cite to support their view is the case of a distant bright jewel which emits lustre. We mistake the lustre for the jewel and, desiring to get the mistaken object of our knowledge, approach it and actually get the jewel. In this case, therefore, the knowledge of lustre as the jewel—which is clearly a false cognition—leads to the attainment of the jewel and therefore satisfies our purpose, though eventually we come also to know that the initial cognition which caused our action was itself false. We can multiply instances of this kind. The hypothesis that the earth is stationary and the sun is moving has been working quite satisfactorily for ages; on the basis of this cognition many of our actions are performed and purposes attained. It is only its conflict with astronomical phenomena that enable us to detect its falsity.

[14] *Vide* PD III: 29. [15] VP I.
[16] *Vide Tattva-pradīpikā* of Citsukhācarya, p. 218.

It is found, therefore, that the pragmatic view of truth is not tenable. The correspondence view has ultimately to fall back on the consilience or coherence theory which, when subjected to strict scrutiny, has to yield the result that truth, as ascertained by it, consists only in its non-contradictedness.'[17]

The definition of valid knowledge (pramā) given by *Vedānta-paribhāṣā*, which we have quoted above, does not exclude memory (smṛti). But, as we have already noted (chap. 3, sec. 11), most Indian philosophers, including the Advaitins, the Mīmāṁsakas, the Naiyāyikas and the Sāṁkhyas, do not recognize memory (smṛti) as valid knowledge (pramā). So the author of *Vedānta-paribhāṣā* has given another definition excluding memory from the category of valid knowledge: '[Valid knowledge (pramā) is] that cognition which has for its object something that is not previously known and is uncontradicted'.[18]

It is to be noted that the term 'uncontradicted' in the definition of valid knowledge means 'not contradicted during the transmigratory state of the jīva'; because all his knowledge of the relative universe is contradicted when he attains Liberation (mōkṣa). So it has been said, 'just as the notion of one's identity with the body is assumed to be valid knowledge, exactly so is this ordinary knowledge [of men, animal, tree, etc.], until the self is realized [that is, until the knowledge of Brahman is attained]'.[19]

The experience of the manifold persists as long as the jīva is subject to ignorance and fails to realize the identity of the self with Brahman. So it is valid in the state of his bondage. In the absolute sense, of course, Brahman alone is uncontradicted. All contradictions cease there. Brahman stays when all else is contradicted. The ultimate Reality is characterized negatively by non-contradictedness. Brahman cannot be described as It is, but as It is not. By rejecting all that is limited, the Śruti points to the Limitless, the Absolute. Transcendentally, Brahman is the sole Reality. But from the standpoint of the embodied self Advaita Vedānta recognizes three orders of existence: (1) the Absolute (pāramārthika), (2) the empirical (vyavahārika), and (3) the illusory (prātibhāsika). Absolute existence is Nondual Brahman. Empirical existence is the objective universe, the world of experience, which endures until Brahman, its substratum, is realized. Illusory existence is the false appearance of something where it does not exist, such as the mirage or the rope-snake, which is erroneous and comes to an end as soon as the obstacles to correct vision are removed.[20]

[17] *The Six Ways of Knowing*, pp. 21, 22.
[18] VP I. [19] *Ibid.*
[20] *Vide* VP II, concluding section.

5. *Psychologically, knowledge includes all forms of cognition—valid, non-valid, and invalid*

While in philosophy knowledge signifies valid cognition, in psychology it includes valid, non-valid, and invalid cognition. From the viewpoint of a psychologist all cognitive states (distinguished from the affective and the volitional), such as sensation, perception, inference, imagination, memory, doubt, dream, illusion, are instances of knowledge. As observed by Dr Chatterjee:

'In psychology knowledge is understood in a wide sense so as to comprise both true and false perception, inference, memory, etc., as well as dream and doubt. Psychology as a positive science of mental phenomena is not so much concerned with the truth or falsity of cognition as with their description, analysis, and explanation. Hence all cognitive facts are regarded as instances of knowledge, no matter whether they are true or false, or neither true nor false. A true or veridical perception is as much a case of knowledge as a false or erroneous one. Illusions, hallucinations, and dreams also are cases of knowledge, since we have in them different kinds of apprehension of objects, although their objects being contradicted, they are classed as invalid or erroneous perceptions.'

'In logic and so also in philosophy, knowledge is understood in a narrow sense and is limited to the definite and assured cognition of an object, which is also true.'[21]

The Sanskrit term 'jñānam' in the widest sense comprehends all forms of cognition, valid, non-valid, and invalid.[22] It all but corresponds with the psychological view of knowledge as explained by Dr Chatterjee. The main point of difference is that jñāna does not comprise any abnormal cognitive state, such as hallucination or fantasy. Indian philosophers include doubt (saṁśaya), error or illusion (bhrama or viparyaya), argument (tarka), indecision (anadhyavasāya), imagination (kalpanā), dream (svapna) in the category of knowledge (jñāna) as cases of apramā (cognition other than valid), which do not necessarily involve any abnormal mental state. They are not valid, because they are contradicted.

The Nyāya school classifies knowledge (jñāna or buddhi) under two main heads: (1) anubhava (awareness or cognition of the object) and (2) smṛti (memory, which is due to the impressions of past cognition).[23] Knowledge as anubhava (awareness or cognition) has

[21] Satischandra Chatterjee, *The Problems of Philosophy*, pp. 58, 60.

[22] Cf. BP 126, 'Jñāna (knowledge) is said to be of two kinds: pramā (valid cognition), and apramā (cognition other than valid).' Apramā includes non-valid and invalid cognition. Memory is a case of non-valid cognition. And so is doubt. Error is a case of invalid cognition.

[23] BP 51; TS 35.

four varieties according to its four means (pramāṇa): perception, inference, comparison, and verbal testimony. To these four Advaita Vedānta adds two more means of knowledge (pramāṇa): postulation and non-apprehension. Thus there can be six varieties of knowledge (anubhava), which can be valid and also invalid. It is valid (pramā) when the means (pramāṇa) to which it is due is free from defects, otherwise it is invalid (apramā) and is contradicted.

As we have noted above, smṛti (memory) is not usually included in valid knowledge (pramā). But this does not mean that it is false (ayathārtha). It is excluded from valid knowledge (pramā) because it is not produced by any of the six means of valid cognition, but by the impressions of past cognition. In fact, it is not a cognition (anubhava) but the reproduction of a cognition, and as such cannot be counted as non-cognition. Smṛti is true (yathārtha) if it arises out of the impressions of valid cognition; it is false (ayathārtha) if it arises out of the impressions of invalid cognition such as error or dream.[24] It can also be said from the popular view-point that smṛti (memory) is right if it is in accord with the past cognition that is recollected, otherwise not. Properly speaking, smṛti (memory) is a case of *non*-valid cognition. Though not valid, yet it is not invalid in the sense in which error (viparyaya) is.

6. *Two main forms of cognition other than valid (apramā)—error and doubt*

According to Nyāya, apramā is the apprehension of something as having what it does not have. Its two main forms are error (viparyaya or bhrama) and doubt (saṁśaya).[25] While error or illusion is attended with certitude, doubt (from Lat. *dubito*, to be uncertain) is attended with uncertainty or indecision. On seeing a stump of a tree in semi-darkness, a person may deliberate 'Is it a man or a stump of a tree?' or he may mistake the stump of the tree for a man and say 'A man is standing there'. The former is a case of doubt, the latter is a case of error or illusion. In either case there is a vague awareness (anubhava) of the subject (tree), without the apprehension of its specific nature.

Patañjali defines error or misapprehension (viparyaya) as 'false knowledge not based on the real nature of the object'. He includes doubt in error (viparyaya), as noted by Vācaspati in his gloss on Vyāsa's commentary. In Patañjali's view doubt is error marked by indecision.[26] Thus, according to him, error is of two kinds, hesitative and unhesitative. But most Indian philosophers differentiate doubt from error because of the difference in the nature of the two. Doubt is not positive error or misapprehension (viparyaya). It is an inde-

[24] *Vide* TS 112. [25] BP 127.
[26] *Vide* YS I: 8, and com. *Tattvavaiśāradī*.

cisive cognition, which is neither true nor false, a wavering of the mind between two contrary judgments, e.g., "Is it this?" or "Is it that?" As defined by Annambhaṭṭa of the Nyāya school: 'Doubt is the simultaneous awareness of contradictory attributes in the same subject, such as the cognition "Is it the stump of a tree or a man?" '[27] In fact, it involves two pairs of contrary judgments: 'Is it the stump of a tree or not?' and 'Is it a man or not?'

Viśvanātha of the same school defines doubt as 'the notion of the presence and absence (of some attribute) with regard to the same subject'.[28] 'The cause of doubt is the knowledge of attributes that are common to two things. For instance, on knowing the height, that is common to the stump of a tree and a man, one doubts whether it is a stump or not.'[29] Thus, doubt is a cognitive mode vacillating between conflicting notions. It is, strictly speaking, non-valid cognition marked by indecision. It neither affirms nor denies anything. It cannot be characterized as belief or disbelief. It is different from misconception. It cannot serve as a means of valid knowledge, as Montague assumes.[30] However, as an interrogatory state of the mind doubt may start the enquiry after truth and open the way to valid knowledge.

There can be doubt associated with any kind of knowledge (perceptual, inferential, or verbal), its means (pramāṇa), and its objects (prameya). Doubts cannot be completely eliminated from the human mind as long as ignorance prevails. It is hydra-headed, so to speak. There can be doubts concerning the Vedic testimony and the truths it conveys. All doubts dissolve when the Truth is realized. So it is said: 'The knot of the heart is broken, all doubts are dispelled, and the impressions of karma eradicated when He is seen, who is immanent and transcendent.'[31]

Error (viparyaya) can be caused by any factor contributing to knowledge, if it be deficient. Broadly speaking, there can be three types of error corresponding to the three means of valid knowledge —perception, inference, and verbal testimony (which are recognized by most thinkers of the world)—when there are defects in them. Erroneous perception or illusion is very common. This is perceptual error (aparōkṣa bhrama). We shall dwell on this in the next chapter. Error due to wrong inference or ambiguous words is non-perceptual (parōkṣa bhrama). The implication of the term adhyāsa (lit. false attribution) in Advaita Vedānta is perceptual error to the exclusion of the non-perceptual. It is with reference to perceptual error that the theory of anirvacanīya-khyāti (apprehension of the indefinable) has been propounded by the Advaitins, as we shall see later.

Error is counteracted by the knowledge of truth or fact. Erroneous

[27] TS 109. [28] BP 130. [29] *Ibid.* com. *Siddhānta-muktāvalī.*
[30] See chap. I, sec. 2. [31] Mu. U. II: 2.8.

cognition is paradoxical. It is, in fact, a phase of ignorance which passes for knowledge. While in error a person hardly knows that he is wrong. He detects the error as the light of truth dispels it, just as a person knows the falsity of dream as he wakes up. Joachim aptly remarks: 'Error is that form of ignorance which poses, to itself and to others, as indubitable knowledge; or that form of false thinking which unhesitatingly claims to be true, and *in so claiming*, substantiates and completes its falsity.'[32] The deceptiveness of error is also evident from the fact that it comes upon a person, who hardly knows how he gets into it, unawares.

7. *Other forms of cognition that are not valid. Distinction of dream from memory and illusion*

In addition to doubt (saṁśaya) and error (viparyaya), Annambhaṭṭa includes *tarka*, argument or indirect proof such as *reductio ad absurdum*, in ayathārtha anubhava (other than valid cognition).[33] It is the indirect or negative method of showing a proposition to be true by proving the absurdity of its contrary. According to Viśvanātha, *tarka* sometimes removes a doubt.[34] On seeing smoke rising from a hill when a person infers that the hill has fire and still has doubt about it, then the argument (tarka) 'had there been no fire on the hill, no smoke would have been there' helps to remove his doubt as to the existence of fire on the hill. Like doubt and error tarka is recognized by Vedānta as a form of apramā (cognition other than valid), which cannot remove doubt altogether. It does not establish the truth of a proposition, but only makes it possible. In his *Khaṇḍana-khaṇḍa-khādya*[35] Śrīharṣa has shown the incapacity of tarka to remove doubt completely, while refuting the realistic ideas of the Nyāya school in order to establish the Advaita view that the nature of the world of experience is indefinable either as real or as unreal (anirvacanīya).

Like perceptual error dream (svapna) is a common instance of false cognition. Dream-objects, though quite real to the dreamer, are contradicted by the facts of his waking state. Dream is similar to memory (smṛti) in that both are caused by the latent impressions of past experiences. But while memory is, as a rule, presentative, dream is, as a rule, representative. Besides, memory is the revival in the waking state of the mental impressions of past experiences, external or internal; it is often due to a stimulus, but can be volitional as well; whereas, dream-imagery is always involuntary, being associated with sleep. There can be memory of dream-experience also.

Dream is more like erroneous perception than like memory. But there is a vital difference between illusion and dream. In the one the

[32] Harold H. Joachim, *The Nature of Truth*, p. 142.
[33] *Vide* TS 108. [34] *Vide* BP 137. [35] See Appendix B, sec. 7.

mind is connected with the sense-organ and the external object more or less, while in the other it is dissociated from them. There is no sense-object contact in dream; it is wholly subjective. The mind does not go out in dream. It is said in the Māṇḍūkya Upaniṣad that in dream state the embodied self is internally conscious; he experiences subtle objects woven out of the mental impressions. As explained by Śaṅkara: 'In the waking state consciousness is associated with many means [such as the sense-organs] and is manifest assuredly in relation to external objects, and, being but the operations of the mind, leave on it corresponding impressions. Ingrained with these impressions like a painted canvas, the mind, being impelled by avidyā, desire, and past karma, appears [in the dream state] as though it is in the waking state, independently of the external means.'[36] That the dream-objects are the creations of the individual self is expressly stated in the *Bṛhadāraṇyaka Upaniṣad*: '(In dream state) there are no chariots, no animals to be yoked to them, nor roads there, but (the individual self) creates the chariots, animals, and roads. There are no pleasures in that state, no joys, nor rejoicings. There are no pools in that state, no reservoirs, no rivers, but he creates the pools, the reservoirs, and the rivers. He indeed is the agent.'[37]

Dream is contradicted by waking experience. Whatsoever objects appear in dream, howsoever real they may appear there to be, all disappear as soon as the waking consciousness is regained. The invalidity of dream is known by the dreamer on waking. Since he remembers the dream he can compare the one state with the other. Similarly, the invalidity of the world-appearance is known when the Truth is realized. All multiplicity of empirical existence is contradicted by the unitary experience of Brahman-Consciousness.

[36] Ma. U. IV, com. [37] Br. U. IV: 3.10.

CHAPTER V

ILLUSION; ITS NATURE AND CAUSE

1. *Illusion (adhyāsa) defined*

The term 'illusion' (from Lat. illudere, to mock, deceive) is used in the sense of illusory perception and illusory object as well. Its Sanskrit synonym adhyāsa applies to both.[1] The two other words adhyārōpa (superimposition) and avabhāsa (appearance) have also the same significance. As defined by Śaṅkara, 'Adhyāsa is the apprehension of something as something else (adhyāsō nāma atasmin tadbuddhih)'.[2] It indicates a twofold perceptual error: (1) apprehending a thing as other than what it is, such as perceiving a rope as a snake; (2) apprehending a thing as different from what it is, such as perceiving a white conch as yellow. The first is the false ascription of one thing to another; the second is the false ascription of the attribute of one thing to another.[3]

A stump of a tree mistaken for a man, a nacre mistaken for a piece of silver, a desert tract mistaken for a lake, Nondual Brahman apprehended as the manifold—are the errors of the first type. A crystal appearing red in the proximity of a red flower, light transmitted through a green glass appearing green, a white conch appearing yellow to a jaundiced eye, trees appearing to move in the opposite direction from a speeding train, the changeless self appearing changeful being identified with the psychophysical adjunct—these are the

[1] It is worthy of note that every case of illusion has these dual aspects: (1) the confusion of one object of cognition with another, and (2) the confusion of one cognition with another. These are called respectively arthādhyāsa (superimposition of object) and jñānādhyāsa (superimposition of cognition). When there is false appearance of a snake on a rope, the snake cognized (which is similar to the snake remembered through some resemblance with the rope) is superimposed on the rope that is vaguely cognized; at the same time the cognition of the snake is superimposed on the cognition of the rope, that is, there is wrong cognition of snake instead of the cognition of the rope. (See VPS, Pt. I, p. 174.)

[2] BS, com. Intro.

[3] Both these are cases of arthādhyāsa (superimposition of object). The definition includes jñānādhyāsa, since there is wrong cognition of snake instead of the cognition of the rope and there is wrong cognition of the yellowness of the conch instead of its whiteness.

errors of the second type. In no case is the substratum of the erroneous cognition the least affected. The rope mistaken for a snake acquires none of its properties. The white conch appearing yellow to the defective vision of the perceiver has not the slightest tinge of yellow.

An illusion (adhyāsa) has invariably an extramental basis. The object presented has a definite external location as in the normal visual perception. 'No illusion is possible without a substratum', says Śaṅkara.[4] In the words of Padmapāda, his chief disciple[5] and exponent of his philosophy: 'A superimposition without a substratum has never been experienced nor is conceivable.'[6] In fact illusion is cognition which mixes two distinct orders of existence. There cannot be any cognition of what is altogether false or non-existent (alīka) like the son of a barren woman. The object superimposed has an apparent existence dependent on the substratum, which is but vaguely apprehended and forms a content of the illusion as 'this'. So the experiencer of an illusory object invariably uses an expression such as 'This is a snake', or 'This is silver', or 'This is a man', while he vaguely cognizes the rope, the nacre, or the stump of a tree forming the basis of the illusion.

As observed by Vācaspati: 'This is an established fact that there cannot be an illusion where the basis is fully apprehended or not apprehended at all.'[7] Illusion disappears with the perception of the specific nature of the substratum. Until then it continues even though the cognizer may be aware of its falsity. Such a person will experience illusion without delusion. He who sees a mirage but knows it as such does not try to quench his thirst with the water that appears to him. An illumined soul living in the world experiences the manifold but is never deluded by it.

Illusion (adhyāsa) differs from memory, dream, and hallucination, which are wholly mental. It is also different from recognition. The distinction of adhyāsa from memory and the rest has been clearly indicated by Śaṅkara: 'Similar to memory, [adhyāsa] is the false apprehension of an object of previous experience on something else.'[8] Adhyāsa is similar to memory in that both are caused by the impres-

4 MK II: 33, com.

5 Śaṅkara's four principal disciples are Padmapāda, Hastāmalaka, Tōṭakācārya, Sureśvarācārya. See also footnote 46, chap. XI.

6 PP, Superimposition (adhyāsa); 'Na hi niradhiṣṭhanah adhyāsō dṛṣṭapūrvah sambhavī vā'.

7 BS, S. com. Intro, *Bhāmatī*, '*Atyantagrahe atyantāgrahe na cādhyāsaḥ*.'

8 BS, com. Intro., Śaṅkara's definition can also be interpreted as 'Similar to the object of memory, [adhyāsa] is the false appearance of an object of previous experience on some other thing'. The first interpretation refers to illusory perception (jñānādhyāsa), the second to the illusory object (arthādhyāsa). As worded by Śaṅkara, the definition covers both the aspects of adhyāsa. (See footnote 1.)

sion of some past experience. But memory is due entirely to the impression of a past experience, while adhyāsa is due partly to the impression of a past experience and partly to the vague apprehension of the substratum, which is other than the object previously experienced. Besides, memory is not an error in itself as adhyāsa is. Like memory, neither dream nor hallucination has an external object as a substratum.[9] In recognition the object of previous experience is apprehended and recalled concurrently, whereas in illusion the object of previous experience is altogether absent and another object forms the substratum.

2. *The seven different theories of illusion (adhyāsa)*

Though a fact of common experience, illusion is a standing puzzle to the human mind. It is undeniable and seems to be inexplicable. It arises as a matter-of-course. No effort, thought, or will on the part of the experiencer is involved in illusory perception. It is difficult to say exactly how it happens. The various schools of Indian philosophy have dealt with the problem of illusion and given different explanations of it. Their interpretations vary according to their epistemological and metaphysical views. Each school has tried to maintain its position by answering the objections of its opponents, and by refuting their theories. The main points of controversy are—What is the nature of the illusory object? How is it caused?

An oft quoted ancient verse enumerates five theories of adhyāsa, each of which has the general appellation of 'khyāti', meaning 'erroneous cognition', or 'false apprehension'. These are:

(1) The Idealistic Yōgācāra theory of ātma-khyāti (apprehension of the subjective cognition).
(2) The Nihilist Mādhyamika theory of asat-khyāti (apprehension of the non-existent).
(3) Prabhākara Mīmāṁsā theory of akhyāti (non-apprehension).
(4) The Nyāya theory of anyathā-khyāti (misapprehension).
(5) The Advaita theory of anirvacanīya-khyāti (apprehension of the indefinable).

Two other well-known theories can be added to this list:

(6) The Sāṁkhya theory of sadasat-khyāti (apprehension of the real-unreal).
(7) Rāmānuja's theory of sat-khyāti (apprehension of the real).

[9] Cf. 'Illusion contrasts with hallucination in which the sensuous ingredients are altogether absent.'—*Dictionary of Philosophy*, ed. by Dagobert D. Runes, New York, Philosophical Library, 1960.

3. *The distinctive character of the Advaita theory*

The Advaita theory of anirvacanīya-khyāti (the apprehension of the indefinable) differs from the rest in that it holds the illusory object to be an instantaneous and apparent creation of ajñāna associated with the substratum which is but vaguely perceived. The illusory object is similar to the object of past experience, which is remembered because of its resemblance to the substratum, but is not the same as that. The rope-snake is not any particular snake experienced before and now recalled. It is something different from memory-image, being cognized as existing outside right there in front of the experiencer.[10] The illusory object is not non-existent, though far less real than the substratum which is a fact of normal experience. It has an apparent existence distinct from the empirical. Unlike the objects of normal experience it lasts only as long as its perception lasts. It arises along with a vague apprehension of the substratum and disappears the instant this comes into full view. It cannot be counted real since it is sublated. Yet it is not unreal, since it is cognized. According to both Sāṁkhya and Vedānta, what is unreal like a human horn, cannot be an object of cognition.[11] The illusory object is, therefore, indefinable (anirvacanīya) as real (sat), or as unreal (asat), or as real and unreal both, which is contradictory.

We have already mentioned (chap. II, sec. 3) that from the standpoint of the embodied self Advaita Vedānta recognizes three orders of existence: (1) the Absolute (pāramārthika), (2) the empirical (vyavahārika), and (3) the illusory (prātibhāsika). The illusory snake is not as real as the snake of normal experience, and yet not unreal as a human horn.

So far we have indicated the nature of the illusory object from the Advaita viewpoint. Later on we shall explain how it is caused. Meanwhile, we shall discuss other theories and see how far they are tenable. To establish its own theory Advaita Vedānta has tried to defend itself from its opponents and also to refute their views.

4. *The nihilistic theory of asat-khyāti (apprehension of the non-existent)*

True to its nihilistic view, the Mādhyamika school of Buddhism holds 'the theory of the apprehension of the non-existent (asat-khyāti-vāda)'. In illusory perception something non-existent is apprehended as existent. In nacre-silver error the silver is cognized as real, although it does not exist at all. Just as the silver is unreal, so is the nacre. On unreal or non-existent nacre appears unreal or non-existent silver. The object of illusion and the substratum both are non-existent. This view is rejected by all the Vedic schools as groundless. The point is this. If the silver and the nacre both be

[10] PP, Superimposition (adhyāsa). [11] *Vide* SD V: 52; BS II: 2.28.

unreal, why should the one be contradicted by the other? Further, what is experienced cannot be non-existent.[12] There cannot be any cognition of the non-existent. The son of a barren woman being non-existent (alīka) cannot be seen either in reality or in illusion.

According to the Mādhyamika school, the object cognized, the cognition, and the cognizer all are non-existent. Vedānta rejects nihilism, the theory of the Void (śūnya-vāda).[13] It is contrary to all means of valid knowledge, such as perception, inference, and the Vedic testimony.[14] Had things been non-existent they would not have been cognized. In fact, however, they are cognized as existent; the tree as existent, the car as existent, the house as existent, the sun as existent, the space as existent, darkness as existent,[15] and so on. The distinction between existence and non-existence depends in the last analysis on our consciousness, which can by no means be denied. Its denial presupposes it. This must therefore be identical with existence or being. The particular forms of existence appear and disappear. But pure existence or being ever remains. Moreover, the theory of Void contravenes the law of cause and effect. Since one object cannot be distinguished from another, each being unspecifically non-existent and characterless, anything could have produced anything in accordance with nihilism. The six Vedic schools and the non-Vedic Jainism have explained the Buddhist śūnya-vāda[16] as

[12] *Vide* BS II: 2.28.

[13] *Vide* BS II: 2.26; Ch. U. VI: 2.1, 2; BG II: 16; S. com.

[14] *Vide* BS II: 2.32, com.

[15] According to Advaita Vedānta darkness is a positive entity. It is not sheer absence of light. It increases and decreases and is perceived by the eyes as something dark blue. (*Vide* VPS, Pt. I, p. 81.)

[16] In the view of many modern scholars the theory of the Void (śūnya-vāda), as expounded by Nāgārjuna and its other teachers, does not actually mean nihilism. Its true intent is not to disprove the reality of all things but to establish the Absolute to the exclusion of the phenomenal. Anything in the relative order can be regarded as śūnya or void in the sense that it has no unconditional or independent existence. As expressed by Nāgārjuna śūnyatā (voidness) means dependent origination; it points to the indeterminable, inexpressible true nature of things.

On Nāgārjuna's view of the world-appearance Dasgupta remarks: 'If the world-appearance has no essence of its own, how is it that it appears to have one, or how is it that the world-phenomena appear at all? To such a question Nāgārjuna's answer is that the appearance of the world is like the appearance of mirages or dreams, which have no reality of their own, but still present an objective appearance of reality. (*Vide* Mādhyamika-kārikā XXIII. 8.) The world is not a mere nothing, like a lotus of the sky, or the hare's horn, which are simply non-existent (avidyamāna). Thus there is not only the ultimate truth (paramārtha); there is also the relative truth of the phenomenal world (lōka-samvṛta-satya); there are, further, the sense-illusions, hallucinations, and the like which are contradicted in ordinary experience (alōka-samvṛta or mithyā-samvṛta) and also that which is merely non-existent, like the hare's horn.'

nihilism, the denial of all existences. This was no doubt its original meaning.

5. *The Idealistic theory of ātmakhyāti* (*the apprehension of the subjective cognition*)

While the nihilistic Mādhyamika school denies the existence of both external objects and internal ideas, the idealist Yōgācāra denies external objects but affirms the existence of internal ideas. There are no external objects apart from internal ideas according to Yōgācāra. Subjective cognitions are all that exist. Inner cognition is apprehended as an external object. The falsity is in its externalization. This happens in illusory as well as in normal perception. Just as the nacre is a form of inner consciousness, so is the illusory silver. Thus, the Yōgācāra school interprets illusory perception as 'the apprehension of the subjective cognition (ātmakhyāti).' This view is untenable. One of the arguments against it is: if the substratum nacre and the illusory silver both be forms of inner consciousness, then there cannot be any distinction between valid and erroneous perception; and in the absence of such distinction there cannot be the sublating and the sublated cognition.

Vedānta rejects the idealism of the Yōgācāra school on more grounds than one. According to the Yōgācāra there is no abiding self, but a stream of momentary consciousness that can divide itself into the cognizer, the cognition, and the object of cognition. With the continuous series of a momentary cognizer (ālaya-vijñāna), there is the continuous series of momentary cognition (pravṛtti-vijñāna). Nothing external exists; it is the inner cognition that is wrongly perceived as an external object. But this is contrary to experience. Śaṅkara remarks: 'Nobody perceives cognition itself as a pillar, as a wall, and so forth. But everybody perceives them as objects of cognition.'[17]

As in dream so in waking states the distinction of the subject and the object is within consciousness itself, contends the Yōgācāra. Śankara points out that the analogy is incorrect; because waking and dream cognitions are not of the same nature; there is a vital difference between them. Dream experiences are falsified by waking experiences, but the latter are not by either dream or hallucination.[18] Again, the Idealists cannot account for the variety of cognitions in the absence of external objects.[19] Further, no recollection or recognition of past experience is possible if the experiencer is momentary.[20]

(Surendranath Dasgupta, M.A., Ph.D., *A History of Indian Philosophy*, Vol. II, Cambridge, University Press, 1952, pp. 4, 5.)

[17] BS II: 2.28, com.

[18] *Ibid.* 29, com.

[19] *Ibid.* 30, 31, com.

[20] *Ibid.* 25, com.

6. *The Mīmāṁsā theory of non-apprehension* (*akhyāti-vāda*)

The Prabhākara school of Mīmāṁsā maintains the theory of non-apprehension (akhyāti-vāda). This theory is also called the theory of non-discrimination (vivekākhyāti-vāda). According to this theory there is no positive error in illusory perception, such as the misapprehension of an object as other than what it is; instead there is lack of discrimination between the object perceived (nacre) and the object remembered (silver). The vague perception of a nacre as something bright like silver by a person of defective eyesight revives in him by association the memory of silver to such an extent that the distinction between the percept and the memory-image is not apprehended. The error consists in his failure to differentiate the two cognitions, perception and memory.[21] It is an error of omission rather than of commission.

Thus in Prabhākara's view there is in this case no presentation of silver, only its representation. He seems to have overlooked the perceptual character of the erroneous cognition. The silver is perceived as something lying 'out there' before the cognizer. The cognition is quite different from the memory-idea. The Naiyāyikas as well as the Advaitins refute this theory on the ground that sheer lack of discrimination between the cognition of the nacre and the memory of silver cannot turn into the positive experience of silver as something present 'here and now', nor can it impel a person to brisk action to procure silver then and there.

7. *The Nyāya theory of misapprehension* (*anyathā-khyāti*)

According to the Nyāya school, in illusion something is perceived as other than what it is, e.g., the nacre is apprehended as silver. It happens in this way. Due to defective eyesight, or insufficient light, or some other cause a person fails to cognize a nacre as nacre and apprehends it as something bright as silver. This knowledge of similarity awakens the vivid memory of silver in his consciousness and leads to the perception of silver in the nacre. Though this silver was perceived by him in some other place at some other time, yet its present perception in nacre becomes possible through a supernormal connection based on knowledge (jñāna-lakṣaṇa-sannikarṣa). The same silver that he perceived before elsewhere he perceives in the nacre. Thus the nacre is mistaken for silver. Falsity consists in relating silver with the nacre where it does not exist. Neither of the two is unreal. The perception of the remote silver is mingled with the vague perception of the nacre present. Thus the error takes the form, 'This is silver'.

The Nyāya theory of the supernormal connection (alaukika

[21] *Vide* BS, S. com. Intro., *Bhāmatī*.

sannikarṣa) of the sense-organ with the object of perception through knowledge is not recognized by Advaita Vedānta. Such connection is said to be formed in this way. The mind is connected with the object through its revival in memory. The sense-organ being connected with the mind is indirectly connected with the object. The means of connection in this case is the previous knowledge of the object. This indirect contact with the sense-organ enables the object to be perceived. The Naiyāyikas of the later school explain by this means illusion and such other extraordinary cases of perception as 'I see a piece of fragrant sandalwood', and 'The cake looks delicious'.[22] (See ch. III, sec. 5.)

The Advaitins contend that there cannot be perception of real silver as 'this is silver', unless it is actually present 'here and now' to the organ of vision. An object of perception must be present to the sense-organ concerned; otherwise the inference of fire from smoke would cause the perception of fire that is not present to the visual organ. So says Padmapāda: 'The object superimposed resembles the object recollected, but is not that. This is evident from its being manifest as existing before the organ of vision.'[23] Without acknowledging the presence of silver in some form in the locus, nacre, the fact of its perception cannot be explained.

8. *The Sāṁkhya theory of sadasat-khyāti* (*apprehension of the real-unreal*)

The Sāṁkhya school of Kapila tries to refute the different theories of illusion.[24] In refuting the Advaita theory of 'the apprehension of the indefinable (anirvacanīya-khyāti)' it contends that the superimposition of something indeterminable as either real or unreal is not possible, because such a thing does not exist; what is not known cannot be superimposed, because superimposition must be consistent with experience. It propounds the theory of 'the apprehension of a real and unreal object (sadasat-khyāti)'.[25] One and the same thing can be regarded as real and also as unreal under different conditions, so the theory is not self-contradictory. In the illusory perception, 'This is silver', silver is real as existent in the silversmith's shop, but it is unreal as superimposed on nacre. So it is the cognition of a real and unreal object. This is Vijñānabhikṣu's explanation of Kapila's theory.

Aniruddha's interpretation is different. According to him, in the illusory perception, 'This is silver', the cognition of 'this' is real,

[22] *Vide* BP 63–65, com. *Siddhānta-muktāvalī*.
[23] PP, Superimposition.
[24] *Vide* SD V: 52–55; Vijñānabhikṣu's com.
[25] *Vide Ibid.* 56; com.

because its object nacre is present to the organ of vision; but the cognition of 'silver' is unreal, because its object is not present to the organ of vision and is sublated by the cognition of the nacre. Thus in Aniruddha's view an illusion is the united cognition of a real and an unreal object. While the Nyāya school explains illusion as the mixed perception of two real objects, Sāṁkhya school explains it as the conjoint perception of a real and an unreal object.

According to the Dualistic Sāṁkhya, the silver is real as it is, but as ascribed to the nacre where it is not, it is unreal. Similarly, the objective universe is real by itself, but as ascribed to the self to which it does not belong it is unreal. Its falsity is in its association with the self. According to Advaita Vedānta the Self alone is real; the phenomenal world is but an appearance dependent on the Self. On the realization of the nondual Self it disappears; until then it endures.

The Sāṁkhya theory of illusion is unacceptable. It is based on the assumption that something non-existent can be perceived. In the nacre-silver illusion, silver is an object of perception, although it does not exist where it appears. The perception of something where it does not exist is absurd. If a non-existent object could be perceived then the son of a barren woman would have been perceivable. The object of perception must be present to the organ of vision.

9. *The Viśiṣṭādvaita theory of sat-khyāti* (*apprehension of the real*)

The Viśiṣṭādvaita school of Rāmānuja criticizes the Advaitin's view of illusory silver and maintains that the silver in the nacre is real. It is composed of the ingredients of silver that exist in the nacre. Similar objects have constituents common to them. So a nacre contains the elements of silver. Because of defective vision and other causes one fails to see a nacre as a nacre, but perceives instead silver composed of the cognate elements therein. When the nacre is perceived, silver resolves into its components. This is called the theory of 'the apprehension of a real object (sat-khyāti)'. According to this theory, the falsity of perception lies not in the unreality of the object, but in its failure to serve any practical purpose. It is based on the cosmological view that all sense-objects are composed of the material elements of five different forms—ethereal, aerial or gaseous, igneous, liquid, and solid, called respectively ākāśa (space or ether), vāyu (air), agni (fire), jala (water), pṛthivī (earth).

The Sāṁkhya and the Advaita school both reject the theory of sat-khyāti as absurd. Had the silver perceived in a nacre been real, it would not have been sublated by the cognition of the nacre. Besides, even though there be rudiments of silver in a nacre they cannot immediately form actual silver and be manifest as such. To take up another instance, had a mirage been actual water, it would have moistened the desert. But never does it moisten a single grain of sand. Even though there be ingredients of water in sand, they are too elementary to create instantly a lake in a desert. A third instance may be given. When a stump of a tree is simultaneously mistaken for a thief by one person, for a policeman by another, and for a sweetheart by a third, does the stump actually turn into these objects of cognition at the same time? Instances can be multiplied to disprove the theory.

10. *The Advaita view of the 'indefinability' of the illusory object explained*

It will be evident from the foregoing discussion that all the schools except the Advaita and the Viśiṣṭādvaita aver that the object of illusory perception (silver in nacre-silver illusion) does not exist where it appears. According to them, it is the direct apprehension of something that is not present. This is absurd. The Advaita Vedānta points out that illusory cognition being direct and immediate, its object (silver) must be present 'here and now'. It is the positive experience of the object as 'This is silver' that incites the experiencer to immediate effort to pick up silver right on the spot. This is neither a case of memory nor of projection. The cognition of silver does not vanish of itself. It is sublated only by the cognition of the nacre. It also differs from recognition, which is not sublated. The Nyāya school recognizes illusion as a case of perception, but holds that the same silver that was experienced before elsewhere is erroneously perceived in the nacre by an extraordinary interconnection with the organ of vision through knowledge (jñāna-lakṣaṇa-sannikarṣa). This view is not tenable, as we have noted above (sec. 7).

The silver perceived 'here and now' must be present where it appears. Yet it cannot be counted real, because it is sublated by the knowledge of the nacre. Nor can it be called unreal, because it is perceived. What is unreal like the son of a barren woman cannot be an object of experience, not even in dream or illusion.[26] The silver in question must therefore belong to a category of objects different from those of normal experience. It has an apparent existence (prātibhāsika sattvam) distinct from the empirical (vyavahārika-sattvam). An empirical object exists prior to its being perceived and afterwards, but the illusory object lasts as long as its perception lasts. It is coterminous with its cognition. But the one is not identical with the other. It is not a case of projection or the objectification of the inner idea. The illusory object is invariably connected with an extramental basis, with the cognition of which alone it disappears. Never does it disappear of itself. Moreover, an illusory object serves

[26] *Vide* MK III: 28.

no practical purpose. It is not real like the object of common experience, nor is it unreal like the son of a barren woman. It is indefinable (anirvacanīya) either as existent (sat) or as non-existent (asat). Nor can it be defined as both existent and non-existent; because these are contradictory attributes and cannot belong to one and the same thing.

11. *The process of illusory appearance*

The illusory object (silver in nacre-silver illusion, for instance) arises from ajñāna[27] associated with the substratum (nacre), which is Pure Consciousness hidden in that form (nacre). As we have mentioned above, Pure Consciousness, the fundamental reality, underlies each and every phase of existence. While It is concealed in all physical objects, It shines as conscious self in sentient beings. All material objects are products of tamas.[28] They are like masses of darkness, unmanifest in themselves. None of them, not even light, shines of itself. It is neither aware of itself nor of anything else. It is wrapped in ajñāna, so to speak. An object is perceived when the light of consciousness that shines in a living individual, being manifest in his mental mode conforming to the object, withdraws its veil of ajñāna and makes it cognizable. This is subsidiary (tula) ajñāna. Its basis is Pure Consciousness qualified by the object, or apparently limited by its form. From this ajñāna arises the illusory object under certain conditions. The primal (mūla) ajñāna is that from which the nacre and all other empirical objects constituting the universe have originated. It rests on Pure Consciousness. Ajñāna has projecting as well as veiling power. It is indefinable (anirvacanīya) either as existent (sat) or as non-existent (asat).

How does the illusory silver appear? Owing to some affection in the organ of vision, such as dimness of sight, or some external cause, such as dimness of light, or both, a person sees at first the bare form of the nacre lying before him and cognizes it as 'this is something bright'. It means that he has the perception of 'thisness' or the bare existence of the nacre qualified by its brightness but not of its specific character as a nacre. This is due to the fact that through the visual organ his mind has located the object and the mental mode identified with 'thisness' and brightness of the nacre has removed ajñāna enveloping these two phases, while the ajñāna hiding the specific

[27] Ajñāna is not nescience or absence of knowledge, but the reverse of knowledge. It is a positive principle removable by knowledge. So it is said to be antiknowledge (jñāna-virōdhi). Ajñāna is *contrary* to Pure Consciousness, its locus or ground, but is *contradictory* to knowledge, which is a manifestation of Pure Consciousness through a mode of the mind corresponding to the object.

[28] See footnote 49, chap. 1, sec. 8.

character of the nacre (nacreness) endures. It is this very ajñāna that gives rise to the illusory silver. In the absence of this ajñāna, that is, in case the specific character of the nacre (nacreness) is perceived there is no room for illusion.

With the vague apprehension of the nacre as something bright there arises in the mind of the perceiver an eagerness to know its specific character, while the consciousness of its similarity with silver awakens the memory of silver by association; all these conjointly impinge on ajñāna hiding the specific character of the nacre. Thus stirred up, ajñāna instantly turns into illusory appearance of silver, which being connected with the mental mode identified with 'thisness' is cognized as 'this is silver'. According to some, the same ajñāna turns into illusory silver and its cognition as well. So the cognition of the illusory silver is not a modification of the mind in their view. Just as ajñāna is indefinable as existent or as non-existent, so is the illusory silver, which is but an appearance of silver.

Thus, the specific character of the nacre (nacreness) serves as the substratum (adhiṣṭhāna) and its bare existence (thisness) as the base (ādhāra) of the illusory silver.[29] In either case, of course, the underlying Consciousness is meant. While the bare existence of the nacre is open to view as 'this', its specific character is apprehended as the illusory silver. This is how a person cognizes the nacre as 'this is silver'.[30] As soon as 'nacreness' is known, the illusory silver disappears, but the perception of 'thisness' continues; so the object is immediately cognized as 'this is a nacre'. Thus, in illusion there is always a bare apprehension of its base. It is not without an element of truth. It is a peculiar conjunction of truth (satya) and untruth (anṛta).

Vedānta-paribhāṣā gives a similar account of illusory appearance:

'When the organs of vision of a person who has such ocular defect as dimness of sight become connected with an object [such as a nacre] in front of him, then he has a mental mode conforming to "this" and "brightness". In that mental mode the consciousness limited by "this" is reflected. The mental mode having been out there in the manner previously stated, the consciousness limited by "this", the consciousness limited by the mental mode and the consciousness limited by the mind [percipient consciousness—pramātṛ-caitanya] coincide.[31] Then the avidyā [ajñāna] that is associated with nacreness and abides in the consciousness limited by the object [nacre] (which is coincident with the percipient-consciousness) is attended with the latent impressions of silver roused by the sight of such similarity as brightness and, being aided by the defective vision,

[29] *Vide* SS I: 31, Rāmātīrtha's com. *Anvayārtha-prakāśikā*.
[30] *Vide* SLS I, sec. 18. [31] See chap. III, sec. 9.

transforms into the [illusory] object silver and also the illusory cognition of the same.'[32]

Nothing but the ajñāna that veils the specific character of the nacre can be the cause of the illusory silver. In case the nacre is known specifically there can be no illusion. The ignorance of the specific character of the object invariably precedes the illusory perception. With the cessation of this ajñāna by the knowledge of the substratum the illusion ceases. The rope-snake disappears when the rope is specifically known. So this ajñāna is directly responsible for illusory appearance. Deficiency of material, physiological, and mental conditions, such as insufficiency of light, defective eyesight, and lack of discrimination between the percept and the memory-image can indirectly contribute to illusory experience, but cannot account for it. The fact of illusory appearance testifies to the existence of ajñāna associated with the object of perception and to its capacity to produce something that does not exist but appears to exist. As the effect cannot be defined as either real or as unreal (anirvacanīya), neither can the cause.

12. *The objectivity of illusion testifies to its origin from ajñāna veiling the substratum*

In every case of illusion the base (e.g., rope in rope-snake, nacre in nacre-silver) is perceived in a general way, while its specific character (ropeness or nacreness) remains unknown. It is the ajñāna hiding the specific character of a thing from the observer that serves as the proximate cause of illusory appearance while other factors indirectly contribute to it. There cannot be any false appearance of a thing when its real nature is cognized. Appearance means misapprehension of reality. It proceeds from the non-apprehension of what is true. It lasts as long as the non-apprehension lasts. It vanishes as soon as the non-apprehension vanishes, as soon as the real nature of the thing is cognized. Since illusion is perceptual cognition, it is counteracted by the direct cognition of the true nature of the thing and not by its mediate knowledge. The sun appears to move despite our knowledge that it is stationary. One can see the mirage while cognizant of the existence of the desert. But one cannot see the mirage and the desert both at the same time. Similarly, none can see the sun moving and unmoving at the same time. A white crystal appears red near a red flower, while its whiteness is unperceived.

Broadly speaking, there are two types of illusion: (1) the ascription of one object to another (such as nacre-silver, rope-snake) and (2) the ascription of the attribute of one thing to another (such as white

[32] VP I, Perception (Illusion).

crystal appearing red near a red flower, a white conch appearing yellow to the diseased eye). In cases of the first type, the ajñāna veiling the specific character of the base (the nacre or the rope) gives rise to the indefinable illusory object (silver or snake) and its cognition as well. These are instances of the identification of the apparent with the real object (tādāmya adhyāsa). In cases of the second type the ajñāna veiling the specific quality (whiteness) of the base (crystal, conch) yields no indefinable illusory object but brings about an indefinable apparent relation (saṁsarga adhyāsa) between two empirical facts that are unrelated and discrete.

When the redness of a flower is reflected in a white crystal the observer sees a red crystal. The crystal does not turn red but becomes red in appearance. This apparent relation between redness and crystal is caused by ajñāna veiling its whiteness, which is unperceived. The crystal and the redness reflected on it are physical facts. But the red appearance of the crystal is an illusion. It is true for the erroneous observer. Like the rising and the setting sun it is an objective experience in which many can share. It is not dependent on the observer's thoughts or feelings. It is not a subjective experience like hallucination, imagination, or memory, but something independent of the mental state of the experiencer. Wherever a person looks at the morning sun he sees it rising. When sunlight is transmitted through a green glass it does not turn green but appears green. At the same time the green glass appears luminous without being so. This is an illusory appearance for which no individual mind is responsible. Such cases of seeming relation are likewise due to ajñāna veiling the specific qualities of the light and the glass referred to. They are not caused by the interference of the observer's mind with its objects. They are due to material conditions rather than to his physiological and mental conditions.

13. *Illusion cannot be explained as a distortion of fact by the observer's mind*

Illusory appearance is not a mental image of something present to, or absent from, the observer's vision. This is what distinguishes an illusion from fancy or phantom. To imagine an aircraft as a bird is one thing. To mistake it for a bird is something different. The latter is a case of erroneous experience not solely dependent on the observer's mental condition. It takes place in a normal state of his mind, while phantom indicates an abnormal mental state. To perceive a white conch as yellow is also a case of illusory appearance. It cannot be explained as a misrepresentation of the fact by the defective mind.

Professor Alexander has mentioned a similar case of illusion, the erroneous experience of a yellow rose as a white rose, but has interpreted the same as a distortion of the fact by the observer's twisted mind. As stated by him:

'Owing to some defect in the erroneous observer, whether of sense or of carelessness or haste, instead of seeing the colour which is before him in the reality, the yellow rose, he as it were squints at reality as a whole, and his mind is compresent with white instead of yellow. One eye sees this rose in its shape; the other sees not the yellow within the shape but a white. Thus two new realities have come into being; one is the union of the real yellow rose with the mind of a true observer; the other is the union of reality, though not merely this particular reality of the yellow rose, with the mind of the observer who squints or has a twist in his mind. That reality is an erroneous belief; it is the artificial product of the mind and reality as a whole, which contains this rose and colours and relation of the rose to colour—the fact that the rose has some colour, as the fact operates on a twisted mind.'[33]

But Vedānta stresses the fact, as we have stated above, that there cannot be an experience of the non-existent, or of unpresented elements. How can a person *perceive* whiteness in a yellow rose where it is altogether absent? He may remember the whiteness of a white rose or imagine it from previous experience but cannot see it right there in the yellow rose in front of him unless it is a case of illusory appearance. Alexander's interpretation has some resemblance to Prabhākara's view of non-apprehension (akhyāti) and the Naiyāyika view of misapprehension (anyathākhyāti), neither of which is tenable as we have already pointed out.

14. *Man's egoism is a case of perennial illusion*

Illusion is not an occasional or unusual occurrence. It is at the root of man's individualism. His egoism is erroneous cognition, being the identification of the self with the not-self. It includes both inapprehension and misapprehension of the self. Not only is man ignorant of the true nature of the self; over and above this he takes himself to be other than what he is. As the cognizer of the body, the organs, and the mind, he is distinct from them all, yet he is under the delusion that he is the aggregate of them all. Consciousness belongs to the cognizer and not to the object cognized. The two are of contrary nature like light and darkness. It is absurd that either should be identified with the other. Yet the mistaken identification

33 S. Alexander, *Space, Time, and Deity*, pp. 254–5, by permission of the University of Manchester and Macmillan and Co., London, 1920.

is made. Conscious spirit and unconscious matter are tied to each other. It is a compound error, a double knot, so to speak. And this is egoism. It involves a co-mingling of the subject and the object and of their attributes as well. It is a multiform illusion natural to man. Its cause is the lack of discrimination between the self and the not-self due to ajñāna or avidyā.

We indicate below some of its prominent features:

(1) Superimposition of the body on the self—such as 'I am a man', 'I am a mortal', 'I am here', 'I move', 'I have a soul'. Just as a rope is mistaken for a snake, so the self is mistaken for the body. This is the identification (tādāmya) of the body with the self.

(2) Superimposition of the self on the body—such as 'I am a conscious being', 'I experience pain and pleasure', 'I feel free', 'I speak with the mouth', 'I see with the eyes', spoken with reference to the body. This is not actual superimposition (adhyārōpa) of the self on the body, but its association (saṁsarga) with the body through its reflection on the mind, similar to the association of the sun with an opaque object through its reflection on a mirror. So in such expressions as 'My body', 'My legs', 'My eyes', the self is falsely related to the body, the limbs, and the organs. It is the apparent that is superimposed on the real and not the real on the apparent. The self, the substratum of appearance, is superimposed on the apparent only through its radiance transmitted by a mode of the mind marked by 'I-ness' or 'my-ness'.

(3) Superimposition of the properties of the body on the self—such as 'I am young', 'I am fair', 'I am tall', 'My health', 'My age', 'I lie down', 'I was born', 'I shall die'. Here the properties of the physical body are falsely ascribed to the changeless, conscious self. The association is apparent. When a crystal appears red in the proximity of a red flower, the relation between the crystal and the redness of the flower is only apparent.

(4) Superimposition of the mental states on the self—'I am happy', 'I am ignorant', 'I am virtuous', 'I am willing', 'I am fearful', 'I think', 'My ego', and so on.

(5) Superimposition of the properties of the organs on the self—'I am deaf', 'I am blind', 'I am active', 'I am eloquent', and so forth.

(6) Through the identification with the body a person identifies himself even with external objects and conditions. 'I am wealthy', 'I am a farmer', 'I am British', 'My home', 'My children', 'My parents', 'My position', and so forth.

Man's real self is ever free, pure, luminous, and united with the universal Self. Yet he is bound to all appearance, because of the erroneous identification of the self with the not-self. Its root-cause is avidyā or ajñāna. The existence of ajñāna cannot be denied. It is evident from such an experience as 'I do not know myself'. While man is under the spell of ajñāna, he is at the same time its witness. The sun manifests the cloud that hides it. As reflected in ajñāna and its modifications, the self is apparently bound and changeful; but as the witness of ajñāna the self is ever free and immutable. The sun appears to move and to shine more or less, although ever stationary and resplendent.

Avidyā has an apparent existence. It imposes forms on the formless. It apparently limits the limitless. Just as a wave is essentially one with the ocean and yet appears to be differentiated from it because of the limitation of a mere form, so avidyā creates a semblance of separation between the individual soul and the supreme Self. One Infinite Self is apparently divided into countless finite selves. Swāmī Vivekānanda aptly remarks:

'According to the Advaitin, this individuality which we have today is a delusion. This has been a hard nut to crack all over the world. Forthwith you tell a man he is not an individual, he is so much afraid that his individuality whatever that may be, will be lost! But the Advaitin says there never has been an individuality, you have been changing every moment of your life. You were a child and thought in one way, now you are a man and think another way, again, you will be an old man and think differently. Everybody is changing. If so, where is your individuality? Certainly not in the body, or in the mind, or in thought. And beyond that is your Ātman, and, says the Advaitin, this Ātman is the Brahman Itself. There cannot be two Infinites. There is only one individual and it is Infinite.'[34]

[34] CW III, p. 347.

CHAPTER VI

THREE MEANS OF NON-PERCEPTUAL KNOWLEDGE: INFERENCE, COMPARISON, AND POSTULATION

So far we have dwelt particularly on perception (pratyakṣa), the first of the six means of valid knowledge recognized by the Kumārila school of Pūrva Mīmāṁsā[1] and Advaita Vedānta. It is the only method of direct knowledge of the physical facts and of the mental states as well. So the perceptual knowledge means direct or immediate cognition. The direct knowledge of the external facts is attainable

[1] Pūrva-Mīmāṁsā, briefly called 'Mīmāṁsā', which means rational investigation (pūjita-vicāra), is one of the six systems of Indian philosophy that accept the authority of the Vedas. The six Vedic systems form three sets of two—(1) Nyāya and Vaiśeṣika, (2) Sāṁkhya and Yōga, and (3) Pūrva-Mīmāṁsā and Uttara-Mīmāṁsā. The system called 'Pūrva-Mīmāṁsā (anterior investigation)' maintains the primacy of the initial or the ritualistic section (karma-kāṇda) of the Śruti, while Uttara-Mīmāṁsā (posterior investigation) maintains the primacy of its concluding or the philosophical section (jñāna-kāṇda), and is known as Vedānta philosophy. The main purpose of the Pūrva-Mīmāṁsā system is to determine the duties of life and uphold Vedic ritualism as the way to liberation, by which it means life in heaven (svarga-lōka). In order to maintain the validity of the Vedic testimony it has dwelt at length on the theory of knowledge and made distinct contributions in the field of logic and epistemology.

The main source of the system is the *Pūrva-Mīmāṁsā-sūtras* of Jaimini (fourth century BC) with the commentary of Sabara Swāmin (first century BC). Its later development into two schools was due to two different expositions of the treatise by two illustrious thinkers, Kumārila Bhaṭṭa and Prabhākara Miśra (seventh century AD). Kumārila acknowledges all the six means of valid knowledge stated above, while Prabhākara (nicknamed 'Guru', a pupil of Kumārila) recognizes only five and denies non-apprehension. Advaita Vedānta is closely related to the Kumārila school as regards the theory of knowledge.

Kumārila's *Ślōka-vārttika* is available in full, but Prabhākara's work is available only in part. Kumārila's *Ślōka-vārttika* and Jaimini's *Mīmāṁsā-sūtras* with Sabara's commentary have been translated into English by Dr Gaṅgānātha Jhā of Allahabad University, India.

Besides these, there are many other notable writings on Pūrva-Mīmāṁsā (also called Karma-Mīmāṁsā), of which *Śāstradīpikā* of Pārthasārathi Miśra (about ninth century, AD), a follower of Kumārila, and *Prakaraṇa-pañcikā*, a compendium of Prabhākara's views, by Śālikanātha Miśra (probably ninth century AD) are well known. For further information see Appendix B, sec. 4.

only by sense-object contact. Whatever knowledge of the physical universe is gained by other means, such as inference (anumāna), comparison (upamāna), and postulation (arthāpatti), is based on sense-perception and is necessarily indirect or mediate. The primary source of the knowledge of the physical world is therefore sense-perception, and this is accepted as a means of valid knowledge (pramāṇa) by all schools of thought, Eastern and Western.

In this chapter we propose to deal with three means of non-perceptual knowledge—inference (anumāna), comparison (upamāna), and postulation (arthāpatti). Since they are dependent on sense-knowledge, their scope is limited to the sensible universe. The two schools of Pūrva-Mīmāṁsā and Advaita Vedānta recognize these three as distinct means of mediate knowledge of the empirical facts. The Nyāya school recognizes the first two—inference and comparison, and treats postulation as a case of inference. But all Indian philosophers—the Vedic and the Non-Vedic, excepting such radical empiricists as the Cārvākas, accept inference as a means of mediate knowledge. In the view of most thinkers of the West it is the sole means of mediate knowledge and ranks next to perception. Its use in everyday life is undeniable.

The two other means of valid knowledge—non-apprehension (anupalabdhi) and verbal testimony (āgama or śabda) have to be treated separately because of their singularities. According to the Kumārila school of Mīmāṁsā and Advaita Vedānta non-apprehension (anupalabdhi) is the sole means of the cognition of non-existence. But the knowledge it conveys is indirect according to the Kumārila school and direct according to Advaita Vedānta. Prabhākara Mīmāṁsā does not acknowledge non-apprehension (anupalabdhi) as a separate pramāṇa.

Verbal testimony (āgama or śabda) has the unique capacity to communicate the knowledge of the suprasensible as well as the sensible. It is generally recognized as a means of mediate knowledge. But in the view of Padmapāda, the founder of the Vivaraṇa school[2] of Advaita Vedānta, it serves in special cases as the means of immediate knowledge (aparōkṣa-jñāna). Because of its extensive range and supreme value verbal testimony has to be dwelt on at length in five chapters under five main headings. This will form the second part of the book.

I. INFERENCE (ANUMĀNA)

1. *The core of inference* (*anumāna*) *is the knowledge of invariable concomitance* (*vyāpti*)

The Sanskrit term for inference is anumāna, literally, knowing after. It means the method by which knowledge is derived from another

[2] See footnote 46, chap. XI.

knowledge. This refers to the logical process of gaining the knowledge. The knowledge thus gained, that is, inferential knowledge, is called in Sanskrit anumiti, literally, 'the consequent knowledge' (from anu=after, and miti=knowledge). It means the knowledge that follows from another knowledge. This is the knowledge that is derived from the knowledge of an invariable relation between what is perceived and what is deduced. The Sanskrit term for this relation is vyāpti (lit., extension or pervasion). In Western logic it is called 'the invariable concomitance'. The core of inference (anumāna) is the knowledge of invariable concomitance (vyāpti), which is gained from experience. Like the English word 'inference' the Sanskrit term anumāna also denotes inferential knowledge, but is generally used in the sense of its method or process. The two words are not, however, quite interchangeable, inasmuch as there are differences in the Indian conception of 'anumāna' and the Western conception of 'inference'.

The Indian dialecticians—the Naiyāyikas—have taken the lead in the systematic study of inference (anumāna). Their methods of reasoning and terminology have considerably influenced the logic of other systems. But though there are agreements among the Indian schools as to the general principles of inference, yet there are sharp differences as regards its particulars. They all agree that the key to inference is the knowledge of invariable concomitance (vyāpti-jñāna). But they differ as to the exact meaning of vyāpti, the way its knowledge is attained, and the method of reaching conclusion through this knowledge. The Buddhist way of determining the invariable concomitance (vyāpti) differs from the ways of the Naiyāyikas and the Advaitins. *Vedānta-paribhāṣā* has pointed out how the Advaitin's interpretation of the process of inference deviates from the Naiyāyika's.[3] There are also divergent views as to the classification of inference. We shall note some of these agreements and disagreements as we proceed.

2. *The meaning of vyāpti (invariable concomitance). Its two different classifications*

The inference that the hill has fire results from the apprehension of smoke as a mark on the hill followed by the recollection of the invariable concomitance between smoke and fire. As we have indicated above, the invariable concomitance between the middle term (hetu, i.e., smoke) and the major term (sādhya, i.e., fire) is the basis of inference, and is called vyāpti (lit., extension or pervasion) in Indian logic. It implies a universal relation of co-existence between the things denoted by the two terms. The knowledge of this is the direct means to inference. As defined by *Vedānta-paribhāṣa*, 'Invari-

[3] VP II, Inference.

able concomitance (vyāpti) is the co-existence of the thing to be inferred [sādhya, e.g., fire] with the mark [sādhana, e.g., smoke] in all substrata in which the mark may exist'.[4] The Naiyāyikas also hold the same view of invariable concomitance (vyāpti).[5] Like the Advaitins they maintain that the invariable concomitance (vyāpti) between two things is not necessarily a relation of cause and effect or their identity of essence (tādāmya), as the Buddhists hold. We shall dwell on this point later (see sec. 6).

The two correlated terms, smoke and fire, are not equal in extension. While smoke is always accompanied by fire, fire is not always accompanied by smoke (as in the case of a red-hot iron ball). Consequently, we can infer the presence of fire from the presence of smoke, but not *vice versa*. The relation between smoke and fire is a case of non-equipollent concomitance (asama-vyāpti), in which fire is the principal concomitant (vyāpaka) and smoke is the subordinate concomitant (vyāpya). As an instance of equipollent concomitance (sama-vyāpti) one may cite the proposition, 'Whatever is knowable is nameable' or 'Whatever is nameable is knowable'. The related terms, 'the knowable' and 'the nameable', are equal in extension.

Besides the above two kinds (sama and asama vyāpti), there are two other varieties of invariable concomitance: (1) the affirmative and (2) the negative (anvaya-vyāpti and vyatireka-vyāpti). Where there is vyāpya (the subordinate concomitant, e.g., smoke) there is vyāpaka (the principal concomitant, e.g., fire)—this is affirmative invariable concomitance, agreement in presence. Where there is no vyāpaka (principal concomitant, e.g., fire) there is no vyāpya (subordinate concomitant, e.g., smoke)—this is negative invariable concomitance, agreement in absence. According to Nyāya, with the knowledge of negative invariable concomitance between two things one can infer the presence of one thing from that of the other. For example, one can infer the presence of fire from the sight of smoke by the knowledge, 'Where there is no fire there cannot be any smoke', as in a lake. Advaita Vedānta explains this as a case of postulation (arthāpatti). It holds that inference (anumāna) is a process of reasoning based on the affirmative invariable concomitance between hetu (the middle term) and sādhya (the major term); e.g., where there is smoke there is fire. So it acknowledges only one kind of inference 'affirmative' (anvayi). We shall discuss this point while dwelling on Postulation (arthāpatti).

3. *The syllogistic forms in Vedānta and the Western logic*

The Naiyāyikas and the Advaitins agree on the twofold classification of inference: (1) svārtha, meant for oneself, and (2) parārtha, meant

[4] VP II. [5] BP 69; TS 59.

for others.[6] In the former case, one argues with oneself for the knowledge of the thing unperceived from the knowledge of its relation with the thing perceived. In the latter case, he puts forth argument to convince others of a truth thus known. To illustrate the former: A person sees a mass of smoke on a hill. He then remembers the invariable concomitance (vyāpti) between smoke and fire; i.e., wherever there is smoke there is fire, or smoke does not exist where fire does not. He concludes that there is fire on the hill.

To demonstrate the truth of the conclusion to others a formal statement of the reasoning process, that is to say, a syllogism is required. According to the Advaitins a syllogism consists of three steps or propositions; according to the Naiyāyikas, of five steps or propositions. The three-membered syllogism of the Advaitins has two alternate forms as illustrated below:

Form I

Proposition to be proved (pratijñā)	The hill has fire.
Reason for this (hetu)	Because it has smoke.
Example (udāharaṇa)	Whatever has smoke has fire, such as a kitchen.

Form II

Example (udāharaṇa)	Whatever has smoke has fire, such as a kitchen.
Application (upanaya)	The hill has smoke.
Conclusion (nigamana)	Therefore the hill has fire.

The second syllogistic form of Vedānta resembles that of the Western logic, which is noted below:[7]

Major premise	Whatever has smoke has fire.
Minor premise	The hill has smoke.
Conclusion	Therefore the hill has fire.

Corresponding to the major, the minor, and the middle term of Western logic, there are in Indian logic the sādhya, the pakṣa, and the hetu. In the above three forms of syllogism, 'fire' is the sādhya (the major term), the thing to be inferred; 'hill' is the pakṣa (the minor term), the subject or that in which the thing is inferred; 'smoke' is the hetu (the middle term), the reason or the ground of

[6] *Vide* VP II, Inference.

[7] A familiar illustration of the Western logic:

Major premise	All men are mortal.
Minor premise	Henry is a man.
Conclusion	Therefore Henry is mortal.

inference. The hetu is also called sādhana, the means of inference, or the liṅga, the mark or the sign that indicates the presence of fire on the hill.

4. *The difference in the Advaita and the Nyāya syllogism*

In the two syllogistic forms of Vedānta cited above there are altogether five propositions. The Nyāya syllogism comprises all these, as illustrated below:

Proposition to be proved (pratijñā)	The hill has fire.
Reason for this (hetu)	Because it has smoke.
Universal proposition supported by an instance (udāharaṇa)	Whatever has smoke has fire, such as a kitchen.
Application of the universal proposition (upanaya)	The hill has smoke, such as is always accompanied by fire.
Conclusion proved (nigamana)	Therefore the hill has fire.

In the Advaitins' view the first three steps or the last three are adequate for the purpose.

According to the Naiyāyikas the fourth step in the above syllogism is the immediate cause of inferential knowledge.[8] Here the presence of smoke on the hill is cognized as correlating the hill with fire. From this cognition arises the knowledge 'the hill has fire'. It is technically called 'the consideration of the mark (smoke) for the third time (tṛtīya liṅga parāmarśa)', in that it is preceded by the first and the second consideration of the mark (smoke). First, smoke is observed in a kitchen and other places and the knowledge of its invariable concomitance with fire is remembered. Second, smoke is perceived on a hill and its invariable concomitance with fire is recollected. Third, the perception of smoke on the hill leads to the knowledge of the hill as containing fire that invariably accompanies smoke. It is this knowledge that yields the conclusion, 'Therefore the hill has fire'.

But the Advaitins disagree with the Naiyāyikas on this point. According to them, 'The instrument of inferential knowledge is the knowledge of invariable concomitance, the latent impression of which [knowledge] is the intermediate operation [that is, cause]'.[9] As soon as a person who has gained from previous experience the knowledge of the invariable concomitance between smoke and fire sees smoke on a hill, the latent impression of this knowledge is revived within him and immediately follows the conclusion, 'The hill has fire'. Hence the interposition of the third consideration of the mark

[8] *Vide* TS 57. [9] VP II.

(e.g., the hill has smoke, such as is always accompanied by fire) is redundant. The fifth step in the syllogism is also unnecessary.

5. *The distinctive character of the Indian method of inference. It is a combined deductive-inductive process of reasoning*

Anumāna (inference) denotes the process of reasoning by which the right conclusion is reached, and not the verbal form of this process. Professor Hiriyanna aptly remarks:

'This syllogistic form, with its five members,[10] is only for leading another to the conclusion in question; and the verbal form, in itself, constitutes no part of inference. It only helps to direct the mind of the listener to think in the required manner, and thereby gives rise to the same process of thought in his mind as the one in that of the speaker. So if the syllogistic *form* is described as anumāna (inference), it is only by courtesy (upacāra). That is, the Nyāya-Vaiśeṣika, like the rest of the Indian systems, rejects the verbal view of logic which is common in the West. It was never forgotten in India that the subject-matter of logic is thought, and not the linguistic form in which it may find expression.'[11]

The invariable concomitance between the middle term (hetu) and the major term (sādhya) is the keystone of the syllogism. On this rests the validity of the conclusion. It lays down the universal proposition showing the connection between the truth to be established and the reason stated. In Indian logic the universal proposition is supported by at least one instance (e.g., whatever has smoke has fire, such as a kitchen, or all men are mortal, such as Socrates, Napoleon, Gandhi). This shows that the knowledge of the invariable concomitance between the middle term (hetu, sādhana, or liṅga) and the major term (sādhya) is acquired by observation and generalization. Thus, the Indian syllogism is not merely deductive. It is a combined deductive-inductive process of reasoning.

The distinctive character of the Hindu method of inference has been thus indicated by Dr Brajendranath Seal:

'Anumāna (inference) is the process of ascertaining, not by perception or direct observation, but through the instrumentality or medium of a mark, that a thing possesses a certain character. Inference is therefore based on the establishment of an invariable concomitance (vyāpti) between the *mark* and the character inferred. The Hindu inference (anumāna) is therefore neither merely formal nor merely

[10] Reference to Nyāya syllogism cited above (sec. 4).

[11] *The Essentials of Indian Philosophy*, p. 101.

material, but a combined Formal-Material Deductive-Inductive process.

It is neither the Aristotelian Syllogism (Formal-Deductive process) nor Mill's Induction (Material-Inductive process), but the real Inference which must combine formal validity with material truth, inductive generalization with deductive particularisation. . . . This Formal-Material Deductive-Inductive process thus turns on one thing—the establishment of the invariable concomitance (vyāpti) between the mark and the character inferred—in other words, an inductive generalization.'[12]

We quote pertinent remarks of D. M. Datta to elucidate the point:

'The various principles on which Western logicians classify inference are conspicuous by their absence from Indian works on Logic. . . . the classification of inference into the mediate and the immediate was never made, owing to the fact that an anumāna *ex hypothesi* involved two premises—the major and the minor.

The necessity of classifying inference into the deductive and the inductive also did not arise, because for the Indian logician no syllogism was of any value unless based on a universal major established through induction; consequently, the processes of induction and deduction blended together to constitute a syllogism. It was no more possible for them to think of classifying inference into inductive and deductive than to think of classifying men into those that have bones and those that have flesh.

This will also explain why the classification of syllogisms into the categorical and the conditional was not made by the Indian logicians. A syllogism with a really conditional major (not a so-called conditional one that is reducible to categorical type) can claim little more than formal consistency. An Indian logician demanded of the syllogism, both formal and material, validity; nothing but a universal major, materially valid, could satisfy him. The hypothetical syllogism could not, therefore, have any place in his logic. With him, therefore, as with Aristotle, every syllogism was necessarily of a categorical nature.'[13]

6. *How to ascertain the invariable concomitance* (*vyāpti*)

The Indian philosophers have different views as to the method of determining the invariable concomitance between hetu (the minor term) and sādhya (the major term). The point is this. How can a

[12] Dr Brajendranath Seal, *The Positive Sciences of the Ancient Hindus*, London, Longmans, Green, 1915, pp. 250–2.

[13] *The Six Ways of Knowing*, pp. 212, 213.

universal proposition be established on the basis of limited observation? For this the Naiyāyikas and the Advaitins both depend on inductive generalization. Unlike the Buddhists, they maintain that the invariable concomitance between two things is not necessarily a relation of cause and effect. The Buddhists derive their knowledge of the invariable concomitance from two *a priori* principles: (1) causality and (2) identity of essence (tādātmya). When two things are found to be related as cause and effect, we can know that there is a universal relation between them. Since smoke is known to be caused by fire and fire alone, it must be universally related to fire. Similarly, if two things have an identical, or a common, essence in them, they are universally related. The proposition, 'A dog is an animal' is universal, because the relation between these two is based on the essence of animality that is common to both.

According to the early Nyāya school the following are the three steps to the knowledge of invariable concomitance (vyāpti-graha-upāya):

(1) Observation of agreement in presence (anvaya), e.g., wherever smoke is present fire is also present.
(2) Observation of agreement in absence (vyatireka), e.g., wherever fire is absent smoke is also absent. This is not applicable in all cases. For instance, the proposition, 'Whatever is knowable is nameable,' is established only by the observation of agreement in presence; because there cannot be the absence of knowability in anything without our knowledge.
(3) Non-observation of the contrary (vyabhicārādarśanam).

The Advaitins do not take into account the second step, because according to them the basis of inference is the knowledge of the co-existence or co-presence (sahacāra) of the mark (e.g., smoke) and the thing to be inferred (e.g., fire), and not of their co-absence. The observation of their co-existence (sahacāra-darśanam) and the experience of no contrary instance (vyabhicārādarśanam) are considered adequate for determining the invariable concomitance between the two; even a single observation of their co-existence can serve the purpose, provided no exception to this is known. As stated in *Vedānta-paribhāṣa*:

'Invariable concomitance is co-existence with the thing to be inferred [e.g., fire] that must abide in all substrata of the mark [e.g., smoke]. It is apprehended by the observation of concomitance when no violation of the latter has been noticed. As to whether this observation of concomitance should be repeated experience or a first experience. no importance need be attached to this distinction, for the deciding factor is simply observation of concomitance.'[14]

The Prabhākara school of Mīmāṁsā and the Nyāya-Vaiśeṣika agree with Advaita Vedānta on this point. How is it possible to establish a universal proposition that smoke is always accompanied by fire by perceiving their co-existence only once? Because, as the Advaitins point out, even a single observation can enable a person to find a general relation between the two universals, 'smokeness' and 'fireness', which is true of all cases of smoke and fire. When there is any doubt as to the validity of the general relation found by the first experience, then repeated observation is necessary. It is a fact of common experience that on seeing a chair for the first time a person can apprehend the universal 'chairness' and recognize as chair whatever has the universal character of 'chairness'.

7. The Advaitins do not accept the threefold classification of inference by Nyāya school. Why they do not

The Advaitins do not agree to the Naiyāyika classification of inference into three different types, namely—

(1) Affirmative-negative (anvaya-vyatireki).
(2) Purely affirmative (kevalānvayi).
(3) Purely negative (kevala-vyatireki).[15]

This classification is based on the nature of the invariable concomitance, which can be either affirmative or negative. The affirmative invariable concomitance (anvaya-vyāpti) is that in which the mark (liṅga, e.g., smoke) is positively related to the thing to be inferred (sādhya, e.g., fire). It is determined by the observation of agreement in presence between the two objects, as for instance, 'Wherever there is smoke there is fire'. The negative invariable concomitance is that in which the mark (liṅga, e.g., smoke) is negatively related to the thing to be inferred (sādhya, e.g., fire). It is determined by the observation of agreement in absence between the two objects, as for instance, 'Where there is no fire there is no smoke'.

The Naiyāyikas' affirmative-negative (anvaya-vyatireki) inference is one in which the invariable concomitance can be either affirmative or negative. For instance, the inference, 'The hill has fire, because it has smoke' can be based on either of the two major premises: (1) Wherever there is smoke there is fire, as in a kitchen; (2) Where there is no fire there is no smoke, as in a lake.

The purely negative (kevala-vyatireki) inference is that which is

[14] VP II. [15] *Vide* TS 66–71; BP 142–4; VP II.

based solely on negative invariable concomitance. For instance, the inference, 'God is Omniscient, because He is the Creator', has for its basis the negative invariable concomitance, 'Whoever is not Omniscient is not the Creator'. No knowledge of affirmative invariable concomitance is possible in this case, because the co-presence of 'Omniscience' and 'Creatorship' is nowhere to be observed. We can observe only their agreement in absence and determine the negative invariable concomitance, 'Whoever is not Omniscient is not the Creator'.

But the Advaitins, like the Mīmāṁsakas, do not acknowledge negative invariable concomitance as the basis of inference. The knowledge of negative invariable concomitance is not possible, according to them, without the knowledge of affirmative invariable concomitance. The conclusion derived from the knowledge of negative invariable concomitance is treated by them under a separate pramāṇa (means of knowledge) called arthāpatti (postulation). Thus, they reject both forms of vyatireki inference—affirmative-negative and purely negative. They admit only one form of inference, anvayi (affirmative), which includes the type of inference designated kevalānvayi (purely affirmative) by the Naiyāyikas. But the Advaitins repudiate the term 'kevalānvayi (purely affirmative)', which is too narrow and not in accord with the nature of Reality as known to them. There is absence of every attribute in Brahman. It is beyond all predication.

The Naiyāyikas define kevalānvayi (purely affirmative) as the type of inference, whereof the sādhya (the thing to be inferred) is present everywhere, in other words, is not a counter-positive (pratiyōgī) of non-existence.[16] 'The jar is nameable, because it is knowable' is an instance of the purely affirmative type of inference, according to them; because 'namability' (the thing inferred) is present everywhere. This inference is based solely on the affirmative invariable concomitance, *viz.*, 'Whatever is knowable is nameable.' Since the absence of 'knowability' and 'namability' is nowhere to be observed, the knowledge of negative invariable concomitance is not possible in this case.

But the Advaitins view every predicate as non-essential in Nondual Brahman, which precludes all affirmation. So they accept only one kind of inference, *viz.*, 'affirmative', but not 'purely affirmative'. To quote *Vedānta-paribhāṣā*:

'That inference is only of one form, namely, "affirmative (anvayi)", but not "purely affirmative (kevalānvayi)", for, according to our view, every attribute is the counter-positive of the absolute non-existence abiding in Brahman, and there is no scope for the *purely*

[16] *Vide* TS 70.

affirmative inference, in which the thing to be inferred must not be the counterpositive of non-existence.'[17]

We have dwelt on the threefold classification of inference according to the later Naiyāyikas. Gautama, the father of Nyāya system, has made a different classification, *viz.*:

(1) Inference *a priori* (pūrvavat), that is, of the effect from the perceived cause.
(2) Inference *a posteriori* (śeṣavat), that is, of the cause from the perceived effect.
(3) Inference from analogy (sāmānyatō-dṛṣṭam), that is, from something perceived as similar.[18]

We shall discuss these three types of inference later (see chap. X, sec. 4).

8. *Inference as a means to suprasensuous knowledge*

Inference is used in Advaita Vedānta to corroborate the metaphysical truths declared by the Śruti. Reason is not an independent means to suprasensuous knowledge, since it cannot decisively establish the transcendental facts, such as Brahman, Ātman, Liberation and its means, but can only show their possibility. Inference is based on sense-perception, which has its own limitations. Like one blind man led by another, they move in darkness and cannot see the pure light of Truth, which is revealed by the Śruti. As regards the inherent incompetence of both Dr Mahadevan remarks:

'The Indian theory of Inference also recognizes the perceptual basis of *anumāna*. If one had not seen the co-presence of smoke and fire in a place like the hearth, one would not be able to infer the presence of fire on the hill from the perceived presence of smoke thereon. It is true that in an ordinary knowledge the pure perceptual element cannot be separated from the element of thought. That is because even perception can be called immediate knowledge only by sufferance. In so far as perceptual knowledge depends on sense-activity, it cannot be independent knowledge nor indubitable. The detected illusions in perception are too many to be ignored. If perception is known to betray us in some cases, the spectra of a doubt that it may betray everywhere can never be exorcized. The immediacy of perception, therefore, is not true immediacy; and the reasoning which relies on perception cannot rise to certitude.

The only knowledge which is immediate and indubitable is self-

[17] Chap. on Inference.
[18] *Nyāya-sūtras* I: 1.5.

knowledge, i.e., knowledge of, or more properly, knowledge which *is* the self. For lack of a better term we shall call this intuitive experience, *ātmasākṣātkāra* or *anubhūti*. It is experience, which is not split up into experiencer, experienced object, and experiencing. It is consciousness *per se*, which is the sole reality according to Advaita.'[19]

Reflection or reasoning on the Vedāntic dictums (such as 'Thou art That') helps the seeker of Truth to grasp their true significance by removing his doubts and misconceptions with regard to them and by reconciling the apparent contradiction in them. Then it becomes possible for him to practise intense meditation on the self (ātman) and realize it as Brahman. Hearing the Vedic dictum (śravaṇa), reflection on it (manana), and meditation (nididhyāsana) are prescribed by the Śruti as a threefold way to Self-realization.[20] We shall dwell on this point at length in the second part of the book (see chap. XI and XII). The self is realized as the sole Reality.

The reality of Nondual Brahman is then established by proving the unreality of the phenomenal world, which is perceived by all. The falsity of the phenomenal world is proved by a syllogism:

Proposition (pratijñā)	The physical universe is unreal.
Reason (hetu)	Because it is contradicted by the knowledge of Brahman.
Example (udāharaṇa)	Whatever is contradicted by knowledge is unreal; such as the silver-in-nacre.

It is to be noted that Advaita Vedānta denies the absolute reality of the phenomenal world, but recognizes its empirical validity. As we have noted above (chap. IV, sec. 4) it maintains three orders of existence from the viewpoint of the apparent manifold: (1) the Absolute, (2) the empirical, and (3) the illusory.

II. COMPARISON (UPAMĀNA)

1. *Upamāna (comparison) explained*

As defined by *Vedānta-paribhāṣā* (chap. III), 'upamāna (comparison) is the instrument of the valid knowledge of similarity'. The Mīmāṁsakas and the Advaitins regard it as a distinct method of mediate knowledge, which is unlike inference as well as perception. Among

[19] T. M. P. Mahadevan, M.A., Ph.D., *Gauḍapāda, A Study in Early Advaita*, University of Madras, India, 1952, pp. 78, 79.

[20] *Vide* Br. U. II: 4.5; IV: 5.6.

other Indian philosophers only the Naiyāyikas recognize upamāna (comparison) as a separate pramāṇa (means of valid knowledge). But the Nyāya interpretation of upamāna[21] is different from the Advaitins' and is not accepted by them.

According to the Mīmāṁsakas and the Advaitins, upamāna (comparison) is the process by which the knowledge of A's similarity to B is gained from the perception of B's similarity to A, which has been perceived elsewhere. To illustrate, a person who has seen his cow at home goes to a forest and sees a gavaya (a wild cow without dewlap). He perceives the similarity of the gavaya to his cow at home, which he remembers, and forms the judgment, 'This gavaya is like my cow.' From this experience he gains additional knowledge in the form of 'My cow is like this gavaya.' Upamāna is the means by which he gains the knowledge of his cow's similarity to the gavaya from the perception of the gavaya's similarity to his cow. The knowledge of similarity thus attained is termed 'upamiti'.

2. *Upamāna is neither a case of perception nor of inference. It is distinct from both*

The Sāṁkhya school views upamāna as a case of perception.[22] But it is not so; because the cow that is known to be similar to the gavaya is not present to the senses. The gavaya and its similarity to the cow are perceived. But in perceiving the gavaya's similarity to the cow one does not perceive the cow's similarity to the gavaya. The cow's resemblance to the gavaya is known neither by perception nor by inference but by a different means, the method of comparison called in Sanskrit 'upamāna'.

As we have noted above (chap. I, sec. 2), the Vaiśeṣika school and the non-Vedic Buddhists recognize only two pramāṇas, perception and inference. They include upamāna in inference. But this position is not tenable. One cannot infer the cow's resemblance to the gavaya from the gavaya's resemblance to the cow. In the first place, the mark (the middle term) and the thing to be inferred (the major term) must be in the same substratum (minor term). The gavaya's resemblance to the cow exists in the gavaya; the cow's resemblance to the gavaya exists in the cow. So the one cannot serve as the mark of the other. Then again, in order to infer the cow's resemblance to the gavaya from the perception of the gavaya's resemblance to the cow one must have the knowledge of the universal proposition (the major premise) that a thing is similar to whatever is similar to it. Such a knowledge cannot be gained without the observation of the two similar things together.

[21] *Vide* TS 92–95; BP 79, 80.
[22] *Vide* SK 5, Vācaspati's com. *Tattvakaumudī*.

Actually, in deriving the knowledge of the cow's resemblance to the gavaya from the perception of the gavaya's resemblance to the cow that is absent such a universal premise is not used. So says *Vedānta-paribhāṣā*, 'For even without the syllogistic inference, the cognition "My cow is like this gavaya" is a matter of common experience. And one has also the consequent apperception (anuvyavasāya), "I am comparing the two things; [I am not inferring]." Hence comparison is a distinct means of knowledge.'[23]

3. *From the Advaita viewpoint upamāna cannot be regarded as a case of 'immediate inference'*

It may be urged that though upamāna is not syllogistic inference, it can be explained from the viewpoint of the Western logic as a case of 'immediate inference by reciprocal relations.'[24] But Advaita Vedānta does not admit immediate inference. All inference (anumāna), according to it, is mediate. The question has been discussed at length by D. M. Datta in his *The Six Ways of Knowing*.[25] As observed by him:

'According to the Indian conception, an inference (anumāna) is essentially an argument from at least *two* premises, one expressing an invariable relation (vyāpti) between the middle and the major terms, and the other a relation between the middle and the minor terms. Thus, according to this view no inference can be immediate. Indian logicians do not seem to realize the possibility of inferring any conclusion from one premise or one term; hence there is no discussion at all regarding the cases of immediate inference, as found in Western philosophy. We find at times, however, some instances of the so-called immediate inference put in the usual syllogistic form. This fact might indicate that the Indian logicians considered most of these cases to be forms of mediate or syllogistic reasoning. But we have no such view explicitly stated.'[26]

4. *The use of upamāna for the knowledge of the suprasensible*

The Advaitins generally explain upamāna as the means to the knowledge of similarity, as we find in *Vedānta-paribhāṣā*. But they do not dissent from the view, usually held by the Naiyāyikas, that like the knowledge of similarity the knowledge of dissimilarity can also be attained by upamāna. In this sense upamāna has been used in Advaita Vedānta to convey the knowledge of ātman (the true self) and Brahman. Ātman (the true self) is declared to be unlike the

[23] Chap. III.
[24] *Vide* M. Hiriyanna, *The Essentials of Indian Philosophy*, p. 141.
[25] See pp. 147–152. [26] pp. 147, 148.

body in every respect so that the seeker can comprehend its true nature by contrast. While the body is mortal, impure, changeful, gross, devoid of consciousness, marked by sufferings and so forth, ātman is immortal, pure, changeless, subtle, conscious, blissful and so on. Similarly, one can comprehend the nature of Brahman by contrasting it with that of the phenomenal world. While the phenomenal world is unreal, changeful, manifold, imperfect, Brahman is real, changeless, nondual, perfect. Brahman is ever untainted by the attributes of the relative order.

Upamāna as a means of the knowledge of similarity is also used to communicate the nature of ātman and Brahman. Ātman (the supreme Self) is said to be all-pervading and unrelated like ākāśa, so that by reflecting on these characteristics of ākāśa, the seeker can form an idea of the nature of the supreme Self. Brahman is said to be resplendent as the sun, so that by perceiving the luminosity of the sun, the seeker can conceive the self-luminosity of Brahman.

III. POSTULATION (ARTHĀPATTI)

1. *Arthāpatti* (*postulation*) *defined*

The word 'postulation' (from Latin *postulare*, to demand) is close to arthāpatti, which means supposition or presumption of fact. Pūrva Mīmāṁsā[27] and Advaita Vedānta[28] sharply differentiate postulation from inference (anumāna) and treat this as a separate means of valid knowledge. It is the method of assumption of an unknown fact in order to account for a known fact that is otherwise inexplicable. *Vedānta-paribhāṣā* defines postulation (arthāpatti) as 'the assumption of an explanatory fact (upapādaka) from the knowledge of the fact to be explained (upapādya).'[29] For instance, from the knowledge of the fact that a stout person A does not eat in daytime, one can assume that A eats at night, otherwise the fact of A's stoutness without eating in daytime remains unexplained. One cannot grow stout by fasting. Since A fasts in daytime, it can be taken for granted that he eats at night. Another typical illustration: On hearing that a person B, who is alive, is not at home, one can assume that B is somewhere outside. The fact of a living person not being at home is otherwise inexplicable. He must be in his house or somewhere else. Since he is not at home, the only alternative explanation is that he is outside his house.

2. *The varieties of arthāpatti* (*postulation*)

Postulation (arthāpatti) is of two types: (1) postulation from what is seen (that is, perceived) and (2) postulation from what is heard (that

[27] *Vide* Kumārila Bhaṭṭa's *Ślōka-vārttika*, chap. on Arthāpatti.
[28] *Vide* VP II, Inference. [29] *Vide* VP V.

is, known from testimony).[30] The first kind means the assumption of a third fact to explain two perceived facts that are apparently incongruous. The above two examples come under this head. Another illustration: When a person apprehends something as 'This is silver,' and subsequently discards the same thing as 'This is not silver,' then he can assume that the silver that appeared to sight was false.

The second type means the assumption of an implied meaning of a sentence (heard or read) on account of the incompleteness or incongruity of its direct meaning. For instance, in the Śruti statement, 'The knower of the Self transcends grief,'[31] since the manifold bonds signified by the word 'grief (śōka)' cannot be destroyed by Self-realization unless they are false, they are assumed to be false.

The second type of postulation (arthāpatti) has again two different forms: (1) that due to incompleteness of verbal expression (abhidhāna), and (2) that due to incompleteness of meaning (abhihita). To illustrate the first form. On hearing a part of a sentence one can assume additional word or words in accord with its intention. For instance, to the utterance of the word 'close' or 'open' one can supplement the term 'the door' in agreement with the context. Similarly, on reading the sign 'slow' on a driveway a person can know that it means 'slow the speed' or 'drive slowly'.

As an example of the second form we may mention that the apparent contradiction in the Śruti text, 'Then the mortal man becomes immortal,' is to be explained by the assumption that the mortality of man is false. Had it been real, it could not be eradicated by Self-realization. The incongruity in the sentence 'One who desires heaven should perform jyōtiṣṭōma sacrifice,' is also to be explained by this type of postulation. The point is this. How can a sacrificial rite that comes to an end here and now bring about a remote result hereafter, e.g., the attainment of heaven? There must be some intervening means between the present act and the ultimate result. It is, therefore, assumed that the performance of the sacrifice, jyōtiṣṭōma, produces in the sacrificer an unseen merit (apūrva) that endures and leads him to heaven.[32] This is the explanation of the Mīmāṁsakas.

We may give a common example of postulation to explain the incongruity of meaning in a statement. The sentence 'The camel is the ship of the desert' is meaningless if the word 'ship' is taken in its primary sense, e.g., 'a vessel to navigate the sea.' It is by the assumption of its secondary or figurative meaning, such as 'a means of transportation,' that we find the significance of the statement.

[30] *Ibid.* [31] Ch. U. III: 1.3. [32] *Vide* VP V

3. *Postulation is not a case of inference. It is not disjunctive reasoning, as the Sāṁkhya school maintains*

The Sāṁkhya school does not recognize postulation (arthāpatti) as a separate means of valid knowledge, but includes it in inference. In his commentary on *Sāṁkhya-kārikā* Vācaspati has explained that a living person Caitra, who is not at home, is known to be outside through inference.[33] His argument is like the 'disjunctive reasoning' of Western logic. It can be summed up as follows:

Caitra who is alive must be either at home or outside.
Caitra is not at home.
Therefore he is outside.

By a similar argument a stout person Devadatta, who does not eat in daytime, is known to be eating at night. It is as follows:

Devadatta who is stout must eat either by day or by night.
The stout man does not eat by day.
Therefore he eats at night.

Mīmāṁsā school, which upholds postulation (arthāpatti) as a separate means of valid knowledge, has maintained by cogent argument that the attempt to reduce arthāpatti to inference involves, a *petitio principii* (begging the question).[34] D. M. Datta has explained how the Mīmāṁsā argument applies to the above disjunctive reasoning:

'The major premise, "Caitra,[35] who is alive, is either at home or is out," here conceals the crux of the whole argument. How could we at all obtain this proposition? We are supposed to know only two facts, namely, that Caitra is alive and that he is not at home, and from these *two* data we are to come to the conclusion that he is out.

But we find that in the inference the major premise contains one datum more, namely, that if the man is alive and yet not at home, he must be out, for this is what the disjunctive proposition contains as one of its meanings.

But the aim of the inference also is to prove the same thing—namely, that the man (who is living and is yet absent from home) must be out. Ultimately we realize, therefore, the truth of the

[33] SK 5 com. *Tattvakaumudī*.

[34] Kumārila Bhaṭṭa's *Ślōka-vārttika*, chap. on Arthāpatti; see also *Śāstra-dīpikā* of Pārtha-sārathi Miśra.

[35] Dr Datta has used the name Devadatta. We have changed it to Caitra in keeping with Vācaspati's statement.

Mīmāṁsaka's argument that the attempt to reduce arthāpatti to inference is vitiated by an unavoidable *petitio principii*.'[36]

4. *The Naiyāyikas' attempt to reduce postulation to the form of inference from agreement in absence (vyatireka-vyāpti) is equally untenable*

The Nyāya school has tried to explain postulation (arthāpatti) as a case of inference from negative invariable concomitance, which means the universal relation between the absence of the thing to be inferred (fire, for instance) and that of the mark (smoke, for instance); for example, where there is no fire there is no smoke, as on a lake.[37] So says Viśvanātha of the Navya-Nyāya (Neo-Logic) school: 'In this system postulation (arthāpatti) is not at all recognized as a separate means of valid knowledge, because its purpose is served by the knowledge of negative invariable concomitance (vyatireka-vyāpti).[38]

But, according to Advaita Vedānta, 'the knowledge of negative invariable concomitance is not a cause of inferential knowledge;'[39] only affirmative invariable concomitance (anvaya-vyāpti) can lead to inference. So it accepts only one kind of inference, affirmative (anvayi), but concedes that negative invariable concomitance can lead to inference in a round-about way, that is, through affirmative invariable concomitance. For, from the knowledge of negative invariable concomitance one can have the knowledge of affirmative invariable concomitance by means of postulation (arthāpatti).[40] From the fact where there is no fire there is no smoke, as in a lake, one can assume that where there is smoke there is fire because the presence of smoke without fire is inexplicable. Then one can infer the presence of fire in a hill from the sight of smoke there.

In neither of the two cases cited above (sec. 3) do we apprehend an affirmative invariable concomitance between the thing perceived and the thing to be inferred, such as between Devadatta's stoutness and eating at night or between Caitra's being alive and staying outside. So these cannot be included in inference, as the Naiyāyikas hold. As stated in *Vedānta-paribhāṣā*:

'This postulation cannot be included in inference. For, since affirmative invariable concomitance cannot be apprehended here, it cannot be classed under affirmative inference, and we have previously refuted the contention that inference through negative invariable

[36] *The Six Ways of Knowing*, p. 236.

[37] This is the view of the later school of Nyāya (Neo-Logicians). The old school treats postulation as a case of inference of the cause from perceived effect (śeṣavat). See Inference; sec. 7. [38] BP 144. [39] VP II.

[40] VP II, V; see also com. *Śikhāmaṇi*.

concomitance is also an inference. Hence in cases of postulation the apperception is not "I am inferring it," but, "I am assuming it from this".'[41]

The difference of attendant apperception is also pointed out as a mark of distinction between the methods of postulation and deduction.

As observed by the Mīmāṁsakas, the Naiyāyika attempt to include postulation (arthāpatti) in inference from negative invariable concomitance (vyatireka-vyāpti), is also vitiated by *petitio principii*. Professor D. M. Datta has dwelt on this point as well:

'It is necessary, therefore, to consider also the categorical form: "The absence of a man from all places outside home, while he is not at home, is a case of the absence of his life. Caitra, while he is not at home, is alive. Therefore, Caitra is not absent from all places outside home, i.e. he is outside home." We find that here also the major premise presents the same puzzle. For it contains the knowledge that "absence from home" and "absence from all places outside home" are incompatible, except on the supposition that the man is not alive. And how such knowledge is acquired is the very problem of arthāpatti (postulation). We have here, therefore, as in the previous case, a *petitio principii*.'[42]

5. *The distinction of postulation (arthāpatti) from hypothesis and deduction*

Thus, postulation, as a method of knowledge, has a distinctive character. It cannot be identified with inference or any other means of valid knowledge. It has other distinguishing marks apart from the difference of attendant apperception that we have noted above. It resembles hypothesis of Western logic, but is different from it. As observed by D. M. Datta:

'On all grounds, therefore, we have to admit that arthā-patti is a distinct method of knowledge; that it cannot be reduced to inference and neither can all inference be reduced to it. But before we conclude, it will be interesting to enquire whether we have any analogue of this process of knowledge in Western philosophy. It may be compared to the hypothesis of Western logic, in so far as both of them are *suppositions* that set out to *explain* given facts. But there are also important points of difference between the two. Like an arthāpatti, a hypothesis may not be always inspired by the motive of solving a conflict or contradiction. What is more important to note is that

[41] VP V. [42] *The Six Ways of Knowing*, p. 236.

"hypothesis" is used to connote a tentative supposition that awaits verification, and does not, therefore, possess absolute certainty. But an arthāpatti, though a supposition, is the supposition of the only possible fact and carries with it absolute certainty. It can claim, therefore, the same place as a method of knowledge as is enjoyed by inference, perception, etc.'[43]

He concludes with the remark: 'Kant's transcendental proof can, therefore, be regarded as an instance of arthāpatti.'[44]

Dr Chatterjee and Dr Datta have clearly distinguished postulation from hypothesis and deduction:

'It will be found that arthāpatti [postulation] resembles a hypothesis as understood in Western logic. It appears to be like an explanatory hypothesis. But the difference is that it lacks the tentative or provisional character of a hypothesis. What is known by arthāpatti is not simply hypothetically supposed or entertained, but is *believed* in as the *only* possible *explanation*. As arthāpatti [postulation] arises out of a *demand for explanation*, it is different from a syllogistic inference, the object of which is to *conclude* from given facts, and not to *explain* given facts. Arthāpatti is a search for *grounds*, whereas an inference is a search for *consequents*.'[45]

6. *Why God's existence and nature cannot be determined by arthāpa*

It is worthy of note that arthāpatti is applicable only when there is but one alternative explanation of the fact to be explained. When there are more than one possible explanation the assumption of any one of them cannot explain the fact assuredly. So this cannot be a case of postulation (arthāpatti), which is a means to valid knowledge (pramāṇa). When a living person is not at home, it can be unquestionably assumed that he is elsewhere; because the fact of his being absent from home cannot be explained otherwise. This is a case of postulation (arthāpatti). From the experience of the manifold the existence of an Omnipotent, Omniscient Creator cannot be ascertained by postulation. Even though the universe be recognized as a creation, there can be more than one explanation of its coming into being. So the following postulation does not hold good:

The world is a creation.
It is not made by a created being.
So it must have a Supreme Maker.

[43] *Ibid.* p. 238. [44] *Ibid.* p. 239.

[45] Satischandra Chatterjee and Dhirendramohan Datta, *An Introduction to Indian Philosophy*, p. 333.

Some may cogently maintain that it is the result of the concerted action of more than one god and not the work of one supreme God. Great achievements are possible by the coordinated efforts of more than one person.

CHAPTER VII

NON-APPREHENSION: THE WAY OF APPREHENDING NON-EXISTENCE

1. *Anupalabdhi (non-apprehension) is the only means to the valid knowledge of non-existence (abhāva)*

According to the Mīmāṁsā school of Kumārila Bhaṭṭa[1] and Advaita Vedānta, the absence of an object or its attribute from a locus is known, neither by sense-perception nor by any other method of knowledge based on it (*viz*., inference, comparison, postulation, or verbal testimony), but by a unique way called 'non-apprehension (anupalabdhi).' It means that the non-existence of a thing is apprehended by its non-perception. By not seeing a jar in a place one knows that it is not there. In all such instances as, 'The teacher is not in the class-room', 'There is no sound here', 'His father has no grey hair', 'The apple is not round', 'This flower has no fragrance', the cognizer is aware of the absence of some object or its attribute by means of non-perception or non-apprehension. The teacher's absence from the class-room is known, not by the perception of his non-existence there, but by the non-apprehension of his presence there. Nor is the teacher's absence cognized by the perception of the room or anything else in the room. Similarly, in other instances; the non-existence of sound, of grey hair, of the roundness of the apple, and of the fragrance of the flower is known by the non-perception of these objects and attributes in their respective places.

It may seem paradoxical that the non-apprehension of a thing is a means to the apprehension of its non-existence (abhāva). But in fact, non-perception as well as perception serve as a means of knowledge (pramāṇa) to the knowing self (pramātā), who is aware of both. They lead to positive and negative experiences. We know both presence and absence of things, the one by perception, and the other by non-perception. I know there is a tree in the yard, because I see it; I know there is no tree in the yard, because I do not see it. A person experiences pain and the absence of pain as well. 'I had a

[1] See footnote 1, chap. VI, and Appendix B, sec. 4.

headache' is a case of memory. 'I have no headache' is a case of experience due to non-apprehension.

Two distinct cognitions find expression in the two statements 'There is a tree in the yard' and 'There is no bird on the tree in the yard.' The one does not lead to the other. The knowledge of the non-existence of the bird on the tree is not a case of perception, because the sense-organ has no contact with non-existence. Nor does it follow from the perception of the tree. It proceeds directly from non-apprehension or non-perception of the bird.

The knowledge of non-existence is not due to another knowledge. Inference (anumāna) is due to the knowledge of invariable concomitance, comparison (upamāna) to the knowledge of similarity, postulation (arthāpatti) to the knowledge of the fact to be explained, and verbal testimony (śabda) to the knowledge of the words conveying intention; but the apprehension of non-existence does not involve any such knowledge as that of concomitance, similarity, etc. Therefore, it is not effected by any of these methods—inference, comparison, etc. Hence non-apprehension is the sole means to the *direct* knowledge of the non-existence (abhāva) of perceptible objects and their attributes. The indirect or mediate knowledge of their non-existence can be attained by other means. For instance, a person who cognizes no jar in a room can inform others of its non-existence there. They will know its non-existence in the room from his report. From the presence of a person in his office one can infer his absence from his residence. So we see the non-existence of sense-objects is known *directly* by non-apprehension (anupalabdhi). It is to be noted that the non-existence of suprasensible objects is usually known by such means as inference and verbal testimony and this knowledge is mediate.

2. *Different views on existence and non-existence, which are both facts of cognition*

According to Advaita Vedānta both existence (bhāva) and non-existence (abhāva) are facts of cognition. This is evident from such expressions as 'There is no book on the desk', 'The rose plant has no roses on it', 'This is a donkey and not a horse', 'A policeman is not a soldier'. In every case of non-existence there is a locus (adhikaraṇa). In the above examples the locus of the non-existence of the book is the desk, the locus of the non-existence of the roses is the rose plant, the locus of the non-existence of the horse is the donkey, and so on. There is no negation without an affirmation. Existence and non-existence are positive and negative facts. As a fact of cognition non-existence cannot be considered false. The counter-positive of non-existence is existence. That of which the existence is denied is the counter-positive (pratiyōgī, lit., the opponent). The counter-positive of the non-existence of a book is the book. The counter-positive of the non-existence of sweetness is sweetness. The counter-positive of the non-existence of destruction is destruction, and so forth.

The Prabhākara school of Mīmāṁsā does not recognize non-existence (abhāva) as a fact distinct from existence (bhāva). Accordingly, it admits the five means of the knowledge of the positive facts (e.g., perception, inference, comparison, postulation, and śabda), and denies the sixth, non-apprehension, which is the means to the valid cognition of non-existence. In its view the non-existence of an object in a particular locus (adhikaraṇa) means the existence of the bare locus. The non-existence of a jar in a place means the existence of the vacant place. Therefore, the cognition of the non-existence of a jar in a place is but the cognition of the place itself.

A similar view has been held by the Sāṁkhya school. As explained by Vācaspati in his commentary on *Sāṁkhya-kārikā*,[1] the non-existence of a jar in a place is no other than the vacant place, unoccupied by anything. Thus, in perceiving the bare place one perceives the non-existence of the jar there. Therefore, according to Sāṁkhya, no separate means of knowledge (pramāṇa) is to be admitted for the cognition of non-existence (abhāva), which is known by the perception of the locus.

In Kumārila's view, which Advaita Vedānta accepts, the non-existence of an object in a particular locus is not identical with the locus itself. It is something more than the existence of the mere locus. In perceiving a bare floor one does not necessarily perceive it as devoid of something. 'I see the floor', and 'I see no jar on the floor', are two different cognitions. The one is the apprehension of existence, the other is primarily the apprehension of non-existence. Moreover, the same place can be perceived as devoid of something else, a bowl for instance. The cognition of the non-existence of the jar in the place cannot be differentiated from the cognition of the non-existence of the bowl in the same place, in case either is identical with the perception of the vacant place.

According to Kumārila, existence (bhāva) and non-existence (abhāva) are two different aspects of one and the same thing. Every object is existence in itself, and is the non-existence or the absence of everything else. It can be viewed as existence and also as non-existence. A positive entity is the negation of everything but itself. When we say 'This is a horse', we perceive the animal as existence. When we say, 'This is a horse and not an ass,' we perceive the animal as it is and also as the non-existence or the absence of the ass. The two aspects are inseparable, but not identical. They have two

[1] *Vide* SK 5, *Tattvakaumudi*.

different meanings. Thus, everything is characterised by existence and non-existence (sadasadātmaka).[3]

3. *The view of the Nyāya school that non-existence can be perceived is not tenable*

The Nyāya system views non-existence (abhāva) as one of the seven categories, of which six are positive.[4] It holds that non-existence (abhāva) can be perceived by the senses. Each sense-organ is capable of perceiving the existence and also the non-existence of its object. The eye can perceive the existence of colour and also its absence. The ear can perceive the existence of sound and also its absence, and so on. Unlike the Prabhākara school of Mīmāṁsā and Sāṁkhya system, Nyāya maintains that the non-existence of an object in a particular locus (adhikaraṇa) is other than the locus. The non-existence of a jar on the floor is different from the floor. It is related to the floor as an attribute (viśeṣaṇa). The floor can be regarded as characterized by the non-existence of a jar. Because of this relation of attributiveness the perception of the floor leads to the perception of the non-existence of a jar on it. The organ of vision has a special kind of contact (sannikarṣa) with the non-existence of a jar in such a case. Thus, the non-existence of a jar on the floor is perceived as the attributiveness of the floor, which is conjoined with the eye.[5]

But the Kumārila school of Mīmāṁsā and Advaita Vedānta reject the idea that the organ of vision which perceives the floor can also perceive the non-existence of a jar there through its relation of attributiveness with the floor. Such an argument leads to *regressus ad infinitum*. In no case can the sense-organ come in actual contact with the non-existence or the absence of an object. Besides, any relation between non-existence and its locus, whether of conjunction (saṁyōga) or of inherence (samavāya), is inconceivable. So the mental mode corresponding to the non-existence of a jar, and the like, is formed not by this means but by another means. As stated in *Vedānta-paribhāṣā*: 'Thus, the mental mode corresponding to the non-existence of a jar and the like [in a locus] is not generated by the sense-organ, which is not in contact with the object [non-existence of a jar and the like], but is generated by a distinct means of knowledge, viz., non-apprehension of the jar and the like. Hence non-apprehension is a distinct means of the valid knowledge [of non-existence].'[6]

[3] *Vide Ślōka-vārttika*, chap. on *Abhāva*, 12–14. 'Everything is positive from its own standpoint, but negative from that of others.'

[4] *Vide* BP 2. These are substance, quality, action, generic attribute, together with ultimate difference, inherence, and non-existence.

[5] *Vide* BP 62, *Siddhānta-muktāvalī*.

[6] VP VI.

The sense-organ comes in contact with the locus of the non-existence of the jar (for instance) but not with the non-existence of the jar. The mental mode corresponding to the locus is generated by sense-activity, but the mental mode corresponding to the non-existence of the jar is not generated by sense-activity but by the non-apprehension of the jar. Thus the non-existence of an object is known by its non-apprehension.

4. *Nor can non-existence be known by inference, as the Buddhist logicians maintain*

Since the non-existence of an object, such as a jar, cannot be apprehended by perception, neither can it be known by inference, which is based on perception. Kumārila has refuted the view that non-existence can be known by inference, as maintained by the Buddhist logician, Dharmakīrti, in his *Nyāya-bindu*.[7] In order to infer the non-existence of an object from its non-perception, one has to know the invariable relation between non-perception and non-existence, namely, what is not perceived in a locus does not exist there. This involves a *petitio principii*, the assumption of that very thing which is intended to be proved. Nor is the knowledge of the non-existence of an object attained by comparison (upamāna), or testimony (śabda), or postulation (arthāpatti), as we have already explained. Therefore, non-apprehension is to be recognized as the sole means to the knowledge of the non-existence of a perceptible object or its attribute.

It may be contended that the knowledge of the non-existence of a book on a desk, for instance, results from the argument: 'Had there been a book on the desk, it would have been perceived; since it is not perceived there, so there is no book on the desk.' But the very proposition 'Had there been a book on the desk, it would have been perceived' presupposes the knowledge of the non-existence of the book on the desk. Now the question arises 'How is this non-existence known in the first place?' 'The knowledge of non-existence proceeds directly from non-apprehension, no inferential process is there involved,' answers the Advaitin.

It is to be noted that non-apprehension (anupalabdhi) in the Advaita view actually means non-perception and not non-cognition in general. It leads to the direct knowledge of the non-existence of the object. The knowledge of the non-existence of a particular cognition is also attained by non-apprehension.

5. *Only* appropriate ***non-apprehension causes valid cognition of non-existence***

But not every case of non-apprehension of an object is a proof of its

[7] **Chap. on Inference (II: 13) and com. by Dharmōttara.**

non-existence. When a person does not see a desk in a dark room, it does not prove that the desk is not there. Hence non-apprehension must be *appropriate* (yōgya). The non-apprehension of a particular object in a locus can be considered *appropriate* (yōgya) provided the object could be perceived under the same circumstances, had it been there. In the above instance, had there been a desk in the dark room, it could not be perceived; therefore it is not a case of *appropriate* non-apprehension that can lead to valid knowledge of the non-existence of a desk in the room. On the contrary, the non-apprehension of a desk in a well-lighted room can be regarded *appropriate* inasmuch as the desk could be perceived if it were there; therefore this leads to valid knowledge of the non-existence of the desk in the room. Again, in a dark room one can feel the existence of a desk by touching it; therefore the non-apprehension of a desk by the organ of touch in a dark room is a proof of its non-existence, being *appropriate*. Further, when a person does not see any fruit on a distant tree, it is not a case of appropriate non-apprehension, because the fruit could not be perceived, even though it were there. If a deaf person does not hear the telephone bell ring, it does not prove that there is no telephone call. Since he would not hear the telephone call had there been any, it is not a case of *appropriate* non-apprehension.

It is worthy of note that appropriate non-apprehension is not a passive state of the mind. It involves a baffled expectation, a failure to find something where it is thought likely to be, a feeling of something missing. We give a few illustrations: 'There is no water in the jar,' 'The secretary is not at his desk', 'The chair has no arms', 'The grapes are not sweet', 'Ours is not a large house', 'The clock makes no sound', 'Their teacher is not a good speaker', 'This is a stump of a tree and no thief', and so on.

Only *appropriate* non-apprehension (yōgya-anupalabdhi) has the capacity to bring about valid knowledge of the non-existence of an object by generating a corresponding mental mode. So it is said: 'Only a non-apprehension that is possessed of capacity is to be regarded as the instrument of an apprehension of non-existence.'[8]

6. *Four different kinds of non-existence; all cognizable by* appropriate *non-apprehension*

As stated in *Vedānta-paribhāṣā*, non-existence is of four kinds: (1) previous non-existence (prāgabhāva), (2) non-existence as destruction (pradhvaṁsābhāva), (3) absolute non-existence (atyantābhāva) and (4) mutual non-existence (anyōnyābhāva).[9]

Previous non-existence is the absence of an effect (e.g., a jar) in its material component (e.g., a lump of clay) before the effect is

[8] VP VI.

[9] *Vide* VP VI.

produced. The non-existence of curd in milk is another instance of previous non-existence. Before a statue is carved out of a block of stone its non-existence in the block is a case of previous non-existence. Previous non-existence has no beginning but comes to an end when the effect is produced. It is the object of the cognition that a thing (a jar, or curd, or a statue, as the case may be) will come into existence. The cognition that a thing does not exist is common to all kinds of non-existence.

Non-existence as destruction is the absence of a thing in its component parts consequent on its destruction. When a jar is broken into pieces, its absence in *those* parts is its non-existence as destruction. When these pieces are further broken, then this destruction is destroyed. But the destruction of destruction does not imply the re-emergence of the jar on the ground that the negation of the negation of a thing implies its affirmation inasmuch as the jar is still cognized as destroyed. Evidently the form of its previous destruction has undergone a change; that is to say, the previous destruction has been destroyed. Thus, according to Advaita Vedānta, the non-existence as destruction has a beginning and also an end. Obviously, the non-existence as destruction has a beginning. But that it has an end is dubitable and is objected to by the Naiyāyikas. In their view non-existence as destruction has a beginning but no end.[10]

This difference of opinion is due to the difference of views regarding the locus (adhikaraṇa) of non-existence as destruction. The Advaitins hold that the non-existence in question cannot be endless unless its locus is eternal. According to them Brahman alone is eternal.[11] So only that kind of non-existence which has Brahman as its locus can be endless. This is the negation of the world-appearance on the realization of Brahman, the substratum. 'The destruction of an imaginary thing is but its being reduced to its substratum.'[12] Therefore, the eternity of the non-existence of the world due to its disappearance in Brahman implies only the eternity of Nondual Brahman.

That which does not exist in a particular locus at any time—in past, present, and future—has absolute non-existence there. For instance, there is absolute non-existence of colour in air, of darkness in fire, of cowness in a horse, of horns on a hare. Like the non-existence as destruction, absolute non-existence also comes to an end, since its locus is subject to destruction, being non-eternal. But the Naiyāyikas hold absolute non-existence to be endless, because according to them such substances as air, ether, etc., are eternal.

[10] *Vide* BP 12, 13, *Siddhānta-muktāvalī*.

[11] It is to be noted Nyāya philosophy recognizes nine fundamental substances (dravya): earth, water, fire, air, ākāśa (ether), space, time, self, and mind. See BP 3.

[12] Quoted in VP VI.

Mutual non-existence is but difference or separateness that is cognized in such cases as 'A jar is not a pan', 'An ass is not a horse', 'This orange is not sweet', 'His eyes are not bright'. Mutual non-existence has a beginning when its locus has a beginning (as the difference of a jar from a pan); but is without beginning when its substratum is without beginning (as the difference of the individual from Brahman, or the difference of Brahman from the individual). All kinds of difference are subject to destruction; for when ajñāna ceases, all that depend on it necessarily cease. Thus, mutual non-existence, whether with beginning or without beginning, has an end.

This four-fold division of non-existence is recognized by the Naiyāyikas also. The first three—previous non-existence, non-existence as destruction, and absolute non-existence—are grouped by them under the non-existence of relationship (saṁsargābhāva), which with mutual non-existence (anyōnyābhāva) form the two main divisions of non-existence.[13]

All these different kinds of non-existence are known by *appropriate* non-apprehension (yōgya-anupalabdhi).

It is to be noted that although the Kumārila school of Mīmāṁsā and Advaita Vedānta recognize appropriate non-apprehension as the sole means of valid knowledge of non-existence, they differ in their conceptions of this knowledge. According to the Kumārila school the knowledge of non-existence gained by non-apprehension is mediate (parōkṣa), whereas according to Advaita Vedānta it is immediate (pratyakṣa).

The Advaita school of Vedānta holds that the absence of multiplicity is known directly by non-apprehension in transcendental experience or immediate apprehension of Nondual Brahman.

13 *Vide* BP 12, 13.

PART TWO

Verbal Testimony (Śabda-pramāṇa): A Means of Valid Knowledge, Sensuous and Suprasensuous

CHAPTER VIII

VERBAL TESTIMONY, A UNIQUE METHOD OF VALID KNOWLEDGE

1. *Sabda-pramāṇa (verbal testimony) defined*

The Sanskrit term śabda, in its widest sense, denotes sound, articulate and inarticulate, called varṇa and dhvani, respectively.[1] In the present context, 'śabda' means an articulate sound, that is, a word with meaning, and applies to a verbal expression consisting of one or more words. It may be uttered or written. The essential part of a word or a combination of words is its meaning. Every word is a symbol of a thought or an idea. Even a single letter having a meaning is a word, e.g., the article 'a' and the pronoun 'I'. Every letter of the Sanskrit alphabet is said to have a meaning.

Śabda as a means of valid knowledge is called śabda-pramāṇa, which is usually rendered into English as 'verbal testimony' or 'authority'. It is also called 'āpta-vākya (the statement of a trustworthy person),' or 'āgama (authentic word).' It must be a declaration in speech or writing consisting of one or more sentences. The unit of human speech is a sentence, which is a single and complete expression of thought. The collocation of words in a sentence is such that it does not leave the hearer in eager expectation of hearing more to get an information complete in itself. Any combination of words that is an incomplete expression of thought is not a sentence. None of the following expressions is a sentence: 'He met', 'While walking on the street', 'Before the sun sets', 'Having arrived home at night', 'A lake near the temple'. Each sentence consists of at least two words, one of which must be a verb, though a single word can constitute a sentence if the remaining word or words can be inferred from the context. To illustrate: 'Go' for 'You go', 'What?' for 'What do you say?', 'Good-bye' for 'God be with you', 'Pray', for 'I pray to you', or 'You pray to God'. An interjection, e.g., 'ah', 'alas', 'goodness gracious', is not to be viewed as a sentence.

A sentence is the unit of śabda-pramāṇa, which has been thus defined: 'That sentence is a means of valid knowledge in which the relation [among the meanings of the words] that is the object of its

[1] *Vide* BP 164.

intention is not contradicted by any other means of valid knowlege.'[1] A sentence signifies more than its constituent words. To grasp its import one has to know not only the meanings of the individual words, but also the relation among the meanings. The significance of a sentence is the relation among the meanings of the words syntactically conjoined. The apprehension of this relation (śābdabōdha) means the verbal cognition of the fact or truth communicated. It is valid if uncontradicted by any other means of valid knowledge. The sentence is, in such a case, śabda-pramāṇa, the verbal instrument of valid knowledge called 'śabda-pramā'. Evidently, knowledge conveyed by such sentences as 'He has seen a hare with horns,' 'This athlete lives on nothing but air', 'An elephant is like a pig', 'The sun moves round the earth', 'Here is empty space', 'Atoms are indestructible', is not valid, being contradicted by one or another means of valid knowledge. Consequently, none of these expressions serves as śabda-pramāṇa (verbal testimony).

A sentence has two essential parts, the subject (uddeśya) and the predicate (vidheya) with substantive-adjective relation between them. In the sentence, 'John has a flower-garden', 'John' is the subject, 'has a flower-garden' is the predicate; 'John' is qualified by 'having a flower-garden'. Similarly, 'The sky is blue' means 'The sky is marked by blueness'; 'The tree lives' means 'The tree is qualified by livingness'; 'He is a ruler' means 'He is qualified by rulership'; and so on. The major part of the predicate is the verb, which must have a subject, but may or may not have an object.

There are instances, rare though they may be, in which the subject and the predicate do not affirm a substantive-adjective relation between the two, but indicate instead a single non-relational entity underlying them. Take, for example, the terse sentence, 'This is that man'. It means 'The man seen at the present time and place is the man seen at some other time and place'. Obviously, the two qualifying terms 'This' and 'That' are incompatible. The sentence points to one and the same individual exclusive of the qualifications. So does the statement 'The most shining one is the moon' refer to a single object 'the moon' to the exclusion of all other objects appearing in the sky at night. The term 'shining' excludes non-luminous things (cloud, airplane, etc.), the term 'most' excludes all other shining things (stars, planets, etc.). Similarly, the pithy sentence 'Thou art That', which declares the identity of 'Thou' (the individual consciousness) and 'That' (the universal consciousness) points to Nondual (akhaṇḍa) Pure Consciousness divested of the attributes, 'the individual' and 'the universal', which are evidently incongruous.

[1] VP IV.

2. *Verbal testimony is different from all other means of valid knowledge*

A verbal statement, uttered or written, is man's most potent instrument for transmitting knowledge. We learn mostly by means of words. An oral or a written message is a universal mode of communication. Through books and magazines, through newspapers, through letters, through conversation, through speeches, through prayers and hymns, through radio broadcasts we constantly acquire new ideas, sentiments, and information. We cannot do without the verbal method. In fact, it is the principal medium of education. Our perception has a limited scope. We perceive only what is 'here and now', that is, what is present to the senses. For the knowledge of what is beyond this limit we depend, as a rule, either on inference from our past experience or on testimony. Though of a much wider scope than perception, inference is quite restricted, being dependent on it. We can infer only what has been previously observed to be invariably related to something that is being perceived. And since the scope of our personal experience is limited, it is the words of the reliable persons such as know truly and communicate correctly that serve as our main source of knowledge. In order to know what happens in our absence we rely primarily on trustworthy reports and records (including history); in other words, on authority. We rarely become acquainted with anything unfamiliar without being taught.

A verbal statement conveying valid knowledge must have an authentic source and must be free from defects. Only a competent person possessed of knowledge can impart accurate knowledge. Ignorance is no authority. The information gained from an authoritative source is valid knowledge. It needs no verification, unless there is cause to doubt its reliability. If all that we learn from testimony were to await confirmation, if authority were not accepted as a source of valid knowledge, then the bulk of human knowledge would have to be regarded as baseless and the advancement of knowledge would be impossible. Among Western philosophers only a few recognize testimony or authority as a separate means of knowledge, but a majority of Indian philosophers do. The Cārvākas deny it. The Vaiśeṣikas explain śabda-pramāṇa as a case of inference,[3] the Buddhists as a case of internal perception similar to memory.

We shall see later that knowledge gained from śabda has a distinctive character. It develops under conditions different from those of perceptual or inferential knowledge. The process of verbal knowledge is not the same as that of inference. It does not involve any knowledge of invariable concomitance. The comprehension of the meaning of a sentence does not proceed from the cognition of an invariable relation between the words perceived and their meanings. It is the

[3] *Vide Vaiśeṣika-sūtras* IX: 2.3, and Praśasta-pāda's com. *The Padārtha-dharma-saṁgraha.*

apprehension of the relation among the recollected meanings of the words.

The Vaiśeṣika view that śabda-pramāṇa can be included in inference has been refuted by the Nyāya school as follows: 'It is a fact of common experience that verbal comprehension takes place even without the knowledge of invariable concomitance. There is certainly no evidence to prove that the hearing of a word is always followed by the knowledge of invariable concomitance [of the word and its primary meaning]. Further, we should consider this: If in every case of verbal comprehension we assume the knowledge of invariable concomitance, then in every case of inference also why should we not assume the knowledge of words, and thereby admit verbal comprehension alone?'[4]

Nor can verbal knowledge be explained in terms of memory, as some philosophers, ancient and modern, maintain. Moreover, śabda can communicate what no other means of knowledge can. Man's inner experiences can hardly be known but through his words. Since śabda serves as a vehicle of suprasensuous experience as well, it does not depend solely on sensory knowledge like other means of mediate cognition, such as inference, comparison, postulation. Thus, for more reasons than one śabda (verbal testimony) is to be recognized as a separate means of knowledge.

A sentence conveys much more than meets the eyes or the ears. To apprehend its meaning is by no means the same as hearing or reading it. Verbal knowledge is not identical with auditory or visual impression. It is far more than an act of perception. The meaning of a sentence also depends on the context. One may say ,'I see no light', while listening to a sermon, or while entering a house at night. The same utterance has two different meanings on two different occasions.

A word can be more suggestive than any other symbol. For examples: 'Right knowledge is the raft to cross the ocean of life', 'The spiritual teacher is the pilot', 'He waged war with a pen', 'His wings are clipped', 'The world offers not a few sugar-coated bitter pills', 'Except a man be born again he cannot see the Kingdom of God', 'I am the bread of life', 'Ye are the salt of the earth'.

In some instances, the significance of a sentence is far deeper than is apparent from the component words. One may know the meanings of the individual words as well as their grammatical arrangement in a sentence and yet may fail to grasp its import. Many know the meaning of every word in such terse sentences, as 'That is the Light of all lights', 'He shining everything shines', 'He is never known, but is the Knower', 'The eye does not go thither, nor speech, nor the mind', 'Thou art That', 'The Light that shines in darkness', 'The

[4] BP 140, 141, *Siddhānta-muktāvalī*.

kingdom of God is within you', yet how few can comprehend the deep significance of any one of these expressions!

While other means of valid knowledge can acquaint us only with the facts of the sensible universe, verbal testimony serves as a vehicle of both sensuous and suprasensuous truth. Just as there are authentic words relating to the order of phenomena, so are there authentic words relating to transcendental principles. Neither sense-perception nor any other means of knowledge based on it can communicate suprasensible facts, such as God, soul, life beyond death, liberation and its means. Man's primary source of the knowledge of the suprasensuous is scriptural testimony. The sacred books are the earliest extant literature of the world, perhaps in every culture. Their survival from hoary antiquity testifies to their enduring intrinsic value. Speculative philosophy is relatively a recent development. And nowhere has it gained the confidence that the scriptural revelation has.

3. *Verbal knowledge is not a case of memory*

The verbal cognition of a fact is different from recollection. In memory a previous experience is reproduced. A person can understand the meaning of the sentence, 'There is a hat on the tree', without ever having seen a hat on a tree. As he hears or reads each word in the sentence he remembers its meaning which has already been known to him. This is the knowledge he gained for the first time from reliable sources. Man invariably learns from others the meanings of words. He accepts authority from the very beginning of his life. This is the first step to knowledge. Learning starts with seeing things and naming them in accordance with usage. It may be contended that the meaning of the sentence, 'There is a hat on the tree', is apprehended by a person by conjoining the meanings of the individual words remembered by him. Even so, the resultant knowledge is not the recollection of a previous experience. Nor is it attained by piecing together the memories of the objects (e.g., hat, tree) that are mentioned in the sentence.

Indeed, the knowledge conveyed by a sentence cannot be explained as memory-synthesis. Several factors other than the recollection of the meanings of the constituent words are involved in it. As a person hears or reads a word he remembers its meaning which he has learnt before. The recollection of its meaning is produced by the word. There is an inseparable relation between a word and its meaning; when the one is cognized the other is recalled through association. The resultant knowledge is the verbal apprehension of the object denoted by the word. It is an idea of the object. It is not the memory of the past experience of the object. It is a well-known fact that one can have verbal cognition of something one has never perceived before. For instance, one can know what a mountain is by hearing or reading about it, without seeing it, vague though the knowledge may be. This shows that the verbal knowledge of an object is different from the memory of it. Since words can convey the knowledge of things unperceived, one can know about Brahman from the scriptures and also from the teacher.

4. *The four conditions of verbal knowledge. Its process is different from that of perception or inference*

The comprehension of the meaning of a sentence is the intermediate cause of the verbal cognition of the truth or fact communicated by it. The sentence is called 'śabda pramāṇam', the comprehension of its meaning 'śābda-bōdhaḥ' and the verbal cognition of the truth or fact communicated by it 'śabda-pramā'. The comprehension of the meaning (śābda-bōdhaḥ) does not depend solely on the knowledge of the meanings of the component words. The meanings of the constituent words are previously known to the cognizer. What he has to know from the statement is the relation of the meanings of the words. It is this fact that distinguishes the process of verbal knowledge from that of perception or inference and characterizes śabda as a separate means of valid knowledge. D. M. Datta aptly remarks:

'The meaning of a sentence is derived from a constructive combination of ideas—a process that takes place under peculiar and specific conditions, which distinguish the knowledge of the meaning of a sentence from ordinary types of knowledge, e.g., perception, memory, memory-synthesis, and inference. This peculiar kind of knowledge is called śābda-bōdhaḥ [comprehension of the meaning of a sentence].'[5]

'Knowledge of meaning [śābda-bōdhaḥ] is an intermediate process that is indispensable to the knowledge of facts [śabda-pramā].'[6]

The comprehension of the meaning of a sentence arises in the following manner: 'The cognition of words is the instrument [of verbal comprehension], the recollection of the meanings of words is the operation there, verbal comprehension is the result, and the knowledge of denotative function is an aid.'[7] Denotative function is the relation of a word to its meaning, something directly meant by the word. Without knowing this relation one cannot recall the meaning of the word cognized by him. The meanings of the constituent

[5] *The Six Ways of Knowing*, pp. 322. [6] *Ibid.* p. 324.
[7] BP 81, *Siddhānta-mukṭāvalī.*

words being known through recollection, one has to apprehend the relation among them. It is the apprehension of their mutual relation that brings out the significance of a sentence. This has four causes: (1) expectancy (ākāṅkṣā), (2) consistency (yōgyatā), (3) contiguity (āsatti), and (4) the knowledge of the purport (tātparya-jñānam).[8] The combination of words in a sentence must fulfill these conditions.

Expectancy (ākāṅkṣā) is defined as 'the capacity of the meanings of the words to become objects of enquiry regarding each other.'[9] On hearing a word signifying action a person invariably enquires about the subject, the performer of action. He also wants to know the object, time, place, etc., connected with the action, according to its nature. If he hears the word 'cut' he naturally asks 'who?' 'what?' 'how?' He may receive the answer: 'The woodcutter cut the tree with an axe'. If he hears the word 'went' he enquires 'who?' 'where?' 'when?' One may satisfy him with the answer 'My friend went home yesterday'.

Similarly, on hearing a word denoting something connected with action a person naturally expects a word signifying action. On hearing the word 'him', one expects some such word as 'call', 'ask', or 'see'. If somebody utters the word 'hurriedly' the hearer expects such conjoining word or words, as 'go', 'he left'. The point is, a single word does not convey a complete thought. It needs other words or word to express its full meaning. The subject needs the verb expressive of an appropriate function; the verb needs the subject and also the object according to the nature of the function. An adjective requires a noun to qualify, an adverb a verb. A preposition expressing relation between two objects needs words denoting the objects related, as in the sentence: 'There is a book *on* the desk'. A significant sentence must fulfill the mutual need or expectancy of the meanings of the constituent words.

The second condition for the combination of words in a sentence is consistency (yōgyatā) of their meanings. This is defined as 'non-contradiction of the relation [between the meanings of the words] that is intended.'[10] It means that the objects or ideas denoted by the constituent words must not be mutually contradictory. The following sentences are lacking in consistency (yōgyatā), being self-contradictory: 'He is moistening the ground with fire', 'This is the only child of the barren mother', 'They lived under a benevolent tyrant', 'He is one of the best speakers I have heard'. Of all the speakers heard by a person only one can be the best and hence the contradiction in the last sentence. Such statements as 'The mortal man becomes immortal', 'Thou art That', 'I and my Father are one', are apparently contradictory, but not actually so. They have other than literal meanings. Their validity rests on their deeper significance.

[8] *Vide* VP IV. [9] *Ibid.* [10] *Ibid.*

The third condition of verbal knowledge is contiguity (āsatti). It is 'the apprehension [recollection] without an interval of the meanings of words that is produced by those words.'[11] The verbal comprehension of their mutual relation is due to this. In cases where particular words are omitted, they have to be supplied for the continuous connection of the meanings. In the following sentences the words to be supplied are shown in parentheses: 'He prays (to God) every day'. 'Your brother is taller than you (are tall).' 'He earns more (money) than he spends.' '(I) Pray (to you to) consider my case.' The words signifying things or ideas intended to be related must not be intervened by incoherent words or word. They should be in close proximity so that there will be no difficulty of construing them. Nor should there be any gap between them. They should not be separated spatially in the case of a verbal statement, nor temporally in the case of a spoken statement. There is lack of contiguity in the following sentence: 'The son of the king became the ruler, who abdicated the throne.' The proper order should be: 'The son of the king, who abdicated the throne, became the ruler.'

The contiguity of sentences forms a passage or a paragraph. As observed by Kumārila Bhaṭṭa: 'Sentences that are complete in themselves as regards the expression of their meanings, again combine in view of their relation of whole and part, etc., and become a unitary passage.'[12] Therefore, if the meaning of the subsidiary sentences are grasped then the meaning of the passage also is grasped; otherwise not.

Besides the above three conditions—expectancy, consistency, and contiguity, the meaning of a sentence also depends on the knowledge of the purport (tātparya-jñānam). According to the Nyāya school, 'the intention of the speaker is called purport;'[13] to find the true import of a sentence one has to know the purpose of the speaker or the writer. But Vedānta defines purport as 'the capacity of a sentence to convey a particular meaning [in accord with valid knowledge].'[14] Even though there be no intention on the part of a speaker, yet his statement will have a purport, in case it has a meaning consonant with established knowledge.

The same word can have different meanings in different cases. From the context one knows its appropriate meaning and the true import of the sentence. For instance, when it is said, 'They won the battle by tanks', one can understand that here the term 'tank' means a special type of combat vehicle and not a receptacle for storing

[11] VP IV; cf. BP 83, *Siddhānta-muktāvalī*, 'The apprehension, without an interval, of the meanings of two words, one of which must be connected with the other [to complete the sense], is a cause of verbal comprehension.'

[12] *Tantra-vārttika*, verse 4, on PMS I: 4.24, quoted in VP IV.

[13] BP 84. [14] VP IV.

water or oil. Similarly, in the sentence 'Man is a rational animal' the word 'man' means 'human being' as distinguished from subhuman creatures, it includes both man and woman; while in the sentence 'Man is virile' the same term 'man' means a male human being as distinguished from a female. Evidently, the word 'salt' has different meanings in the following sentences: 'The curry is not seasoned with salt', 'Ye are the salt of the earth', 'I take his words with a grain of salt'. The validity of a sentence depends on its purport and not on its literal meaning.

5. *The relation between a word and its meaning is natural and not conventional*

A word has the inherent power (śakti) to call up its meaning on being heard or read. Its power is inferred from the effect it produces, e.g., the apprehension of its meaning. This is the direct or primary meaning of the word. This may be a thing, an attribute, an action, or a relation. Some words have the potency to convey more than one meaning. A word does not convey its meaning to the hearer, unless he knows the relation between the two.

The same word may have several meanings; yet its relation with each of them is natural, just as a father has natural relation with each of his several children. Evidently, proper names and the conventional (pāribhāṣika) words coined by men or established by usage are not intended here.

According to Vedānta, the relation between a word and its meaning is natural, and not conventional; it is eternal.[15] It is to be noted that a word denotes the generic nature of a thing and not an individual thing. The term 'cow' represents 'cow-ness' or the class 'cow' and not an individual cow. So the relation between the word 'cow' and its meaning signifies the relation between 'cow' and the universal 'cow-ness'. Words exist with the universals prior to the particulars. As the universals are eternal so are the words. It is the particulars that are created and not the universals, which endure in Prakṛti, the potential cause of the universe.

According to Nyāya, the relation between a word and its meaning is fixed by the will of God. 'It is of the form of a divine will that such and such a word should denote such and such a thing.'[16] But this does not mean that the relation between an expressive word and the thing expressed is extrinsic or accidental. It is eternal, being unvaried in successive cycles of creation. The expressiveness of a word is not the work of usage. Commenting on Patañjali's Yōga Aphorism, 'The word that signifies Him [Īśvara] is Om,'[17] Vyāsa observes: 'The usage

[15] *Vide* BS I: 3.28, S. com.

[16] BP 81, *Siddhānta-muktāvalī*; see also TS 99, 100.

[17] YS I: 27.

as determined by Īśvara declares its existent meaning, as the relation of father and son that is existent is expressed by verbal statements—"This is his father", "This is his son".' On the same aphorism Swāmī Vivekānanda remarks:

'Every idea that you have in the mind has a counterpart in a word; the word and the thought are inseparable. The external part of one and the same thing is what we call word, and the internal part is what we call thought. No man can, by analysis, separate thought from word. The idea that language was created by men—certain men sitting together and deciding upon words—has been proved to be wrong. So long as man has existed there have been words and language. What is the connection between an idea and a word? Although we see that there must always be a word with a thought, it is not necessary that the same thought requires the same word. The thought may be the same in twenty different countries, yet the language is different. We must have a word to express each thought, but these words need not necessarily have the same sound. Sounds will vary in different nations.

Our commentator says, "Although the relation between thought and word is perfectly natural, yet it does not mean a rigid connection between one sound and one idea." These sounds vary, yet the relation between the sounds and the thoughts is a natural one. The connection between thoughts and sounds is good only if there be a real connection between the thing signified and the symbol; until then that symbol will never come into general use. Symbol is the manifestor of the thing signified, and if the thing signified has already an existence, and if, by experience, we know that the symbol has expressed that thing many times, then we are sure that there is a real relation between them. Even if the things are not present, there will be thousands who will know them by their symbols. There must be a natural connection between the symbol and the thing signified; then, when that symbol is pronounced, it recalls the thing signified.'[18]

6. *Words refer directly to universals and indirectly to particulars*

The Advaitins' view of universals (jāti) and particulars (vyakti) differs from that of the Naiyāyikas. According to both each of the three categories—substance (dravya), attribute (guṇa), and action (karma)—signified by words has universal and particular aspects.[19] The universals are more or less general. Existence is the most general concept. According to Nyāya school universals are eternal and independent of their respective particulars, to which they are related through samavāya (inherence). As defined by this school a universal

[18] CW I, pp. 217–8. [19] *Vide* BS I: 3.28, S. com.

(sāmānya or jāti) is 'eternity coupled with inherence in many things'.[20] It is the eternal common characteristic inhering in all the individuals of a class, e.g., cow-ness in all cows, tree-ness in all trees. It abides in substance, attribute, and action.[21] It is one of the seven categories.[22] As maintained by Advaita Vedānta, a universal is not a separate entity, nor is it related to its particulars by samavāya (inherence); it stands for the essential attributes common to all of them.[23] Though distinct, it is inseparable from the particulars, as regards essence. It is related to them by way of identity. It signifies the generic shape and also the generic nature.

The Indian philosophers are divided in their opinion as to whether the primary meaning of a word is a universal (jāti) or a particular (vyakti). Does the word 'cow', for instance, directly refer to an individual cow or to the universal 'cow-ness', the generic nature of the cow? In a general way it can be said that, according to Sāṁkhya and Nyāya, a word signifies a particular (vyakti), while, according to the Kumārila school of Mīmāṁsā, Advaita Vedānta, and Jainism, a word signifies a universal (jāti). As observed by Śaṅkara, 'Truly, it is the particulars of substance, attribute, and action that originate and not their generic nature (ākṛtis). Words are related to the universals (ākṛtis) and not to the individuals.'[24]

It may be argued: 'If the primary meaning of the word *cow* be *cow-ness*, how does it then apply to an individual cow? In actual practice the term is used for an individual cow and not for the class as a whole. When a person says "Here is a cow", it invariably means the presence of a single member of the species *cow*. Therefore, the Neo-logicians[24a] rightly hold that the primary meaning of a word is an individual possessed of a certain generic attribute and form.'[25]

But it is to be noted that the word 'cow' signifies no particular cow but any individual of the species 'cow'. This indicates that the word 'cow' refers to the generic nature, or the common characteristics, of the class 'cow'. To recognize a particular being as a cow one has to apprehend at first the common characteristics of the class cow. The word 'cow' directly refers to the concept 'cow-ness', which enables a person to distinguish a certain animal as a cow; it indirectly refers to an individual cow. It is the knowledge of the universal (jāti) that leads to the knowledge of the particular (vyakti). In the Vedāntic view a universal (cow-ness) is inseparable from an individual (cow). While signifying the universal a word signifies the individual.

[20] BP 8, *Siddhānta-muktāvalī*. [21] *Vide* TS 127.

[22] See footnote 4, chap. VII.

[23] *Vide* VP IV, com. *Āśubōdhinī* by Kṛṣṇanātha Nyāyapañcānana.

[24] BS I: 3.28, com. The word 'ākṛti' is often used in Vedānta in the sense of 'jāti (genus)'. It refers to the generic nature as well as to the generic shape.

[24a] The Navya (modern) Nyāya School.

[25] *Vide* BP 81, *Siddhānta-muktāvalī*.

With regard to the universal its significance is direct; with regard to the individual its significance is indirect. Each individual is characterized by the universal, that is, by the essential attributes of the class to which it belongs. We invariably cognize the universal as we cognize an individual. This is why by knowing one cow a person can recognize any other cow. It is said, 'The same cognition that comprehends a generic attribute also comprehends the individuals.'[26] The fact that the term 'cow' is applicable to all individuals of the class 'cow' shows that it signifies something common to them. It directly refers to their generic nature and not to their individual peculiarities. To refer directly or primarily to an individual cow means to particularize it. The term cannot in that case refer to any other cow, because each cow is different from every other cow. So a word primarily means a universal (jāti) and secondarily an individual (vyakti) of the same class. Or, we may say that a word explicitly means the universal and implicitly the particular.

7. *Primary and implied meanings of words and sentences*

Besides primary meanings words have implied meanings. Primary meaning[27] is something directly meant by a word. It is known through its significance (*śakti*, lit., inherent power). As held by the Mīmāṁsakas, the meaning of a word is to be obtained from no other source than the word itself. An implied meaning[28] is something implied by a word. It is its secondary meaning. In case the primary meanings of the words of a sentence prove inadequate for the apprehension of their logical connection and its import, then implied meanings are sought. Take, for instance, the sentence 'There is a cowherd colony on the river'. Evidently, there cannot be a colony of the cowherds on 'the stream of water', which is the primary meaning of the word 'river'. So its implied meaning 'the bank of the river' has to convey the import of the sentence. Similarly, in the sentence 'The city mourned over the death of the mayor', the word 'city' implies 'citizens'.

It is actually the intention of the sentence rather than the logical connection of the words that necessitates implication. As pointed out by *Vedānta-paribhāṣā*, 'The root of implication, however, is the frustration of intention alone, and not that of logical connection [of words].'[29] In the sentence 'Protect the bowl of curd from the crows' there is no frustration of logical connection, but of intention, which is the protection of curd not only from the crows but also from other creatures that are likely to spoil curd, (such as dog, cat, etc.).

[26] VP IV.
[27] It has different names: mukhyārtha, vācyārtha, śakyārtha, abhidheyārtha.
[28] This is called 'lakṣyārtha' or 'gauṇārtha'.
[29] VP IV.

So the term 'crows' implies 'all creatures that can spoil curd'. In the sentence 'There is a cowherd colony on the river' the frustration of intention is consequent on the frustration of the logical connection. The frustration of intention is common to both the sentences. When it is said, 'He was free from all attachment to gold', gold implies material possessions; the implication is necessary not for the logical connection but for the intention.

Thus, sentences as well as words have implied meanings (lakṣyārtha). Of these there are different types. According to one classification, implication (lakṣaṇā) is of three kinds: (1) exclusive (jahat), (2) inclusive (ajahat), (3) quāsi-inclusive (jahat-ajahat).[30] When the implied meaning of a word or an expression excludes the primary meaning, then it is a case of exclusive implication (jahat lakṣaṇā). An instance of this type is 'There is a cowherd colony on the river'. Its implied meaning is 'There is a cowherd colony on the bank of the river'. Here, the direct meaning of 'river', 'the stream of water', is replaced by the indirect meaning, 'the bank'. If the implied meaning includes the primary, then it is a case of inclusive implication (ajahat lakṣaṇā). When it is said, 'The red flag is rushing forward', the implication is 'Someone with the red flag is rushing forward'. Here the primary meaning 'the red flag' is included in the implied meaning.

In the case of quasi-inclusive implication (jahat-ajahat lakṣaṇā) the primary meanings of terms are partly excluded and partly included. For instance, 'This is that man'. Here, the primary meaning of 'this' is 'the man seen at this time in this place'; the primary meaning of 'that man' is 'the man seen at some other time in some other place'. The primary meanings of the two terms being incompatible, their identity points to a single individual devoid of the temporal and the spatial qualifications. Similarly, the Vedāntic dictum, 'Thou art That' is an instance of quasi-inclusive implication. The primary meaning of 'Thou' is 'the individual consciousness'. The primary meaning of 'That' is 'the universal Consciousness'. The two are obviously incompatible. In declaring their identity the text affirms the reality of Nondual Pure Consciousness, exclusive of the superimposed limiting adjuncts, 'the individual' and 'the universal'.

8. *According to most Indian philosophers a word presents its meaning directly and not through sphōṭa (a latent unitary medium of expression), as the Grammarians hold*[31]

In the view of the Grammarians a word consisting of letters and syllables cannot directly convey its significance. Corresponding to

[30] VP IV.

[31] As far as we can trace, the theory of sphōṭa was established by the celebrated (Sanskrit) grammarian, Pāṇini (tenth or ninth century BC) on the

each word there is a sphōṭa (a latent unitary medium of expression), which underlies the constituent letters and has no component parts. It is this unitary, unchanging sphōṭa latent in the word, which, being evoked as the letters and syllables are successively uttered or heard, produces the cognition of its meaning.[32] The utterance may be either audible or inaudible as in reading mentally. The term sphōṭa literally means 'that from which breaks forth [the meaning of a word when uttered]'. It is due to the invariability of sphōṭa [the latent unitary medium of expression] that the differences in the pronunciation of a particular word by different persons cause no variation in its meaning. Sphōṭa can be defined in the words of Professor S. Radhakrishnan as 'the indivisible unitary factor latent in every word as the vehicle of its significance'.[33]

The advocates of the theory of sphōṭa argue that in pronouncing or hearing a word (garden, for instance) we do not grasp it as a whole. As the letters (g,a,r,d,e,n) are successively uttered, each preceding letter-sound vanishes with the utterance of each succeeding letter. Evidently, the significance of the word is apprehended with the utterance of the last letter. But the last letter-sound, that is to say, its perception, even though connected with the successive impressions of preceding letter-sounds cannot convey the meaning of the word. The letter-sounds being successively perceived, they cannot be remembered together as a whole. Therefore, something other than the sound-series that is entire and present throughout must serve as the vehicle of the significance of the word. And this is the indivisible (niravayava) and unvarying (nitya) sphōṭa latent in the word (pada-sphōṭa). There is also sphōṭa corresponding to every sentence (vākya-sphōṭa), which conveys a complete meaning.

The upholders of the theory recognize one ultimate Sphōṭa, which is infinite, eternal, and self-existent. Each particular sphōṭa latent in a word or a sentence is but an apparent variation of the universal, immutable Sphōṭa. So Sphōṭa is essentially one and is identical with

Mīmāṁsā doctrine of the eternity of word. It was later developed by Patañjali, the great commentator on the *Pāṇini-sūtras* (See *Mahābhāṣya* I: I.I), Bhartṛhari, the author of *Vākyapadīya*, and other grammarians. The Pāṇini system, though not of much philosophical significance, is included in Mādhavācārya's *Sarvadarśana-saṁgraha*, a compendium of sixteen philosophical views (written in the first part of the fourteenth century, AD). There is no proof of the identity of Patañjali, the grammarian, and Patañjali, the author of *Yōga-sūtras* (see Professor Woods' Introduction to *The Yōga System of Patañjali*, Harvard Oriental Series). In the opinion of Professor Surendranath Dasgupta their identity cannot be disproved (*A History of Indian Philosophy*, Vol. I, p. 232). According to some authorities, the author of the *Mahābhāṣya* lived in the second century BC. Professor Woods assigns the date of the *Yōga-sūtras* to some time in the fourth or the fifth century, AD.

32 *Vide* Bhartṛhari's *Vākya-padīya*, Brahmakāṇḍa, 48 ff.

33 *Indian Philosophy*, Vol. II, p. 28.

Brahman. Thus, the advocates of the sphōṭa theory conceive imperishable Brahman, without beginning and without end, as the eternal principle of word (śabda-tattva), which means the essence of all letters, words, sentences, and their meanings,[34] and may be likened to Plato's absolute Idea.[35]

Except Patañjali's Yōga system none of the six systems of Indian philosophy accepts the Grammarians' theory of sphōṭa as the latent vehicle of a word's significance.[36] Śaṅkara rejects the theory as unsatisfactory and unnecessary.[37] It is unsatisfactory, because it is liable to the very objection which it proposes to obviate. According to this theory, the letters of a word cannot convey its meaning, because the successive letter-sounds cannot be apprehended as a whole. At the same time it holds that sphōṭa, being evoked by the successive letter-sounds, yields the meaning of the word. In case the sound-series be incapable of manifesting the meaning of the word, they must also be incapable of manifesting sphōṭa. If they can manifest sphōṭa, why should they not be able to manifest the meaning of the word? Thus, the hypothesis of sphōṭa is redundant. It denies the obvious and proposes the dubious.

Śaṅkara points out that although the letter-sounds of a word are successively perceived, yet the synthesizing power of buddhi (intellect) apprehends the entire sound-series as a single act of cognition. The letter-sounds being thus grasped as a whole yield the meaning of the word. It is evident from experience that when we turn our eyes to a group of trees we apprehend the whole group as a unit, even though we do not see all the trees at a time. Similarly, an army passing before the eyes is grasped as a whole, although the entire body is not looked on simultaneously. The same thing happens when we watch a line of ants. These are facts of common experience and need no special theory for explanation. Therefore, the postulation of sphōṭa to explain the verbal-series is untenable.

9. *The distinctive character of verbal knowledge and its method*

Verbal knowledge has a speciality that clearly distinguishes it from both perceptual and inferential knowledge. The one and the same fact, such as the hill has fire, can be known in three different ways—

[34] *Vide Vākya-padiya*, I. 1, and SDS, Pāṇini System.

[35] Cf. *Plato's The Republic*. Trans. by B. Jowett, Bk. VI, New York, The Modern Library, 1941, pp. 246–7, 'And there is an absolute beauty and an absolute good, and of other things to which the term "many" is applied there is an absolute; for they may be brought under a single idea, which is called the essence of each.'

[36] Reference to sphōṭa-theory is noticeable in YS III: 17, Vācaspati's com. *Tattvavaiśāradī*. See also Dasgupta's *A History of Indian Philosophy*, Vol. I, p. 232.

[37] *Vide* BS I: 3.28, com.

by perception, by inference, and by verbal testimony. In the first case, one actually sees fire on the hill. In the second case, one sees only smoke arising from the hill and infers the co-presence of fire from the knowledge of its invariable concomitance with smoke, which has been gained from previous experience. In the third case, one sees neither fire, nor smoke, nor even the hill, but only hears the report, 'the hill has fire' and gains knowledge of the fact thereby; evidently, the knowledge is derived wholly from the statement, 'the hill has fire'. While perceptual knowledge is based on the direct cognition of the object (fire), and inferential knowledge on the apprehension of the invariable concomitance of the mark (smoke) and the object inferred (fire), verbal knowledge is based on the comprehension of the meanings of the pertinent words and their relation. The character as well as the process of knowledge being different in each case, each of the three ways has to be recognized as a distinct means of valid knowledge. On the same ground Vedānta accepts the three other means of valid knowledge, e.g., comparison, postulation, and non-apprehension, which we have already dealt with.

As observed by Śaṅkara: 'A means of knowledge is or is not a means according as it leads or does not lead to valid knowledge.'[38] Since 'śabda' (verbal testimony) leads to valid knowledge independently of perception and inference, so far as the object of knowledge is concerned, why should it not be regarded as a separate means of valid knowledge?

Nor can śabda be rejected as an independent means of knowledge on the ground that its validity has to be ascertained by perception or inference when there is doubt as to the reliability of the report. In that case perception and inference have also to be discarded as independent means of knowledge; inasmuch as perceptual as well as inferential knowledge need verification whenever there is doubt as to their validity. The point is that the method of verification of any knowledge does not produce the knowledge in question. It only proves or disproves the information that is already gained. Therefore, śabda remains an independent means of valid knowledge just as perception or inference does. As observed by D. M. Datta:

'Any source, which gives us information about facts, can be and should be considered a method of knowledge, irrespective of the question whether its validity is ascertained intrinsically or by some external method. For otherwise even perception cannot stand as an independent method. When the validity of perception is doubted, it has to be established through inference. Then perception also has to be brought under inference. Neither can it be said that as the validity of perception is not always doubted, at least in those cases of absence

[38] Br. U. II: 1.20, com.

of doubt, it can be accepted as a method. For if this be granted, exactly for a similar reason verbal testimony, the validity of which also remains very often undoubted and unchallenged, should also be accepted as a method at least for those cases. And if inference or perception is necessary to validate testimony, testimony also is, at times, employed to validate inference and perception. Nay, at times either of them may be rejected in deference to testimony. We perceive the sun to be moving, but in deference to the authority of the astronomers we disbelieve our perception. Thus we find that the grounds on which śabda, as a method of knowledge, is discarded lead us to absurdities. In fact, however, for a method to be so considered it is sufficient that it should give some information which *is* not derived from (even though it may be *derivable* from) other sources.'[39]

According to Nyāya, the validity of every method of knowledge has to be established by inference, yet it accepts śabda as a means of valid knowledge for the reasons we have stated above. Professor Dasgupta aptly remarks:

'The same thing which appears to us as the object of our perception, may become the object of inference or śabda (testimony), but the manner or mode of manifestation of knowledge being different in each case, and the manner or conditions producing knowledge being different in each case, it is to be admitted that inference and śabda are different pramāṇas, though they point to the same object indicated by the perception. Nyāya thus objects to the incorporation of śabda (testimony) or upamāna [comparison] within inference, on the ground that since the mode of production of knowledge is different these are to be held as different pramāṇas.'[40]

10. *Knowledge gained from authority cannot be discounted as mere belief*

The information gained from an authoritative statement is valid cognition of a fact or truth. Though mediate like inferential knowledge, it should not be regarded as mere belief, and consequently something different from knowledge. Unfortunately, the Western thinkers have shown a general tendency in this direction. The words of the trustworthy (āptavākya) are a veritable source of human knowledge. They carry conviction without proof. When a person learns from another's report that the hill has fire, he usually believes

[39] *The Six Ways of Knowing*, pp. 329–30.

[40] Surendranath Dasgupta, *A History of Indian Philosophy*, Vol. I, p. 333. The passage is based on the view of *Nyāyamañjari* cited in the footnote of the book.

it, unless there is a cause of doubt as to its reliability. 'To hear is to believe,' as Montague says,[41] is true in the sense that it is a general tendency of man to believe in what he hears or learns from authority.

In case the information that the hill has fire proves to be valid on the ground of the reliability of the reporter or on the evidence of the hearer's own experience, the method of verification confirms the cognition, but is not its actual cause. When the hearer accepts the information as true without verification on the ground of the reliability of the reporter it may be characterized as belief. But such belief or faith is a mode of valid knowledge, and not something different from it. Knowing from an authoritative source is, as a rule, attended with confidence. There cannot be any knowledge as long as doubt prevails in the mind of the cognizer. A doubtful cognition cannot rank with knowledge. No information gained is valid knowledge for the cognizer unless he is convinced of its truth.

Montague, though critical of the authoritarian method, tacitly accepts belief as a form of knowledge: 'We get more of our beliefs from the testimony of our fellows than from any other source. Little of our knowledge of the universe is directly tested by our own intuition, reason, experience, or practice. We accept on trust nine-tenths of what we hold to be true.'[42]

According to Vedānta, implicit belief or faith (śraddhā) is the acceptance of, or the reliance on the words of the trustworthy, which need no verification. It is other than credulity or gullibility. It is conviction of truth and tantamount to valid knowledge. As such it is distinct from feeling, volition, imagination, or assumption. Śabda as a source of valid knowledge means āgama, authentic word that is free from all defects. It is a canon of knowledge recognized by most Indian systems of thought that the words of such persons as are free from delusion, error, deceit, and defects of the senses and the mind are a source of valid cognition. Thus, reason is implicit in faith. It is not unreasonable to rely on the reliable.

Moreover, Advaita Vedānta as well as the Mīmāṁsā school hold that true knowledge has not to be verified by any other knowledge. It is its own proof. Its validity is due to the very conditions that cause it and is certified by them. Thus, the knowledge of a fact or truth is intrinsically valid and its validity is self-evident. It carries conviction. Doubt arises in the mind of the cognizer only when he is aware of some drawback in the conditions that produce the knowledge. In that case verification is needed for the removal of the doubt and not for establishing the validity of the knowledge in question. We have dwelt at length on the Advaita theory of the self-evidence of the validity of knowledge in chapter IV.

[41] William Pepperell Montague, *The Ways of Knowing*, p. 39.
[42] *Ibid.*

11. *Certain facts of everyday life are made known only by means of śabda (verbal testimony)*

It is worthy of note that some common experiences of life cannot be communicated but through *śabda*. Neither perception nor inference can help us in these matters. Take, for instance, the case of man's dream-experience. How can one know about another's dream without being told? At best, a person can guess from his own experience that others also dream. But by no means can he know what dreams they dream, unless they recount their respective dreams to him. Indeed, one can know very little about another's inner experience without hearing from him.

Even the ordinary experience of a person (e.g., how he feels physically or mentally) can hardly be known but through his words. This may be one of the reasons why it is a general custom to greet a person with such queries as 'How do you do?' 'How are you?' 'How do you feel?' If a person appears to be sick, others can guess from his behaviour that he has some physical or mental trouble, but they can hardly determine the nature of the ailment unless he discloses it himself. Even though there be an indication of his pain, it is not possible to ascertain whether he is suffering from headache, or toothache, or stomach-ache, or heartache, until he expresses himself. It is true that the internal states can be judged to some extent by their symptoms. But no physical mark or behaviour is as expressive of the inner experiences as genuine self-disclosure. We cannot even know definitely whether a person has appetite or not without asking him. Says Śaṅkara: '[Internal states] of bondage, liberation, satisfaction, anxiety, recovery from ailment, hunger, and such other things are known only to the man concerned, and the knowledge of these to others is conjectural.'[43] This means that others can only guess at them through their physical expressions. It is only the words of the experiencer that can truly acquaint others with the nature of his inner experience.

12. *Śabda (verbal testimony) can even serve as a means of immediate knowledge (aparōkṣa-jñānam)*

Another distinctive mark of śabda-pramāṇa (verbal testimony) is that in certain instances, rare though they may be, it can serve as a vehicle of immediate (aparōkṣa) knowledge. Like all inferential knowledge, verbal knowledge (śabda-pramā) is usually mediate (parōkṣa). As held by some Nondualistic philosophers, śabda-pramāṇa (verbal testimony) can also lead to immediate or direct cognition, when the knowledge of the self, empirical or transcendental, is concerned. For example, a king, who under the spell of

[43] VC 475.

amnesia forgets that he is a king and imagines himself to be a commoner, can recognize himself as the king on being repeatedly told, 'Thou art the king', 'Thou art the king'. The words remove his delusion regarding himself and unveils his true status. Similarly, on hearing the Vedic dictum 'Thou art That' a qualified spiritual aspirant can get rid of ajñāna and realize the true nature of the self as Nondual Brahman. We shall further dwell on this point later. The fact is illustrated in Vedāntic literature by a classical story that can be narrated as follows:

'Thou Art the Tenth'

Once ten young men, living in the desert province of Rājputana, left home and travelled on foot to the Gangetic plain. There they came across for the first time a brook, which had overflowed its banks on account of a recent rainfall. Never before had they seen such an expanse of water; because in their native place the only source of water was the deep wells. After much pondering they decided to wade the stream. With slow and steady steps they proceeded. Despite their caution their feet slipped a number of times. When they reached the other side of the brook, they were exhausted mainly because of nervousness. In order to be sure that all of them were safe, one of the ten young men counted the number in the party and found only nine. 'Where is the tenth?' cried he, 'He must have been drowned.' Then a second young man counted with the same result. In this way each of them counted the party excluding himself, and did not find the tenth person. Then they were all wailing over his death, presuming that he had been drowned in the stream.

Just then a man was riding by. He saw the distressed young men from a distance, rode up to the place, and asked them what had happened. 'Our tenth one is missing; he must be dead,' all cried out in one voice. The horseman saw at a glance that all the ten persons were present there. He at once understood the situation and told one of them to count all in the party. The young man did the same, but could not find the tenth one. 'Thou art the tenth,' shouted the man on horseback. At once the young man realized that he himself was the tenth person that was missing. In this way each one in the party found that the tenth that was missing was he and felt happy.[44]

From the foregoing discussion it is evident that śabda-pramāṇa (verbal testimony) is a unique means of valid knowledge. Indeed, śabda is the only vehicle that conveys profound truths, sublime ideas, delicate shades of thought, finest and deepest sentiments, and the subtlest moods of the mind.

[44] The story has been briefly referred to by Śaṅkara in his Br. U. com. (I: 4.7) and US (XII: 3, XVIII: 176).

CHAPTER IX

VERBAL TESTIMONY AS THE MEANS OF SUPRASENSUOUS KNOWLEDGE; THE SPECIALITY OF THE VEDIC TESTIMONY*

1. *The twofold capacity of verbal testimony. It is the only vehicle of suprasensuous knowledge. It precedes intuitive perception*

Śabda-pramāṇa, word as a means of valid knowledge, has a twofold capacity: it can communicate the facts of the sensible universe, and can also enlighten us on suprasensible truths; whereas other vehicles of knowledge are capable of acquainting us only with the sensible. Thus there are two kinds of verbal testimony: the secular and the scriptural, conveying the knowledge of the sensible and the suprasensible respectively. As observed by Sāyaṇa, the great Vedic commentator, it is the special purpose of the scriptural texts to disclose truths that are beyond man's normal experience.[1] 'The scripture is the only source of the knowledge of the truths regarding the suprasensible,' says Śaṅkara.[2]

Neither sense-perception, nor any of the other means of knowledge dependent on it, can impart knowledge of suprasensible facts, e.g., God, soul, their relation, soul's journey after death, heaven, hell, the origin of the universe, merit and demerit accruing from righteous and unrighteous deeds, their fructification, man's highest destiny and its fulfilment. However, the existence of the suprasensible cannot be denied. The explanation of the seen is in the unseen. Perception does not exhaust reality. With the experience of an object one is aware of the experiencing self that is invariably present. The finite betokens the infinite, the changeful the changeless, the temporal the eternal, the imperfect the perfect. Indeed, reality far exceeds the four dimensional objective universe.

* For a short account of the Vedic texts see Appendix A.

[1] Intro. to com. on the Ṛg-Veda (*Ṛg-Veda-bhāṣya-bhūmikā*).
[2] BS II: 1.27; see also BS II: 3.1, com.

Reason, which is founded on common experience, necessarily fails to unveil what is beyond it. Swāmī Vivekānanda rightly observes:

'The field of reason, or of the conscious workings of the mind, is narrow and limited. There is a little circle within which human reason must move. It cannot go beyond. Every attempt to go beyond is impossible, yet it is beyond this circle of reason that there lies all that humanity holds most dear. All these questions, whether there is an immortal soul, whether there is a God, whether there is any supreme intelligence guiding this universe or not, are beyond the field of reason. Reason can never answer these questions. What does reason say? It says, "I am agnostic; I do not know either yea or nay". Yet these questions are so important to us. Without a proper answer to them, human life will be purposeless. All our ethical theories, all our moral attitudes, all that is good and great in human nature, have been moulded upon answers that have come from beyond the circle. It is very important, therefore, that we should have answers to these questions.'[3]

How does man know the truths that are beyond the range of the senses and out of the reach of reason? According to most religions, great saints and seers intuit these truths in a superconscious state above reason. As declared by Patañjali, 'In that state [of samādhi] knowledge can be said to be "filled with truth". The knowledge that is gained from testimony and inference is about common objects. The knowledge gained from samādhi is of a much higher order, being able to penetrate where inference and testimony cannot go.'[4] Many Eastern and Western philosophers concur on this point that the human mind can develop a suprasensuous and suprarational faculty of 'intuition', which is far superior to intellect and can perceive facts that are otherwise inaccessible. As observed by S. Radhakrishnan:

'We have to pass beyond thought, beyond the clash of oppositions, beyond the antinomies that confront us when we work with the limited categories of abstract thinking, if we are to reach the real where man's existence and divine being coincide. It is when thought becomes perfected in intuition that we catch the vision of the real. The mystics the world over have emphasized this fact. Pascal dwells on the incomprehensibility of God, and Bossuet bids us not to be dismayed by the divergencies, but regard them all trustfully as the golden chains that meet beyond mortal sight at the throne of God.

According to the Upaniṣads there is a higher power which enables us to grasp this central spiritual reality. Spiritual things require to be spiritually discerned. The yōga method is a practical discipline

[3] CW I, p. 181. [4] YS I: 48, 49.

pointing out the road to this realization. Man has the faculty of divine insight or mystic intuition, by which he transcends the distinctions of intellect and solves the riddles of reason. The chosen spirits scale the highest peak of thought and intuit the reality.'[5]

Of course, one has to undergo the necessary disciplines to develop the supernal vision. It is the intense practice of meditation on the nature of the Self or God that leads to the intuitive realization of the same. Other spiritual disciplines are the preparatory steps. For the practice of meditation it is absolutely necessary for the seeker to have the previous knowledge of the Self or God from a reliable source. The sacred texts and the words of a qualified teacher are the only authentic source. The seeker should also convince himself of the truth of the verbal statements by reasoning on them. 'Seek, and ye shall find,' says Jesus Christ.[6] But without a clear comprehension of the nature of God and His abode one cannot seek Him even, far less find.

The purpose of meditation is to turn the mediate knowledge into the immediate apprehension. In consequence of the long-continued steady practice of meditation on God or the Supreme Self with a yearning heart, when the seeker's mental mode fully conforms to the object of meditation, then the illumination is attained. One may ponder on the nature of the Self or God through sheer imagination, heedless of any authoritative account, but this cannot lead to the desired end. In such a case one is likely to be subject to fantasy, which cannot remove ignorance and reveal the Truth. Without a definite knowledge of the Truth, right meditation is not possible. So it is said, 'One attains the supreme state of yōga by developing intuition (prajñā) in a threefold way—hearing of the authentic words (āgama), reasoning on them, and the ardent practice of meditation.'[7] A spiritual aspirant meditates on God particularly as the innermost Self, since no other knowledge leads to Liberation. 'Behold, the kingdom of God is within you', says Jesus Christ.[8]

Thus, the verbal knowledge invariably precedes the superconscious experience. Before one can develop the intuitive perception one must know about God or the Self from the scriptures, or from a qualified teacher, or from both. So the questions arise: 'Where do the scriptures come from?' 'Who is the first teacher of spiritual knowledge?' 'How did man first know God?' Some may hold that the scriptures are the records of the superconscious experiences of the seers. Even then one can pertinently ask, 'How could the seers experience truth without being taught about it?' So, in the last resort, it is to be admitted that the All-knowing, Self-existent Supreme Being is the

[5] *Indian Philosophy*, Vol. I, p. 176.
[6] Matt. 7: 7; Luke 11: 9.
[7] Quoted in Vyāsa's commentary on YS I: 48.
[8] Luke 17: 21.

Teacher of all teachers and that the scriptures are initially His Divine revelations.

Patañjali rightly says, 'He is the Teacher of even the ancient teachers, being not limited by time.'[9] Swāmī Vivekānanda comments on this aphorism:

'It is true that all knowledge is within ourselves, but this has to be called forth by another knowledge. Although the capacity to know is inside us, it must be called out, and that calling out of knowledge can only be done, a yōgī maintains, through another knowledge. Dead insentient matter never calls out knowledge, it is the action of knowledge that brings out knowledge. Knowing beings must be with us to call forth what is in us, so these teachers were always necessary. The world was never without them, and no knowledge can come without them. God is the Teacher of all teachers, because these teachers, however great they may have been—gods or angels—were all bound and limited by time, while God is not.'[10]

2. *The Śruti is the only means to the knowledge of Nondual Brahman*

The knowledge conveyed by the six pramāṇas (perception, inference, comparison, testimony, postulation, and non-apprehension) is broadly speaking, of two distinct orders: (1) relating to conditional reality, and (2) relating to absolute reality.[11] Nondual Brahman is absolute reality, being uncontradictable. All else, the sensuous and the suprasensuous as well, belong to the temporal order, which is conditionally real, being uncontradicted until the experiencer realizes his identity with Brahman. Nondual Brahman is revealed only by the Upaniṣads, and by no other pramāṇa. So says the sage Yājñavalkya, 'I ask you of that Being who is to be known only from the Upaniṣads, who definitely projects those beings [that comprise the phenomenal world] and [again] withdraws them unto Himself, and who is at the same time transcendent.'[12] The Upaniṣadic texts, with one accord, declare the reality of Brahman free from all distinctions and differences.[13] 'That is the Brahman taught by the Upaniṣad; yea, that is the Brahman taught by the Upaniṣad.'[14] Indeed, it is the Vedas that have revealed to mankind the ultimate reality of Brahman, One only without a second. As the primary source of the knowledge of Nondual Brahman they are distinct from all other scriptures.

Even reason independently of the Śruti cannot determine the nature of the ultimate Reality. Śaṅkara firmly maintains that human reason is incapable of ascertaining the fundamental reality, let alone sense-perception. As stated by him,

[9] YS I: 26. [10] CW I, pp. 216–7. [11] *Vide* VP VII.
[12] Br. U. III: 9.26. [13] *Vide* BS I: 1 4, S. com. [14] Sv. U. I: 16.

'Although in certain cases [relating to empirical facts] reason is found to have a stable ground, yet in the present case [the determination of the cause of the universe] it cannot but be subject to its defect of instability. Independently of the scriptures one fails even to imagine this most profound, nondual Cause of the manifold, the attainment of which is Liberation. Because of the absence of color and the like this entity cannot be known by sense-perception; because of the absence of an indicatory mark this cannot be known by any such method as inference: this is what we declare.

Moreover, it is the consensus of all who uphold mōkṣa (Liberation) that this is attainable by true knowledge. And true knowledge must be unvaried, being in conformity with Reality. That is Reality which is invariable. The knowledge of this is considered true knowledge in the world, like the knowledge that fire is hot. Therefore, the difference of views in the case of true knowledge is absurd. But the conclusions reached by reasoning, being mutually contradictory, are well-known to be divergent.'[15]

That the Upaniṣadic texts consistently point to the reality of Nondual Brahman is evident from the six characteristic marks of the treatment of a subject-matter. According to an ancient authority, 'In ascertaining the purport [of a treatise] the tests are—the consistency of the introduction and the conclusion, frequent reference to the theme, its originality, fruitfulness, commendableness, and reasonableness.'[16] The sage Uddālaka's instruction to his son Śvetaketu in the sixth chapter of the Chāndōgya Upaniṣad is often cited as an example, where one can see by these marks that the import of the entire discourse is Nondual Brahman, One only without a second.

The chapter begins with the words, 'In the beginning, my dear, this [the universe] was Being alone, One only without a second,' and ends thus: 'In That all that exists has its self. That is the true. That is the Self. That thou art, O Śvetaketu.' Brahman is again and again referred to by the same statement: 'Now, in that which is the subtle essence all that exists has its self. That is the true. That is the Self. That thou art, O Śvetaketu.'

The fruitfulness of the knowledge of Brahman is thus stated: 'A man who has found a teacher to instruct him gains the true knowledge. For him there is delay only so long as he is not liberated [from the body], then he attains perfection.' The knowledge of Brahman is thus commended: 'Have you, my dear, ever asked for that instruc-

[15] BS II: 1.11, com.

[16] The verse is quoted from the *Bṛhatsaṁhitā* in the *Sarvadarśana-saṁgraha*, chap. on Pūrṇaprajñā-darśanam, p. 59, Ananda-ashrama, Poona, 1950.

tion by which one hears what is unheard, contemplates what is uncontemplated, and knows what is unknown?'

The uniqueness of the theme is evident from the son's question 'What is that instruction, venerable sir?' The reasonableness of the statement that all is known by knowing Brahman is evinced by the following illustration: 'Just as, my dear, by one clod of clay all that is made of clay is known, the modification being only a name, arising from speech, while the truth is that all this is clay . . . even so, my dear, is that instruction.'

Indeed, the purport of the Vedic texts is to affirm the reality of Nondual Brahman, which cannot be known by any other means. Even the Śruti passages relating to Saguṇa Brahman and the diversified universe have that one end in view. The knowledge of Saguṇa Brahman as the Creator, as the Ruler of all things and beings, can be gained from other scriptures as well, but the knowledge of Nirguṇa Brahman cannot be attained from any other source but the Śruti and the scriptures that consistently follow it.

The all-transcendent Nondual Brahman is the One Self of the apparent manifold. This is the Supreme unity underlying all diversity. Here is the culmination of human knowledge. It is the ultimate ground of all metaphysical conceptions, religious doctrines, scientific truths, and ethical principles. Swāmī Vivekānanda rightly observes:

'You must remember the one theme that runs through all the Vedas—"Just as by the knowledge of one lump of clay we know all the clay that is in the universe, so what is that, knowing which we know everything else?" This, expressed more or less clearly, is the theme of all human knowledge. It is the finding of a Unity towards which we are all going. Every action of our lives, the most material, the grossest as well as the finest, the highest, the most spiritual, is alike tending towards this one ideal, the finding of Unity. . . . Irresistibly we are impelled towards that perfection which consists in finding the Unity, killing this little self and making ourselves broader and broader. . . . That is the foundation of all morality. It is the quintessence of all ethics, preached in any language, or in any religion, or by any prophet in the world. . . . This is the theme that runs through the whole of Vedānta, and which runs through every other religion.'[17]

3. *It is by implication that the Śruti conveys the knowledge of Nondual Brahman that is beyond description*

As declared by the Upaniṣad, Nondual Brahman is beyond the range of thought and speech. That is Brahman 'wherefrom words along with ideas turn back without reaching It.'[18] Necessarily, the

[17] CW VI, pp. 2–4. [18] Tai. U. II: 9.1.

Upaniṣads indicate Its nature by negative expressions, such as—

'That Brahman is without prior or posterior, without interior or exterior.'[19]

'It is neither gross nor minute, neither short nor long.'[20]

'Other than righteousness and unrighteousness, other than cause and effect, other than what has been and what is to be.'[21]

But while declaring Brahman to be beyond speech, the Upaniṣads also describe It by positive expressions indicative of Its intrinsic characteristics (svarūpalakṣaṇa), such as—

'Brahman is Truth, Consciousness, Infinite.'[22]

'Brahman is Consciousness, Bliss.'[23]

'Supreme Brahman is Being-Consciousness-Bliss.'[24]

Yet there is no self-contradiction in this dual account; because the positive expressions refer to Brahman only by implication, and not by their primary significance. 'Brahman is beyond speech' actually means 'Brahman cannot be directly signified by words.' Speech cannot define, but can indicate, Brahman. As observed by Śrī Rāmakṛṣṇa, 'What the Vedas say about Brahman is only a hint.' All positive expressions with reference to Brahman have negative connotations. 'Being (sat)' excludes the idea of non-being with regard to Brahman, 'Consciousness (cit)' excludes the idea of unintelligence or materiality, and 'Bliss (ānanda)' excludes the idea of imperfection, or grievance of any kind whatsoever. The expression 'Being-Consciousness-Bliss' is used, lest the ultimate Reality beyond thought and speech be conceived as non-being, or as unconscious or imperfect existence.

Usually, the Upaniṣads define Brahman by extrinsic characteristics (taṭastha lakṣaṇa), which do not inhere in It, but differentiate It from all else. Brahman is characterized as 'That from which are the projection, the preservation, and the dissolution of the universe.'[25]

'That from which these beings are born, That by which, when born, they live, That into which [at the time of dissolution] they enter, they merge; seek the knowledge of That. That is Brahman.'[26]

'He is the Lord of all. He is the Knower of all. He is the Inner Controller. He is the source of all; for from Him all beings originate and in Him they finally disappear.'[27]

The sole reality of Brahman is affirmed by declaring It as the basis and being of the world-appearance, as the unitary existence transcending all names and forms.

'All this is Brahman.'[28]

'The immortal Brahman alone is before, that Brahman is behind,

[19] Br. U. II: 5.19. [20] Br. U. III: 8.8. [21] Ka. U. I: 2.14.
[22] Tai. U. II: 1.3. [23] Br. U. III: 9.28. [24] NPT U. I: 6.
[25] BS I: 1.2. [26] Tai. U. III: 1. [27] Ma. U. VI.
[28] Ch. U. III: 14.1.

that Brahman is to the right and to the left. Brahman alone pervades everything above and below; this universe is that Supreme Brahman alone.'[29]

4. *The identity of the individual self and the Supreme Self pointing to the sole reality of Nirguṇa Brahman is the Supreme Truth revealed by the Vedas*

Of all the Upaniṣadic teachings the most significant is the declaration of the identity of the individual self with the Supreme Self. This is the kernel of the Vedas. While disclosing the oneness of the individual consciousness and the universal consciousness that sustains and manifests the manifold, the Śruti points to the sole reality of nondual, non-relational Pure Consciousness that Brahman is. The whole truth is contained in a terse sentence of three words. There are four such pithy sentences in the four Vedas. Each sentence is called a 'mahāvākya,' lit., the great saying.

The four Vedic mahāvākyas (the great sayings) are—

(1) 'Consciousness [manifest in an individual] is Brahman,' as stated in the Aitareya Upaniṣad of the Ṛg-Veda.[30]

(2) 'I am Brahman,' as stated in the Bṛhadāraṇyaka Upaniṣad of the Yajur-Veda.[31]

(3) 'Thou art That,' as stated in the Chāndōgya Upaniṣad of the Sāma-Veda.[32]

(4) 'This ātman [the individual self] is Brahman,' as stated in the Māṇḍūkya Upaniṣad of the Atharva-Veda.[33]

Each of these terse sentences declares the identity of the individual consciousness and the universal or the Divine Consciousness. So the implied meaning of each is the sole reality of Nondual Consciousness that Brahman is. Hence, this great teaching (mahāvākya) is said to be *akhaṇḍārtha-bōdhaka* (indicative of the undivided Absolute Being free from all distinctions).'

This supreme Vedic teaching imparts a twofold knowledge attainable by no other means: on the one hand, by affirming ātman as Brahman, it removes man's deep-rooted misconception regarding himself, namely, that he is bound, finite, imperfect, and mortal, and points to his true self as self-existent, self-shining, ever-pure and ever-free. On the other hand, by proclaiming Brahman as ātman it removes man's equally indomitable misconception regarding the Supreme Being, namely, that He is remote, unattainable, hidden, if not non-existent, and reveals Him as the innermost Self, ever-manifest, immediate and direct. Thus, what is conceived as the farthest is revealed as nearer than the nearest, what appears to be unattainable

[29] Mu. U. II: 2.12. [30] III: 1.3. [31] I: 4.10.
[32] VI: 8.7, *passim*. [33] II.

as already attained, what is ever hidden as self-manifest. So it is said:

'That Brahman is vast, self-luminous, inconceivable, subtler than the subtle. That shines forth. That is far beyond what is far, and yet here very near at hand. That is seen here, dwelling in the cave of the heart of conscious beings. Brahman is not grasped by the eye, nor by the organ of speech, nor by other organs or senses, nor by penance or good work. Being pure-minded through the purity of understanding, as a person practices meditation, thereby he beholds Him, who is whole and without component parts.'[34]

The mahāvākya presents in a nutshell the Vedic view of God, the Vedic view of man, and the Vedic view of man's approach to God. It furnishes the clue to his spiritual life. By knowing the self one knows God, the One Self of all. The way to the Supreme Being is an inner approach. It is the gradual realization of the innate Divinity. In fact, the great Vedic dictum makes the inaccessible accessible, the incomprehensible comprehensible, the unknowable knowable.

5. *The knowledge of the identity of the jīva and Brahman is the only direct approach to ultimate Reality*

The teaching of the identity of the jīva and Brahman is the only direct instruction that can be given to a seeker of the Highest of the high, the all-transcendent Being. There can be no other direct approach to Brahman than knowing Him as the very Self. Any instruction that does not unveil Brahman as the Self of the seeker is indirect, because of its remote reference to the Supreme Being. It fails to bring Brahman within the reach of the seeker. A few instances of indirect instruction are cited below:

'That from which these beings are born, That by which, when born, they live, That into which [at the time of dissolution] they enter and merge, seek That, That is Brahman.'[35]
'From Him [the Immutable Brahman], who has general and detailed knowledge of everything, whose austerity consists in knowledge [and not in effort], arise Brahmā [the cosmic soul], name, form, and food.'[36]
'From fear of Him [Brahman] fire burns, from fear of Him the sun shines, from fear of Him Indra, Vāyu, and Death, the fifth, run.'[37]
'No one can grasp Him above, across, or in the middle. There is none equal to Him, His name is great glory.'[38]

[34] Mu. U. III: 1.7, 8. [35] Tai. U. III: 1. [36] Mu. U. I: 1.9.
[37] Ka. U. II: 3.3. [38] Sv. U. IV: 19.

It is evident that the seeker, while receiving the knowledge of Brahman through these teachings, becomes conscious of His remoteness. He feels that Brahman is far out of his reach. Even those Śruti texts that relate Brahman to the seeker's self, but set forth the immense difference between the two, are indirect instructions, for they do not dispel from his mind the remoteness of Brahman. The gap between the seeker and the Goal is not bridged over. For examples:

'That great, birthless Self is the eater of food [in all living beings] and the giver of wealth [the fruits of the actions of all]. He who knows Him as such receives wealth [those fruits].'[39]
'That Brahman is Tadvana, the Adorable of all; He should be worshipped by the name of Tadvana. All creatures desire him who worships Brahman thus.'[40]
'Therefore, having reached this border [the Self], he who is blind ceases to be blind, he who is miserable ceases to be miserable, he who is afflicted ceases to be afflicted.'[41]
'One attains supreme peace by realizing the self-effulgent adorable Lord, the bestower of blessings.'[42]
'On knowing Him—who is the bestower of virtue, the destroyer of sin, the Lord of the six great attributes, who is the support of the universe—as dwelling within [one attains Liberation].'[43]

Of the direct instruction on Brahman the Vedas are the primary source. The identity of the jīva and Brahman pointing to the absolute reality of Nondual Consciousness beyond the tripartite relative order (comprising the individual souls, the universe, and Īśvara) is the central theme of the Upaniṣads. This is the fountain-head of the Vedic teachings. The direct instruction being the very essence of the Vedas, they are rightly called the 'Śruti'. The term 'Śruti', lit., hearing, implies 'direct teaching (aparōkṣa upadeśa)'; whereas the term 'smṛti', lit., remembering, implies 'indirect teaching (parōkṣa upadeśa)'. All scriptures derived from the Vedas are generally called the Smṛti. In them is the predominance of the indirect teaching regarding the Supreme Being. In this sense all sacred texts other than the Vedas come under the category of the 'Smṛti'. Their authority depends on the authority of the Śruti. They are to be accepted as far as they are consistent with the Vedic teachings. In case of any contradiction between the Śruti and the Smṛti, the Śruti has to be followed. In a restricted sense the term Smṛti is applied to Dharma-śāstras, the scriptures that deal particularly with rules of conduct in different spheres of life, such as the Manu-Smṛti, the

39 Br. U. IV: 4.24. 40 Ken. U. IV: 6. 41 Ch. U. VIII: 4.2.
42 Sv. U. IV: 11. 43 *Ibid.* VI: 6.

Yājñavalkya-Smṛti, the Parāśara-Smṛti. As stated by Manu, 'By "Śruti" is meant the Veda, while by "Smṛti" the codes of laws."[44]

The identity of ātman and Brahman cannot be known by any other means of knowledge. No human being can discover this supramental truth. The real nature of the self beyond the ego cannot be determined either by perception or by inference. As observed by Śaṅkara, 'Being different from objects of perception, the existence of the self cannot be proved by this means. Similarly, inference, too, is powerless.'[45] Nor can the mystical intuition of the innermost Self be developed without the previous knowledge of the Upaniṣadic truth. In order to realize the identity of the self with Brahman the seeker has to be conversant with the Vedic dictum. The Śruti is prior to mystical perception. It is Divine revelation. It did not originate from the superconscious experience of the seers, as is generally presumed by modern thinkers. The seers are those who perceive the suprasensuous truths disclosed by the Vedas. (See sec. 1).

In the beginning the Vedic truths were transmitted orally by the teacher to the disciple. The Supreme Lord, the Teacher of all teachers, imparted the Vedas to the first created being, Hiraṇyagarbha, the cosmic soul, whose limiting adjunct is the universal mind. So it is said, 'Longing for Liberation I seek refuge in the Supreme Being, the revealer of Self-knowledge, who created Brahmā in the beginning and delivered the Vedas to him.'[46] Being at first transmitted orally through a succession of teachers and disciples the Vedas have been called 'anuśravaḥ', that which is heard from the utterance of the teacher.

Being the repository of the Truth of truths revealed by the Supreme Lord, the Śruti is an independent means of knowledge. It is authority by itself. It requires no proof. It can be corroborated, and not contradicted, by other means of knowledge. As observed by Śaṅkara, 'Śruti is the primary source of our knowledge of the suprasensuous facts.'[47] Just as inference is dependent on perception, so the authoritativeness of the Smṛti, which consists of inspirational writings, is dependent on the Śruti, the primary revelation. Because of this difference the Vedas are also called 'pratyakṣa' (the direct or the first-hand knowledge), while other scriptures are termed 'anumāna' (the indirect or the derivative knowledge).[48] Even the Bhagavad-gītā (lit., the Song of God), delivered by Śrī Kṛṣṇa, God incarnate in human form, falls into the category of the Smṛti and cannot rank with the Śruti.

The message of the identity of ātman and Brahman is based on the recognition of oneness of existence underlying all diversity. It is evident from the sage Uddālaka's instruction to his son Śvetaketu:

[44] MS II: 10. [45] Br. U. com. Intro. [46] Sv. U. VI: 18.
[47] BS II: 3.1, com. [48] *Vide* BS I: 3.28, S. com.

'Of all these created things and beings, my child, Pure Existence is the origin, Pure Existence is the support, Pure Existence is the end. . . . In that subtle essence all this has its being. That is Reality. That is the Self. That thou art, O Śvetaketu.'[49] As we have noted above, it is the Śruti that has revealed to man the absolute oneness of existence.

6. *The mahāvākya signifies a twofold approach to Nondual Brahman, the one is the direct, the other is the indirect*

The sole purpose of the Vedas, comprising the Mantras and the Brāhmaṇas,[50] is to lead human individuals step by step, to the attainment of Nondual Brahman through the realization of the identity of the self with the Supreme Self. The great Vedic dictum (the mahāvākya) signifies the two main approaches to Nondual Brahman, the direct and the indirect, which are, in fact, the two main courses of man's spiritual journey. For instance, the dictum, 'I am Brahman' being resolved into the two factors 'I am He' and 'I am His', signalizes two distinct methods of God-realization, the way to Nirguṇa Brahman and the way to Saguṇa Brahman. The formula, 'I am He', signifying the identity of the individual soul with the Supreme Self, marks the direct approach to Nirguṇa Brahman (the Impersonal Godhead). It is a straight, but steep course. Since intellect plays a major part in it, this is characterized as the path of knowledge (jñāna-mārga). But it is not purely an intellectual process; there is room for devotional feeling in it. None can see the face of Truth without ardour and consecration. The second formula, 'I am His', signifying the relation between the individual soul and the Supreme Self marks the direct approach to Saguṇa Brahman (the Personal God), and the indirect approach to Nirguṇa Brahman, because the realization of Saguṇa Brahman can lead to the realization of Nirguṇa Brahman. On account of the predominance of devotional feeling in this course, it is characterized as the path of devotion (bhakti-mārga). It covers all theistic religions of the world; inasmuch as the relation between man and God is the keystone of all of them. Each one of them is based on some form of relation between the worshipper and the worshipped. But this is not purely an emotional approach. There is enough scope for intellect in this path. Without a clear understanding of the nature of God and the nature of the soul, the worshipper cannot apprehend his spiritual relation with the Divine Being and hold to Him as the Supreme Goal or the Ideal.

[49] Ch. U. VI: 8.6, 7.

[50] 'The Mantras and the Brāhmaṇas together are called the Veda.' (Āpastamba's *Yajña-paribhāṣā-sūtram,* 38).

According to the Nondualistic philosophers, an average spiritual aspirant cannot follow the direct approach to Nirguṇa Brahman. He has to worship Saguṇa Brahman and realize Him before he can attain Nirguṇa Brahman. The worship of Saguṇa Brahman is an indirect means to the realization of Nirguṇa Brahman. So says Śaṅkara: 'The Vedāntic texts teach one and the same Brahman as the object of worship in relation to the adjuncts and as the goal of knowledge without any relation to the adjuncts.'[51] As stated in *Vedānta-paribhāṣā*: 'Meditation on the Conditioned Brahman is also a cause of the realization of the Unconditioned Brahman through the concentration of the mind. So it has been said, "Persons of ordinary intelligence who are unable to realize the Unconditioned Brahman are done a favor by the delineation of the Conditioned Brahman. When their minds are brought under control by the practice (of meditation) on the Conditioned Brahman, that very Unconditioned Brahman, divested of the superimposition of limiting adjuncts, directly manifests Itself".'[52] In his gloss on Śaṅkara's commentary on the *Bhagavad-gītā* Ānandagiri expresses the same view: 'The knowledge of the Conditioned Brahman is the doorway to the knowledge of the Unconditioned.'[53]

7. *The universal sympathy and all-comprehensiveness of the Śruti. Its object is to lead men and women at all levels of life to the Highest Goal by providing methods suited to their individual capacities*

A spiritual aspirant worships God for God's sake. Whether he conceives Him as Saguṇa or Nirguṇa, he accepts Him as the Ideal, as the Goal. But there are many more believers in God who worship Him not for His sake, but for secular interests here and hereafter. Indeed, a vast majority of human beings hanker after the temporal, and not the eternal. The Vedas have not been callous to such men and women, but have taken their case into full consideration, and laid progressive courses for their spiritual unfoldment. The Vedic religion is, broadly speaking, a twofold way: the path of prosperity and the path of perfection, characterized respectively by desire and dispassion. It teaches how the seeker of prosperity and pleasure, by the legitimate fulfilment of his desires through the performance of duties and righteous deeds, can gradually outgrow sense-attachment and develop the spirit of renunciation and a yearning for God-realization. Thus, the path of prosperity, regulated by ethical principles and religious observances, is intended to lead the seeker to the path of perfection, regulated by spiritual disciplines and ideals;

[51] BS I: 1.11, com.

[52] VP VIII, quoting *Vedānta-kalpataru*, verses 1, 2, on BS I: 1.20. See Appendix B, sec. 7.

[53] X: 7.

the ultimate goal of the two ways being one and the same—the attainment of Nirguṇa Brahman.

Both sections of the Vedas, karma-kāṇḍa, dealing with sacrificial rites and duties, and jñāna-kāṇḍa, dealing with spiritual knowledge, have one common end in view: to lead human individuals of varying capacities and conditions of life to final Liberation. For this supreme purpose they have prescribed many forms of ritualistic worship, duties of different social orders and stages of individual life, and gradations of moral ideals and spiritual disciplines including methods of meditation. Says Śaṅkara, 'The section of the Vedas dealing with knowledge has the same import as that dealing with rites.'[54] The reason is, the rites and duties are preparatory to knowledge by which Brahman is attained. They purify and quiet the mind.

The Vedas have prescribed sacrificial rites and ceremonies not only for specific results in a man's life here, but also for more durable and satisfying results in his life hereafter. By these latter observances a seeker of welfare can acquire merit even for attaining to svarga-lōka, the celestial region, which is the highest plane of sense-fulfilment. But the aspirant has to meet two pre-conditions. In the first place, he must have faith in the continuity of the soul's existence after death. Secondly, he must follow the path of virtue. 'The Vedas [the Vedic rites] do not sanctify an unrighteous person,' says an ancient law-giver.[55] 'A man devoid of good conduct is not entitled to the Vedic rituals,' remarks Śaṅkara in citing the above passage.[56]

'One should practice non-injury to all living beings,' is a general Vedic precept. But this can be followed especially by those who are capable of self-control. In order to encourage others lacking in self-restraint to abstain from violence provision has been made for the killing of animals in certain sacrificial rites as an exception to the general instruction.[57] Such relaxation of hard and fast rules often serves as an incentive to the practice of self-restraint by those who are not used to it. In the Vedic culture righteousness is the essential pre-requisite for secular well-being as well as for spiritual attainment.

It is evident from the foregoing discussion that a special characteristic of the Śruti is its universal sympathy and all-comprehensiveness. We have seen that it recognizes the differences in the capacities of the aspirants (adhikāri-bheda) and prescribes a variety of moral and religious courses to suit different types and grades of individuals. Various are the approaches to one and the same Goal—this is the keynote of the Vedic way of life. The same Supreme Being is variously

[54] Br. U. IV: 4.22, com.

[55] *Vāśiṣṭha Dharma-sūtra* or *Dharma-śāṣtra*, VI.3.

[56] BS III: 1.10, com.

[57] Cf. *Bhāmatī* on Adhyāsa-bhāṣya in the context that the Śāstras are for the unillumined.

conceived by the human mind according to its capacity. One transcendental Reality underlies all diversity and is the indwelling self in every living being. On this insight rests the universality of the Vedas. From time immemorial the Śruti has declared to all humanity this eternal truth: 'The Reality is One, the sages call It by different names,'[58] 'One Reality is variously conceived,'[59] 'One effulgent Being is manifest in many ways,'[60] 'Thou art One, but hast penetrated diverse forms,'[61] and so on. The authoritativeness of the Śruti is due as much to the affirmation of incontrovertible Truth as to its Divine origin.

Says Swāmī Vivekānanda:

'And as the Vedas are the only scriptures which teach this real absolute God, of which all other ideas of God are but minimised and limited visions; and as the *sarva-lōka-hitaiṣiṇī Śruti* [the Veda, the well-wisher of all the world] takes the devotee gently by the hand, and leads him from one stage to another, througn all the stages that are necessary for him to travel to reach the Absolute; and as all other religions represent one or other of these stages in unprogressive and crystallised forms, all the other religions of the world are included in the nameless, limitless, eternal Vedic religion.'[62]

'Although the suprasensuous vision of truths is to be met with in some measure in the Purāṇas [mythologies] and Itihāsas [the Epics] and in the religious scriptures of other races, still the fourfold scriptures known among the Aryan race as the Vedas being the first, the most complete, and the most undistorted collection of spiritual truths, deserve to occupy the highest place among all scriptures, command the respect of all nations of the earth, and furnish the rationale of all their respective scriptures.'[63]

8. *Not only Brahman (the Supreme Being), but also dharma (moral ideal) is beyond the scope of normal experience and reason, being rooted in suprasensuous truth*

The Vedas are the original source of the knowledge of Brahman and of the knowledge of dharma (moral ideal).[64] Spiritual and moral ideals leading to the ultimate Goal are based on man's entire life—here, heretofore, and hereafter. They cannot be discovered by human reason dependent on normal experience. Neither mōkṣa (Liberation and its means) nor dharma (moral ideal) can be determined by perception or inference. Truly speaking, man cannot know what is right and what is wrong, until the mind becomes unbiased and free

[58] Ṛg-V. I: 164.49. [59] *Ibid.* X: 114.5. [60] Tai. Ar. III: 14.1.
[61] *Ibid.* III: 14.3. [62] CW IV, p. 289. [63] CW VI, p. 155.
[64] Sāyaṇa's com. on Ṛg-V., Intro. (*Ṛg-Veda-bhāṣya-bhūmikā*).

from egoism. His capacity for moral judgment requires some inner development, which is not possible without the practice of righteousness. It is the consensus of the Vedic teachers that virtue brightens intellect, while vice darkens it. Without the practice of virtue reason does not grow, far less insight. In order to develop moral consciousness a person has to make his life conform to ethical rules, which he must know from an authoritative source. If he depends on himself from the very beginning his mind will be liable to self-deception; he will have a tendency to justify his wrong behaviour knowingly or unknowingly. Hence, it can be reasonably held that man's moral evolution has not been purely a natural process. It must have been initiated by ethical principles set by a divine agency.

Morality in its lower forms, such as obedience to the government laws, or observance of social rules and conventions, or adherence to ethical conduct conducive to common secular interest, can be determined by normal intelligence. But the universal standard of morality, which is goodness for goodness' sake, which accepts disinterested love for all as an ideal in itself, is based on the recognition of the spiritual relation among all beings irrespective of their physical and psychical differences, and cannot be established by ordinary human experience or reason. It requires the vision of one Supreme Being dwelling in the heart of each and every individual as the inmost self. Basically, morality is the attunement of the individual self to the Supreme Self. Unselfishness is the fundamental moral principle. Human reason, which is egoistic and secularistic in its outlook, cannot go beyond the ethics of enlightened self-interest.

Thus, in the last resort, the revealed texts have to be recognized as the final authority on man's moral ideal. So it is wise to hold to them for guidance. This is evident from Śrī Kṛṣṇa's instruction to Arjuna: 'He who, disregarding the directions of the Śāstra, acts under the impulse of desire, attains no ability, nor happiness, nor the supreme Goal. Therefore, let the Śāstra be your authority in determining what ought to be done and what ought not to be done. Having ascertained what is prescribed or prohibited by the Śāstra, you should act here [in this world].'[65] A person has to depend on the authority of the Śāstra for moral guidance until he is capable of discriminating the self from the not-self and is free from the delusion of the body-idea. With the development of spiritual consciousness morality becomes a part of his nature. No more does he need any direction for right conduct. So says Śrī Kṛṣṇa to Arjuna: When your understanding will cross the bewilderment of delusion [identification of the self with the not-self] then you will be unconcerned as to what you have heard and what you have to hear.'[66] Even then the seeker has to hold to the Śāstra for spiritual knowledge and discipline.

[65] BG XVI: 23, 24. [66] *Ibid.* II: 52.

9. *The Vedic conception of Ṛta, the cosmic moral principle*

In the Vedic view the cosmic order is controlled by a fundamental moral principle. An eternal law or unity, which can be conceived as the principle of rightness or justice, regulates all phenomena. This is called Ṛta, which means 'the fixed way or course', in other words, 'the settled order of things'.[67] It governs the animate and the inanimate. As stated in the *Ṛg-Veda*, 'The whole universe is founded on Ṛta and moves in it.'[68] It keeps all things and beings in their respective courses. Consequently, nothing deviates from its own nature. Because of Ṛta fire burns, wind blows, water flows, plants grow, human beings think, and seasons revolve. Ṛta maintains regularity in the movements of the sun, the moon, the planets and other luminaries. It manifests itself as the universal law of causation, which finds expression in the human plane as the law of karma. It establishes unity between the cosmic forces and the individual powers. It is the basis of all laws, physical, biological, psychical, moral, and spiritual.

Ṛta is presided over by the all-pervading, all-knowing, almighty Being. It is born of the luminous Supreme Self, as He reflects on the creation in the beginning of a cycle.[69] Īśvara plans the creation in view of the jīvas' karma and the unfoldment of their inner nature. The new creation is a readjustment of the physical order to the psychical. To quote Śaṅkara: 'He reflected concerning the order and the arrangement of the world to be created. Having thus reflected He created the universe with time and space, names and forms, as required by the karma and other conditions of the living beings. This is the universe that is being experienced by all creatures in all states according to their perception.'[70]

Ṛta regulates dharma, the principle of equity, the moral law that governs human life. Because of this, right deed inevitably produces good result, whereas wrong deed leads to evil consequences. There is no unmerited happiness or misery, gain or loss, in man's life. Ṛta also provides the standard of morality. Right conduct must be in conformity with the cosmic law. Adherence to truth is the primary moral virtue. Untruth is 'anṛta', deviation from Ṛta. The word 'dharma' is often used in the restricted sense of right conduct or deed. Truthfulness (satya), performance of duties, in other words, the fulfilment of all obligations (yajña), and self-control (tapas) are particularly enjoined by the Vedas. 'Ṛta (rightness)' is sometimes used in the restricted sense of right thought and 'satya (truth)' in the restricted sense of right speech.[71] Right thought (ṛta), right speech (satya), and right deed (dharma) are essential moral traits. The two

[67] *Vide* Ṛg-V. I: 1.8, I: 23.5, I: 24.8, IV: 21.3, X: 121.1; *passim*.
[68] *Ibid.* IV: 23.9. [69] *Ibid.* X: 190.1. [70] Tai. U. II: 6, com.
[71] *Vide* Mn. U. I: 6.

precepts: 'Speak the truth (satya)' and 'Practice virtue (dharma)'—form a part of the farewell instruction given by a Vedic teacher to his pupil after his graduation.[72] According to the Vedic moral code, 'non-injury, truthfulness, non-stealing, cleanliness, control of the senses, charity, self-restraint, kindness, calmness, are the moral rules for all.'[73] Shortly, practice of virtue is the one universal duty of all human beings. It is imperative on the seekers of perfection and the seekers of pleasure as well.

10. *Even the law of karma is disclosed by the Śruti. It cannot be determined by perception or inference*

The term 'dharma' and its antonym 'adharma' are also used in the sense of puṇya (merit) and pāpa (demerit) accruing from work. Whatever karma is done with desire, or secular motive, leaves on the doer's mind some subtle impression (saṁskāra) that has the potency of bearing fruit, good or evil, according to the nature of the deed, in course of time. In this context, *puṇya* (merit) signifies the subtle impression of a virtuous deed, having the potency of bearing good fruit, and *pāpa* (demerit) signifies the subtle impression of a sinful deed, having the potency of bearing evil fruit. Generally speaking, the cumulative effect of such impressions (saṁskāras) determines an individual's course of life here and hereafter.

According to the Vedas, karma produces a twofold result: seen (dṛṣṭa) and unseen (adṛṣṭa), in other words, known and unknown. The result of karma, as known to us, does not explain the inequalities and calamities of life. The Śruti says there are unseen, future effects of a man's karma which he reaps in another incarnation in this world or in the world beyond. Evidently, each karma is of short duration, the physical or the mental operation it involves ceases 'here and now'. How does it bring about a remote result? It is the subtle impressions (saṁskāras) left by karma on the mind of the doer that cling to him wherever he may be, here or beyond, and fructify in due course. As a man sows, so does he reap.

Declares the Śruti:

'As an individual acts and behaves, so he becomes; by doing good he becomes good, by doing evil he becomes evil. He becomes virtuous through virtuous deeds and vicious through sinful deeds.'[74]

'And then the vital force udāna, moving upward by the one upward nerve (suṣumnā), leads the departing soul to the domain of the virtuous in consequence of virtuous deeds, to the domain of the sinful in consequence of sinful deeds, or to the human world in consequence of both.'[75]

[72] Tai. U. I: 11. 1.
[73] *Yājñavalkya-Smṛti* I: 4.122.
[74] Br. U. IV: 4.5.
[75] Pr. U. III: 7.

The result of karma is inevitable. Time cannot erase it, distance cannot avert it, nor can death annul it.

Truly, perceptual knowledge does not solve the riddle of karma. Nor can inference based on it help us. One may assume an inevitable relation between karma and its effect to explain the anomalies of life. But assumption is not inference; the one makes the conclusion possible, the other certain. The point is this. We do not observe in human life any invariable relation between karma and its result, such as—good karma necessarily produces good result and evil karma evil result, and that in the absence of karma there is no result. Without the observation of such relation no law of karma can be established. Indeed, many are the facts noticeable that belie the theory of karma. Not infrequently does it happen that the wicked prosper and the honest suffer, that one enjoys the fruits of another's labour, and that one is born an idiot and another a genius, for no obvious reason. There are also mishaps and catastrophes in life which we cannot account for and so dismiss as 'accidents'. Plainly speaking, with our limited knowledge of human life we cannot propound the law of karma. Further, it requires the recognition of man's survival after death, which is beyond empirical knowledge. Indeed, the truth about karma imparted by the Śruti cannot be known from common experience.

'How did then the Buddha, who denied the authority of the Vedas, establish the law of karma?' one may pertinently ask. In the first place, we should say, that, though the Buddha did not acknowledge the authority of the Vedas, he accepted the Upaniṣadic teachings and presented them in his own way.[76] He must have received the idea of karma from the Śruti and verified it by intuitive perception; but he found a rational ground for it from the observation of natural phenomena. He applied the causality observable in the physical universe to human life. This involves an assumption, as far as we can see. No doubt, a sequence of cause and effect is noticeable in the physical world. Every effect is preceded by causal factors, in the absence of which, there can be no effect; and the effect corresponds with the cause.[77] Yet, what is true of non-human nature may or may not be true of human life. There is a gulf of difference between the

[76] Cf. *A Source Book in Indian Philosophy*, ed. by Sarvepalli Radhakrishnan and Charles A. Moore, New Jersey, Princeton University Press, 1957, p. 272. 'The Buddha takes up some of the thoughts of the Upaniṣads and gives to them a new orientation. The Buddha is not so much formulating a new scheme of metaphysics and morals as rediscovering an old norm and adapting it to the new conditions of thought and life.'

[77] Cf. The Buddha's law of 'dependent origination' (pratītyasamutpāda): 'I will teach you the dharma,' says he, 'that being present, this becomes; from the arising of that, this arises. That being absent, this does not become; from the cessation of that, this ceases.' (Majjhima Nikāya, II.32).

two. In fact, karma prevails only on the human plane. It does not exist on the subhuman level, let alone inanimate nature. The law of karma is a moral law, while the law of causality is a physical law. There is no moral life below the human level. Karma means volitional conscious operation, physical or mental. It implies self-determination, which is lacking in non-human nature. All development in the non-human region can be characterized as a natural process, whereas the development of human life is primarily a cultural operation, that is, due to volitional deliberate action. Man's intellectual, aesthetic, moral, or spiritual life does not grow without cultivation. Thus, karma belongs particularly to man's psychical nature. Its way cannot be deduced from the way of inanimate nature.

11. *The supremacy of the Vedas is due to the fact that they are the only source of incontrovertible truths, the knowledge of which is the highest and most fruitful*

The validity of the Vedic testimony is evident from the fact that it discloses truths which can neither be contradicted nor established by any other means of knowledge. The Vedic truths are not determinable by reason based on sense knowledge, nor are they contradictory to it. They admit of rational interpretation. In fact, the Vedānta philosophy developed out of an attempt to systematize the Vedic teachings. The Vedas reveal, as we have noted above, two fundamental truths.

(1) The identity of the individual self and the Supreme Self.
(2) The ultimate reality of Nondual Brahman, Pure Being-Consciousness-Bliss.

The two are intimately connected. The one points to the other. The Vedic mysticism, philosophy, religion, and ethics are rooted in them. In fact, they form the ultimate ground of all human knowledge, of all religious experiences and disciplines, and of all ethical principles.

Man's search for Truth is bound for Absolute Oneness. It cannot go beyond, nor stop short of, this. Here is the culmination of human knowledge. The ideal of knowledge can be neither duality nor relativity, where ignorance prevails in some form or other. It must reach non-relational Consciousness beyond all distinctions and differences, including the duality of the subject and the object. Until then the mystery of human knowledge remains unsolved, because 'otherness' persists and the Truth, the Absolute, is unattained.[78] The ultimate must be nondual and non-relational. This is what is indicated by some great mystics of the East and the West as the

[78] Cf. D. M. Datta, *The Six Ways of Knowing*, p. 73. 'From the epistemological standpoint the existence of an 'other' means also a possible source of ignorance about that other.'

attainment of intuitive or immediate awareness that transcends the duality of the subject and the object. It is actually the realization of the unitary Self beyond the bifurcation of the self and the not-self. So the Śruti declares: 'Then what delusion and what grief can there be for one who sees unity?'[79] 'It is from a second [entity] that fear comes.'[80]

It is the more or less hazy vision of unity in diversity, of the absolute in the relative, that serves as the impelling force in philosophy, science, and religion.[81] While philosophy may remain satisfied with the conceptual comprehension of the absolute and science with the never-ending search for it,[82] religion points out the way to its immediate apprehension. For it declares what is real in an atom is real in man and shines as his innermost self. By realizing the self one can realize the truth of the universe, and this is the way to the attainment of the Highest Good.

The realization of the identity of the self with Brahman is the highest and the most fruitful of all knowledge. It means the culmination of all that man can aspire after. It removes forever all his delusions, doubts, fears, bondages, and sufferings. He ceases to be a transmigratory being. He becomes free—in every sense of the term. He attains the Highest End. On attaining the knowledge of Brahman there remains nothing more to know, nothing more to achieve. 'He who knows the Supreme Brahman verily becomes Brahman.'[83] 'Verily, the Imperishable, Supreme Being he attains who knows that Pure, Imperishable One free from darkness, free from adjuncts, free from attributes. He becomes all-knowing, he becomes all.'[84] 'When all the desires lodged in his heart drop, then a mortal becomes immortal and here attains Brahman. When all the knots of the mind

[79] Is. U. 7. [80] Br. U. I: 4.2.

[81] Cf. Aldous Huxley, *The Perennial Philosophy*, New York, Harper, 1945, p. 5. 'It is from the more or less obscure intuition of the oneness that is the ground and principle of all multiplicity that philosophy takes its source. And not alone philosophy, but natural science as well. All science, in Meyerson's phrase, is the reduction of multiplicities to identities. Divining the One within and beyond the many, we find an intrinsic plausibility in any explanation of the diverse in terms of a single principle.'

[82] Cf. Max Planck, *The New Science*, Cleveland, Meridian Books, 1959, p. 150. 'How can we say that a scientific concept, to which we now ascribe an absolute character, may not at some future date show itself to have only a certain relative significance and to point to a farther absolute? To that question only one answer can be given. After all I have said, and in view of the experiences through which scientific progress has passed, we must admit that in no case can we rest assured that what is absolute in science today will remain absolute for all time. . . . The absolute represents an ideal goal which is always ahead of us and which we can never reach. . . . To bring the approach closer and closer to truth is the aim and effort of all science.'

[83] Mu. U. III: 2.9 [84] Pr. U. IV: 10.

are broken here, then a mortal becomes immortal. Only this much is the teaching [of the Vedānta].'[85]

The Unity of the individual self with the Supreme Self, the Omnipresent Being, is the goal of all religious disciplines. The direct knowledge of the Supreme Being, the Soul of all souls, cannot be attained except by union, which means complete surrender of the self-regarding ego. By denying the apparent self one finds the real Self. The relationship between the adorer and the Adorable One, which is the keynote of every theistic religion, ultimately leads to their oneness.

Says Meister Eckhart:

'Any soul that sees God must have forgotten herself and have lost her own self; while she sees and remembers herself she nor sees nor is conscious of God. But when for God's sake she loses herself and abandons all things then in God does she refind herself, for knowing God she is knowing herself and all things (which she rids herself of) in God in perfection.'[86]

'She [the soul] is one with God and not united: where God is there is the soul and where the soul is there is God.'[87]

The realization of the oneness of the individual self with the Supreme Self is the way to Universal Love, which is the one goal of all ethical disciplines. Indeed, it is the ultimate ground of all moral ideals. To quote the Vedāntic texts:

'When a person following the instructions of a teacher directly realizes this effulgent Self, the Lord of all that has been and will be, [as identical with his own self] he no longer finds fault with anyone.'[88]

'He who sees all beings as the very self and the Self in all beings in consequence thereof abhors none.'[89]

'The knowers of the self look with an equal eye on a Brāhmaṇa, endowed with learning and humility, a scavenger, a cow, an elephant, or a dog.'[90]

'With imperfections exhausted, doubts dispelled, senses controlled, engaged in the good of all beings, the seers obtain absolute Freedom.'[91]

As observed by Paul Duessen:

'The gospels postulate quite correctly as the highest law of morality: love your neighbor as yourself. But why should I do so, since by the

[85] Ka. U. II: 3.14, 15.
[86] *Meister Eckhart*, Trans. by C. de B. Evans, Vol. I, London, John M. Watkins, 1956, p. 173.
[87] *Ibid.* Vol. II, p. 89.
[88] Br. U. IV: 4.15.
[89] Is. U. 6.
[90] BG V: 18.
[91] BG V: 25.

order of nature I feel pain and pleasure only in myself, not in my neighbor? The answer is not in the Bible (this venerable book being not yet quite free from Semitic Realism), but it is in the Veda, in the great formula *Tat Tvam Asi*—"Thou art That", which gives in three words all of metaphysics and morals. You shall love your neighbour as yourself because you are your neighbour, and mere illusion makes you believe that your neighbour is something different from yourself.'[92]

So says Vidyāraṇya: 'The knowledge of the Self leads to the identification of oneself with others as closely as one identifies oneself with one's body.'[93]

12. *Being the divine revelation of indisputable truths, the Vedas are intrinsically valid. They do not contradict perception or inference*

The two sources of knowledge, the Vedic and the empirical (perception, inference, etc.)—refer to two distinct orders of facts, suprasensible and sensible. They are authoritative in their respective spheres. The Vedas do not contradict other means of knowledge, nor can be contradicted by them. Just as the fundamental Reality is out of the scope of the empirical sciences, so the order of phenomena is out of the scope of the Vedas. Most great thinkers acknowledge that neither sense-perception nor any reasoning based on it can determine the nature of the fundamental reality. Metaphysical speculation is more or less conjecture or guess-work. It makes things possible, but not actual. While the Śruti refers to the facts of common experience in order to communicate suprasensuous knowledge, it does not intend to impart instruction on them or to pass verdict on them. In interpreting the revealed texts the exact relation between revelation and reason has to be borne in mind.

The truths declared by the Śruti have to be known by reasoning on the texts and not by arguments independent of them. The function of reason is not to judge the truth of the Vedic statements, but to determine their true import, free from inconsistencies and in conformity with established facts. They are not to be accepted dogmatically, but through intelligent interpretation compatible with perceptual and inferential knowledge. There are also in the Vedas primary and subsidiary truths and statements with literal and implied meanings. A valid and independent source of knowledge as it is, the Śruti awaits rational analysis to yield its true import. To quote Gauḍapāda: '[Of the two contrary views mentioned in the Śruti] that which is ascertained by the Śruti and corroborated by reason is the import, and not the other.'[94]

[92] *The Philosophy of the Vedānta*, Madras, Theosophical Publishing House
[93] PD VI: 285. [94] MK III: 23; see also BS II: 1.11, S. com.

Thus, the acceptance of scriptural authority in Advaita Vedānta is by no means denial of reason. Truth is not irrational. Reason is inherent in revelation. So the alliance of revelation and reason does not mean a compromise. Authority and reason can be harmonious. One can reasonably trust the trustworthy. There is no inherent conflict between faith and reason. Truly speaking, the one rests on the other. Reason is the key that unlocks the scriptural truths and paves the way to their intuitive perception. According to Nondualistic philosophers, revelation, reason, and realization form the triple means to the full knowledge of Brahman. Thus, revelation is supported by reason and verified by the seers' immediate apprehension or mystical awareness. We shall elaborate on these points in the succeeding chapters. Throughout the ages the Vedic revelations have been confirmed by the intuitive perceptions of the illumined souls.

13. *From rational theology Medieval Scholasticism turned into dogmatic theology.*

The alliance of revelation and reason was the keynote of Scholasticism in medieval Europe. The Schoolmen succeeded in achieving this, more or less. But their ideas of revelation and reason varied. So the relation between the two was conceived by them diversely. Johannes Scotus Erigena, the founder (about the middle of the ninth century), set reason above faith. He recognized that truth cannot be unreasonable; revelation must be the revelation of truth; so it cannot contradict reason. In his view speculative reason could independently evolve a system of the universe which would coincide with the teaching of the scripture. Indeed, he was more of a Neoplatonist than a Scholastic doctor. But the Schoolmen, as a rule, followed the method of allying logic with faith, in other words, reason with authority. Scholasticism declined, not that the very principle was wrong, but because its application was inappropriate. The Church dogmas passed for revelation and refused to be put in the rational garb, for which they were not intrinsically fit. This was evident 'from the withdrawal of doctrine after doctrine from the possibility of rational proof and their relegation to the sphere of faith'. External causes also contributed to the decline of Scholasticism.

14. *The Vedas have no author. They are without beginning and without end. They are not produced, but revealed, by Īśvara in the beginning of each new cycle.*

The Vedic testimony is infallible, inasmuch as its validity is intrinsic. The truths it embodies are eternal and universal and invariably conformable to reason. Just as Īśvara, the Supreme Lord, and the universe (comprising the animate and the inanimate) are without beginning, so are the Vedas. But all the three belong to the relative order. None but Nondual Brahman has absolute reality. In the beginning of creation Īśvara manifests the universe from its causal state in undifferentiated prakṛti, His creative power. Likewise are the Vedas manifested from their potential state in His power of knowledge. Īśvara does not produce the Vedas. The Vedas of the previous cycle are revealed in each new cycle. Īśvara manifests the already existing Vedas to the cosmic soul (Brahmā) as the process of creation starts. He is the first teacher of the Vedas, but not their originator. Throughout the ages the Vedas have been transmitted orally through a succession of teachers and pupils.

According to the orthodox view, the Vedic words embodying the knowledge of God are inseparable from it. They endure as potencies with the universals in God's power of knowledge or omniscience during the period of the dissolution of the cosmos. We have noted above (ch. VIII, sec. 5), that a word (cow, for instance) represents the universal (cow-ness) and is inseparable from it. The Word of words is the syllable 'Om', the verbal symbol of the Divine Idea of creation, the Idea of ideas. This is the seed of the universe as well as of the Vedas.

Since the Vedas have no author and are without beginning, they are called apauruṣeya, lit., unconnected with a person. As stated in *Vedānta-paribhāṣā*:

'In the beginning of cosmic projection, the Lord produced the Vedas having a sequence of words similar to that which had already existed in the Vedas in the previous cosmic projection, and not the Vedas of a different type. Hence the Vedas, not being the object of utterance that is independent of any utterance of the same kind, are not connected with a person [apauruṣeya]. The utterance of the *Mahābhārata*, etc., however, is not at all dependent on any utterance of the same kind. Hence they are connected with a person [pauruṣeya]. Thus two kinds of scriptural testimony have been determined, *viz.*, that which is connected with a person, and that which is not.'[95]

Even the *Bhagavad-gītā* (the Song of God) delivered by Śrī Kṛṣṇa, God incarnate in human form, is not Divine revelation in the sense in which the Vedas are. Being composed by a human being (Veda-Vyāsa) it is pauruṣeya (lit. connected with a person), that is, has an author; while the Vedas having no author, are apauruṣeya (lit., unconnected with a person). So the *Bhagavad-gītā*, like all other scriptures composed by human beings, is included in the Smṛti.

According to Nyāya school, the Vedas are the means of valid

[95] V P IV.

knowledge, because they are produced by the Supreme Lord, who is eternal and omniscient. According to the Mīmāṁsakas, who deal with sacrificial rites, the Vedas are the means of valid knowledge, because they are eternal, and as such free from all human defects. According to Nondualistic Vedānta, the Vedas issue from the Supreme Being spontaneously in the beginning of creation. 'They [the Vedic texts] are like the breath of this [the Supreme Being]', says the Upaniṣad. They are coeval with time. As explained by Śaṅkara:

'It is the eternally composed and already existent Vedas that are manifested like a man's breath without any thought or effort on his part. Hence they are an authority as regards their meaning independently of any other means of knowledge. Therefore, those who aspire after their well-being must accept the verdict of the Vedas on knowledge or on rites, as it is. . . . Since the Vedas issue without effort like a man's breath, they are an authority; they are not like other books.'[96]

Says Swāmī Vivekānanda:

'The Vedas do not owe their authority to anybody, they are themselves the authority, being eternal—the knowledge of God. They were never written, never created, they have existed throughout time; just as creation is infinite and eternal, without beginning and without end, so is the knowledge of God, without beginning and without end. And this knowledge is what is meant by the Vedas (from *vid*, to know).'[97]

'This knowledge comes out at the beginning of a cycle and manifests itself; and when the cycle ends, it goes down into minute form. When the cycle is projected again, that knowledge is projected again with it.'[98]

'The whole body of suprasensuous truths, having no beginning or end, and called by the name of the Vedas, is ever-existent.'[99]

It is worthy of note that the Vedic teachings relating to the rites and ceremonials and certain duties are not of universal application. It is the teachings regarding the fundamental truths and principles that hold good at all times and in all climes. These are conveyed by the knowledge-portions of the Vedas, well-known as the Upaniṣads. The crown of the Vedas is the Upaniṣads, also called Vedānta, the end or the culmination of the Vedas.

96 Br. U. II: 4.10, com.
97 CW III, p. 119.
98 CW V, p. 325.
99 CW VI, p. 154.

CHAPTER X

SENSE-PERCEPTION, REASON, AND THE VEDIC TESTIMONY

1. *There is no contradiction betwen the Śruti and sense-perception. The one deals with the suprasensible, the other with the sensible. They are valid in their respective spheres*

The distinctiveness of the Vedas as a means of knowledge lies in the fact that through them we can know what cannot be known by any other means.[1] The transcendental oneness of Being is established by the Śruti alone. Neither perception nor inference can convey this knowledge. In declaring the absolute reality of Nondual Brahman the Śruti does not repudiate the apparent manifold. It accepts the empirical validity of perception, but denies its ultimateness. There is no contradiction in this. 'Empirical experiences are valid until the identity of the self with Brahman is realized, as are dream-experiences until awakening', says Śaṅkara.[2] As long as the jīva (the individual) is under the spell of ajñāna he invariably experiences multiplicity, but as soon as he is free from ajñāna he realizes Nondual Brahman, where there is no distinction of any kind. Dream-experience is real until one wakes up. Scriptural knowledge does not controvert empirical experience, but relegates it to the state of ajñāna. The one dwells on the fundamental reality, the other on the world of appearance. Either is valid in its own sphere. Sureśvara aptly remarks: 'Each of the pramāṇas has the inherent capacity to convey knowledge. Their intrinsic validity cannot be maintained in case one is regarded as complementary to another.'[3]

Sense-perception is limited to the world of phenomena. It does not communicate what is beyond. Vedānta does not question the validity of perceptual knowledge so far as the world of experience is concerned but denies its authoritativeness in the suprasensuous realm. Empirical facts can be known by sense-perception and by all other means of knowledge that are based on it. As regards transcendental truths the Śruti is the sole valid source of knowledge. Yet to convey this knowledge it refers to the world of experience. Śaṅkara rightly observes:

[1] *Vide* Sāyaṇa's com. on the Ṛg.-Veda, Intro. (*Ṛg-Veda-bhāṣya-bhūmikā*).
[2] BS II: 1.14, com. [3] NS III: 86.

'Things in the world are known to possess certain fixed characteristics such as grossness or fineness. By citing them as examples the scriptures seek to tell us about some other thing which does not contradict them. They would not cite an example from life if they wanted to convey an idea of something contradictory to it. Even if they did, it would be to no purpose, for the example would be different from the thing to be explained. You cannot prove that fire is cold, or that the sun does not give heat, even by citing a hundred examples, for the facts would already be known to be otherwise through another source of knowledge. And one source of knowledge does not contradict another, for it only tells us about those things that cannot be known by any other means. Nor can the scriptures speak about an unknown thing without having the recourse to conventional words and their meanings.'[4]

The Śruti is the authoritative source of knowledge in suprasensuous matters, but not in matters within the range of perception. The scriptural text cannot controvert facts of experience. Any statement that is obviously contradictory to them should not be taken literally. It must have an implied or secondary meaning. So says Śaṅkara, 'Even though a hundred Śruti texts may declare that fire is cold or that it is dark, yet they cannot have any authority in the matter. Should there be any such statement that fire is cold or that it is dark, then it has to be assumed that a meaning different from the apparent one is intended by the Śruti, because its authority cannot be otherwise maintained. But no meaning of the Śruti should be contradictory to itself or to any other valid source of knowledge.'[5]

Vedānta philosophy does not accept the authority of the Śruti against the evidence of perception. On the contrary, it utilizes perceptual knowledge and the reasoning based on it to explain the supramental truths declared by the Śruti. The purpose of the Śruti is to communicate what cannot be known by other means of valid knowledge and not to contradict their findings. It is the sole authority on the suprasensuous truths, which are beyond the province of other means of knowledge.

As stated by Madhusūdana Sarasvatī in his *Advaita-siddhi*,

'Only the empirical validity of perception and other allied means of knowledge is a proven fact; this is not controverted by the scriptures (āgama). What is controverted is its ultimateness, which is by no means a proven fact. Therefore there is no conflict between perception and the scriptures (āgama).'[6]

4 Br. U. II: 1.20, com.
5 BG XVIII: 67, com.
6 Chap. I, sec. 18, Bombay, Nirnaya-sagar Press, 1937, pp. 373–4.

Most philosophers and scientists recognize the inherent incapability of perception to probe into the fundamental reality. Its province is the world of appearance.[7] It is with regard to the ultimate Reality that the Śruti declares: 'There is no diversity whatsoever in this [Brahman].'[8] So it does not contradict sense-knowledge. When one person says 'The sun moves', and another with his astronomical knowledge says 'The sun does not move', the two statements do not contradict each other, but represent two different view-points regarding the sun.

It is a normal human experience that the self is variable; it suffers from hunger and thirst; it grows and decays; it becomes happy and unhappy, weak and strong, active and dull, righteous and unrighteous, conscious and unconscious; it is born and it dies. But the Śruti declares that the self is 'birthless, changeless, eternal';[9] that it is 'sinless, decayless, deathless, sorrowless, free from hunger and thirst';[10] that it is 'beyond righteousness and unrighteousness';[11] that it is 'luminous and pure'.[12] Evidently, the Śruti contradicts the common human knowledge regarding the self. Yet there is no conflict between the two; because they refer to different aspects of the self; the apparent and the real.[13] The referent of common experience is the self conjoined with the limiting adjuncts of the body, the senses, and the mind; whereas the Upaniṣads point to the innermost self differentiated from all the adjuncts. Though the same term 'aham' or 'I' is used with reference to the self by a human individual and by the Śruti as well,[14] yet in the one case it signifies the self identified with the adjuncts; while in the other case it implies the transcendental self dissociated from all the limiting adjuncts.

The common knowledge of the self, valid though it be empirically, is not fundamentally true. It endures as long as the jīva (the individual) continues to be in the migratory state under the spell of ajñāna. But when he is awakened to the real nature of the self as declared by the Śruti, then all contrary notions regarding this from whatever source prove to be fallacious. It is a fact of common experience that the sun moves round the earth, or that the sky is like a blue canopy, yet either proves to be a myth when the truth is known to be otherwise. The central truth regarding the self is imparted by the mahāvākya, the great saying (e.g., 'I am Brahman', 'This Ātman is Brahman', 'Thou art That', 'Consciousness is Brahman').[15] The true import of the dictum, as ascertained by the six

[7] Cf. Sir James Jeans, *Physics and Philosophy*, Cambridge University Press, 1942, p. 15. 'Our studies can never put us into contact with reality; we can never penetrate beyond the impressions that reality implants in our minds.'

[8] Br. U. IV: 4.19. [9] Ka. U. I: 2.18. [10] Ch. U. VIII: 7.1.

[11] Ka. U. I: 2.14. [12] Mu. U. III: 1.5. [13] *Vide* NS III: 44, 45

[14] e.g., 'I am Brahman'. [15] See Ch. IX, sec. 4.

tests,[16] is the identity of the jīva and Brahman. When this is known all dualistic conceptions of the self are disproved. 'The authority of the Śruti being inviolable, a Vedic passage must be taken exactly in the sense that it is tested to bear, and not according to the ingenuity of the human mind', observes Śaṅkara.[17]

2. *Nor is there any contradiction between the Śruti and reason. The suprasensuous is suprarational, but not irrational*

It is true that the Śruti is the only valid source of knowledge regarding the transcendental truths, that neither Brahman (Nirguṇa or Saguṇa) nor dharma (moral ideal) can be established by inference or by any other process of reasoning based on empirical experience.[18] But though reason cannot determine transcendental truths, independently of the Śruti, yet it serves as the key to unlock that treasury. It is the seeker's indispensable guide for the scriptural knowledge. Without the exercise of reason the seeker cannot ascertain the import of the sacred texts simply by hearing or reading them. In the first place, he has to know beyond doubts and misconceptions what the Śruti declares and, secondly, he has to be convinced of the declared truths. Reasoning is indispensable to both these ends. It is also necessary to refute contrary views and strengthen the seeker's own position.

Hearing of the truth from the Śruti, reflection on it, and constant meditation on the same have been prescribed as the threefold means of Self-realization.[19] But 'hearing' does not mean tacitly assenting to what is heard or read. It implies a thorough investigation into the texts in order to find their import. To understand the Śruti it is not enough to know the literal meaning of its statements; one has to grasp their drift, their inner significance.[20] As defined by Sadānanda, 'Hearing (śravaṇa) is the ascertainment through the six characteristic marks[21] of the purport of the entire Vedānta as the affirmation of

[16] These are (1) the correspondence of the introduction and the conclusion, (2) frequent reference to the theme, (3) its originality, (4) fruitfulness, (5) commendableness, and (6) reasonableness. See Ch. IX, sec. 2.

[17] Br. U. III: 3.1, com.

[18] Besides syllogistic inference (anumāna) there is hypothetical reasoning called 'tarka', assumption to reach a conclusion. While anumāna leads to certain knowledge (so far as the empirical facts are concerned), the result of tarka is conjectural knowledge. So tarka is not recognized in Indian logic as a pramāṇa, but as its aid. Tarka has been used by the Advaita philosophers in different forms for such purposes as—to ascertain the true import of the Śruti, to remove the seekers' mistrust and misconceptions with regard to its teachings by refuting contrary views, and to convince them of the true nature of the self as declared by it.

[19] *Vide* Br. U. II: 4.5; IV: 5.6.

[20] Cf. 'For the letter killeth, but the spirit giveth life', says St Paul, 2 Corinthians, 3: 6.

[21] See footnote 16.

Nondual Brahman.'[22] That the intention of the Śruti cannot be determined without the guidance of reason is thus indicated by *Vedānta-paribhāṣā*: 'The intention is determined with regard to the Vedas only by reasoning rectified by the principles of interpretation, while with regard to the secular sentences, by means of the context, etc., such as the reliability of the source. Of these, secular sentences are of the nature of restatements, since their meanings are primarily apprehended through other means of knowledge; but with regard to the Vedas, since the meanings of the Vedic sentences are known at first hand, they are not of the nature of restatements.'[23]

Through 'hearing' the seeker removes from his mind all doubts and misconceptions as regards the purport of the sacred texts. For, by the application of the above-mentioned six tests he finds answers to such questions as 'Does Vedānta teach the difference or the non-difference of the jīva and Brahman?' 'Is the duality or the non-duality of reality the purport of Vedānta?' Next to hearing (śravaṇa) is reflection (manana). When the import of the texts is known, then the seeker has to reflect on it through reasoning in order to be assured of its truth. When it is ascertained that the nonduality of Brahman is the purport of Vedānta, then the seeker's next step is to comprehend through appropriate argument the sole reality of Brahman. The purpose of hearing (śravaṇa) is to ascertain beyond doubt what Vedānta teaches. The purpose of reflection (manana) is to grasp the truth of this teaching by argumentation and constant contemplation on it.[24]

Faith, according to Vedānta, must be grounded on reason. It is not credulous acceptance of the teachings of the Vedas or the seers, authoritative as they are. As stated by Śaṅkara, 'A firm conviction through discerning intellect of the truth of the teachings of the scriptures and of the spiritual guide is called by the sages "faith (śraddhā)", which leads to the realization of Reality.'[25] It comes through śravaṇa (hearing) and manana (reflection). Through 'faith' the seeker gains the power to meditate on the Self as Brahman. It is the intense practice of meditation that is the direct means to Self-realization in nirvikalpa samādhi, the superconscious state, in which the tripartite distinction of the subject, the object, and the process of knowing that characterizes all relative knowledge vanishes and Nondual Absolute Consciousness shines. This is the experience of Supreme Bliss of Brahman in this very life.

Acceptance of authority does not mean the rejection of reason. In most secular matters we depend on authority. Why not in religion? Man's knowledge is limited. He cannot know everything, nor can he know equally well all that he knows. So he has to depend on especially

[22] VS, sec. 30; AV 29.
[23] VP V, Verbal Testimony, Intention.
[24] *Vide* VS, sec. 30 and AV 43
[25] VC 25.

qualified, trustworthy persons more or less. Just as there are specialists in secular subjects so are there specialists in religion. In religion there is a greater need for dependence on authority, because it deals with suprasensuous truths, which are beyond perception and inference.

As we have noted above, the truths unveiled by the Śruti, though beyond the limit of reason, are not contrary to it. Being valid, they are in agreement with reason, and admit of rational interpretation. The nature of Ātman or Brahman declared by the Śruti cannot be determined by abstract reasoning, but can be explained in terms of reason. Though subordinate to the Śruti, reason plays a very important part in the Vedāntic systems. It is admitted on all hands that there cannot be any authoritative teaching contrary to reason. As observed by Dr Mahadevan: 'It is true that Scripture is appealed to as the ultimate authority in matters spiritual by the teachers of Vedānta. But the appeal itself is for a reason; and reason comes in as an aid at every stage in the process of selection and interpretation of scriptural passages.'[26]

There is no place for illogical authority in the Vedāntic thought and culture. Even in determining ethical conduct (dharma) one has not to follow the scriptural instructions blindly, but has to grasp their full significance and their adaptability to varying conditions of life. So says Manu, a highly venerated authority on Hindu ethics, 'He who investigates into the Śruti and the Smṛti according to the canons of reason that do not defy the Vedic authority knows dharma ethical conduct], and not he who proceeds otherwise'.[27]

Any Vedic teaching that is obviously inconsistent or contrary to reason is not to be taken in the literal sense. It must have a secondary meaning in conformity with reason. It is true that there are dualistic or pluralistic passages in the Śruti, but their purpose is not to establish any kind of distinction or difference, but to lead the mind of the seeker gradually to the comprehension of Nondual Reality. So says Gauḍapāda, 'The delineation of creation [in the Śruti] by the examples of earth, iron, sparks, etc., or otherwise, is like a stepping-stone [to the comprehension of Non-duality]. No difference of any kind whatsoever really exists. There are three grades of men according to inferior, mediocre, and superior understanding. Out of compassion for them the spiritual course [comprising work, worship, and meditation] has been taught.'[28]

3. *The allegiance to the Śruti has not militated against philosophic thought in India*

It is through reasoning that one has to determine the meaning of the Śruti. There are apparently contradictory views in the Upaniṣads.

[26] T. M. P. Mahadevan, *Gauḍapāda, A Study in Early Advaita*, p. 77.
[27] MS XII: 106.
[28] MK III: 15, 16.

But the one that is corroborated by reason is to be accepted. Says Gauḍapāda, 'Whether the creation is actual or apparent [modification of the Cause], both [processes] are described by the Śruti. That which is supported by the scripture and confirmed by reason is true and not the other.'[29] While acknowledging the authority of the Śruti, the Vedāntic teachers have at the same time put it to the test of reason. They have rationally explained the Vedic teachings. Revealed texts, authoritative as they are, do not supplant reason. Revelation allied with reason determine the truth. According to Śaṅkara, scripture and reasoning together reach a decisive conclusion; by itself reasoning is useless, while by themselves mere scriptural statements cannot clear doubts and produce conviction. A thing that is ascertained by the scriptures and reasoning deserves credence on account of its proving universally true. Indeed, scriptural revelation awaits rational interpretation for universal acceptance.

The inherent incapacity of reason to communicate transcendental truths is acknowledged by many eminent philosophers of the East and the West. Reason recognizes its own inadequacy, so to speak. The subordination of reason to the revealed texts, which are corroborated by the direct experience of the seers, is by no means unreasonable. Speculative knowledge is indecisive; it requires confirmation by intuitive perception based on scriptural knowledge. Intuition, without the orientation of scriptural revelation can hardly attain the desired end. But the revealed texts do not yield their true meanings without the aid of reason. Though subsidiary to scriptural revelation reason is indispensable to the realization of Truth. According to Vedānta, revelation (Śruti), reason (yukti), and realization (anubhūti) must harmonize to carry full conviction to the seeker. By this triple approach he overcomes ajñāna completely and attains the Nondual Self beyond all trace of the not-self. So says Śaṅkara, 'Realizing thyself as the Self of all by means of the Śruti, reasoning, and thy own experience, do away with what is superimposed on thee even when the least shade of it appears'.[30]

The welding of revelation and reason is the special characteristic of the Vedic systems of philosophy, of which six are well-known: Sāṁkhya of Kapila, Yōga of Patañjali, (Pūrva) Mīmāṁsā of Jaimini, Vedānta of Bādarāyaṇa Vyāsa, Vaiśeṣika of Kaṇāda, and Nyāya of Gautama.[31] In accepting the Vedic authority these philosophers have

[29] MK III: 23. [30] VC 281.

[31] Mādhavācārya in his *Sarvadarśana-saṁgraha* has outlined sixteen different systems of Indian philosophy, of which three—Cārvāka, Bauddha, and Jaina—are Non-Vedic, and the rest are Vedic. He lived in the fourteenth century A.D., and was well known as Vidyāraṇya in his monastic life. Of his numerous treatises we may mention particularly, *Pañcadaśī*, *Vivaraṇa-prameya-saṁgraha*, and *Jīvanmukti-viveka*. The traditional identity of Mādhavācārya and Vidyāraṇya is disputed by some modern Indian scholars.

not decried reason, but have made legitimate use of it. This has saved the Vedic systems from turning into dogmatic theology. Indeed, their allegiance to the Vedas has not stunted their speculative thought. Two of them, Sāṁkhya and Mīmāṁsā do not even recognize Īśvara (the Supreme Lord) in the traditional sense, still they are regarded as āstika (theistic), because they accept the authority of the Vedas, the keynote of which is that man's real self is pure, free, and immortal. Two contemporary philosophers, Eastern and Western, aptly remark:

'India has produced a great variety of philosophical doctrines and systems. This has been true despite universal reverence for and acceptance of the authority of the ancient seers as the true discoverers of wisdom. The variety of the systems, even in their basic conceptions, looked at in the light of the prevalent acceptance of authority, reveals the fact that this reverence has not made Indian philosophy a dogmatic religious creed, as is often alleged, but rather a single tone or trend of thought on basic issues. How completely free from traditional bias the systems are is seen, for example, by the fact that the original Sāṁkhya says nothing about the possible existence of God, although it is emphatic in its doctrine of the theoretical undemonstrability of his existence; the Vaiśeṣika and the Yōga, especially the latter, admit the existence of God, but do not consider him to be the creator of the universe; the Mīmāṁsā speaks of God but denies his importance and efficacy in the moral ordering of the world.'[32]

Although all the six systems mentioned above profess their allegiance to the Śruti, they do not depend on its authority in the same sense. They argue freely and give different interpretations of its validity. According to Vedānta, Sāṁkhya, and Prabhākara school of Mīmāṁsā, the validity of the Śruti is intrinsic, while according to Nyāya and the Kumārila school of Mīmāṁsā it is extrinsic. We have already dwelt on the extrinsic and the intrinsic validity of knowledge and of the means of knowledge. (See ch. IV, sec. 2.) All the Vedic systems except Vedānta and Mīmāṁsā are engaged mainly in the speculation of the categories of existence. In their view fundamental realities can be determined by inference.[33] They have sought the Vedic authority in corroboration of their conclusions. So they are characterized as 'primarily dependent on argument (yukti-pradhāna)'.

[32] *A Source Book in Indian Philosophy*, Ed. by Sarvepalli Radhakrishnan and Charles A. Moore, General Introduction, p. xxv.

[33] *Vide* BS I: 1.5, S. com

But Vedānta and Mīmāṁsā are devoted specially to the rational exposition of the Vedic texts. To investigate into their true import is the main task of these two systems. They base their arguments on the Vedas, which according to them are the perennial source of suprasensuous knowledge. So they are characterized as 'primarily dependent on the Śruti (Śruti-pradhāna)'. But there is a fundamental difference between the two. While Mīmāṁsā holds particularly to the karma-kāṇḍa (work-section), Vedānta holds particularly to the jñāna-kāṇḍa (knowledge-section) of the Vedas. The two systems are also called 'Pūrva Mīmāṁsā (prior investigation)' and 'Uttara Mīmāṁsā (posterior investigation)' respectively. The main theme of the one is karma, and of the other is Brahman.

The system of Vedānta, which comprises six main schools, has developed out of an attempt to systematize the teachings of the Upaniṣads.[34] The extant remarkable attempt made in this direction is Bādarāyaṇa's *Brahma-sūtras* (aphorisms on Brahman).[35] It is an enquiry into the nature of the ultimate Reality as a means to Liberation. The existing Vedānta systems—monistic and monotheistic—are primarily different interpretations of the *Brahma-sūtras*, in the course of which the metaphysical problems are dealt with. Besides the monistic or the Nondualistic system, the greatest exponent of which is Śaṅkara, there are five principal monotheistic systems of Vedānta belonging to the schools of Vaiṣṇavism. These are (1) Viśiṣṭādvaita of Rāmānuja, (2) Dvaitādvaita of Nimbārka, (3) Śuddhādvaita of Vallabha, (4) Dvaita of Madhva, (5) Acintya-bhedābheda of Baladeva, a follower of Śrī Caitanya. In expounding their views the Nondualistic philosophers refer more often to the Śruti than to the Smṛti, while the monotheistic or the Vaiṣṇava philosophers lean more on the Smṛti, although both schools acknowledge the supremacy of the Śruti. Despite many points of agreement there are sharp differences of views among them. This testifies to the wide scope of their metaphysical reflection and subtle reasoning.

[34] As observed by Professor F. Max Muller, 'The most extraordinary feature of this Vedānta philosophy consists in its being an independent system of philosophy, yet entirely dependent on the Upaniṣads, a part of the Veda, nay, chiefly occupied with proving that all its doctrines, to the very minutest points, are derived from the revealed doctrines of the Upaniṣads, if only properly understood, that they are in perfect harmony with revelation, and that there are no contradictions whatever between the various Upaniṣads themselves'. (*Three Lectures on Vedānta Philosophy*, p. 23, delivered at the Royal Institution, in March, 1894; published in London in 1894; reprinted by Susil Gupta Calcutta, 1950.)

[35] Also called '*Vedānta-sūtras*', '*Vedānta-darśana*', '*Śārīraka-Mīmāṁsā*', '*Śārīraka-sūtras*'. In this treatise there are references to earlier attempts made by Āśmarathya, Kāśakṛtsna, Kārṣṇājini, Ōuḍulōmi, Ātreya, Bādari, and so on. *Vide* BS I: 2.29; I: 2.30; I: 4.21, 22; III: 1.9; III: 1.11; III: 4.44, 45. Their works are not available now.

As observed by Dr Sircar in his comparative study of the six schools of Vedānta:

'Vedāntic teachers have thought in concepts similar to those of Western thinkers, have shown the highest logical acumen and have not been lacking in philosophic boldness in pressing, as they do, their conclusions to a logical end. Though their works may sometimes be thought deficient in the scientific analogies, employed in the philosophy of the day, yet their acuteness in logic, their depth of metaphysical reflection and their keenness of intuitive penetration, and, above all, their deep conviction in, and whole-hearted call to the life of transcendent bliss do not leave the least trace of doubt that they have established a sufficient claim to be heard.'[36]

4. *Why reason independently of the Śruti cannot determine the nature of God. Neither syllogistic inference nor analogical argument is capable. The views of Sāṁkhya, Nyāya, and Vedānta*

In Vedānta philosophy reasoning is based on the Śruti texts (Śrutyanugṛhīta). Its purpose is to ascertain their import without contradicting them. It is by means of the Upaniṣads and by means of reasoning in accord with them (Vedāntānuguṇa) that self-intelligent Brahman is established as the efficient and material Cause of the universe. It has been cogently explained why reason by itself cannot lead to the knowledge of the First Cause. The main type of the reasoning process is syllogistic inference. It is based, as we have explained (ch. VI), on the previous experience of the invariable relation (vyāpti) between the object perceived (hetu) and the object inferred (sādhya). From the perception of smoke on a hill one can infer the presence of fire there, because it has been previously observed that smoke is invariably associated with fire. While the universe is an object of perception, God, the Omnipotent and Omniscient Being, is not. So a constant relation between the two cannot be observed. To quote Śaṅkara: 'Since Brahman is not an object of sense-knowledge, its relation with the world of effects cannot be perceived.'[37] In the absence of the knowledge of an invariable concomitance (vyāpti), how can one infer from the perception of the universe the existence of an All-knowing, All-powerful Being as its cause?

As we have noted (ch. VI, sec. 7), Gautama, the father of the Nyāya system (the Indian school of logic), has mentioned three kinds of inference:[38]

[36] Dr Mahendranath Sircar, *Comparative Studies in Vedāntism*, Preface, Humphrey Milford, Calcutta, Oxford University Press, 1927.

[37] BS I: 1.2, com.

[38] *Nyāya-sūtras* I: 1.5.

(1) Inference *a priori* (pūrvavat), that is, of the effect from the perceived cause, such as the inference of imminent rain from seeing masses of lowering clouds.
(2) Inference *a posteriori* (śeṣavat), that is, of the cause from the perceived effect, such as the inference of a preceding rainfall from seeing a swollen rushing creek.
(3) Inference from analogy. Neither the cause nor the effect is its ground, but something perceived as similar (sāmānyatōdṛṣṭam).

When two characteristics of a certain type of object are found to be invariably associated, then by perceiving one of the characteristics in a similar object a person can infer the presence of the other characteristic also. To illustrate: When a person knows from observation that an animal with horns has cleft hoofs, then by seeing a strange animal with horns he can infer that this, too, has cleft hoofs. By this third kind of inference which does not depend on the previous experience of an invariable relation between what is perceived (hetu) and what is inferred (sādhya), Nyāya school has tried to establish the existence of the creator of the universe. It is a fact of common experience that every created object, e.g., a jar, a cloth, a chair, has a living being as its agent, as an efficient cause, that knows all about it. The world as a whole is also perceived as a created thing. From this one can conclude that like any other created object, it must have a corresponding efficient cause. Thus, by this type of inference the Nyāya school determines the existence of the Omniscient and Omnipotent Creator of the world. They also quote the Vedic texts as proof of the existence of God.[39]

According to the Sāṁkhya school, the existence of certain suprasensuous principles, e.g., puruṣa (the intelligent self), prakṛti (the ultimate, unintelligent cause of all objects physical and psychical), and the like, is ascertainable by the inference from analogy (sāmānyatōdṛṣṭam) and also by the inference from the effect (śeṣavat); other suprasensibles which cannot be determined even by these means are established by the testimony of the trustworthy persons and the scriptures.[40]

Evidently, the inference from analogy (sāmānyatōdṛṣṭam) narrows the scope of the Vedic testimony. If any knowledge of the suprasensible can be attained by such means, then the Śruti cannot be regarded as its only source. But Advaita Vedānta does not recognize this type of inference. It views this method of reasoning as a case of argument (tarka), and not as a case of inference (anumāna). Inference has no scope in the realm of the suprasensuous. Inferential knowledge, mediate as it is, bears the mark of certitude, while the

[39] *Vide* BP, Invocation, *Siddhānta-muktāvalī*.
[40] *Vide* SK 6 and Vācaspati's com. *Tattvakaumudī*.

conclusion reached by argument (tarka) is only a probability. By analogical argument one cannot attain certain knowledge. It can make God's existence probable, and not decisive. The same type of reasoning by which the Naiyāyikas conclude the existence of one Omniscient and Omnipotent Creator of the world can lead others to the conclusion that the world has more than one creator. It is a matter of common knowledge that many a thing, small as well as great, is made by a number of persons working in coordination. Therefore, one can as well hold that this vast, variegated universe is the result of the cooperation of more than one god. There are, of course, replies and counter-replies on this issue.

Indeed, argument can neither prove nor disprove the existence of God. It is indecisive so far as the knowledge of the suprasensuous is concerned. It is particularly so with regard to the knowledge of the ultimate Reality. 'This knowledge cannot be gained by argument', says the Upaniṣad.[41] The conclusive knowledge of Brahman can be attained only from the Śruti with the aid of reason. True knowledge must be unvaried. Only such knowledge can lead to Liberation. This is why reasoning based on the Śruti has been recommended as a means to the realization of the Self.[42] The truth about the Self cannot be known by any other means.

5. *The empirical and the transcendental self. The Śruti as a means to the knowledge of the Self*

Neither perception nor inference can determine the true nature of the self, which has a dual aspect—the changeful and the changeless, the empirical and the transcendental. The one is apparent, the other is real. It is the reflected empirical self identified with the body and the mind and characterized as the doer and experiencer that is perceived by the senses as an individual, but not the real transcendental self, the unchanging witness of the ever-changing body and the mind. Indeed, the sense-organs are not meant for Self-knowledge. They are created with outgoing tendencies; so a person perceives through them only external objects and not the Self within.[43] 'The eye does not go thither, nor speech, nor the mind.''[44] Being the knower *per se*, the inmost Self cannot be an object of knowledge. So the Śruti points to It as the immutable witness (sākṣī, draṣṭā) of the physical and the psychical events: 'You cannot see that which is the witness of vision; you cannot hear that which is the hearer of hearing; you cannot think that which is the thinker of thought; you cannot know that which is the knower of knowledge. This is your Self that is within all; everything else but that is perishable.'[45]

[41] Ka. U. I: 2.9. [42] *Vide* BS II: 1.6, 11, S. com.; Br. U. II: 4.5; IV: 5.6.
[43] *Vide* Ka. U. II: 1.1. [44] Ken. U. I: 3. [45] Br. U. III: 4.2.

Such means of knowledge, as perception and the rest based on it, deal only with the knowables and not with the Self, the knower *per se*.[46] The Knower is contrary to all that is known including the body and the mind. While the known are many, limited, changeful, and non-conscious, the knower is one, unlimited, changeless, and self-aware. So says Sureśvara: 'The inmost Self, which is perpetual awareness, which is not dependent on any other proof [being self-evident], which is without attributes, such as sound, form, etc., as to whose existence there is no room for doubt, which is supreme blessedness, which is immeasurable, which is the innermost being, cannot be determined by such means of knowledge as perception and the rest engendered by despicable desire.'[47]

Man's inmost Self is self-manifest. Being of the nature of Pure Consciousness, it shines of itself, so to speak. Therefore, each and every individual is spontaneously aware of his own existence. No process of knowledge is involved in his self-awareness. It is immediate and direct presentation (sākṣāt aparōkṣāt). Self-awareness is the central fact from which all thoughts, all cognitions, and all actions of an individual proceed. Before he thinks, or sees, or acts he knows that he is. It is not inferential knowledge. The luminous self is prior to all mental operations. One does not deduce one's existence from them. It is self-evident, being of the nature of consciousness. The point is, 'I am, therefore I think', and not 'I think, therefore I am', as Descartes said. But the great French philosopher did not mean the dictum *cogito, ergo sum* as an inference, but as an axiomatic truth, which is perceived immediately prior to cogitation.[48]

None needs proof of his own existence. A man is sure of his existence before he is sure of anything else. He invariably accepts this as the established fact, and makes it the nucleus of all other facts. The self is self-revealing. It is authority by itself. Each and every form of existence presupposes the conscious self. The first thing real to an individual is his own self. On the basis of this he accepts, or denies, or doubts whatever he does. A man can disavow anything, even God, but not his self. In repudiating the self he has to acknowledge it as the repudiator. So says Śaṅkara, 'Being the basis of all proof and disproof, the self is established prior to them. It is not possible to deny an entity of this nature. What is extraneous can be denied, but not the self. For, he who denies that is the self.'[49]

Though aware of his own existence, man is not aware of his real

[46] *Vide* NS III: 45. [47] NS III: 47, 48.

[48] Cf. *History of Philosophy*, by Alfred Weber, Trans. by Frank Thilly, New York, Scribners, 1925, p. 246. 'Descartes's motto (*cogito, ergo sum*) is not, however, an inference, and he does not wish us to regard it as such. As an inference it would be a vicious circle; for the conclusion is really identical with the major premise. It is a simple analytical judgment, a self-evident proposition.' [49] BS II: 3.7, com.

nature. He is vaguely conscious of the fact that he does not know himself as he is. Sometime or other he likes to ponder on such questions as 'Who am I?' 'Where am I from?' 'Whither am I to go?' It is with reference to man's real nature that Socrates gave the instruction, 'Man, know thyself'. It is enigmatic that man with all his pretensions to knowledge does not know himself. Nay, he knows himself wrongly. He identifies himself more or less with anything other than the self, such as the body, the senses, the mind, the vital principle, the kindreds, and even with the pets and possessions. All his miseries are due to this wrong knowledge, the root cause of which is ajñāna (antiknowledge).[50] He attains supreme blessedness through Self-knowledge on the removal of the veil of ajñāna. 'Know yourself and you shall then know God', says Śrī Rāmakṛṣṇa.[51]

Though veiled by ajñāna (antiknowledge), man's inmost self shines as its witness (sākṣī) and is unaffected by it. It is the light that manifests darkness. The sun manifests the cloud that hides it. A person can be aware of his ignorance regarding the real nature of the self by introspection. During deep sleep when all mental operations cease, the self beyond the ego stays as the witness of unspecified ignorance (ajñāna) that engulfs the mind. The luminous self has no sleep, being its witness.

The psychophysical adjunct of an embodied soul is rooted in ajñāna, which forms his causal body. Just as the resplendent sun being reflected in a water-surface partakes of some of its qualities and appears to be different, similarly, the effulgent self, being associated with the psychophysical adjunct through its reflection in ajñāna functions as the experiencer and as the doer without losing its transcendental character as the unchanging witness. While aware of himself as the knower, the reflected self gets identified with the known, such as the body, the senses, the vital principle, and the mind, and ascribes to himself what actually belongs to them. Being subject to ajñāna, not only does he fail to apprehend his real nature as Pure Consciousness, but even misapprehends himself as other than what he is. The purpose of the Śruti is to eliminate all contrary notions of an individual regarding the self, with their root-cause ajñāna. The realization of the self does not mean the attainment of something unattained. It is the recognition of the self on the removal of the veil of ajñāna. Self-knowledge does not mean knowing an unknown object, but the manifestation of the knower free from all

[50] Ajñāna or avidyā, usually translated as ignorance or nescience, does not mean the absence or the negation of knowledge, but its reverse, antiknowledge, which terminates with the knowledge of Reality. It is the cause of both inapprehension and misapprehension of the self. The superimposition of the not-self on the self is due to it.

[51] Swāmī Brahmānanda, *Words of the Master* (Select Precepts of Śrī Rāmakṛṣṇa), eighth edition, Calcutta, Udbodhan Office, 1938, p. 1.

superimposition. So says Sureśvara, 'Just the removal of ajñāna is regarded as the whole result of the Vedic testimony and not the knowledge of something unknown, which is absurd in the case of ātman that is awareness itself'.[52]

The embodied soul is apparently changeful but really changeless, apparently impure but really pure, apparently mortal but really immortal, apparently bound but really free. The various names and forms and states that characterize an individual actually belong to the limiting adjuncts constituting his three bodies—the gross, the subtle, and the causal—but are falsely ascribed to the indwelling self. Throughout the varying conditions, physical and psychical, that he undergoes as the experiencer and doer, the inmost self (pratyak ātmā) ever shines as their witness distinct from them. Thus, the indwelling self has two main aspects: As subject to the limiting adjuncts it is the experiencer and doer; as their transcendent witness it is immutable Pure Consciousness. Underlying all mental operations and their intervals, the witness, 'sākṣī', is ever present as their illuminator. Being perpetually the same despite all variations of the psychophysical adjunct, this is also called 'kūṭastha' (lit. firm as an anvil). As stated in the *Pañcadaśī*, 'It is the immutable self (kūṭastha) that has been defined by the foregoing teachers everywhere as the witness of the mind (antaḥkaraṇa) and its modes and in many other ways'.[53]

6. *An individual (the jīva) is basically the unchanging witness of all changes—psychical and physical*

It is 'kūṭastha', the immutable self ever shining as the witness of the jīva's ajñāna, the causal body, that being reflected in it assumes a specific form and emerges as the individual self with the subtle body as its limiting adjunct. The individual self becomes particularly manifest through buddhi (the cognitive mind), which is the main component of the subtle body. It is called 'cidābhāsa (the reflected self)', which being identified with the mind (antaḥkaraṇa) apparently acquires its attributes. Thus, the immutable self of the nature of Pure Consciousness, because of the jīva's ajñāna, seems to be endowed with tendencies and desires, merits and demerits, which actually dwell in the mind (antaḥkaraṇa), somewhat in the way a person's face appears to assume some qualities of a mirror being identified with its reflection in the mirror by mistake. In the words of Śaṅkara, 'Just as the properties of a mirror assumed by the reflection of a face in it are attributed to the face, so the properties of the cognitive mind (buddhi) assumed by the reflection of the self are superimposed on the self'.[54]

[52] NS II: 105. [53] *Vide* PD VIII: 25. [54] US XVIII: 70.

Further, being identified with the mind the reflected self gets identified with the physical body and the organs, cognizes agreeable and disagreeable objects, performs good and evil deeds, and experiences pain and pleasure. This is the empirical or the apparent self that functions as the cognizer (pramātā), as the doer (kartā), and as the experiencer (bhōktā). At the back of this ever shines the immutable self of the nature of Pure Consciousness. The one cannot exist without the other. The term 'jīva' includes both. It signifies the central principle of consciousness, the immutable self, which appears to be the experiencer, while shining as the witness of all experiences. Simultaneously, the mind (antaḥkaraṇa), naturally unconscious, becomes tinged with consciousness, so to speak, like a crystal appearing effulgent in association with a luminous object. The body and the senses also appear to be conscious through their contact with the mind tinged with consciousness.

The individual self finds expression as the ego (aham) primarily through "I-ness" (aham-vṛtti or ahaṅkāra), a mode of the mind that transmits consciousness. To all appearance the ego functions as a conscious agent. It is through "I-ness" or the ego-consciousness that the immutable self becomes more or less identified with the mental processes, the bodily organs, the vital principle (prāṇa), and the physical conditions. This is evident from such expressions as 'I remember', 'I doubt', 'I am determined', 'I am deaf', 'I was eloquent', 'I am lazy', 'I am still alive', 'I am sick', and so forth. Indeed, "I-ness" (ahaṅkāra) is the knot that ties together the conscious spirit and the unconscious matter, in other words, the self and the not-self. So there is an intermingling of the two. The knower becomes identified with the known and the known with the knower. It is not easy to discriminate one from the other. The light of consciousness transmitted through "I-ness" makes the mental states, the organs, and the body appear to be conscious in themselves. So it is said: 'My mind knows this to be true', 'As far as the eyes can see', 'My hands work day and night', 'My body feels tired'.

By introspection and an act of withdrawal, a person can apprehend himself as the witness of his mental states. He can know his hope and fear, pain and pleasure, love and hatred, virtue and vice, before disclosing them. He can also observe the passive state of the mind free from all modifications. Being intrinsically the immutable witness-self, a person can know what he knows and what he does not know. The inmost self is the witness of his knowledge and ignorance as well.[55] The mental states and the cognizing self both are directly manifest to the transcendental self, the witness (sākṣī). While knowing, an individual knows that he knows. When he does not know, he knows that he does not know. When he sees, he knows that

[55] See footnote 52, ch. II.

he sees. When he does not see, he knows that he does not see. When he feels happy he knows that he feels happy. When he feels unhappy, he knows that he feels unhappy.

Similarly, the doer is cognizant of his doership as well as the deed. When he acts he knows that he acts. When he does not act he knows that he does not act. All the while he receives the light of consciousness from the unchanging self (kūṭastha), whether he recognizes it or not. The luminous self as the witness (sākṣī) illuminates the cognizer, the cognition, and the object cognized. It manifests the doer, the doership, and the deed. None of them is self-luminous. So says Sureśvara: 'The cognizer, the cognition, and the objects cognized do not know themselves nor can they know one another. Therefore, their manifestation is due to something [the immutable self] distinct from them.'[56]

As pointed out by Vidyāraṇya, in the cognition of an external object, such as a jar, the statement 'this is a jar' is by virtue of the cidābhāsa [the reflected self, the perceiver]; the statement 'the jar is known' is by virtue of the kūṭastha, the immutable self.[57] Thus, the cognition of a jar is due to both the self as the perceiver (pramātā) and the self as the witness (sākṣī). So it is said, 'The cognition of an external thing, such as a jar, is produced by buddhi [cognitive mind] illuminated both by cidābhāsa [the reflected self, the perceiver] and the kūṭastha [the immutable self, the witness]'.[58] In the internal perception of a mental mode (whether in the form of a cognition, or doership, or feeling) the mind (antaḥkaraṇa) does not go out as in the case of the perception of an external thing. The percipient self lies with the mental mode inside, and both are manifest to the immutable self, their witness (sākṣī). Thus, when a person cognizes a jar, he is at the same time cognizant of the cognition. So he says, 'I know the jar', 'The jar is known to me', or 'I have the knowledge of the jar'. When he is the doer, he is aware of his doership. When he is happy, he knows that he is happy.

It is to be noted that the knowledge of an object, such as a jar or fire, can be either perceptual or inferential, that is, immediate or mediate; but the knowledge itself is invariably an immediate apprehension due to the luminous self as the witness (sākṣī). So the cognition of a cognition is always direct. For the cognition of an external object a mental mode in the form of the object is necessary. For the perception of its cognition, which is itself a mental mode, no other mental mode is necessary. It is directly manifest to the sākṣī (the witness-self), without being objectified. This is what is meant by the self-manifestedness (svaprakāśattva) of knowledge in the true sense (see ch. IV, sec. 1).

In the waking state the jīva (the individual self) dwells primarily

[56] NS II: 106. [57] PD VIII: 16. [58] LVV, st. 6, com. *Puṣpāñjali*.

in the physical body being identified with it through egoism or I-ness. The body and the organs appear to be conscious in association with the conscious self. The ego-idea is formed in the mould of the body and is well defined. It is the waking ego that perceives external objects, performs various deeds, and experiences different conditions of life. The form of the ego changes in the dream state. The dream-ego has no definite shape. It is amorphous and fickle. So there is lack of volition in dream. In deep sleep the ego subsides, an individual does not know who he is or what he is. But the same individual self, which finds definite expression as the waking ego, and plays the inconstant dream-ego, persists as the cognizer of all the three states. So a person can say, 'I sleep', 'I dream', 'I wake up'. All the while the jīva, the cognizer, has its being in the kūṭastha, the immutable self, but is unaware of its nature due to ajñāna.

Indeed, ajñāna, is the basic limiting adjunct of an embodied being. It forms his causal body, which is the root of the subtle and the gross body.[59] Ajñāna rests on the kūṭastha, the immutable self, its witness (sākṣī), which is uncontaminated by it. It is the inmost self that holds the three bodies (the limiting adjuncts), and not the three bodies the inmost self. The kūṭastha (the immutable self) is the inmost, because it penetrates the adjuncts (the three bodies), and nothing can penetrate it. While the inmost self is unaffected by the adjuncts, being their witness; the reflected self is subject to them, being involved as their experiencer. Ajñāna obstructs the vision of the experiencer (the empirical self), and not of the witness (the transcendental self), to whom it is manifest. One and the same indwelling self is the experiencer (as reflected consciousness) and the witness (as immutable consciousness).

7. *The real self (ātman) is the knower whose knowledge is intrinsic. It is its own proof. It needs no proof. The meaning of the Vedic testimony as the source of the knowledge of ātman*

After knowing from the Śruti the nature of the self (ātman) one can be convinced of its truth by reflecting on this through reasoning. That the inmost self of man is immutable pure consciousness is evident from the fact that it never loses self-awareness and that it illuminates all that we cognize directly or indirectly. 'In Its light all this shines.'[60] 'It is the Ear of the ear, the Mind of the mind, the Speech of [the organ of] speech, the Life of life, the Eye of the eye.'[61] When the light of consciousness recedes from the body, as in the dream state, the ear cannot hear, the mouth cannot speak, the eyes

[59] Cf. LVV, st. 1, 2, 'Ajñāna is the causal body. Pure Consciousness supports the three bodies as their witness and illuminator'.

[60] Ka. U. II: 2.15; Mu. U. II: 2.10; Sv. U. VI: 14.

[61] Ken. U. I: 2.

cannot see, the legs cannot move. When the light of consciousness further recedes from the mind in dreamless sleep, all mental operations stop. In that state the animation of the body gets very low and subsides completely when the conscious self, its source, departs.

Self-awareness is the central fact on which rest all other facts. Consciousness is primary. It cannot be a derivative.[62] It is self-manifest. That which is self-manifest must also be self-existent. Truly, each and every form of existence presupposes consciousness. It is the light that reveals itself in every form of cognition.[63] Nay, it shines through all mental operations and through all functions of the sensory and the motor organs. All our thoughts, feelings, volitions, imaginations, memories, deliberations, and determinations are but varied expressions of consciousness through different modes of the mind. All perceptions and all actions of the organs are due to consciousness transmitted to them through the mind. Livingness of an organism implies purposive behaviour, which is not possible without consciousness being implicit in it, if not explicit.

In dreamless deep sleep (suṣupti), when the mind with all its features and functions—desires, tendencies, thoughts, ideas, feelings, memories, doubts, imaginations, and worries, including the ego, their pivot—merges in a state of unspecified ignorance (the causal ajñāna), in which a father is no father, a mother is no mother, a king is no king, a thief is no thief, a hermit is no hermit, even then the witnessing consciousness endures as its illuminator. This has no sleep. Being ever wakeful, the witness-self (sākṣī) manifests sleep—a state of complete inapprehension, wrapped in which the empirical self reposes on the witness-self, its basis. Released from all physical and mental strain due to its identification with the not-self (the body, the senses, and the mind, etc.), during waking and dream states, the empirical self returns to its own self, but without realizing its nature as blissful consciousness, lies in blissful ignorance that enfolds it. Even then the witness-self (sākṣī) is the illuminator of both—the empirical self and ajñāna. It shines alone when the ego subsides. The immutable self is the light that shines in darkness as its sole witness. It manifests the ego, the cognizer. The ego, apparently the source of consciousness, draws its light from the witness-self.

So when an individual wakes up he recollects the experience and says, 'I slept happily and did not know anything'. With reference to dreamless sleep it is said: 'That it [the self] does not see in that state

[62] Cf. 'I regard consciousness as fundamental. I regard matter as a derivative from consciousness. We cannot get behind consciousness. Everything that we talk about, everything that we postulate as existing requires consciousness. Professor Planck in an interview with J. W. N. Sullivan, which appeared in the *Observer*, January 25, 1931. (Quoted by C. E. M. Joad in his *Guide to Modern Thought*, London, Faber, 1933, pp. 94–5).

[63] Ke. U. II: 4.

is because although seeing then, it does not see. For the vision of the witness can never be lost, because it is immortal. But there is not that second thing separate from it which it can see.'[64] As observed by Vidyāraṇya: 'Various modifications of the mind arise in succession being mutually exclusive. They all disappear in sleep, swoon, and samādhi. The immutable consciousness that reveals the intervals of the mental modes and their cessation is called "kūṭastha".'[65] 'Unvaried consciousness penetrates the modifications of the mind like the thread in a string of pearls', says Śaṅkara.[66]

The inmost self is immutable pure consciousness. The agency of seeing or knowing is not possible in what is absolutely changeless and without attributes. Yet the self is said to be the seer (draṣṭā), or the knower (vijñātā) in the sense of the illuminator of the cognitive and other modes of the mind. But it does not illuminate them as the agent (kartā). They become manifest to the self by reason of their proximity to its intrinsic luminosity, which is constant and unvaried. Thus, the self is regarded as their illuminator (avabhāsaka). For instance, the resplendent sun, which is devoid of 'I-ness' and 'my-ness' and of desire and effort, is looked upon as the illuminator of things, which become manifest in contact with its natural radiance. So the self is the seer or the knower in relation to the modes of the mind, which exist and shine in the light of consciousness.[67] Being allied with the psychophysical vehicle through 'I-ness', a mode of the mind, the self finds expression as the cognizer (pramātā), as the doer (kartā), and as the experiencer (bhōktā). Intrinsically, it is immutable Pure Consciousness. The immutability of the self is thus indicated by Sureśvara: 'That which is impartible in the tripartite division of the cognizer, the cognition, and the object cognized, and is also the witness of their origin and dissolution, must be free from all these conditions.'[68]

The Self is the basic fact. It is the ultimate knower. As declared by the Upaniṣad: 'He is never seen, but is the Witness; He is never heard, but is the Hearer; He is never thought, but is the Thinker; He is never known, but is the Knower. There is no other witness but Him, no other hearer but Him, no other thinker but Him, no other knower but Him.'[69] 'By what should one know the Knower?'[70] 'You cannot know that which is the knower of knowledge.'[71] According to Schopenhauer, that which knows all things and is known by none is the subject. The self needs no proof. It is the datum of all proof. Truly speaking, it is its own proof, being self-evident. As pointed out by Śaṅkara,

[64] Br. U. IV: 3.23. [65] PD VIII: 20, 21. [66] LVV, st. 9.

[67] *Vide* Śaṅkara's *Ātmajñānōpadeśa-vidhi*, Pt. II, sec. 12, and com. by Ānandajñāna. [68] NS II: 108.

[69] Br. U. III: 7.23. [70] *Ibid.* II: 4.14. [71] *Ibid.* III: 4.2.

'Therefore the self is not established by any means of knowledge. That which is unknown can be made known and requires proof, but not the self [the knower]. If it be granted that the self requires proof, then who will be the knower [because in that case the self becomes one of the knowables, and in the absence of the knower there can be no application of proof]. It is settled that the knower is the self. "Is not the self proved by āgama [the Vedic testimony]?"—it may be argued. No, not even by āgama. By removing from ātman all contrary attributes superimposed on it, the Śruti leads to the knowledge of its identity with Brahman. The evidence of the Śruti has to be understood in this sense. It serves as a proof not by disclosing ātman, which is self-evident, but by disclosing the unknown meaning [the implied meaning, that is, the identity] of the two entities, ātman and Brahman, whose direct meanings are known.'[72]

Ātman and Brahman are not unknown, but wrongly known. The Śruti removes this wrong knowledge and the consequent misery by disclosing their identity.

8. *The process of reasoning in Vedānta to prove that the Self is the light that never fails*

By distinguishing the self from the not-self a seeker of self-knowledge can be assured of its nature as immutable consciousness. The Vedāntic teachers have usually followed this method of reasoning to con vince their pupils of the self-luminosity of ātman, as declared by the Śruti. This is characterized as the discrimination of the self from the not-self (ātmānātma-viveka), in other words, the differentiation of the knower (jñātā) from the known (jñeya), or of the seer (draṣṭā, dṛk) from the seen (dṛśya). The self is recognized by all as the knower. Each individual regards himself as a knower of the external objects and as such holds himself distinct from them all. For the same reason the inner man must be distinct from the physical body, of which he is the knower. This means that the knowing self is other than the body. Consequently, neither the body, nor any of its properties—size, shape, colour, sex, race, nationality, youth, old age, health, sickness, birth, death, etc.—inhere in the self.

A person is also aware when he hears with the ears and when he does not hear, when he sees with the eyes and when he does not see, when he speaks with the mouth and when he does not speak, when he works with the hands and when he does not work. He, the knower, must, therefore, be distinct from all the organs, and their functions —hearing, seeing, touching, talking, grasping, and so forth. Nor do their attributes, such as keenness or dullness of sight, dumbness or

[72] *Ātmajñānōpadeśa-vidhi*, Pt. IV, sec. 10, 11.

eloquence, lameness or wholeness, actually belong to the knowing self. The knower is characteristically different from all that is known. Consciousness is its very nature. While the knower is self-aware and is aware of all else; the object cognized is devoid of consciousness. No external object, nor the body, nor any of the organs, has consciousness inherent in it.

Not even the mind (antaḥkaraṇa) is the knower *per se*. For the mental modes are invariably known. Whatever thought, feeling, desire, doubt, or determination arises in the mind becomes manifest to the witness-self. There cannot be an unknown desire or fear except in its potential state. The knowing self is therefore distinct from the mind and all its modifications. So says Śaṅkara: 'Just as the perceiver is different from colors, etc., which are perceivable, so the knower, the self, is different from the modifications of the mind, which are cognizable. Just as a lamp revealing things is different from them, so is the knower different from the things known.'[73] Such opposites as virtue and vice, wisdom and folly, pain and pleasure, deliberation and determination, hope and despair, concentration and distraction, attachment and detachment, characterize the mind and not the inmost self, their witness.

As observed by Patañjali, 'The mind is not self-luminous, because it is cognizable.'[74] Consciousness is intrinsic in the knower and not in the known. Therefore, the inmost self, the knower *per se*, alone is self-luminous. Truly speaking, it is immutable pure consciousness unrelated to all the adjuncts (including ajñāna) that illuminates them, so to speak. Being in association with the mind (antaḥkaraṇa) the inmost self appears to be a knower. So says Śaṅkara:

'The buddhi [the cognitive mind] has no consciousness and the self no action. The word "knows" can, therefore, reasonably be applied to neither of them.'[75]

'The self is said to be knowing things on account of the superimposition of the agency of the buddhi on It. Similarly, the buddhi is called a knower owing to the superimposition of consciousness on it.'[76]

During deep sleep when the self recedes from the body and the mind, the vital principle (prāṇa) continues to operate, yet there is no indication of consciousness in any of them. This shows that the vital principle is devoid of consciousness like the body, the organs, and the mind. The inmost self is other than the vital principle, but being associated with it appears to live, to breathe, to have biological urges, such as hunger, thirst, instincts of self-preservation, self-propagation, and so forth. Truly speaking, the self is unaffected by

[73] US XVIII: 152. [74] YS IV: 19.
[75] US XVIII: 54. [76] *Ibid.* 65.

vital processes, being beyond them all. Similarly, being in association with the organs, the inmost self seems to hear, see, taste, talk, grasp, walk, and so forth. In itself the self is immutable pure consciousness, the unchanging witness of the mental modes, the bodily states, and the functions of the organs and the vital principle. Unobscured by them, the self shines with constant effulgence, like the sun under the cloud. As observed by Śaṅkara:

'Unlike the knowledge gained through the eye, the knowledge of the knower does not cease to exist. It is said that the knowledge of the knower does not go out of existence.'[77]
'The knower, therefore, is always of the nature of homogeneous consciousness.'[78]

It is distinct from all that is known, the body, the organs, the vital principle, the mind, and their attributes.

Another method of reasoning adopted by the Vedāntic teachers to convey the knowledge of the self is the discrimination of the invariable from the variable. That which is invariable in the midst of the variable must be other than the variable. If any of the variables inheres in it, then it is bound to be variable. While all else varies, the knower *per se* remains the same. Changes betoken an unchanging observer that relates the succeeding to the preceding events. External conditions change, so does the body, and so does the mind, even beyond recognition; yet an individual maintains his identity. It is because the inmost self, the witness of all changes, is constant. It is not the everchanging psychophysical personality, but the indwelling self, its constant observer, that asserts—'I was a grandchild, now I am a grandfather; the golden dreams of my youth have vanished; now I am facing hard realities.' As stated by Patañjali, 'The modes of the mind are invariably known, because its master, the intelligent self, is immutable.'[79] So the self is distinct from the ever-changing psychophysical constitution.

Waking, dream, and dreamless sleep are the primary states of the mind (antaḥkaraṇa). The luminous self as the witness underlies them all. It is the one observer of all the three states. Even in deep sleep when the organs and the mind cease to function, its light does not fail. The luminous self is ever present. Nothing else endures. All else comes and goes, appears and disappears. Waking is contradicted by dream. Dream is contradicted by sleep. And sleep is contradicted by waking or dream, and so on. But the conscious self as the witness persists throughout. It alone is uncontradicted. What is uncontradicted is the real self. What is contradicted cannot be the self. It cannot exist independently of the self. The knower existing, the

77 Br. U. IV: 3.23, com. 78 US XV: 18. 79 YS IV: 18.

known exists. In the absence of the knower nothing can be established. Thus, by discriminating the invariable from the variable, the witness from the witnessed, unvaried consciousness is found to be the true self, distinct from the three states and the three bodies.[80]

9. *Neither the ancient nor the modern view of the impermanence of the self is tenable*

To all appearance, an individual is a psychophysical complex in a state of flux. The indwelling self is the only constant entity that sustains it. This is the central principle of consciousness that cognizes and appropriates the inconstant factors, such as the body, the organs, the vital force, the mind. Not only that, it unifies them all and develops them as a system. Like the spokes of a wheel fixed to the nave, all physical and psychical constituents of the system are held by it. Had there been no permanent subject underlying the impermanent elements in man, had he been simply an aggregate of the five skandhas (the bodily and the mental constituents of an individual), as Nāgasena, the well-known Buddhist dialectician, maintained,[81] then a human being could by no means behave as a self-conscious identical individual despite all changes internal and external.

The self coordinates all experiences and synthesizes them into knowledge. While the experiences pass away the knowledge stays. This would not have been possible had there been no enduring knower other than the fleeting experiences. Not only is the self distinct from the varied objects of experience, but also from the experiences themselves—the functions of the sense-organs and the mind. It underlies all sense-perceptions and mental operations. Just as a big fish swims freely from one bank of a river to another, being unrelated, so does the self pass smoothly from waking experience to dream experience, from dream experience to sleep experience, and from sleep experience back to dream or waking experience, being distinct

[80] This type of reasoning is generally known as 'anvaya-vyatirekī yukti' (argument by agreement and contrariety) and is applied to the discrimination of the self from the not-self, and the real from the unreal. Śaṅkara in his *Upadeśa-sāhasrī* (XVIII: 96, 180, 182, 191) and Sureśvara in his *Naiṣkarmya-siddhi* (III: 22, *et seq*) have made use of this argument in expounding the mahāvākya, 'Thou art That'.

[81] *Vide The Questions of King Milinda* (Milindā Pañhā), Bk. II, chap. I, pp. 40 ff., translated from the Pali by T. W. Rhys Davids, The Sacred Books of the East, Vol. XXXV, London, Oxford University Press, Humphrey Milford, 1925. (It is an interesting dialogue between Nāgasena and Baktrian Greek king, Minander, who ruled the Indus territory and the valley of the Ganges from about 125 to 95 BC. It represents a phase of Buddhism that developed about four centuries after the Buddha). 'This Nagasena says there is no permanent individuality (no soul) implied in his name', reported the king.

from them all.[82] The self is not just a unity of complex experiences, but a distinct principle that unites them all and turns them to account. Nay, it illuminates them all. Consequently, such a view of the self as expressed by Professor Stout does not seem to be tenable. 'The unity of the self seems to me indistinguishable from the unity of the total complex of its experiences', he remarks.[83]

According to David Hume, an individual is 'nothing but a bundle or collection of different perceptions, which succeed each other with an inconceivable rapidity, and are in a perpetual flux and movement'.[84] Hume does not recognize the perceiver in his perception. How can he? For he himself is the perceiver. The perceiver cannot be perceived. So he says, 'For my part, when I enter most intimately into what I call *myself*, I always stumble on some particular perception or other, of heat or cold, light or shade, love or hatred, pain or pleasure. I never can catch *myself* at any time without a perception, and never can observe anything but the perception'.[85] However, he admits that he is the observer of perception. Indeed, with each act of perception there is the perceiver. So a person says, 'I see', 'I hear', 'I touch', 'I smell', 'I feel cold', 'I feel happy', 'I love my son', and so forth. While the perceptions vary the perceiver remains the same. It is evident from such statements as 'I see the flower I smell', 'I touched the garment I saw', 'This is the man I met yesterday', 'I like the music I hear'.

Underlying the fleeting experiences external and internal there is the inmost self that remains ever the same. The one immutable self functions as the doer as well as the knower. This hears through the ears, sees through the eyes, speaks through the mouth, works with the hands, thinks through the mind, comprehends through the intellect, and so on. One self plays different parts through different organs. In the words of the Upaniṣads: 'It is he that sees, that touches, that hears, that smells, that tastes, that thinks, that cognizes. He is the doer. He is the knowing self of the essence of consciousness that penetrates the whole system.'[86] It is a fact of common knowledge that a person who hears about something can recognize it when he sees it. There is nothing incongruous in such a statement as 'I see the house I heard about; I like it'. This shows that the same intelligent self that heard about the house in the past, now sees it, and likes it. Even after losing the eyesight a person can recollect what he saw twenty years ago. This shows that it is the one abiding self that sees and recollects, and not the organ of vision.

[82] Cf. Br. U. IV: 3.18.

[83] G. F. Stout, *Studies in Philosophy and Psychology*, paper on *Some Fundamental Points in the Theory of Knowledge*, London, Macmillan, 1930, p. 358.

[84] David Hume, *A Treatise of Human Nature*. Bk. I, pt. IV, chap. on 'Personal Identity', Oxford, The Clarendon Press, 1896, p. 252.

[85] *Ibid.*

[86] Pr. U. IV. 9.

The self is beyond the ego-idea. It cannot be reduced to a rapid succession of perceiving egos. Had there been no abiding self, personal identity would have been meaningless and memory would have been an impossibility. In the absence of memory none could recognize things and gain knowledge. The Buddhist Idealists' view that there is no permanent self but a series of momentary consciousness serving as the cognizer was long ago rejected by the *Brahma-sūtras*: 'And because of the fact of memory [the immutability of the cognizer has to be recognized].'[87] The Idealists of the Yōgācāra school of Buddhism explained the continuity of the self with the illustration of a torch that gives the appearance of a circle of light when twirled rapidly.

The theory that there is no enduring self but a series of momentary subjects has been supported by William James. In his view each subject of the series lasts but for a moment; its place is immediately taken by another which exercises its function, that is, to act as the medium of unity; the successor for the time being knows and adopts its predecessor, and by so doing appropriates what its predecessor adopted.[88] In his commentary on the *Brahma-sūtras* quoted above Śaṅkara anticipates this argument and refutes it in refuting the Buddhist Idealists' theory of the cognizer as a series of momentary consciousness. His observation is partly as follows: Recollection results from the previous experience. This is not possible unless the experiencer endures until recollection. One cannot remember what another experiences. A passing consciousness would last at least two moments to connect recollection with experience. So the theory of momentariness is untenable. Further, in case it is contended that the continuity of the series is due to the fact that a preceding momentary consciousness gives the cue to the succeeding consciousness, then also it must be admitted that a fleeting consciousness must endure at least two moments. Thus the theory of momentariness falls to the ground.

It may be noted here that the contiguity of succession is inconceivable without any connection between the preceding and the

[87] II: 2.25.

[88] *Vide* Professor William James, *Principles of Psychology*, New York, Holt, Rinehart and Winston, 1920, p. 215: 'The consciousness of Self involves a stream of thought, each part of which as "I" can remember those which went before, know the things they knew, and care paramountly for certain ones among them as "Me" and *appropriate to these* the rest. This *Me* is an empirical aggregate of things objectively known. The *I* which knows them can not itself be an aggregate; neither for psychological purposes need it be an unchanging metaphysical entity like the Soul, or a principle like the transcendental Ego, viewed as "out of time". It is a *thought*, at each moment different from that of the last moment, but *appropriative* of the latter, together with all that the latter called its own.'

succeeding event. This necessitates an enduring principle underlying them.

According to some eminent psychologists and philosophers of modern times there is no such conscious entity as the knowing self, but a continuous flow of psychical states; the identity of personality is an illusion like the appearance of continuity of a motion picture. But the point is, the mental states are not conscious in themselves. There must be an abiding self-luminous principle, intrinsically conscious, for their unification and objectification, that is to say, illumination. It is to be noted that the motion pictures have an unmoving background to connect them. There is a screen to hold them together. Not only that, the retina in the eyeball serves to connect the disconnected pictures by retaining each image till the next one is received.

It is evident from the foregoing discussion that the Vedic dicta are not meant to be accepted as dogmas. It is by reasoning on them that their true meanings have to be found and grasped before they can be followed as guiding principles with inner conviction. A clear comprehension of the true nature of the self as declared by the Upaniṣads, free from doubts and misconceptions, is a prerequisite for the realization of Nondual Brahman.

CHAPTER XI

'THOU ART THAT', THE TRUTH OF TRUTHS

1. *The dictum 'Thou art That' is the key to the realization of the ultimate Unity, which is the goal of human knowledge. It signifies the distinctive character of the Vedic monism*

As we have indicated above (chap. IX, sec. 4), the final truth about the self (ātman) has been given out by the Śruti in each of the four mahāvākyas, affirming the identity of the individual soul and the Supreme Self, which is the Truth of truths. We shall dwell at length on one of the four, namely, 'Thou art That', as typical. In declaring the identity of 'Thou' and 'That', the Śruti points to the sole reality of Pure Being-Consciousness-Bliss, undivided and undiversified, divested of all superimposition of differences and dualities, including the distinction of the adorer and the Adorable, nay, of the knower and the known. Thus, the realization of the identity of the self (ātman) and the Supreme Being means the attainment of Nirguṇa Brahman, the One without a second. This is the culmination of knowledge. Human knowledge cannot go beyond undifferentiated absolute Oneness. It has, of course, unlimited scope, as regards details, in the realm of phenomena marked by endless variety, comprising innumerable universals and particulars.

It is to be noted that Pure Being, Pure Consciousness, and Pure Bliss are identical. Pure Existence is Consciousness Itself and is Bliss Itself. They imply one and the same undifferentiated Reality. They are not the aspects or attributes of Brahman, but Its three different appellations indicative of Its absolute flawlessness. It is the very perfection of existence. The Real is the Ideal. As declared by the Upaniṣad, 'The Infinite is Bliss. There is no Bliss in anything finite. Only the Infinite is Bliss. It is the Infinite that one should desire to know.'[1]

To find unity in diversity is the goal of knowledge. It is the one aim of science, philosophy, and religion. While different sciences seek unity in their respective spheres, philosophy seeks the unity of all unities. The end of religion is the realization of the ultimate Oneness.

[1] Ch. U. VII: 23.1.

'What is that on knowing which all this becomes known?'[2] This is the central theme of the Upaniṣads. So it is said:

'To the knower of Truth, all things have verily become the Self. What delusion, what sorrow can there be for him who realizes that oneness?'[3]
'Where one sees nothing else, hears nothing else, understands nothing else—that is the Infinite. Where one sees something else, hears something else, understands something else—that is the finite. The Infinite is immortal, the finite is mortal.'[4]
'He who knows Supreme Brahman verily becomes Brahman.'[5]
'The knower of Brahman attains the Highest.'[6]

As observed by Śrī Rāmākṛṣṇa: 'God is the ocean of Infinite Bliss. There is no fear of being drowned there. By being immersed in this, one becomes immortal.'

Man has a clearer vision of unity in diversity with the deepening of his insight. To common human experience various things and beings appear as distinct entities. With the growth of knowledge man discovers general laws and principles underlying and unifying them. As he reaches higher and higher generalizations, all created things, divergent as they are, are found to be interrelated; the universe proves to be a system in which the living and the non-living, the physical and the psychical, form an organic whole. With the furtherance of knowledge the manifold turns out to be a continuous existence without the least break anywhere, and is conceived as the varied forms of one all-pervasive Reality. In the Nondualistic (Advaita) view the One does not transform into the manifold, but appears as such.

Though the monistic thinkers of the East and the West maintain that the fundamental reality underlying all diversity is one and the same, yet they have divergent views on three important points:

(1) What is the nature of the ultimate Reality? Is it a material, or a vital, or a spiritual entity?
(2) What place has the perceptible manifold in the underlying unity? Does the one inhere in the other? Is multiplicity actual modification of the unitary principle?
(3) Can the fundamental unity be directly perceived? Or, is it ever 'unknown and unknowable'? Is unity only a subject of speculation, while manifoldness endures as a fact of experience?

As maintained by the Nondualistic Vedānta, the Upaniṣadic dictum 'Thou art That' holds answers on all these points that are

[2] Mu. U. I: 1.3. [3] Is. U. 7. [4] Ch. U. VII: 24.1.
[5] Mu. U. III: 2.9. [6] Tai. U. II: 1.3.

clear, convincing, and strikingly distinctive. As we expound the terse formula, its following implications will be borne out:

In the first place, it indicates, as we have noted above, that the ultimate Reality is Pure Spirit, Self-effulgent Consciousness, which is All-Bliss and the very perfection of existence. As affirmed by the *Aitareya Upaniṣad* of the *Rg-Veda*, 'All this [the entire universe of the living and the non-living] is moved by Consciousness, supported by Consciousness, guided by Consciousness, and has its being in Consciousness. Consciousness is Brahman.'[7]

Secondly, it implies that the manifold has no actual position in Nondual Brahman, even as a mirage has no existence in the desert, being only an appearance. It is a mere superimposition that disappears with the dawning of the knowledge of Reality. As stated in the *Bṛhadāraṇyaka Upaniṣad*, 'There is no difference whatsoever in this [Brahman]. From death to death moves he who sees in this [Brahman] the seeming diversity'.[8]

Thirdly, the dictum 'Thou art That' discloses the direct approach to Nondual Brahman. This is its main purpose. It is the realization of the ultimate Oneness that demonstrates the first and second points. Inasmuch as an individual is essentially identical with Brahman, he can realize the same by realizing his inmost self. As declared by the *Muṇḍaka Upaniṣad*: 'The stainless, indivisible Brahman shines in the golden innermost sheath[9] [as the luminous self]. It is all-pure. It is the Light of lights. It is that which *they* know who know the inmost self.'[10]

2. *The beatific experience of Absolute Oneness as delineated in the Upaniṣads. Nirvikalpa and savikalpa samādhi. Śaṅkara's account of Nondual Brahman as perceived in samādhi.*

In realizing Brahman the jīva becomes identified with It. For Brahman is his very being and can by no means be objectified. The individual soul withdrawn from all limiting adjuncts realizes his essential unity with the all-pervading Supreme Self. The knower and the knowable become fused into indivisible unitary Consciousness. All-blissful, pure, simple Awareness, real to Itself (svasaṁvedya), shines. In every form of knowledge, direct or indirect, there is a distinction between the knower and the object of knowledge, but in the realization of Brahman no such distinction prevails. Here there is complete obliteration of the triple distinction of the knower, the known, and the process of knowledge (tripuṭī-vilaya). This transcen-

7 Ai. U. III: 1.3. 8 Br. U. IV: 4.19.

9 The cognitive mind (buddhi) with the five subtle sense-organs is called 'vijñānamaya kōṣa,' the sheath of intelligence. Being radiant with the radiance of consciousness it is conceived as golden. 10 Mu. U. II: 2.10.

dental experience is altogether different from the three normal states of experience—waking, dream, and deep sleep—that an individual goes through almost every day under the spell of ajñāna. It is called 'the fourth [turīya]' in relation to the other three states, though it is the only state native to the jīva. While the other three states perpetuate man's bondage, being superimposed by ajñāna, the fourth (turīya) eradicates ajñāna and makes him free forever.

The transcendental experience of the Self is thus delineated by the *Māṇḍūkya Upaniṣad*:

'The wise consider that to be the fourth [turīya], which is not internally conscious [as in dream], nor externally conscious [as in waking state], nor conscious both ways [as in a state intermediary between waking and dream]; which is not a mass of consciousness [dormant state of the conscious processes as in profound sleep], nor all-consciousness, nor unconsciousness; which is imperceptible [by the sense-organs], ungraspable [by the organs of action], and inaccessible [by any empirical means]; which is uninferable, inconceivable, indefinable; which is Pure Self-awareness; which is the cessation of the manifold; which is nondual, calm. and blissful. This is the Self. This is to be realized.'[11]

It is to be noted that this is not just a state of complete isolation of the Self from the entire objective universe including the experiencer's body, the sense-organs, the vital principle, the mind, and the ego. It is far more than that. The whole phenomenal world, physical and psychical, melts away like bubbles, as it were, into an ocean of blissful awareness. In this unitary consciousness there is no other. The manifold drops out of existence. So says the sage Yājñavalkya to his wife Maitreyi:

'Just as a lump of salt dropped into water dissolves, as water mingles in water, and no one is able to pick it up, but from whatever part one takes that water it tastes salty, even so, my dear, this immense, endless, boundless Reality is but Pure Consciousness. The finite self that arises because of the elements constituting its limiting adjuncts disappears with their disappearance. When freed from them it no longer has [individualized] consciousness [being united with Pure Consciousness].'

'When there is appearance of duality then one smells something, one sees something, one hears something, one speaks something, one thinks something, one knows something. But when to the knower of Brahman everything has become the Self, then what should one smell

[11] Ma. U. VII.

and through what, what should one see and through what, what should one hear and through what, what should one speak and through what, what should one think and through what, what should one know and through what? Through what should one know that because of which all this is known, through what, O Maitreyi, should one know the Knower?'[12]

This is the acme of spiritual experience, according to Nondualistic Vedānta, and is called 'nirvikalpa samādhi', being free from all ideation. As stated by Śaṅkara, 'The truth of Brahman is clearly and decisively realized by nirvikalpa samādhi, and not by any other way, in which it is apt to be mixed up with alien ideas because of the fluctuation of the mind'.[13] The next lower type is savikalpa samādhi, in which the individual consciousness retains its distinctness, and the experiencer realizes his unity or inmost relation with the Divinity, Saguṇa Brahman, the Goal of the path of devotion. Rare spiritual aspirants attain savikalpa samādhi. Nirvikalpa samādhi is even rarer. The one can lead to the other. In fact, most spiritual aspirants have to reach the nirvikalpa state through the savikalpa. It is said in the *Muṇḍaka Upaniṣad*: 'When the spiritual aspirant perceives the self-luminous Creator, the Lord, the Omnipresent Being, the Origin of Brahmā [the cosmic soul],[14] then the wise one gets rid of merit and demerit (due to karma), becomes stainless, and attains supreme unity beyond dualities.'[15]

It is said that the great seer-philosopher, Śaṅkarācārya, who lived, according to the orthodox view, from A.D. 686 to 718, was barely twelve when he had his first experience of nirvikalpa samādhi at the feet of his guru, Gōvindapāda, near the temple of Oṅkāranātha on the river Narmada. His delineation of Nondual Brahman as realized in nirvikalpa samādhi is reminiscent of his personal experience:

'The illumined one realizes in his heart, through samādhi, the Infinite Brahman which is something of the nature of immutable Consciousness and Pure Bliss, which is incomparable, which transcends all limitations, which is ever-free and without activity, which is like the boundless sky indivisible and absolute.

'The illumined one realizes in his heart, through samādhi, the infinite Brahman, which is free from the relation of cause and effect, which is the Reality beyond all ideations, which is the same at every point, and has no parallel, which is beyond the range of proofs, but established by the pronouncements of the Vedas, and ever known to us through the ego-consciousness.

'The illumined one realizes in his heart, through samādhi, the

12 Br. U. II: 4.12, 14; IV: 5.13, 15.

13 VC 365.

14 The expression 'Brahma-yōni' in the original may also mean 'Brahman, the Origin of the universe'.

15 Mu. U. III: 1.3.

Infinite Brahman, which is undecaying and immortal, the positive entity which precludes all negations, which resembles the placid ocean and is without a designation, where the modifications of the guṇas subside, which is eternal, calm, and nondual.'[16]

3. *The immediate intuition of the all-transcendent Being cannot be characterized as ancient or modern, as Eastern or Western. The transcendental experiences of Plotinus and Śrī Rāmakṛṣṇa*

The acme of spiritual experience is the realization of the all-transcendent Being. It is as boundless as Reality. It is neither Eastern nor Western, neither ancient nor modern. Any mystical experience that can be determined as such cannot be the highest. An individual has to go beyond all bounds in order to reach the Absolute One. According to both Plotinus and Śaṅkara, 'the One can be indicated only in negatives'. So says the Upaniṣad: 'Hence the instruction on Brahman as "not this", "not this". There is no other or more apropriate mode of expression with regard to Brahman than this "Not this". Reality of realities is Its name.'[17]

With regard to the Supreme Reality and Its experience Plotinus observes:

'In our self-seeing There, the self is seen as belonging to that order, or rather we are merged into that self in us which has the quality of that order. It is a knowing of the self restored to its purity. No doubt we should not speak of seeing; but we cannot help talking in dualities, seen and seer, instead of, boldly, the achievement of unity. In this seeing we neither hold an object nor trace distinction; there is no two. The man is changed, no longer himself nor self-belonging; he is merged with the Supreme, sunken into it, one with it; centre coincides with centre, for on this higher plane things that touch at all are one; only in separation is there duality; by our holding away, the Supreme is set outside. This is why the vision baffles telling; we cannot detach the Supreme to state it; if we have seen something thus detached we have failed of the Supreme which is to be known only as one with ourselves.'

'There is thus a converse in virtue of which the essential man outgrows Being, becomes identical with the Transcendent of Being.'[18]

It is evident from Porphyry's account that Plotinus had samādhi four times in his life and that Porphyry himself had it once.[19] The

[16] VC 408–410. [17] Br. U. II: 3.6. See also S. com.

[18] *Plotinus, The Ethical Treatises*, The Enneads VI: 9.10, 11. Trans. by Stephen MacKenna. Boston, Branford, 1916.

[19] *Ibid.* Vol. I, p. 24. 'There was shown to Plotinus the Term ever near: for the Term, the one end, of his life was to become Uniate, to approach to the God over all: and four times, during the period I passed with him, he achieved

differences of mystical experiences, of ways and methods indicate only lower phases and outer manifestations of mystical life. But the heart of mysticism is quietism. Faith, devotion, reasoning, charity, contemplation—all have their due places in spiritual life, though they do not become equally manifest in all mystics. But none can realize the inmost Self until the mind is completely tranquil and transparent and suffused with Its light. So prays Meister Eckhart, 'O Eternal Light of Divine Glory, since thou art in my innermost depths, since thou transcendest all things, be to me *That thou art*, a turning away from all things into the ineffable Good that thou art in thy naked self'.[20]

The transcendental experience of Śrī Rāmākṛṣṇa in the modern age also testifies to the ultimate reality of nondual, non-relational Consciousness. In his own words as recorded by Swāmī Sāradānanda, one of his close disciples and biographers, 'I hold forcibly to one or two trifling desires, with the help of which I keep the mind low down for you all; otherwise its natural inclination is to remain united and identified with the Indivisible One'.[21] Indeed, the natural resting ground of his mind was the nondual Reality. Says Swāmī Sāradānanda: 'As the result of his being established in the plane of nirvikalpa consciousness, the memory of nonduality used to be suddenly awakened in him off and on by the sight of things and persons within the bounds of the plane of duality, merging him in the Absolute. We saw that state brought on him by the slightest association of ideas even without his desiring it. It is, therefore, superfluous to add that he could ascend any moment to that plane by a mere wish.'[22] In fact, samādhi was a daily occurrence in the later life of Śrī Rāmakṛṣṇa. Sometimes he remained in samādhi an hour or an hour and a half at a stretch.[23]

Occasionally, he voiced his experience of nirvikalpa samādhi in the course of his conversations. As recorded by Mahendranath Gupta, an intimate lay disciple:

'Reaching it, the mind merges in Brahman. The individual soul and the Supreme Soul become one. The aspirant goes into samādhi. His consciousness of the body disappears. He loses the knowledge of the

this Term, by no mere latent fitness but by the ineffable Act. To this God, I also declare, I Porphyry, that in my sixty-eighth year I too was once admitted and entered into Union.'

[20] *Meister Eckhart*, Vol. II, p. 143, Trans. by C. de B. Evans.

[21] Swāmī Sāradānanda, *Sri Ramakrishna the Great Master*, Trans. from Bengali original by Swāmī Jagadānanda, Madras, Sri Ramakrishna Math, 1952, p. 221. [22] *Ibid*. p. 265.

[23] See *Dharma-prasaṅge Swāmī Brahmānanda* (Swāmī Brahmānanda's Conversations in original Bengali), Calcutta, Udbodhan Office, 1936, p. 28.

outer world. He does not see the manifold any more. His reasoning comes to a stop.'

"Brahman is immovable, immutable, inactive, and of the nature of Consciousness. When a man merges his *buddhi*, his intelligence, in *Bōdha*, Consciousness, then he attains the knowledge of Brahman; he becomes *buddha*, enlightened. Naṅgtā [Śrī Rāmakṛṣṇa's nondualistic preceptor] used to say that the mind merges in *buddhi*, and the *buddhi* in *Bōdha*, Consciousness. The aspirant does not attain the knowledge of Brahman as long as he is conscious of his ego.'

'Ah, what a state of mind I passed through! My mind would lose itself in the Indivisible Absolute.'

'As a result of the discrimination that Brahman alone is real and the world illusory, the aspirant goes into samādhi. Then for him, the forms and attributes of God disappear altogether. Then he does not feel God to be a person. Then he cannot describe in words what God is. And who will describe it? He who is to describe does not exist at all; he no longer finds his "I". To such a person Brahman is attributeless. In that state God is experienced only as Consciousness, by man's inmost consciousness. He cannot be comprehended by the mind and intelligence.'[24]

The following remarks of Swāmī Sāradānanda on the attainment of the nondual experience are illuminating:

'The plane of the nondual Consciousness indirectly implied by the words "void" and "all" has been described in the Upaniṣads and Vedānta as the state beyond all ideation. For, perfectly established in It, the mind of the sādhaka [spiritual aspirant] transcends the limits of all other planes of consciousness, produced by God's play of creation, preservation, and dissolution, and merges in homogeneity. Therefore, the nondual state of consciousness is something nonrelational, different from the five moods [devotional attitudes], such as śānta, dāsya, sakhya, vātsalya, and madhura,[25] with the aid of which the limited human mind enters the spiritual relation. Only when the man of the world becomes absolutely indifferent to all kinds of enjoyment, whether of this world or of the next, and attains, on the strength of purity, a position higher than that of gods, he comes

[24] M. (Mahendranath Gupta), *The Gospel of sri Ramakrishna* trans. by Swāmī Nikhilānanda, New York, Ramakrishna-Vivekananda Center, 1942, pp. 245, 430, 767, 859.

[25] These are the different types of relationship between the adorer and the Adorable One, characterized respectively by serenity (awe and veneration), service, friendship, parental affection, and ardent love. The relationship of service has three different forms: (1) between the protected and the protector, (2) between the servant and the master, and (3) between the child and the parent.

to the nondual mood, with the help of which he realizes the attributeless Brahman, in which the whole universe together with Īśvara, its creator, preserver, and destroyer, has its eternal being and on the attainment of which the acme of life is reached.'[26]

4. *To the seer who returns from nirvikalpa samādhi, Nondual Brahman shines in and through the manifold*

Rare, indeed, is the spiritual personage who returns from nirvikalpa samādhi to the plane of empirical experience. It is the Divine Incarnations and the elect who have the special capacity to live as free souls after the realization of Nirguṇa Brahman for the upliftment of humanity. Most of the aspirants who attain nirvikalpa samādhi leave their bodies as they merge in Brahman. They generally reach the nirvikalpa state when the life's term is almost over. Only the illumined souls that return to the normal plane after nirvikalpa samādhi have the true knowledge of the universe and the Supreme Lord (parameśvara). They actually see the One in the many and the many in the One. They are rightly called the seers. Their vision of nondual Consciousness is never lost. It shines in and through everything as the sole Reality. To them is demonstrated the Upaniṣadic message, 'All this is verily Brahman.'[27] They can affirm from experience: 'All this that is before is but immortal Brahman. What is behind is Brahman. It is Brahman that is to the right, that is to the left. Brahman exists above and below. This universe is verily this Supreme Brahman.'[28] The unillumined often parrot the sublime truth; some even delude themselves with the idea that they see Brahman everywhere while their life betrays their ignorance.

The seers live in a transcendental plane beyond dualities. They experience eternal Bliss. Says Śrī Rāmakṛṣṇa: 'A man should reach the Nitya, the Absolute, by following the trail of the Līlā, the relative. It is like reaching the roof by the stairs. After realizing the Absolute, he should climb down to the Relative and live on that plane in the company of devotees, charging his mind with the love of God.[29] As declared by Śrī Kṛṣṇa: 'He who sees Me in all things, and sees all things in Me, he never becomes separated from Me, nor do I become separated from him. He who being established in unity, worships Me, who am dwelling in all beings, whatever his mode of life, that yōgī abides in Me.'[30]

It is the seers of this type that realize Nondual Brahman as transcendent and immanent as well. To their vision the Undiversified is apparently diversified, the Unconditioned is apparently conditioned,

[26] *Sri Ramakrishna, the Great Master*, pp. 221–2. [27] Ch. U. III: 14.1.
[28] Mu. U. II: 2.11. [29] *The Gospel of Sri Ramakrishna*, p. 257.
[30] BG VI: 31, 32.

the Static is apparently dynamic, the Nirguṇa is apparently Saguṇa. In some Upaniṣadic passages both the aspects have been presented side by side. So says Śaṅkara, 'Two kinds of Brahman are stated; the one having as its adjuncts the diversities of the universe, the modifications of name and form; the other, its contrary, completely free from all adjuncts.'[31] As declared by the Upaniṣads:

'Just as the same undiversified fire, when it has entered the world, becomes different according to what it burns, even so the same undiversified innermost Self becomes different according to whatever It enters; and It is also beyond.

'Just as the same undiversified air [cosmic energy] when it has entered the world, becomes different according to whatever body it goes in, even so the same undiversified innermost Self becomes different according to whatever body It enters; and It is also beyond.

'Just as the sun which helps all eyes to see, is not tainted by the defect of the eyes or the external objects revealed by it, even so the same undiversified innermost Self is not contaminated by the misery of the world, being beyond it.'[32]

'It moves and It does not move. It is far and It is also near. It is inside all this and It is also outside all this.'[33]

'For it is from Bliss [of Brahman] that all these beings are born, by Bliss, when born, do they live; into Bliss [at the time of dissolution] do they return and merge.'[34]

'One effulgent Being is hidden in all creatures. He is all-pervading, and is the innermost Self of all. He presides over all actions, and all beings reside in Him. He is the witness. He is Pure Consciousness free from the guṇas. He is transcendent.'[35]

Throughout the varied experiences of an individual the one unvaried, indivisible, immutable, Consciousness shines. The objects of experience—waking, dream, and deep sleep—widely differ; but the Light that manifests them is ever the same. It is the Light that shines as the knower and reveals all that is known, but is never known. 'Through what should one know the Knower?' asks the Upaniṣad.[36] We do not have dual experience. The subject is not known side by side with the object. They are not two coordinate existences. The same nondual self-effulgent Consciousness, being manifest as the knower, manifests the known. It is the sole independent existence. The knower is identical with It. It is also the ultimate ground of the known. Once Swāmī Vivekānanda was asked: 'If unity is the only reality, how could duality, which is perceived by all every moment,

[31] BS I: 1.11, com. [32] Ka. U. II: 2.9–11. [33] Is. U. 5.
[34] Tai. U. III: 6. [35] Sv. U. VI: 11.
[36] Br. U. II: 4.14; IV: 5.15.

have arisen?' His answer was—'Perception is never dual, it is only the representation of perception that involves duality. If perception were dual, the known could have existed independently of the knower, and *vice versa*.'[37] So says the Upaniṣad: 'This [Brahman] alone ever existing in one's own self is to be known. Truly, beyond this there is nothing else to be known. On knowing the triad—the experiencer, the world of experience, and their Ruler, the seers declare all this to be Brahman.'[38]

5. *The triple approach to Nondual Brahman—hearing the Vedic dictum, reasoning on it, and meditation*

It is evident from the foregoing discussion that Vedānta has followed a triple approach to Nondual Brahman: (1) revelation (Śruti), (2) reason (yukti), and (3) realization (anubhūti), in other words, hearing the Vedic mahāvākya, such as 'Thou art That', reasoning on it, and meditating on the Self. These are the three successive methods constituting a single course. So they must be in full accord with one another. As stated in a well-known Purāṇic verse, 'The seeker should first hear [about ātman] from the Śruti texts, then reflect [on it] through reasoning, and after reflection constantly meditate upon [it]. These are the means of Self-realization.'[39] The Śruti text which the seeker of Liberation is particularly concerned with is the declaration of the identity of the jīva and Brahman; because it sets the way to the ultimate Goal. In realizing the Self one realizes Brahman. By realizing Brahman one becomes immortal; for it eradicates ajñāna and reinstates the Self in its pristine purity and freedom. This is Liberation (mōkṣa), the cessation of all sufferings and the attainment of Supreme Bliss. The sage Yājñavalkya thus speaks of the triple method. 'The Self, my dear Maitreyi, should be realized—should be heard of, reflected on, and meditated upon. By the realization of the Self, my dear, through hearing, reflection, and meditation, all this is known.'[40] For, the Self is Brahman, Being-Consciousness-Bliss Absolute, the One only without a second; there is nothing else to know but this.

The three steps to Self-realization and their mutual relation are thus indicated by *Vedānta-paribhāṣā*:

'Hearing is a mental activity leading to the conviction that the purport of the Vedāntic texts is the reality of Brahman, the One only without a second. Reflection is a mental operation producing ratiocinative knowledge that leads to the refutation of any possible

[37] CW V, p. 238. [38] Sv. U. I: 12.
[39] Quoted in VPS (1) and com. *Vidvanmanōrañjinī* on VS, sec. 4.
[40] Br. U. II: 4.5; IV: 5.6.

contradiction from other sources of knowledge regarding the meaning established by the scriptural testimony [such as "Thou art That"]. Meditation is a mental operation helping to fix the mind on the Self by withdrawing it from objects, when it is drawn towards them by latent wrong impressions, no beginning of which can be traced. Of these, meditation is the direct means to the realization of Brahman, for we have the Śruti texts like, "Following the yōga of meditation they discovered [as the cause of the universe] the [creative] power, which has no existence apart from the self-effulgent Being, and is hidden by [the manifestations of] its own guṇas [sattva, rajas, and tamas]". Reflection is a means to meditation; because it is not possible for a person who has not reflected to meditate on the meaning of what has been heard of, for he lacks a conviction about it. And hearing is a means to reflection; because in the absence of hearing, the intention [of a passage] cannot be ascertained, and consequently no verbal comprehension can take place, with the result that there cannot be reflection leading to a certitude about the reasonableness or otherwise of the meaning of what has been heard of.'[41]

The above view of the triple method, comprising śravaṇa (hearing), manana (reflection), and nididhyāsana (meditation), is held especially by Vācaspati Miśra and his followers.

According to the Vācaspati school[42] the knowledge gained by hearing the Śruti text and by reasoning on it is invariably mediate. It can remove the seeker's ignorance regarding the existence of Nondual Brahman and his doubts and misconceptions regarding Its nature and the means of Its attainment, but cannot unveil It to him. Nor can the mediate knowledge of the Self do away with his inveterate ego-idea, his persistent self-consciousness as an individual, as a doer and experiencer. The seeker's present self-consciousness is direct, wrong though it be. It can be eliminated only by immediate

[41] VP VIII.

[42] One of the two main schools of Advaita Vedānta founded on Śaṅkara's commentary on the *Brahma-sūtras*. The other school is called the Vivaraṇa school (see footnote 46). Vācaspati Miśra, well-known as the unbiased master of all Indian systems of thought ('sarvatantra-svatantra'), lived in Mithilā (in modern Bihar) in the ninth century AD. His luminous exposition of Śaṅkara's commentary on the *Brahma-sūtras*, which is called *Bhāmatī* ('the lustrous'), forms the pillar of the school named after him. Many are the commentaries written on this commentary on Śaṅkara's commentary. The most famous of them all is Amalānanda's *Vedānta kalpataru* of the thirteenth century AD. An elucidation of this commentary written by Appayadīkṣit in the sixteenth century AD is well known as the *Vedānta-kalpataru-parimal*. Besides *Bhāmatī*, Vācaspati wrote commentaries on Patañjali's Yōga Aphorisms, Iśvarakṛṣṇa's *Sāṁkhya-kārikā*, Gōtama's Nyāya philosophy, Kumārila Bhaṭṭa's Mīmāṁsā philosophy, and so on.

apprehension of the true nature of the self.[43] To give an illustration: The illusory perception of the mirage is counteracted only by the experience of the desert, not through another's instruction, nor through reasoning. The innermost experience of the Self gained in samādhi through constant meditation removes all contrary notions of It with their root-cause ajñāna and makes It free from all superimpositions. Says Śaṅkara:

'In the realization of the Self (ātman), which is Pure Being-Consciousness-Bliss, through the breaking of one's connection with the bondage of avidyā, scriptures, reasoning, and the words of the preceptor are the means, while one's own experience attained in the inmost being [through the complete absorption of the mind in samādhi] is the evidence.'

'The preceptor as well as the Śruti instruct the pupil standing on the shore; while the man of realization crosses [the ocean of avidyā] through illumination alone supported by the grace of God.'

'Himself knowing his indivisible Self through his own experience and thus becoming perfect, a person should abide in the Self [ātman] with his mind free from all dualistic ideas.'[44]

The seeker's intuitive experience (aparōkṣānubhūti or sākṣātkāra) is the final proof or demonstration of the fundamental facts—that his very self is identical with Brahman, that Brahman is the sole reality, and that abiding in Brahman is Liberation (mōkṣa).[45] It corroborates the truths revealed by the Śruti, but does not constitute a separate means of knowledge with regard to them. According to Vedānta the Śruti is the only independent means to the knowledge of Brahman. The seeker's immediate awareness of the self as Brahman is invariably dependent on the Śruti text. It is the hearing of the mahāvākya aided by reasoning and meditation that leads to the realization of Brahman, which is the end of knowledge and not its means (pramāṇa). Therefore, the Vedic testimony is the primary means to the knowledge of Brahman, mediate or immediate.

6. *The different views of the Vācaspati and the Vivaraṇa school regarding the triple approach. The one holds 'meditation' and the other 'hearing' as the means to the direct knowledge of Brahman*

There is a difference of opinion among the followers of Śaṅkara

[43] *Vide Bhāmatī*, BS I: 1.1, S. com.

[44] VC 474, 476, 477. Cf. *Yōga-vāśiṣṭha Rāmāyaṇa*, Nirvāṇaprakaraṇa, Pt. I, 118.4, 'The Supreme Being is shown neither by the scriptures nor by the teacher. The Self is seen by one's own self through one's own mind resting on itself [being free from I-ness and my-ness].'

[45] Cf. VP VIII, 'The attainment of Brahman, which is Bliss as also the cessation of grief, is Liberation'.

regarding the position of śravaṇa (hearing) as a means to the knowledge of Brahman. According to Vācaspati Miśra, śravaṇa (hearing) is the cause of the mediate knowledge of Brahman and an indirect means to Its immediate knowledge, which is attained through nididhyāsana (meditation). Evidently, he has followed in this respect Maṇḍana Miśra, a direct disciple of Śrī Śaṅkarācārya. In their view śravaṇa (hearing) is the stepping-stone to manana (reflection) and nididhyāsana (meditation). The mediate knowledge gained through śravaṇa is confirmed through manana and turned into immediate knowledge through nididhyāsana.

But, according to the Vivaraṇa school[46] śravaṇa (hearing) is the direct means to the immediate knowledge of Brahman. Manana (reflection) and nididhyāsana (meditation) are subsidiary to it. They consolidate the knowledge gained through śravaṇa (hearing), by eradicating whatever doubts and false notions may be associated with it.[47] For though immediate, this knowledge is not, as a rule, firm in the beginning.[48] It is somewhat vague like the perception of a stump of a tree from a distance or in semi-darkness. It is through one of the mahāvākyas, such as 'Thou art That', that the pupil receives the direct knowledge of Brahman. It is said, 'The knowledge that Brahman exists is mediate; the knowledge, "I am Brahman", is immediate'.

Prakāśātma Yati, the author of the *Pañcapādikā-vivaraṇa*, (shortly *Vivaraṇa*) thus explains the relation of śravaṇa (hearing) to manana (reflection) and nididhyāsana (meditation):

'The comprehension [through hearing] of the words [such as "Thou" and "That"] that have primary and implied meanings is the immediate cause of the knowledge of the thing to be known [Brahman]; for

[46] Named after the *Pañcapādikā-vivaraṇa* (called in short 'Vivaraṇa'), a brilliant interpretation of Padmapāda's *Pañcapādikā* by Prakāśātma Yati, who lived in the thirteenth century AD. It is the pillar of this school. Padmapāda was one of the chosen four disciples of Śrī Śaṅkarācārya. His *Pañcapādikā* is a masterly exposition of Śaṅkara's commentary on the first four aphorisms of the *Brahma-sūtras*. Though far from complete, the treatise is so profound that commentaries upon commentaries have been written to elucidate it. The most famous of the explanatory treatises on Prakāśātma's *Pañcapādikā-vivaraṇa* are Vidyāraṇya's *Vivaraṇa-prameya-saṁgraha* (about AD 1350) and Rāmānanda Saraswatī's *Vivaraṇōpanyāsa* (early AD 1600). Another well-known work of the school is *Prakaṭārtha-vivaraṇa* by an anonymous author of the thirteenth century. It is an elucidation of Śaṅkara's entire commentary on the *Brahma-sūtras* in accordance with the *Pañcapādikā-vivaraṇa*. Padmapāda's *Pañcapādikā* deals with the fundamental doctrines of Nondualistic Vedānta in nine Varṇakas or discourses. An English translation of the *Pañcapādikā* by D. Venkataramiah has been published by Oriental Institute, Baroda, India; Gaekwaḍ's Oriental Series, Vol. CVII, 1948.

[47] *Vide* VPS (1); VP VIII. [48] *Vide* PD VII: 97.

the means of knowledge is the immediate antecedent to the knowledge of an object. But reflection and meditation contribute to the realization of Brahman by developing a concentrated state of the mind with regard to It in consequence of the latent impressions due to the prevailing mental tendency towards the inmost self. Hence, with respect to the comprehension of the words having primary and implied meanings [through hearing], which is the immediate cause of the result [the knowledge of the identity of the self with Brahman], reflection and meditation, being further removed, are recognized as subsidiary to it.'[49]

Thus, in the view of the author of the *Vivaraṇa*, a verbal statement (śabda), which is widely recognized as a means of mediate knowledge (parōkṣa jñānam), can also serve as the vehicle of immediate knowledge (aparōkṣa jñānam) when the knowledge of the self is concerned. The point is illustrated by a classical story 'Thou art the tenth', which we have recounted at the end of chapter VIII, sec. 12.

The same view with regard to śravaṇa (hearing) has been upheld by Sureśvarācārya, the second of the chosen four disciples of Śrī Śaṅkarācārya.[50] He maintains that through reasoning based on the Śruti texts the seeker can discriminate the immutable Self (kūṭastha) from the ever-changing not-self, but the removal of the primal ignorance (mūlājñāna) that hides the true nature of the Self is effected through hearing the dictum that declares the identity of the jīva and Brahman. He refers to the story 'Thou art the tenth' to illustrate how by listening to the Śruti teaching such as 'Thou art That', the seeker realizes the Self. Says he, 'Just as the utterance, "Thou art the tenth", led to the discovery of the tenth person by the distressed seeker, who found nine omitting himself, similarly the dictum, 'Thou art That', conveys to the seeker the right knowledge of the Self.[51] The same view has been expressed by Sureśvara in his monumental work, the *Bṛhādaraṇyaka-Upaniṣad-bhāṣya varttika*.[52] His disciple, Sarvajñātma Muni, also maintains that hearing the Vedic dictum is the primary means to the direct knowledge of Brahman.[53]

But Vācaspati is emphatic on the point that Brahman cannot be realized through śravaṇa, nor through manana, nor through śravaṇa attended with manana, but only through nididhyāsana preceded by śravaṇa and manana. According to him, the mind is the chief instrument of the knowledge of Brahman. As observed by him, 'The mind

[49] Quoted in VP VIII.
[50] These are Padmapāda, Sureśvarācārya, Hastāmalaka, and Tōṭakācārya.
[51] NS III: 68.
[52] A versified exposition of S. com. on Br. U., *Vide* Pt. I, 206–214.
[53] *Vide* SS I. 341 and com. *Anvayārtha-prakāśikā*.

prepared by the perfection of meditation on the meaning of the great saying ["Thou art That"] ascertained beyond all doubts eliminates the superimposed adjuncts of "Thou" and "That" and manifests the identity of "Thou", the self that is directly perceived, with "That".'[54] It is said in the *Muṇḍaka Upaniṣad*: 'Brahman is not reached by the eye, nor by the organ of speech, nor by any other organ, nor by austerity, nor by work. When the seeker's mind is purified by the purification of his understanding then through meditation he realizes indivisible Brahman.'[55]

According to the Vivaraṇa school, the mahāvākya is the primary means of the direct knowledge of Brahman, and not the mind. It recognizes, however, that this knowledge, though immediate, appears as mediate when there are such obstacles as doubts and wrong notions in the seeker's mind. In conveying the immediate knowledge, śabda, as a rule, depends on the removal of all these obstacles from the seeker's mind by the practice of manana and nididhyāsana. Thus, according to this school, the mind serves as an aid to śabda in the realization of the Self; but as it is an indirect means, there is no contradiction with such Śruti passages as 'Through the mind alone [Brahman] is to be realized',[56] 'This subtle ātman [the Self] has to be known by the mind',[57] 'The Self is seen by men of keen vision with their sharp, one-pointed intellect (buddhi).'[58] It is also pointed out by the school that, although the mind is the indirect means of seeing and hearing, yet the Śruti says, 'It is through the mind that one sees, through the mind one hears'.[59]

7. *Though holding different views as to the relative importance of the three methods, both schools recognize the necessity for the practice of all of them*

It is worthy of note that, though there is difference of opinion among the Nondualistic teachers[60] as to the respective merit of the three methods of Self-realization—śravaṇa, manana, and nididhyāsana—yet they agree on the point that all the three should be practised by a seeker, not once but repeatedly until the goal is attained. They all accept the authority of Bādarāyaṇa on this point, who says: 'The repeated practice [of hearing, reflection, and meditation] is imperative on account of the repeated instruction by the Śruti.'[61] As stated by Śaṅkara, 'Until one is established in the knowledge of the dictum "I am Brahman", one should continue the practice of hearing,

[54] *Bhāmatī*, BS I: 1.1, S. com.
[55] Mu. U. III: 1.8.
[56] Br. U. IV: 4.19.
[57] Mu. U. III: 1.9.
[58] Ka. U. I: 3.12.
[59] Br. U. I: 5.3.
[60] For the different views see SLS III, sec. 9, 10.
[61] BS IV: 1.1.

reflection, and meditation, being possessed of such virtues as control of the mind, control of the senses, and so forth.'[62]

There may be cases of exceptionally qualified pupils who may be able to realize Brahman in samādhi just on hearing the mahāvākya (such as, 'Thou art That') from a competent teacher, a knower of Brahman *par excellence*, prior to the practice of reflection (manana) and meditation (nididhyāsana). But even these rare individuals are acknowledged to have repeatedly practised the triple method in their previous incarnations. As observed by Śaṅkara, 'No one is seen freed from sorrows simply by comprehending the meaning of the sentence ["Thou art That"]. If, however, a person is ever seen to be freed from sorrows on the mere hearing of the sentence, it is to be inferred that he must have gone through the repeated practice of the triple method in previous lives.'[63]

8. *Only the seeker of Liberation with the fourfold qualification is capable of following the triple approach. Other auxiliary virtues of the seeker*

The triple approach to Brahman is intended only for the seeker of Liberation (mumukṣu).[64] The seeker of temporal values is not eligible for it. Not even the seeker of the academic knowledge of Brahman has the competence to pursue the course. The point is, the one precondition for the direct knowledge of Brahman is the seeker's acceptance of it as the supreme Ideal, as the ultimate Goal of life. Only the seeker of Liberation develops this attitude, for Liberation is the immediate result of the realization of Brahman. A person with academic interest in the knowledge of Brahman can at best proceed on the first two steps—śravaṇa (hearing) and manana (reflection)—but cannot practise nididhyāsana, intent meditation on the self as Brahman, even though he may gain an intellectual comprehension of their identity. Intent meditation on the self as Brahman, that is, as the sole Reality, is not possible unless the mind is impressed with the unreality of the diversified universe. As long as the world of phenomena is counted as real the mind is sure to be preoccupied with it in some way or other. It can by no means be wholly concentrated on the nondual Self. The freedom from all attachment to the manifold is a characteristic mark of the seeker's yearning for the realization of Nondual Brahman (Brahma-jijñāsā).

As observed by Śaṅkara, a spiritual aspirant possessed of the following fourfold means of attainment (sādhana-catuṣṭaya) develops the yearning for the direct knowledge of Brahman and also the capacity for the same.[65] These are:

62 VV 49. The verse is reproduced by Vidyāraṇya in PD VII: 98.
63 US XVIII: 15, 16.
64 *Vide* VP VIII.
65 *Vide* BS I: 1.1, com.; VC 16–30, AV 23–57.

(1) The discrimination between the Real and the unreal, that is, a firm conviction of the mind to the effect that Brahman is real and the manifold is unreal.
(2) A dispassion for the enjoyment of all fruits of action here and hereafter including the life of Brahmā (the cosmic soul), as a result of the understanding of their futility.
(3) The sixfold asset, namely, (1) control of the mind (śama), (2) control of the senses (dama), (3) withdrawal of the mind (uparati), i.e., the cessation of distractions, (4) fortitude (titikṣā), that is, being unaffected by the pairs of opposites, (5) faith in the words of the preceptor and the Vedānta (śraddhā), (6) concentration of the mind on Brahman (samādhāna).
(4) Yearning for Liberation or freedom from all bondages superimposed by ajñāna.

Of course, all seekers of the direct knowledge of Brahman do not develop these qualities equally well. A person with dull or moderate desire for Liberation can gradually intensify it by the practice of dispassion and the cultivation of the six virtues mentioned above.[66] The guidance of a competent teacher also helps him in this operation. According to most Vedāntic teachers, an individual belonging to any of the four stages of life (āśrama), be he a student, a householder, a hermit, or a monk, can acquire the necessary qualifications for the realization of Brahman. But in no other stage of life is there as much scope for their development as in the monastic. This is why the monks (sannyāsins) are found to be specially qualified for the knowledge of the Self or Brahman. It is true, there are instances of Kṣatriya kings excelling Brāhmaṇa priests in Brahma-vidyā. But the sannyāsins have been from the very beginning the traditional custodians of this knowledge, as is evident from the Upaniṣad:

'By virtue of self-discipline and through the grace of the Supreme Lord, the sage Śvetāśvatara realized Brahman and imparted the sacred, supreme knowledge, fully cherished by an array of seers, to the all-renouncing, ideal sannyāsins.'[67]
'This ātman (the Self) luminous and pure, whom the stainless sannyāsins see, is to be realized within the heart through the constant practice of truthfulness, self-discipline, right knowledge, and continence.'[68]

But none can acquire the fourfold qualification of a seeker of Brahman without adequate purification of the mind through such measures as moral observances, practice of charity, the worship of

[66] *Vide* VC 28. [67] Sv. U. VI: 21. [68] Mu. U. III: 1.5.

God, association with spiritual personages, the performance of duties with equanimity, the cultivation of dispassion, the study of the Vedic texts, and so forth.[69] It is said, 'The Brāhmaṇas grow the desire to know It [the Self] through the study of the Vedas, sacrificial rites, charity, and austerity in the form of dispassion'.[70] Even the preparatory methods followed by a seeker in his past incarnations bear result in his present life. Although a person may be lacking in some of the prerequisites for the cultivation of Brahma-jñāna, still he will be benefited by whatever knowledge he can gain from the practice of śravaṇa (hearing), manana (reflection), and the discrimination of the Self from the not-self.[71]

But a seeker of Self-knowledge must be possessed of physical and mental vigour, a keen understanding and dispassion to begin with. As stated in the Upaniṣad:

'This ātman (the Self) cannot be realized by him who is devoid of strength, or who is without vigilance, or who has no spirit of renunciation along with his knowledge. But if an intelligent person strives by these means, then his soul enters into Brahman, the Abode.'[72] 'The Self hidden in all beings does not appear. But it is seen by men of keen vision with their sharp, one-pointed intellect (buddhi).'[73]

Śaṅkara stresses the reasoning power of the seeker as well:

'The intelligent and wise man skilled in arguing in favor of the scriptures and refuting counter arguments against them—one who has the above characteristics is the fit recipient of the knowledge of the ātman.'[74]

9. *The imperative need of a competent teacher for the seeker of Liberation*

A seeker of truth who has developed a yearning for the direct knowledge of Brahman, well qualified as he is, should duly approach a teacher (guru) for the same. This is an inviolable behest of the Śruti, for otherwise he has little possibility of success. In the Vedāntic

[69] As defined in *Vedānta-sāra*, 'A qualified student [of the knowledge of Brahman] is the enquirer who is possessed of the fourfold means of attainment [sādhana-catuṣṭaya], who, after having studied the Vedas with the auxiliary courses [Vedāṅgas], has vaguely apprehended the purport of the entire Vedas, whose mind has been thoroughly purified, being purged of all impurities through the performance of worship, penance, and the obligatory rites for every-day life and special occasions, carried on in the present life or in the past incarnations while abstaining from acts that are forbidden and that are recommended for the fulfilment of sense-desires'.

[70] Br. U. IV: 4.22. [71] *Vide* AV 59. [72] Mu. U. III: 2.1.4.

[73] Ka. U. I: 3.12. [74] VC 16.

tradition, spiritual knowledge has invariably been transmitted by the teacher (guru) to the disciple (śiṣya). Even though well versed in the Vedas, the aspirant should not seek the knowledge of Brahman independently.[75] He should learn from the teacher as well as from the Śruti.[76] The triple method of śravaṇa (hearing), manana (reflection), and nididhyāsana (meditation) should be practised under the guidance of a competent teacher, who according to the Śruti, must be 'śrōtriya' (thoroughly grounded in the Vedic knowledge) and 'Brahma-niṣṭha' (settled in Brahman).[77] It is necessary that the teacher should be fully established both in the mediate and the immediate knowledge of Brahman. Even a knower of nirguṇa Brahman, unless he is thoroughly acquainted with the arguments for and against the Vedic teachings, cannot dispel all doubts and misconceptions of the seeker.

The Supreme task of a worthy teacher is to impart to a worthy disciple Self-knowledge, which eradicates his avidyā and sets him free forever. This knowledge is not to be found in the Śruti, which dwells on it, but does not hold it, just as a treatise on milk does not contain milk. It is the seer of Truth that has the knowledge. Not only that; he is able to transmit it to an earnest seeker. As observed by Śaṅkara, 'For when knowledge is firmly grasped it conduces to one's own good and is capable of transmission. The transmission of knowledge is helpful to the seeker like a boat to one who wants to cross a river.'[78] So right knowledge has been called 'the bark (plava)' and the teacher 'the pilot (plāvayitā)'. This is why it is imperative on the seeker to approach the seer for the direct knowledge of Brahman. There are other reasons also for which the seeker needs the guidance of the teacher.

Even an intellectual comprehension of the Self, the finest of all existences, is not easy to achieve. Contrary to all current conceptions of it, the self is changeless, birthless, deathless, beyond hunger and thirst, beyond pain and pleasure, beyond virtue and vice, all-pure, ever free and resplendent, and identical with Limitless Being-Consciousness-Bliss. It is said in the *Katha Upaniṣad*: 'Many do not have the opportunity even to hear about the Self. Though hearing of it, many cannot comprehend its nature. Wonderful is the teacher, rare is the learner. Rare, indeed, is the knower taught by an adept.'[79] Unless the teacher expounds or elucidates the sacred texts it is quite hard for the seeker to find their true meaning and harder even to grasp the spiritual truths signified by them.

Even in acquiring secular knowledge every individual mind has difficulties peculiar to itself. The teacher takes the student by the hand, as it were, solves his problems at every step and guides him

[75] *Vide* Mu. U. I: 2.12, S. com. [76] *Vide* Br. U. II: 4.5; IV: 5.6; S. com.
[77] *Vide* Mu. U. I: 2.12. [78] US, Pt. I. chap. 1.3. [79] Ka. U. I: 2.7.

through all the mazes of intellectual confusion. All this help cannot be received from written pages, lucid though the writing may be. No author can anticipate all the difficulties of all the readers for whom his treatise is intended. There are innumerable books in every branch of knowledge, yet the teacher's services cannot be dispensed with. In case the students could receive from books all the help they need, then the universities could be replaced by huge libraries and the erudite professors could devote their talents wholly to literary pursuits. If a seeker of empirical knowledge cannot do without a teacher, how can a seeker of suprasensuous knowledge? Even for the mediate knowledge of spiritual verities one needs the guidance of a teacher. How much more guidance should one have for their immediate perception! The necessity for a spiritual teacher has been stressed in Vedānta, particularly because its keynote is the direct knowledge of Brahman.

10. *The way the pupil should approach the teacher. The qualifications of each*

The importance of the teacher and the way the seeker should approach him for knowledge have been reiterated in the Vedāntic texts throughout the ages:

'Having examined the worlds attainable through work, a Brāhmaṇa should renounce desires for them; the eternal, the uncaused, cannot result from work. For the *knowledge* of that he should, sacrificial fuel in hand,[80] invariably approach a teacher who is śrōtriya [thoroughly grounded in the Vedic knowledge] and Brahma-niṣṭha [settled in Brahman].

To that pupil who has duly approached him, whose mind is perfectly calm, whose organs are under control, the illumined teacher imparts the knowledge of Brahman wholly and rightly, by which is realized the true and immutable all-pervading Being.'[81]

'Learn it by prostration, by inquiry, and by service. The sages who have seen the Truth will teach you that knowledge.'[82]

'He who has faith, who is ardent, who has controlled his senses attains knowledge. Having attained knowledge he attains Supreme Peace immediately.'[83]

'The seeker of Self-knowledge who is possessed of the fourfold means of attainment mentioned above should approach an illumined teacher, who removes bondage, who is sinless and free from sense-desire, who is thoroughly grounded in the Vedic knowledge and a perfect knower of Brahman, who is withdrawn to Brahman and is

[80] Symbolic of the offering of service by the pupil.
[81] Mu. U. I: 2.12, 13. [82] BG IV: 34. [83] *Ibid.* 39.

calm like fire that has consumed all its fuel, who is an ocean of spontaneous grace and a friend of all virtuous persons who humbly seek his guidance. Serving the teacher with devotion, the pupil should sit near him as he is pleased with his reverence, humility, and service, and ask him what should be known about the Self.'[84]

The knowledge of Brahman is the highest that man can aspire to. A seeker of this knowledge must be possessed of the best qualities of head and heart. His moral virtues are even more conducive to Self-knowledge than his intellectual capabilities. Śrī Kṛṣṇa has mentioned the following qualities as means to right knowledge.

'Humility, unpretentiousness, non-injury, forbearance, uprightness, service to the teacher, cleanliness, steadfastness, and self-control;

Dispassion towards sense-objects, absence of egoism, reflection on the evil of misery in birth, death, decrepitude, and disease;

Non-attachment, non-identification of one's own self with son, wife, home, and the rest, and constant even-mindedness in agreeable and disagreeable situation;

Unswerving devotion to Me through constant meditation on Me alone, resorting to solitude, dislike for the society of men;

Constant striving for Self-knowledge, keeping in view the end of the knowledge of Truth:

All this is declared as conducive to knowledge and the reverse is ignorance.'[85]

11. *The genial, intimate relation between the teacher and the pupil is a natural development of spiritual life.*

Not only should the disciple and the teacher both be well qualified; there should also be a genial and intimate relation between the two. While the disciple should be humble, obedient, reverent, and willing to render personal services, the teacher should be compassionate, tolerant, and unsparingly beneficent. In the absence of such a relationship the one cannot receive any inspiration or upliftment from the other. Moral and spiritual development depends more on inspiration than on instruction. Neither moral nor spiritual help can be given or received mechanically, but through mutual sympathy, understanding, and esteem. In ancient India the disciple used to carry in his hand a sacrificial faggot while approaching a teacher. This was symbolic of his spirit of service in those days when the sacrificial fire was always kept burning.

Association with the teacher serves as a source of moral and spiritual inspiration for the pupil. It is to be noted that in ancient

[84] VC 32–34. [85] BG XIII: 7–11.

India the student invariably lived with the teacher as a celibate during the whole period of training. It is also the duty of the teacher to point out to the pupil his short-comings and failings. Śaṅkara observes how the teacher helps the pupil by admonition:

'When the teacher finds indications that knowledge has not been grasped by the disciple, he should remove the causes of non-apprehension, which are past and present sins, lack of self-restraint [in talking, eating, etc.], want of previous firm knowledge of the self and the not-self (that form the subjects of discrimination between the eternal and the non-eternal), courting popular esteem, vanity of caste, etc. and so forth.

[In what way?] By means contrary to those causes—that are enjoined by the Śrutis and the Smṛtis—namely, "yama", the negative courses, such as avoidance of anger, non-injury, etc. and "niyama", the positive courses that are not contrary to knowledge. He should thoroughly impress upon the disciple qualities like humility that are the means to knowledge.'[86]

Then again, the teacher should always have the pupil's well-being in his heart. His blessings, his disinterested love, his parental solicitude for the pupil's good, serve as uplifting forces and sustain the latter's spiritual ardour even though his moods may vary. For all these reasons the Śruti declares: 'Only the knowledge which is learnt from a teacher leads to the highest good.'[87] 'He who has a teacher can know Brahman.'[88]

The sage Uddālaka illustrates with a story how the teacher liberates the pupil:

'Just as someone, my dear, might abduct a person blindfolded [from the country of] the Gāndhāras, and leave him in a place where there were no human beings; and just as that person would turn toward the east, or the north, or the south, or the west, shouting: "I have been brought here blindfolded. I have been left here blindfolded."

And as therefore someone might remove the bandages from his eyes and say to him, "Gāndhāra is in that direction; go that way"; and as therefore, having received advice and being wise, he would by asking his way from one village to another, arrive at last at Gāndhāra—in exactly the same manner does a person who has found a teacher to instruct him attain true knowledge in this world.'[89]

A pupil's reverence and gratitude for the teacher are the natural result of his inner development. They are far from conventional.

[86] US Pt. I, chap. 1.4, 5.
[87] Ch. U. IV: 9.3.
[88] *Ibid.* VI: 14.2.
[89] *Ibid.* VI: 14.1, 2.

Whoever chooses God-realization or Liberation as the supreme Ideal of life and intends to pursue the course to the very end cannot but have steadfast devotion to his unfailing guide, the guru, his greatest benefactor who removes all obstacles on the way and leads him to the Goal.

One of the Upaniṣads ends with an encomium on the devotion to the guru: 'In the heart of that high-minded person who has true devotion to God and as much devotion to the guru as to God, these truths, when told, will shine forth, will shine forth.'[90]

12. *It is especially through the* mahāvākya *that the teacher imparts the knowledge of the Self to the pupil*

To a worthy pupil who has duly approached him for the means of Liberation, the teacher expounds the mahāvākya, such as 'Thou art That', which is the only key to the direct knowledge of Nondual Brahman.[91] Liberation follows immediately from this knowledge. By declaring the identity of the individual self with the universal Self, the Vedic dictum points to the non-relational, nondual Consciousness that Brahman is. In realizing the oneness of the inmost self that is directly perceived with the all-pervading Self, the seeker realizes Being-Consciousness-Bliss Absolute beyond all distinctions and differences. The identity of the jīva and Brahman cannot be maintained without acknowledging the ultimate oneness of existence. It implies the falsity of all distinctions between an individual and the Supreme Being, which means the unreality of all limiting adjuncts of jīvahood and Īśvarahood. So it is said: 'In the sentence "Thou art That", neither the mutual connection of the two terms "Thou" and "That", nor the qualification of one by the other is the intended meaning. The intention of the sentence, according to the wise, is an absolute Being beyond all differences and distinctions.'[92]

The monotheistic philosophers, who hold the distinction between the jīva and Īśvara to be ultimate, explain the mahāvākya to signify some relation between "Thou' and 'That', and not their identity. But their interpretations, apart from misconstruing the text, contradict such Śruti passages as:

'All this is Brahman. From It the universe arises, in It the universe merges, and in It the universe lives.'[93]

[90] Sv. U. VI: 23. [91] *Vide* SS III: 302–4.

[92] VV 38; PD VII: 75. In the sentence 'It is a blue lotus', while blue qualifies 'lotus', 'lotus' qualifies 'blue', because here 'blueness' of lotus is meant, not of the sky, nor of a cloth, etc. This is mutual qualification or connection (saṁsarga). Or, it may be said that only one of the terms qualifies the other. The sentence 'Thou art That' has a different import than such qualification of the terms. Here, 'Thou' does not qualify 'That', nor does 'That' qualify 'Thou'.

[93] Ch. U. III: 14.1.

'There is no difference whatsoever in It [Brahman]. He goes from death to death, who sees the seeming difference in It [Brahman].'[94] 'To the seer, all things have verily become the Self: what delusion, what sorrow, can there be for him who realizes that oneness?'[95] 'The wise consider that to be the fourth (turīya) . . . which is uninferable, inconceivable, indefinable; which is Pure Self-awareness; which is the cessation of the manifold; which is nondual, calm, and blissful. This is the Self. This is to be realized.'[96] 'As flowing streams disappear in the sea, losing their names and forms so a knower of Brahman, free from name and form, attains the resplendent transcendent Being greater than the Great [qualified Brahman].'[97]

The relation between man and God is the keynote of all theistic faiths. Relation implies a distinction between the related. According to Nondualistic Vedānta all distinction is in the domain of ajñāna. It is not final. It persists until Brahman, the One without a second, is realized. However, Nondualistic Vedānta holds that the recognition of the relation between the jīva and Īśvara eventually leads to the apprehension of their complete unity. As we have already stated, the worship of Saguṇa Brahman is a stepping-stone to the realization of Nirguṇa Brahman. And this is the approach that suits the spiritual aspirants in general. (See ch. IX, sec. 6.)

13. *The meaning of the* mahāvākya, *'Thou art That'*

The proposition 'Thou art That' is evidently absurd, so far as the primary meanings of 'Thou' and 'That' are concerned. 'Thou' signifies an individual being. 'That' signifies the Supreme Being. How can an individual being and the Supreme Being be identical? In other words, how can man and God be the same? What is an individual? As we have already noted, man's ideas of man widely differ. An individual is not a mere physical being possessed of the bodily organs, nor is he merely a psychophysical being—an aggregate of the body, the organs, and the mind. He is primarily an experiencer with consciousness as the central principle of his being. Daily he experiences three different states—waking, dream, and deep sleep. Whatever is experienced varies, but not the experiencer, being of contrary nature. When he experiences dream the physical organs do not operate. When he experiences sleep, the mind does not function. As their experiencer, he is distinct from the mind as well as the body. Truly speaking, an individual is embodied consciousness. It is consciousness that underlies all his thoughts, feelings, imaginations, memories,

94 Br. U. IV: 4.19; Ka. U. II: 1.11.
95 Is. U. 7.
96 Ma. U. VII.
97 Mu. U. III: 2.8.

perceptions, and actions. The same unvaried consciousness has varied expressions through his mind, the organs, and the body. Thus, in the Vedāntic view an individual is this central principle of consciousness which, being reflected in his psychophysical system and identified with it through a particular mode of the mind, becomes manifest as the ego, the cognizing self that functions in various ways.

An individual endures even after he leaves the physical body at death. He is not shorn of the subtle body, of which the mind is the main component. It is with the subtle body as a vehicle that the individual soul transmigrates, repeatedly undergoing birth and death and experiencing pain and pleasure in consequence of his karma. As the repository of his latent tendencies, desires, and capacities, the subtle body betokens the jīva's past lives and is therefore called 'liṅga śarīra (the index body)'. Every individual has a mind of his own. It is the mind rather than the body that distinguishes one individual from another. The twin brothers or sisters prove to be two distinct individuals despite closest physical resemblance. Indeed, a continuous limiting adjunct of an individual is his subtle body.

An individual or the jīva is thus defined:

'The principle of consciousness that is the ground of the subtle body, its reflection in the subtle body, and the subtle body—the combination of these three is termed "the jīva".'[98]

In the words of Śaṅkara:

'The principle of consciousness united with the mind (antaḥkaraṇa) which is the basis of the ego-idea, and is signified by the term "I", is the primary meaning of the word "thou".'[99]

Now, what is the primary meaning of "That"? As defined by Śaṅkara:

'The Supreme Being-Consciousness-Bliss, whose limiting adjunct is māyā, who is the cause of the universe and is possessed of such attributes as omniscience, omnipotence, etc., who is qualified by remoteness or mediately known, is the primary meaning of the word "That".'[100]

Evidently, the two words, 'Thou' and 'That', in their primary sense, do not refer to one and the same entity. So there is an apparent contradiction in the statement 'Thou art That'. As we have already noted (ch. VIII, sec. 7), in case the primary meanings of the words of a sentence prove inadequate for the comprehension of their logical connection and the import of the statement, then their

[98] PD IV: 11. [99] VV 44. [100] *Ibid.* 45.

implied meanings have to be sought. The implication of 'Thou' and 'That' in the dictum 'Thou art That' is veritably the same. The ground of both 'Thou' and 'That' is unqualified Pure Consciousness beyond all limitations, and this is implied by either term. Therefore, there is no contradiction in the sentence 'Thou art That'. The implied meaning of a word is inevitably connected with its direct meaning. Pure Consciousness, or Being-Consciousness-Bliss associated with māyā, the cosmic principle of appearance and becoming, is the omnipresent Lord of the manifold. This is the primary meaning of 'That'. Pure Consciousness associated with individual ajñāna and reflected in it and its modifications turns into a transmigratory being that experiences pain and pleasure because of non-discrimination between itself and its adjuncts. This is the primary meaning of 'Thou'. Obviously, Pure Consciousness is the Reality underlying both, 'Thou (the jīva)' and 'That (Īśvara)'. They point to one and the same Nondual Consciousness (Brahman).

We have explained in the previous chapter that the empirical self is basically immutable consciousness (kūṭastha caitanya). Though associated with individual ajñāna, the kūṭastha (the immutable self) is not limited or qualified by it, but only betokened by it. Just as the same limitless sky seen from different windows appears to be different in relation to each window, similarly, the same all-pervading Consciousness being associated with different individual minds appears to be diverse kūṭasthas (immutable selves). In fact, the kūṭastha or the sākṣī caitanya (consciousness as the witness-self), though apparently different in the case of each individual, is by no means limited. Thus, the empirical self is fundamentally the transcendental Supreme Self. This truth is beautifully illustrated in the Upaniṣad by an imagery. 'Two birds, always united, and of the same name (ātman) abide in the same tree. One of them eats fruits of different tastes. The other looks on without eating. Being attached to the same tree the jīva is deluded and grieves helplessly. But when he perceives the other [the transcendental Self] the Lord that is worshipped, and His glory as his own, then he becomes free from grief.'[101]

Indeed, the same transcendental Consciousness, being reflected in each individual ajñāna and its product, the subtle body (comprising the mind, the ego, the ten organs, the five vital forces), is apparently divided into countless individual souls. By negating the limiting adjuncts as 'not this', 'not this', an individual knows the self to be 'self-effulgent Consciousness, the knower, the inmost reality free from actions and directly perceived, the Witness, the bestower of consciousness [to mind, organs, etc., which receives Its radiance], the One that is all-pervading, eternal, attributeless, and without a second.'[102]

[101] Mu. U. III: 1.1, 2; Sv. U. IV: 6, 7.

[102] US XVIII: 26.

14. *Being convinced of the true import of the* mahāvākya *through hearing and reasoning, the pupil has to practise intent meditation (nididhyāsana) for Self-realization*

Thus, by hearing and reasoning the seeker knows the right meaning of the dictum 'Thou art That', and by contemplating on the message with reasoning he becomes convinced of its truth. It is said, 'The teaching "Thou art That" will surely be useless in the absence of the knowledge "I am Brahman". This teaching is of use only to those who are acquainted with the discrimination between the self and the not-self.'[103] We have explained this method of reasoning in the preceding chapter (sec. 8).

The next step for the seeker of Liberation is to intently meditate on the Self as Brahman, and realize their identity in nirvikalpa samādhi. We shall dwell on this theme in the following chapter. We close with a pertinent observation by Śaṅkara:

'As gold purified by thorough heating on the fire gives up its impurities and attains to its own lustre, so the mind, through meditation, gives up its impurities of sattva, rajas, and tamas, and attains to the reality of Brahman.'

'When the mind thus purified by constant practice, is merged in Brahman, then the samādhi passes on from the savikalpa to the nirvikalpa state, and leads directly to the realization of the Bliss of Brahman, the One without a second.'

'Reflection [manana] should be considered a hundred times superior to hearing [śravaṇa] and meditation [nididhyāsana] a hundred thousand times superior to reflection even, but the nirvikalpa samādhi is simply infinite in its results.'[104]

[103] *Ibid.* 90. [104] VC 361, 362, 364.

CHAPTER XII

'THE KNOWER OF BRAHMAN ATTAINS THE HIGHEST'*

1. *Meditation on the Self is the direct approach to Brahman. Its culmination is immediate experience. Scriptural study, reasoning, and all other disciplines are subsidiary means*

Once the seeker is fully convinced that his inmost self is Brahman, Pure Being-Consciousness-Bliss, then his whole mind centres upon the sole idea of the realization of Brahman, which means Liberation. No longer does he remain occupied with scriptural study and ratiocination. He puts away the books, ceases to argue, closes his eyes, and plunges into meditation on the inmost Self, which is the direct and immediate means to the realization of Brahman. As stated in the Kaṭha Upaniṣad: 'Rare is the wise man [capable of discriminating the Self from the not-self) who, desirous of immortality, sees the innermost Self with the eyes turned inward.'[1] Further, 'This Ātman [the Self] cannot be attained by the study of the Vedas, nor through intelligence, nor by much hearing of the sacred texts. He who chooses Ātman—by him alone is Ātman attained. To him this Ātman reveals Its true nature.'[2]

So says the *Bṛhadāraṇyaka Upaniṣad*: 'The intelligent seeker of Brahman, knowing about this alone [the real nature of the self] should attain intuitive knowledge (prajñā). [He] should not think of too many words; for it is particularly fatiguing to the organ of speech.'[3] Commenting on this Śaṅkara remarks: 'This restriction on too many words implies that a few words dealing exclusively with the unity of the Self, are permissible. The *Muṇḍaka Upaniṣad* has it: "Meditate upon the Self with the help of the syllable Ōm" [II: 2.6] and "Give up all other speech" [II: 2.5].'

Just as one cannot be cured of an ailment only by knowing the remedy without applying it, similarly, one cannot get rid of ajñāna (the primal ignorance) by knowing about Brahman from the sacred

* Tai. U. II: 1.3.

[1] Ka. U. II: 1.1. [2] Ka. U. I: 2.23; Mu. U. III: 2.3.
[3] Br. U. IV: 4.21.

texts and the teacher only without striving after Its realization. In the words of Śaṅkara:

'For one who has been bitten by the serpent of ignorance (ajñāna) the only remedy is the knowledge of Brahman. Of what avail are the Vedas and the śāstras, mantras, and medicines to such a one? A disease does not leave off if one simply utters the name of the medicine, without taking it; similarly, without direct knowledge one cannot be liberated by the mere utterance of the word Brahman.'[4]

By scriptural study and reasoning only one cannot realize Brahman without spiritual discipline, such as discrimination between the Real and the unreal, dispassion for the temporal, self-control, serenity of the mind, steadfast devotion, and above all meditation. The need of spiritual practice for a seeker of God has been very much emphasized in this age by Śrī Rāmakṛṣṇa. In his view the study of the sacred texts and argumentation have a minor place in spiritual life. Says he:

'What will you achieve by mere study of scriptures? The scriptures contain a mixture of sand and sugar, as it were. It is extremely difficult to separate the sugar from the sand. . . . One should learn the essence of the scriptures from the guru and then practise sādhana [spiritual discipline]. If one rightly follows spiritual discipline, then one directly sees God. The discipline is said to be rightly followed only when one plunges in. What will a man gain by merely reasoning about the words of the scriptures? Ah, fools! They reason themselves to death over information about the path. They never take the plunge. What a pity!'[5]

Addiction to even scriptural study causes distraction. So says Śaṅkara: 'The scriptures consisting of many words are a dense forest which causes the mind to ramble.'[6] Like the desire for physical comfort or social recognition, the desire for the sacred lore forms an obstacle to Self-realization. So a seeker of Self-knowledge has to overcome it. As observed by Śaṅkara:

'Owing to the desire to walk after society, the passion for too much study of the scriptures, and the desire to keep the body comfortable, people cannot attain to proper realization. For one who seeks deliverance from the prison of transmigratory existence, these three desires have been designated by the wise as strong iron fetters to shackle one's feet. He who is free from them truly attains Liberation.'[7]

[4] VC 61, 62.
[5] *The Gospel of Sri Ramakrishna*, p. 543.
[6] VC 60.
[7] VC 271, 272.

Meditation is the innermost spiritual discipline. It is through this that Illumination is attained. Brahman that is unmanifest becomes manifest when the mind is purged of ignorance in perfect meditation.[8] All other spiritual courses are intended to prepare the mind for the practice of meditation. Usually the mind is concentrated on the object of meditation through a symbol. In deep meditation the mind becomes focused on the object and stays still without flickering like a steady flame of light in a windless cell. This culminates in samādhi, which closes the gap between the meditator and the object of meditation, his innermost Self, and unites the two. In meditation there is the tripartite distinction of the meditator, the object of meditation, and the act of meditation, in other words, of the knower, the knowable, and the process of knowledge. But in samādhi this distinction subsides. The three are fused into an integral consciousness. The less marked the distinction, the deeper is the samādhi. So there are different states of samādhi. They are broadly classified under two main heads: savikalpa (with distinction) and nirvikalpa (without distinction). The one is the realization of Saguṇa Brahman, the other of Nirguṇa Brahman.

Since God is the Soul of all souls, the innermost Self of all, He cannot be objectified. Knowing Him means either knowing one's essential unity with Him or realizing one's identity with Him. In savikalpa samādhi the distinction between the knower and the known, in other words, between the meditator and the object of meditation, is not obliterated. The self is perceived as inseparable from, but not identical with, the Supreme Self. It is the realization of the adorer's deepest relationship or union with the Adorable One. As the wave is inseparably connected with the ocean, so is the individual soul with the Supreme Self. This is the goal attained by the worshippers of Saguṇa Brahman.

In nirvikalpa samādhi the distinction between the knower and the known is lost. The mind becomes modeless and blends with Brahman. The veil of ajñāna completely disappears. One unbroken, limitless Consciousness beyond the duality of the subject and the object prevails. It is said, 'The distinction of the knower, knowledge, and the goal of knowledge does not endure in the all-transcendent Self. Being of the nature of Bliss that is Pure Consciousness, It shines of Itself.'[9] Thus, in realizing the identity of the self and Brahman in nirvikalpa samādhi, the seeker is immersed in a limitless ocean of effulgent Bliss. 'When the Ātman, the One without a second, is realized by means of nirvikalpa samādhi, then the heart's knot of ignorance is totally destroyed.'[10]

[8] *Vide* BS III: 2.24.

[9] AB 41.

[10] VC 353.

2. *The way the seeker meditates on Nondual Brahman*

In starting meditation the seeker envisages Brahman as the Supreme Goal, as the Highest Ideal: It is That beyond the attainment of which there is no greater attainment, beyond the joy of which there is no greater joy, beyond the knowledge of which there is no greater knowledge; It is That on seeing which there remains nothing more to see, on realizing which one is not reborn, on knowing which there remains nothing more to know; It is That which is Pure Being-Consciousness-Bliss without a second, which fills above and below and all other directions, which is One, infinite, and eternal. Then he meditates on the identity of the self with Brahman.

A preceptor thus exhorts his pupil to meditate on Brahman:

'That which, though One only, is the cause of the many; which refutes all other causes, but is Itself without cause; distinct from Māyā and its effect, the universe; and independent;—that Brahman art thou, meditate on this in thy mind.

That which is free from duality; which is infinite and indestructible; distinct from the universe and Māyā;—supreme, eternal; which is undying Bliss; taintless;—that Brahman art thou, meditate on this in thy mind.

That Reality which [though One] appears variously owing to delusion—taking on names and forms, attributes and changes, Itself always unchanged, like gold in its modifications;—that Brahman art thou, meditate on this in thy mind.

That beyond which there is nothing; which shines even above Māyā, which again is superior to its effect, the universe; the inmost Self of all, free from differentiation; the Real Self, the Existence-Knowledge-Bliss absolute; infinite and immutable;—that Brahman art thou, meditate on this in thy mind.'[11]

While repeating the sacred formula, 'I am Brahman', within himself, the seeker at first concentrates his mind on the unchanging self, the kūṭastha, the immutable consciousness, which is implied by the term 'I'. Next he ponders on the immutable self as distinct from and devoid of all limiting adjuncts, such as the gross body, the subtle body, and the causal body, which have no existence apart from the witness-self (sākṣī), being rooted in ajñāna. Then he meditates on the self as Brahman, Pure Being-Consciousness-Bliss, beyond all distinctions and limitations.

3. *The process of meditation that leads to the realization of Brahman in nirvikalpa samādhi*

Through intense meditation (nididhyāsana) on the immutable self with the thought 'I am Brahman' the seeker's mind conforms to

[11] VC 260–263.

Brahman. It becomes tranquil and transparent and absorbed in Brahman, but not unified with It, because the veil of ajñāna endures. This mental modification suffused with the knowledge of the identity of ātman and Brahman is called Brahmātmākārā vṛtti. It destroys ajñāna and brings about the realization of Brahman. So says Śaṅkara, 'It is to the buddhi [the cognitive mind] and not to the Self which is immutable that the knowledge "I am Brahman" belongs. Moreover, the Self is changeless, because It has no other witness.'[12] In fact, it is the seeker's individualized self, consciousness reflected in the mind and apparently limited (pramātṛ-caitanya) that realizes its oneness with Brahman as 'I am Brahman'. The seeker endures as an individual as long as the mind endures. The light of Brahman manifest in the mental modification called 'Brahmātmākārā vṛtti' is indirect, being reflected Consciousness. The seeker's individual consciousness becomes allied with it. Brahman is not yet directly perceived as the nondual Self.

We have mentioned before (ch. III, sec. 7, 8) that in the perception of an external object, the mental mode coincident with the object serves a twofold purpose. Firstly, it uncovers the object for the perceiver by removing the veil of ajñāna that envelops it. Secondly, Consciousness underlying the object being manifest in the mental mode illumines the object for the perceiver, and this proves to be the knowledge of the object (phala-caitanya). But in the realization of Brahman the eradication of the veil of ajñāna by the mental modification (Brahmātmākārā vṛtti) is all that is necessary. Brahman being self-effulgent nothing is needed for Its manifestation. The mental mode coincident with It removes the veil of ajñāna but does not objectify It.[13] By no means can Brahman be an object of cognition.

With the eradication of ajñāna the mental modification (Brahmātmākārā vṛtti) subsides; then the mind coalesces in Brahman and is suffused with Pure Consciousness, where the seeker's 'I'-consciousness merges. As the mind of the seeker gets into this modeless state, self-luminous Brahman is unveiled and is directly perceived as 'I am Brahman'; instantly, the Self is realized as indivisible, limitless Pure Consciousness in nirvikalpa samādhi. This is illumination (prajñā), or immediate awareness (aparōkṣānubhūti) beyond the distinction of the knower and the known, the self and the not-self. In this transcendental experience there is no other; the mind is fused with Brahman, Pure Being-Consciousness-Bliss; the order of phenomena disappears altogether.[14]

[12] US XVIII: 159. [13] *Vide* PD VII: 90–92.

[14] *Vide* Br. U. II: 4.14. Cf. S. Radhakrishnan: *An Idealist View of Life*, London, Allen & Unwin, 1957, p. 138. 'This intuitive knowledge arises from an intimate fusion of mind with reality. It is knowledge by being and not by

When the knower's mind dissolves into this state, the individual consciousness, divested of its limiting adjuncts, merges in Absolute Brahman, indivisible Being-Consciousness-Bliss (akhaṇḍa Saccidānanda). His body drops; he attains immediate Liberation. Being released from the body he is not reborn.[15] The individual soul is restored to its true nature as limitless Being-Consciousness-Bliss. In nirvikalpa samādhi the mind stays as coalescent in Brahman, but dissolves in Liberation at death. Then Brahman alone shines. There is a difference between the realization of Brahman and Absolute Brahman.

Only a few among the seekers of Liberation attain nirvikalpa samādhi. Fewer still attain it during the continuation of their life-terms and return to the normal plane of consciousness. The rest reach this state at the close of their life-time. Their experience of nirvikalpa samādhi is, as a rule, of short duration and is hardly repeated. They leave the body in that state and attain Liberation (videha-mukti). In exceptional cases the body stays alive in nirvikalpa samādhi for twenty-one days at the most, and then drops like a dry leaf.

One may ask, how can the mental modification (Brahmātmākārā vṛtti) destroy primal ajñāna, its material cause? The answer is, it is not actually the mental modification that destroys ajñāna, but the light of Pure Consciousness (Brahma-caitanya) that is manifest in it. Just as fire arising from wood consumes different things as well as wood and then becomes extinct; similarly, the knowledge of Brahman as the inmost Self, manifest through the mental mode, mediate as it is, consumes ajñāna and the mental mode as well, and then becomes extinct.[16] It is true that Pure Consciousness (Brahma-caitanya), the locus of ajñāna, is contrary, and not contradictory, to it. But the same Consciousness shining through the mental mode (Brahmātmākārā vṛtti) proves contradictory to ajñāna, and annihilates it. To give an illustration: The same sunlight that illumines a piece of straw can burn it if focused through a concave lens.[17]

The state of the mind in nirvikalpa samādhi can be contrasted with the state of the mind in profound sleep (suṣupti). In dreamless deep sleep all the functions and the features of the mind, including even the ego-idea, subside into a state of unspecified, undifferentiated unawareness, or homogeneous ignorance, beyond the distinction of the experiencer and the experienced. As stated in the Upaniṣad, 'In this state a father is no father, a mother no mother, the worlds no worlds, the gods no gods, the Vedas no Vedas'.[18] When a person

senses or by symbols. It is awareness of the truth of things by identity. We become one with the truth, one with the object of knowledge.'

15 *Vide* Ka. U. II: 2.1.

16 *Vide* SLS III: 12. Cf. SB XI: 13.7.

17 SLS III: 12.

18 Br. U. IV: 3.22.

awakes from deep sleep he recalls the experience, because the immutable self (kūṭastha), the basis of the ego, stays as the witness of that homogeneous ignorance, or causal ajñāna, which is pure and simple inapprehension.

In nirvikalpa samādhi, contrary to deep sleep, all the features and functions of the mind, including even the ego-idea, are absorbed in unspecified, undifferentiated awareness, or Pure Consciousness beyond the distinction of the knower and the known. Whereas in deep sleep the mind is completely engulfed in ignorance or darkness, in nirvikalpa samādhi it is thoroughly suffused with the light of Pure Consciousness. This makes all the difference between the two states. In nirvikalpa samādhi, the immutable self beyond the ego stays as the witness of undifferentiated consciousness, while in deep sleep it endures as the witness of unspecified ignorance or inapprehension. So in either case the experiencer can recall the experience on his return to the physical plane. But the two experiences produce diametrically opposite results. From sleep a person returns with all his ignorance. His doubts, fears, wrong notions, and tendencies rooted in ajñāna remain just the same. But from nirvikalpa samādhi one returns as an illumined person freed from ajñāna. As declared by the Muṇḍaka Upaniṣad: 'When That which is transcendent and immanent is perceived then are all knots of the heart cut asunder, all doubts dispelled, and all latent impressions of karma eradicated.'[19]

4. *Rare individuals 'attain Brahman here' and live as free souls. A knower of Nirguṇa Brahman merges in Brahman at death*

As we have noted above, rare is the seeker who attains nirvikalpa samādhi during the continuation of the term of life. This means that the impressions of past karma to which his present bodily existence is due are not exhausted. Some are still in force. Because of the remnant of these impressions (prārabdha-karma-śeṣa) such a knower of Brahman regains body-consciousness. In his case the mental mode manifesting the identity of ātman and Brahman (Brahmātmākārā vṛtti) eradicates the veiling power (āvaraṇa-śakti) of ajñāna. But a vestige of ajñāna (avidyā-leśa) with the projecting power (vikṣepa-śakti) persists on account of the residue of the past impressions that are to bear fruit in this life.[20] An illumined person of this type is free even though living in the body. He is said to be jīvan-mukta (liberated-in-life).

It is the projecting power of ajñāna that is responsible for the superimposition of the subtle and the gross body on the self. The veiling power of ajñāna functions in two distinct ways: (1) hiding the

[19] II: 2.8. [20] *Vide* SLS IV: 1.

existence of Brahman (asattvāpādaka) and (2) hiding the revelation of Brahman (abhāṇāpādaka). The first phase of the veiling power is removed by the knowledge of Brahman gained through śravaṇa (hearing) and manana (reflection). Then the seeker becomes convinced of the existence and nature of Brahman, but cannot perceive Brahman. The second phase of the veiling power is removed by the aforesaid mental modification (Brahmātmākārā vṛtti) developed by nididhyāsana (meditation).[21] In consequence of this, Brahman is revealed to the seeker in nirvikalpa samādhi. It is worthy of note that the removal of the veil of ajñāna and the realization of Brahman are not two different processes. The one means the other. Thus, Liberation is but the cessation of ajñāna. It is the reinstatement of the self in its pristine freedom and blissfulness. It is not a new attainment or a new knowledge, It is like the regaining of kingship by a king on waking from a dream in which he lost it.

An illumined person who regains body-consciousness after nirvikalpa samādhi identifies himself with the not-self in no form whatsoever. He experiences the manifold; but in and through everything he perceives Brahman as the One Self of all. He dwells in the body, but is never deluded by the ego-idea. He gets along with a semblance of the ego, being ever aware of his identity with Brahman. Though not impelled by the ego, yet the body runs its course because of the momentum of the past impressions that have caused it, somewhat like the potter's wheel that continues to revolve even after the rod that turns it is withdrawn. The knower of Brahman has nothing to desire. Being established in Self-knowledge he has constant serenity of mind which is unaffected by physical and environing conditions. So it is said, '*If* a man knows the Self as "I am this", then desiring what and for whose sake will he suffer in the wake of the body?'[22] Śaṅkara remarks, 'The word "if" shows the rarity of Self-knowledge'.

Being himself free, such an illumined person leads others to freedom. He is declared to be the best knower of Brahman. 'The seer who knows [as his Self] Him who is the life of all, who shines forth variously in all beings, cannot be a declarer of truth beyond [this]. Delighted in the Self, ever devoted to the Self, and steadily active, he is the foremost of the knowers of Brahman.'[23] His thoughts and actions are naturally pure, for he is united with the All-pure. Scriptural regulations do not apply to him. 'What prescriptions and what prohibitions can there be for him who traverses the path beyond the triad of the guṇas?' says Śaṅkara with regard to Śukadeva, who was born a free soul. Even a seeker of the knowledge of Brahman does not deviate from the path of virtue, how can a knower of Brahman? As observed by Śaṅkara: 'No one likes to eat poison even if pressed

[21] *Vide* PD VII: 56. [22] Br. U. IV: 4.12. [23] Mu. U. III: 1.4.

by hunger. So, no one but an idiot will knowingly wish to eat it when his hunger has been appeased by eating sweetmeats.'[24]

The body of the jīvanmukta (the living-free) drops as soon as the remnant of those impressions of past karma to which its existence is due runs out. Forthwith his individualized self freed from the limiting adjuncts rooted in ajñāna, merges in Brahman; he attains final Liberation (videha-mukti). So it is said, 'For him there is delay only so long as he is not released [from the body] and then immediately he is absorbed in Brahman'.[25] A jīvanmukta is free from all the fetters that bind a human being to the phenomenal world. No sooner does he attain Illumination than the unfructified impressions of his past karma, the seed-forces of future births, become annihilated with the destruction of ajñāna, their root-cause. Neither merits nor demerits accrue from what actions he performs after the Illumination.[26] Consequently there remain no more impressions of karma to bind him. It is to be noted that karma produces impressions in the form of merits (puṇya) and demerits (pāpa) so long as it is impelled by the ego-idea.

A knower of Nirguṇa Brahman does not depart from the body: 'As pure water poured in pure water becomes verily the same, so also does the self of the sage who realizes Brahman.'[27] His subtle body readily dissolves, whereas the physical body is cast off, like the slough of a snake, and disintegrates in due course. So it is said:

'Of him who is without desires, who is free from desires, the objects of whose desires have been attained, and to whom all objects of desire are but the Self—the organs [the components of the subtle body] do not depart. Being but Brahman, he is merged in Brahman.

Regarding this there is this verse: "When all the desires that dwell in his heart are rooted out, then the mortal man becomes immortal, and *attains Brahman here* [in this very body]."

Just as the slough of a snake lies dead and cast away on an anthill, so does the body lie. Then the Self becomes disembodied and immortal, becomes the Supreme Self, Brahman, the Light.'[28]

Commenting on the text, 'attains Brahman here', Śaṅkara remarks, 'While living in this very body he attains oneness with Brahman, that is, Liberation'. This is also evident from what the Vedic seers say about themselves: 'Perceiving the higher light in the sun that is beyond darkness [cosmic consciousness] as identical with the higher light within us [individual consciousness], perceiving the

[24] US XVIII: 232; Cf. NS IV: 62–7.
[25] Ch. U. VI: 14.2; Cf. VV 52, 53.
[26] *Vide* BS IV: 1.13–15; S. com. on 15.
[27] Ka. U. II: 1.15.
[28] Br. U. IV: 4.6, 7.

Light that is higher than all other lights, we have attained the Supreme Light, the self-luminous One, shining in all shining deities.'[29]

'On the exhaustion of prārabdha-karma [the impressions of past karma that are bearing fruits in the present life] the jīvanmuktas are not reborn', Śaṅkara clearly states.[30] The gradual stages of overcoming ajñāna by a seeker of Liberation has been thus indicated: 'The indirect knowledge of the Self gained from the scripture removes his notion of the reality of the world of phenomena [including the gross and the subtle body]. The direct knowledge of the Self removes his engagement in this with such contrary notions as "I am an experiencer", "I am a doer". The cessation of prārabdha removes its very appearance. Thus, the seeker's ignorance of the Self is destroyed by stages.'[31] Jīvanmukti (Liberation-in-life) is recognized by all Advaita philosophers excepting a few, among whom Maṇḍana Miśra, the author of the *Brahma-siddhi*, and Sarvajñātma-muni, the author of the *Saṁkṣepa-śārīraka* are well known. Madhusūdana Sarasvatī, the celebrated author of the *Advaita-siddhi*, supports it.[32]

5. *The illumined ones living as free souls demonstrate the truth 'Thou art That'*

A concrete demonstration of the sublime nondualistic dictum 'Thou art That' is jīvanmukti—Liberation-in-life. Not only do the seers realize the Supreme Truth in the inmost depth of their being and declare it unequivocally, but also live as its shining exemplars. The Vedāntic literature is replete with the delineation of the ways of the Illumined that attain Liberation-in-life. We quote a few passages from different sources:

'The Light that is Brahman, the Light that is clear as broad daylight, the Light that is eternal, the Light that is the source of the world, the knowers of Brahman see that Supreme Light everywhere.'[33]

'He who realizes the bliss of Brahman—from where words together with thoughts turn away unable to reach—has nothing whatsoever to fear from. He is not distressed by the thought, "Why did I not do what is good? Why did I do what is evil?" Such an illumined person cherishes the Self which underlies both [good and evil]. For he who knows that both these [good and evil] are [fundamentally] but this [the Self] cherishes the Self. This, indeed, is the Upaniṣad [the sacred knowledge].'[34]

'Dwelling in this very body, we have somehow realized That [Brah-

[29] Ch. U. III: 17.7; quoted from the *Ṛg-Veda* I: 50.10.
[30] *Ajñānabōdhinī*, 209. [31] *Ibid.* 210 (quoted by Śaṅkara).
[32] AS IV: 5, pp. 890–2.
[33] *Ṛg-Veda* VIII: 6.30; quoted in Ch. U. III: 17.7. [34] Tai. U. II: 9.

man]; otherwise, we would have been ignorant and great calamity would have overtaken us. Those who know Brahman become immortal, while others only suffer misery.'[35]

'The seer does not see death or disease or sorrow. The seer sees everything and obtains everything everywhere [because he realizes the all-pervading Self].'[36]

'Resting in Brahman, with settled conviction, and without delusion, the Knower of Brahman neither rejoiceth on receiving what is pleasant, nor grieveth on receiving what is unpleasant. His mind being unattached to the sense-objects he finds the joy that is in the Self. With the mind devoted to the meditation on Brahman he attains undying Bliss.'[37]

'A friend of all beings, tranquil-minded, having the firm conviction due to knowledge and realization[38] and beholding the universe as consisting of nothing but Me [the Supreme Self] the illumined person no more undergoes misery [does not transmigrate].'[39]

'Where is activity or inactivity, where is Liberation or bondage, for me who am ever immutable and indivisible and established in the Self?'[40]

'Sometimes a fool, sometimes a sage, sometimes possessed of regal splendour; sometimes wandering, sometimes behaving like a motionless python, sometimes wearing a benign expression; sometimes honoured, sometimes insulted, sometimes unknown: thus lives the man of realization, ever happy with Supreme Bliss.

Though without riches, yet ever content; though helpless, yet very powerful; though not enjoying sense-objects, yet eternally satisfied; though unequalled, yet looking upon all with an eye of equality.

Though doing, yet inactive, though experiencing fruits of past actions, yet untouched by them; though possessed of a body, yet without identification with it; though limited, yet omnipresent is he.'[41]

6. *A brilliant example of the attainment of nirvikalpa samādhi in the modern age is set by Śrī Rāmākṛṣṇa. Two eye-witnesses' report on his state of samādhi*

A graphic account of the attainment of the nirvikalpa samādhi by Śrī Rāmakṛṣṇa in this very modern age has been given by his direct disciple and biographer, Swāmī Sāradānanda. It happened in the year 1865, when Śrī Rāmakṛṣṇa was twenty-nine years old. After initiating him into sannyāsa (the monastic ideal of complete renunci-

[35] Br. U. IV: 4.14. [36] Ch. U. VII: 26.2. [37] BG V: 20, 21.

[38] 'Knowledge' means mental grasp of the oneness of the Self, 'realization' direct perception of the same. [39] SB XI: 7.12.

[40] *Aṣṭāvakra-saṁhitā* XX: 12. [41] VC 542–4.

ation) his teacher, Tōtā Purī, who had realized Nondual Brahman, instructed him to be identified with Brahman. In the words of Swāmī Sāradānanda:

Śrī Tōtā tried to make the Master [Śrī Rāmakṛṣṇa] attain samādhi on that day with the help of various arguments and conclusive quotations from the Śāstras. The Master said to us that Śrī Tōtā girt up his loins, as it were, to make the experiences gained by him from his life-long sādhanā [spiritual practice] enter into the Master's mind on that occasion and put him immediately into the nondual mood of samādhi.

'After initiating me', said the Master, '"the naked one"[42] taught me many dicta conveying the conclusion of the Vedānta, and asked me to make my mind free of function in all respects and merge in the meditation of the Self. But, it so happened with me that when I sat for meditation I could by no means make my mind go beyond the bounds of name and form and cease functioning. The mind withdrew itself easily from all other things but, as soon as it did so, the intimately familiar form of the Mother of the universe, consisting of the effulgence of Pure Consciousness, appeared before it as living and moving and made me quite oblivious of the renunciation of names and forms of all descriptions. When I listened to the conclusive dicta and sat for meditation, this happened over and over again. Almost despairing of the attainment of the nirvikalpa samādhi, I then opened my eyes and said to the naked one, "No, it cannot be done; I cannot make the mind free from functioning and force it to dive into the Self". Scolding me severely, the naked one said very excitedly, "What, it can't be done! What utter defiance!" He then looked about in the hut and finding a broken piece of glass he took it in his hand and forcibly pierced its needle-like pointed end into my forehead between the eyebrows and said, "Collect the mind here to this point". With a firm determination I sat for meditation again and, as soon as the holy form of the Divine Mother appeared now before the mind as previously, I looked upon knowledge as a sword and cut it mentally in two with that sword of knowledge. There remained then no function in the mind, which transcended quickly the realm of names and forms, making me merge in samādhi.'

Tōtā remained sitting for a long time beside the Master who entered into samādhi in the manner mentioned before. Then coming out of the hut silently, he locked the door up lest someone should enter the hut without his knowledge and disturb him. He took his seat under the Pañcavaṭī, not far from the hut and was awaiting the Master's call to open the door.

[42] Since Tōtā Purī put on only a loin-cloth, Śrī Rāmakṛṣṇa endearingly called him 'Naṅtā (the nude, the naked one)'.

The day passed into night. Slowly and calmly days rolled on. At the end of three days, when Tōtā did not still hear the Master's call, he was filled with curiosity and astonishment and left his seat to open the door. With a view to knowing the condition of his disciple, he entered the hut and saw that the Master was sitting in the same posture in which he had left him and that there was not the slightest function of the vital force in his body, but that his face was calm and sedate and full of effulgence. He understood that the disciple was completely dead to the external world and that his mind, merged in Brahman, was calm and motionless like an unflickering lamp in a windless place. . . .

Tōtā then undertook the process of bringing the disciple back to the consciousness of the external world.[43]

Śrī Rāmakṛṣṇa's life was a complete demonstration of both nirvikalpa and savikalpa samādhi. Throughout the rest of his life he had almost daily experience of the one or the other, or of both. Once being asked about the nature of Śrī Rāmakṛṣṇa's samādhi Swāmī Brahmānanda, his most intimate and beloved disciple, said 'He remained absorbed in different states of samādhi at different times'.[44] Indeed, the Divine Master was capable of moving up and down the different stages of ecstatic experience from its acme in nirvikalpa samādhi to the varying devotional moods with more or less external consciousness. This was due to the fact that the usual resting ground of his mind was somewhere between Nirguṇa and Saguṇa Brahman, the line of demarcation of the Absolute and the relative, whence all individuations proceed. This is technically called 'bhāva-mukha', the starting-point of all ideations.

Śrī Rāmakṛṣṇa's 'I-consciousness' was ever united with the universal consciousness. Says Swāmī Sāradānanda,

'In nirvikalpa samādhi, the Master's "I-consciousness" disappeared totally; his pulse, heart-beat, etc., stopped simultaneously. Śrī Mahendralal Sarkar and other doctors examined him with the help of instruments and found no sign of the functioning of his heart. Not satisfied with that, his friend, another doctor, went further and touched with his finger the Master's eye-ball, and found it insensitive to touch like that of a dead man.'[45]

The present writer heard from an authentic source that the only indication of the livingness of the body in this state was its heat.

[43] *Sri Ramakrishna, the Great Master*, pp. 255–6.
[44] *Dharma-prasaṅge Swāmī Brahmānanda*, p. 26.
[45] *Sri Ramakrishna, the Great Master*, p. 341.

The above incident took place in October, 1885, when Śrī Rāmakṛṣṇa was staying in a rented house at Shyāmpukur in Calcutta for medical treatment.

Another eye-witness, Mr Nagendranath Gupta, a journalist of considerable fame (sometime editor of the *Tribune* of Lahore), writes about Śrī Rāmakṛṣṇa's samādhi:

'Rāmakrishna Paramahaṁsa[45a] frequently passed into a trance or samādhi. The exciting cause was invariably some spiritual experience or some new spiritual perception. On one occasion —it was in 1881— I formed one of a party that had gone with Keshub Chunder Sen by river to see the Paramahaṁsa. He was brought on board our steamer, which belonged to Maharaja Nripendra Narayana Bhup of Kuch Behar, Keshub's son-in-law. The Paramahaṁsa, as is well known, was a worshipper of the goddess Kālī, but just about that time he was engaged in the contemplation of Brahman, the formless (nirākāra), and had some previous conversation with Keshub on this subject. He was sitting close to Keshub facing him, and the conversation was practically a monologue, for either Keshub or someone else would put a brief question, and in answer the Paramahamsa with his marvellous gift of speech and illustration would hold his hearers entranced. All of us there hung breathless upon his words.

And gradually the conversation came round to nirākāra (formless) Brahman, when the Paramahaṁsa, after repeating the word "nirākāra" two or three times to himself, passed into a state of samādhi. Except the rigidity of the body there was no quivering of the muscles or nerves, no abrupt or convulsive movement of any kind. The fingers of the two hands as they lay in his lap were slightly curled. But a most wonderful change had come over the face. The lips were slightly parted as if in a smile, with the gleam of the white teeth in between. The eyes were half closed with the balls and pupils partly visible, and over the whole countenance was an ineffable expression of the holiest and most ecstatic beatitude. We watched him in respectful silence for some minutes, after which Trailokya Nath Sanyal, known as the singing apostle in Keshub Chunder Sen's party, sang a hymn to the accompaniment of music and the Paramahaṁsa slowly opened his eyes, looked inquiringly around him for a few seconds, and then resumed the conversation. No reference was made either by him or anyone else to his trance (samādhi).'[46]

[45a] Paramahaṁsa (lit. the great swan) is an epithet of a knower of Brahman whose soul sports like a swan in the placid ocean of Pure Being-Consciousness-Bliss. During his life-time Śrī Rāmakṛṣṇa was renowned as a Paramahaṁsa.

[46] *Ramakrishna-Vivekananda* by Nagendranath Gupta, Bombay, Sri Ramakrishna Math, 1933, pp. 59–60.

7. The triple approach to Nirguṅa Brahman is meant for the specially qualified seekers. The difference between jñāna (knowledge) and dhyāna (meditation). Nididhyāsana is a special case of meditation that partakes of both

The triple course, consisting of śravaṇa, manana, and nididhyāsana, is the direct approach to Nirguṇa Brahman with no mediating means. It is a steep, straight way without any curve or slope or resting-place. It does not befit all seekers of Liberation, earnest though they be. Only the most qualified spiritual aspirants (uttama adhikāris) are capable of following it. They are the seekers who have developed by preliminary disciplines an intense longing for the realization of Nirguṇa Brahman along with complete detachment from all that is temporal or conditioned. Over and above, they are possessed of such reasoning power and penetrating insight as to be able thoroughly to dissociate the Self from all its adjuncts and comprehend it as Pure Being-Consciousness-Bliss that Brahman is.

It is to be noted that the term 'nididhyāsana' in this context does not mean the kind of meditation (dhyāna) that is usually practised with a symbol. It is more like a process of knowledge or right apprehension. In the Upaniṣadic text we notice that the sage Yājñavalkya, while prescribing śravaṇa (hearing), manana (reflection), and nididhyāsana (meditation) as the threefold means of Self-realization has substituted in the next sentence the word 'vijñāna' (right apprehension) for 'nididhyāsana': The passage is quoted below:

'The Self, my dear Maitreyi, should be realized—should be heard of, reflected on, and "meditated upon". By the realization of the Self, my dear, through hearing, reflection, and, "right apprehension (vijñāna)", all this is known.'[47]

The term 'vijñāna' usually signifies the immediate apprehension of Brahman (aparōkṣānubhūti), but in this context it is used as a means to that end. As noted by Sureśvarācārya in his *Vārttika*,[48] the purpose of the substitution is to indicate that 'nididhyāsana' is used here not in the usual sense of meditation (dhyāna), but in the special sense of right apprehension or knowledge (vijñāna) which, unlike meditation (dhyāna), depends on the nature of the thing known rather than on the knower's mind.

As pointed out by Śaṅkara, there is a marked difference between meditation (dhyāna) and knowledge (jñāna).[49] Both are mental processes. But while knowledge (jñāna) depends on its means and its object, meditation (dhyāna) depends on the directions of the scripture and the teacher and the aspirant's faith and will. For instance, when an image of a deity is before the eyes of a person, he will see it

[47] *Vide* Br. U. II: 4.5; IV: 5.6. [48] ***Br. U. bhāṣya-vārttika*** **II: 4.233.**
[49] *Vide* BS I: 1.4, S. com.

as it is, whether he wants to or not. The knower has no option in it. But the practice of meditation on the image as symbolic of the deity rests on the scriptural prescriptions, the aspirant's faith in them, and his determined effort. He may or may not practise it, or even practise it differently. Moreover, in meditation there is a scope of imagination in conformity with the object of knowledge, but in the cognition of an object there is no room for imagination. As pointed out by Vidyāraṇya, the difference between knowledge and meditation is this: 'While knowledge is determined by fact, meditation is dependent on the seeker.'[50]

In practising 'nididhyāsana' strictly as 'vijñāna (right apprehension or knowledge)' the seeker of Liberation does not meditate on the self as Brahman, but aims to *apprehend* it as Brahman by repudiating all limiting adjuncts superimposed on it through ajñāna. By discarding every contrary notion that apparently differentiates the one from the other, the self is grasped as Pure Being-Consciousness-Bliss. Sureśvara points out in his *Naiṣkarmya-siddhi*: 'Just as a person who mistakes a stump of a tree for a man being told "this is not a man but a stump" gets out of his error and perceives the stump as a stump, similarly, the instruction "Thou art That" removes the seeker's wrong notion of jīvahood and manifests the Self as Brahman.'[51] This is not in his view a case of meditation (prasaṁkhyāna), but of right apprehension (vijñāna); meditation cannot change one thing into another, nor can make the unreal real.[52]

But usually 'nididhyāsana' is regarded as a special case of meditation (dhyāna) which includes 'vijñāna' and in which ātman is apprehended as Brahman by distinguishing it from all limiting adjuncts, and contemplating it as devoid of them all, which it really is. This is not possible without full concentration of the mind on the self. The essential part of meditation (dhyāna) is the concentration of the mind. In his commentary on the Bhagavad-gītā,[53] Madhusūdana has explained 'dhyāna' as 'nididhyāsana', continuous contemplation on the self as the result of 'hearing' and 'reflection'.

As illustrative of the practice of 'nididhyāsana' in the sense of 'vijñāna' we quote below in part Śaṅkara's poem *Nirvāṇa-ṣaṭkam* (also called *Ātma-ṣaṭkam*):

'I am not the mind, nor its function—deliberation,
determination, egoism, or memory.
I am not the organ of hearing, nor of taste, nor of smell, nor of sight.
None of the elements—ether, earth, fire, or air—am I.
I am Pure Consciousness-Bliss. I am the Absolute,
I am the Absolute.[54]

[50] PD IX: 74. [51] NS III: 73. [52] *Vide Ibid.* 89–92. [53] *Vide* BG XIII: 24.

[54] Śaṅkara has used the word 'Śiva' in the sense of Nirguṇa Brahman, the Absolute.

I have neither virtue nor vice, I have neither pleasure nor pain.
Neither sacred word nor place have I; neither the Vedas
nor the sacrificial rites.
I am not the eater, nor eating; nor am I the food.
I am Pure Consciousness-Bliss. I am the Absolute.
I am the Absolute.

I have no death nor danger. I have no distinction of caste.
Neither father, nor mother, not even birth have I;
Neither friend nor companion, neither teacher nor disciple.
I am Pure Consciousness-Bliss; I am the Absolute;
I am the Absolute.

I have neither form nor ideation; all-pervading am I.
Beyond all the senses I exist everywhere.
No bondage nor Liberation for me; nor fear.
I am Pure Consciousness-Bliss; I am the Absolute,
I am the Absolute.'

8. *Dhyāna or upāsanā (meditation with the help of a symbol), which is distinct from nididhyāsana, i the way for the less qualified aspirants*

For the less qualified seekers of Liberation the Śruti has recommended the way of constant contemplation and meditation, which is usually termed 'upāsanā', 'dhyāna', or 'prasaṁkhyāna', as distinct from the way of 'manana and nididhyāsana (reflection and right apprehension)'. They, too, aim at the realization of Nirguṇa Brahman, but their reasoning power and the capacity for withdrawing the self from the not-self are not as effective as those of the specially qualified. As a matter-of-fact, faith (śraddhā) is predominant in them rather than reason. They are characterized in Advaita Vedānta as spiritual aspirants of the mediocre type (madhyama adhikāris). As stated by Vidyāraṇya: 'He who is not capable of 'vicāra' should constantly *meditate* on the Self.'[55] By "vicāra" he evidently means both 'manana (reflection)' and 'nididhyāsana (right apprehension)'. He has also pointed out that the Ātma-gītā as well as the Upaniṣads support the view that such seekers of Liberation as are not capable of attaining Nirguṇa Brahman by vicāra, that is, manana and nididhyāsana (reflection and right apprehension), are entitled to the practice of dhyāna (meditation) on the same.[56] The primary method of 'hearing (śravaṇa)' is, of course, common to both—vicāra (reflection and right apprehension) and dhyāna (meditation). The term 'upāsanā' is often used as a synonym of 'dhyāna', which means

[55] PD IX: 151, 155. [56] Cf. Pr. U. V: 5–7; BS III: 3.33; SLS III: 8.

continuous, uninterrupted concentration of the mind on a chosen object.[57]

In the practice of 'nididhyāsana' preceded by śravaṇa and manana, the mind is invariably directed to Nirguṇa Brahman and no symbol of any kind is used. But meditation, as denoted by dhyāna or upāsanā, is generally practised on Saguṇa Brahman, and rarely on Nirguṇa Brahman, and in either case some symbol of the object of meditation is used to hold the mind. As is well known, it is less difficult to concentrate the mind on a concrete object than on an abstract entity. The second grade seekers of Liberation, 'madhyama adhikāris (the mediocres)' as they are called, are instructed to practise meditation on Nirguṇa Brahman with the help of the verbal symbol Ōm (aum) to support the mind. The Upaniṣads have prescribed other symbols also for the meditation on Brahman, such as the mind, the sky, the sun,[58] and the words like 'tat', 'sat'. Yet from the earliest times the syllable Ōm, which is called 'praṇava', has been regarded by the Vedic seers as the greatest verbal symbol of both Saguṇa and Nirguṇa Brahman. As observed by Śaṅkara:

'Although such words as Brahman, Ātman, and the like signify Brahman, yet, on the authority of the Śruti, Ōm stands as the nearest designation of Brahman. Therefore, it is the supreme means to the realization of Brahman; and it is so in two ways: (1) as an image [visual symbol] and (2) as a name [audible symbol]. As an image: just as the image of Viṣṇu or any other deity is regarded as identical with deity, so is Ōm to be regarded as Brahman.'[59]

9. *The significance and efficacy of the symbol Ōm (aum)*

The Vedāntic texts resound with the eulogy of praṇava. As declared by the *Kaṭha Upaniṣad*:

'The goal which all the Vedas proclaim, which all austerities aim at, seeking which men live the life of continence, I [the King of death] will tell you that briefly. It is Ōm.
This syllable [Ōm] is indeed [Conditioned] Brahman. This syllable is the Supreme [Unconditioned Brahman]. By knowing this one attains all that one desires.
This is the best support [means of attaining Saguṇa Brahman]. This is the highest support [means of attaining Nirguṇa Brahman]. By knowing this support one is adored in the world of Brahmā [as the knower of Brahman].'[60]

[57] *Vide* BS IV: 1.7, 8; S. com. [58] Ch. U. III: 18.1; 19.1.
[59] Br. U. V: 1.1, com.; Cf. Pr. U. V: 2, com. [60] Ka. U. I: 2.15–17.

The *Praśna Upaniṣad* recommends Ōm for meditation on Nirguṇa and Saguṇa Brahman:

'The sage Pippalāda was asked: "O venerable sir, if someone among men should devoutly meditate on the syllable Ōm until death, which world verily would he win thereby?"
He replied: "O Satyakāma, this syllable Ōm is the Unconditioned Brahman and also the Conditioned Brahman. Therefore, he who knows it attains by this very means either of the two".'[61]

The *Māṇḍūkya Upaniṣad* thus points to the all-comprehensiveness of Ōm:

'The syllable Ōm is all this [the whole universe]. A clear explanation of this follows. All that is past, present, or future is, indeed, Ōm. And what else exists beyond the three divisions of time is also verily Ōm'.[62]

The *Chāndōgya Upaniṣad* refers to Ōm as the matrix of all articulate sounds and as symbolic of the whole existence covered by human speech:

'Just as every leaf is held together by its mid-rib, so is all speech held together by Ōm. Verily Ōm is all this. Verily, Ōm is all this.'

The syllable Ōm, constituted of the three letters—a (pronounced as in 'all'), u (pronounced as in 'put'), and m (pronounced as 'ma' in 'maul')—each with a meaning, is the most comprehensive of all verbal symbols. Specifically, it signifies the English *Word*, Sanskrit *Vāk*, Greek *Logos*, from which the whole cosmic order started. But its connotation is far beyond this. As declared by the Vedas:

'Verily, in the beginning Prajāpati [the creator, lit., the Lord of creatures] alone existed here (Prajāpatirvai idam agre āsīt ekah eva).'[64]
'Prajāpati alone was this universe. He had vāk, too, as his own, as a second to him (Prajāpatirvai idam ekah āsīt. Tasya vāg eva svam āsīd vāg dvitīyā.'[65]
'Vāk is Brahman (vāgvai Brahman).'[66]
'Vāk is coextensive with Brahman (yāvad Brahman tiṣṭhati tāvatī vāk).'[67]

[61] V: 1, 2. [62] I. [63] II: 23.3. [64] Sat. Br. VII: 5.2.6.
[65] *Pañcaviṁśa Brāhmaṇa* XX. 14.2. (See John Muir's *Original Sanskrit Texts*, Vol. V, London, Trubner, 1884 pp. 391–2.)
[66] Ṛg-V. I: 3.21. [67] *Ibid.* X: 114.8.

'All was made by vāk and likewise all that was made was vāk.'[68]

The same Vedic truth seems to be restated by St John in the New Testament:

'In the beginning was the Word, and the Word was with God, and the Word was God.'
'The same was in the beginning with God.'
'All things were made by him; and without him was not anything made that was made.'

'It is known from the Śruti and the Smṛti that the world originates from the Word [śabda, that is, vāk)', says Śaṅkara.[69] 'The Word [vāk] is the mother of the Vedas (Vedānām mātā)', declares the Veda.[70] What is the Word? It is the creative idea of God, the Idea of ideas, which is inseparable from God. As observed by Swāmī Vivekānanda, 'The external aspect of the thought of God is the Word, and as God thought and willed before He created, creation came out of the Word'.[71]

Ōm is the name of the Word. As the creative idea of the Lord the Word is the seed-force that evolves as the universe. Since a word and the thought conveyed by it are inseparable, so Ōm is inseparable from the Word, the cosmic ideation, God's thought of creation, the matrix of all ideas. It is the first manifestation of His omniscience. As a vehicle of thought, each word is a form of consciousness. Thus, Ōm is the embodiment of cosmic consciousness that appears as the diversified universe through names and forms. It is to be noted that in the Nondualistic view the manifold is essentially Pure Consciousness diversified by names and forms, the Supreme Being is both efficient and material cause of the universe.

Being intermediary between God and the world, Praṇava, as the syllable Ōm is called, stands for both. It is symbolic of the all-embracing Consciousness, the Supreme Self. It represents Brahman immanent (Saguṇa) and Brahman transcendent (Nirguṇa) as well. In fact, it is the potent seed of the knowledge of both. Being spiritual consciousness in the most concentrated form, it germinates and grows when sown in the right soil and nurtured by meditation. It is well-known that a word has the capacity to call forth the idea it embodies. Praṇava is regarded as a sacred seed-word (vīja-mantra). There are other sacred seed-words, but none is as fully representative of the Supreme Being as this.

[68] Sat. Br. VIII: 1.2.9. Quoted by Max Muller in *Three Lectures on Vedānta Philosophy*, p. 78, from Albrecht Weber's *Indische Studien*, Vol. X, p. 479 (18 vols. 1849–98).

[69] *Vide* BS I: 3.28, com.

[70] Tai. Br. II: 8.8.5.

[71] CW I, p. 72.

Ōm is the basic sound, of which all other sounds are but diversified or particularized forms. The utterance of Ōm, usually called Ōṅkāra, covers the whole process of articulation, as we shall see later. It is like the long-drawn peal of a gong which starts voluminously and tapers to a point (bindu), that is, reaches the subtlest, the all-pervading entity, the infinite, the eternal. The sound embraces all levels of existence from the grossest to the finest. It signifies the correlation between the microcosm and the macrocosm in all aspects. Its three letters or morae (mātrās)—a, u, m—represent respectively the gross, the subtle, and the causal aspects of the individual and the cosmic being. The culminating point (bindu) represents Pure Being underlying the three aspects, which is the partless, the fourth (the turīya), the transcendental nondual Self, where is the cessation of all phenomena, which has no limit, which is all bliss.[72]

No verbal symbol but this mystic syllable conveys such profound significance of the Supreme Being. Indeed, Ōm is the most comprehensive and most potent name of God. Any other name of God preceded by Ōm attains these qualities. As observed by Swāmī Vivekānanda:

'There are hundreds of words for God. One thought is connected with a thousand words; the idea, God, is connected with hundreds of words, and each one stands as a symbol for God. Very good. But there must be a generalization among all these words, some substratum, some common ground of all these symbols, and that which is the common symbol will be the best, and will really represent them all. In making a sound we use the larynx and the palate as a sounding board. Is there any material sound of which all other sounds must be manifestations, one which is the most natural sound? Ōm (aum) is such a sound, the basis of all sounds. The first letter, A [pronounced as in "all"] is the root sound, the key,[73] pronounced without touching any part of the tongue or palate; M [pronounced as "ma" in "maul"] represents the last sound in the series, being produced by the closed lips, and the U (pronounced as in "put"] rolls from the very root to the end of the sounding board of the mouth. Thus, Ōm represents the whole phenomena of sound-producing. As such it must be the natural symbol, the matrix of all the various sounds. It denotes the whole range and possibility of all the words that can be made. . . . Take, for instance, the English word God. It covers only a limited function, and if you go beyond it, you have to add adjectives to make it Personal, or Impersonal, or Absolute God. So with the words for God in every other language; their signification is very small. This word Ōm, however, has around it all the various significances.'[74]

[72] *Vide* Ma. U. XII.

[73] 'A (Ô)' is the first letter of the Sanskrit alphabet. It is the least differentiated of all sounds. Śrī Kṛṣṇa says, 'I am "A (Ô)" among letters'. (BG X: 33).

[74] CW I, pp. 218, 219.

10. *Practice of meditation with the symbol Ōm*

The efficacy of praṇava is a proven fact. It is accepted as the highest symbol of the Divinity by all Vedic schools.[75] Some non-Vedic schools also use it. From time immemorial praṇava has been fruitfully used in India and some adjacent countries by an unbroken line of spiritual aspirants for meditation on Nirguṇa as well as Saguṇa Brahman. As we have noted above, the Śruti has instructed the second grade spiritual aspirants, 'madhyama adhikāris (mediocres)' as they are called, to practise meditation on Nirguṇa Brahman by means of the symbol Ōm, and has prescribed different methods for the same. These are all intended for the realization of the identity of the individual self with the Supreme Being, which is the direct way to Liberation. Praṇava proves to be the intermediary or the link between the two, the individual self and the Supreme Being, in all of them. It stands for both ātman (the self) and Brahman. It is used as the auditory and also as the visual symbol (in Sanskrit characters, of course).

The *Muṇḍaka Upaniṣad* thus instructs the seekers of Brahman: 'Meditate thus on the Self with the help of Ōm. May your way to reach the other shore beyond darkness be free from obstacles.'[76]

The *Māṇḍūkya Upaniṣad* has explained how by means of the symbol Ōm (aum) a seeker of Liberation can meditate on the correlation between the individual and the cosmic self as the experiencers of waking, dream, and dreamless sleep, and attain the one transcendental Self, the fourth (the turīya), beyond the three states, which is 'Pure Awareness, where is the cessation of the manifold, which is nondual, calm, and blissful.'[77]

The *Muṇḍaka Upaniṣad* has illustrated by an analogy how the self being meditated upon as Brahman by means of praṇava assuredly attains Brahman. Just as a sharp arrow fitted to a bow, being fully drawn and intently aimed, hits the target without fail, even so the self with the mind purified and completely withdrawn from sense-objects through the practice of meditation by means of the symbol Ōm, being focused on Brahman, inevitably reaches Brahman. So it is said:

'Taking hold of the bow, the great weapon, well-known in the Upaniṣads, fix to it the arrow sharpened by meditation; then drawing it with the mind absorbed in the thought of Brahman, hit that mark the Immutable, O my good friend.

Ōm is the bow, the self (ātman) is the arrow. Brahman is said to be the mark. It is to be aimed at with unerring attention. Then the self (ātman) becomes one with Brahman as the arrow with the target.'[78]

[75] *Vide* YS I: 27. [76] II: 2.6. [77] Ma. U. VII. [78] Mu. U. II: 2.3, 4.

The *Śvetāśvatara Upaniṣad* has given another simile. Just as in the sacrificial rite the upper piece of fire-wood being rubbed repeatedly on the lower piece brings out the latent fire, even so a person by constant meditation with the help of the symbol Ōm can realize the luminous Self hidden like fire, so to speak, in the body.

'By making the body the lower piece of wood, and Ōm the upper piece, and by the continuous practice of meditation, as the process of rubbing, one should see the luminous Self hidden like the fire in the wood.'[79]

A qualified spiritual aspirant can meditate on the individual self as Brahman with the help of the symbol Ōm. This type of meditation is called 'aham-graha upāsanā (lit., meditation on I-consciousness)'. The mind is focused on the individual self, the ego-consciousness, which is essentially Brahman-Consciousness and is realized as such through intense meditation by means of the symbol Ōm. 'Brahman is ever familiar to us as the ego-consciousness', says Śaṅkara.[80] The basis of the ego-consciousness, as we have noted above, is the immutable self (the kūṭastha), which is identical with Brahman (the Supreme Self) as Pure Consciousness divested of all limiting adjuncts. Knowing this, the seeker meditates on the self as Brahman and on Brahman as the self.[81]

Praṇava (Ōm) serves as the medium of unity between the individual self and the Supreme Self. As the symbol of both it signifies Pure Consciousness underlying them and manifests their essential oneness beyond all distinctions.[82] Truly speaking, this monosyllabic word is the embodiment, nay, the potent seed of spiritual consciousness in the highest sense. Being the symbol of a thought or an idea, each word is a phase of inner consciousness and has the capacity to evoke the same. As the seeker continually repeats the sacred word (Ōm) and intently contemplates on its deep significance, his mind gets purified and apprehends the self as Pure Consciousness and its unity with Brahman-Consciousness. With the complete absorption of the mind in Brahman, as the result of ardent practice of meditation with the symbol Ōm, the self becomes unified with Brahman and all but merges therein. This leads to immediate perception of Nirguṇa Brahman in nirvikalpa samādhi. The individual self does not lose itself in Nondual Brahman as long as the mind endures.

Besides the methods of meditation indicated above there are other methods prescribed for the seekers of the mediocre type. For example, the Chāndōgya Upaniṣad has recommended meditation on Brahman in the space within the heart, where He dwells as the internal ruler.[83] The repetition of the symbol Ōm will be helpful in this case also.

79 Sv. U. I: 14. 80 VC 409. 81 *Vide* BS IV: 1.3.
82 *Vide* Ma. U.; Pr. U. V. 83 VIII: 1.1–3.

II. *Gradation of spiritual disciplines to suit different types of individuals with the same ultimate Goal in view.*

For the seekers of Liberation below the mediocre type, that is, for inferior or dull aspirants (adhama or manda adhikāris), who are not capable of fixing the mind on Nirguṇa Brahman, Vedānta recommends the practice of meditation on Saguṇa Brahman with the help of the syllable Ōm, which can be used both as auditory and visual symbol. Failing in that, a spiritual aspirant has to worship, and meditate on, some aspect of Saguṇa Brahman, such as Viṣṇu, Śiva, or Śakti, as his Chosen Deity with a symbolic name and a form. It is to be remembered that each and every aspect represents the Divinity as a whole, just as each photograph of a house, from whatever angle, represents the whole house. Or, the aspirant may choose any of the Divine Incarnations like Rāma, Kṛṣṇa, and others as the special object of adoration. It is worthy of note that in practising meditation on Brahman with a symbolic form (pratīka) the symbol is to be viewed as Brahman, and not *vice versa*.[84]

By steadfast and fervent worship of Saguṇa Brahman in any aspect and intent meditation on Him as the innermost Self of all, the aspirant can realize Him through His grace. As a matter-of-fact this is the method that suits a majority of spiritual aspirants. Following the same method an ardent seeker can even have immediate perception of Nirguṇa Brahman in nirvikalpa samādhi.[85] Śrī Kṛṣṇa has clearly indicated to his disciple Uddhava how intense meditation on Personal God with form (of Viṣṇu, for instance) leads to the realization of the formless, attributeless, Impersonal Brahman:

'The man of self-control should withdraw the organs from the sense-objects with the help of the mind, and with the intellect as guide direct the mind to my entire form.
Then one should concentrate that mind—distributed all over My body—on one part, and think of the smiling countenance alone and nothing else.
Drawing the mind which is concentrated on that, one should fix it on the Supreme Cause. Then leaving that too, one should rest on Me [as Nirguṇa Brahman] and think of nothing whatsoever [the meditator then becomes united with the object of meditation].
With one's mind thus absorbed, one sees Me alone in oneself and sees oneself united to Me, the Self of all—like light united to light.
A yōgī[86] who thus concentrates his mind through intense medita-

[84] *Vide* BS IV: 1.5. [85] *Vide* BS III: 2.24–30.

[86] Śrī Kṛṣṇa has used the term 'yōgī' in the wide sense of a spiritual aspirant given to meditation and not in the restricted sense of a follower of the Yōga system of Patañjali.

tion will soon extinguish the delusion about objects, finite knowledge, and action [that is, the entire realm of relativity, the apparent manifold].'[87]

To prepare the devotee's mind for the practice of meditation on the form of the Deity various modes of worship—physical, verbal, and mental—have been prescribed. The repetition (preferably inaudible) of the symbol Ōm, or any other sacred word or formula, is considered very efficacious in this respect. According to the sage Patañjali, the repetition of the symbol Ōm and contemplation of its meaning are conducive to the comprehension of tne innermost self and the elimination of all obstacles to its realization.[88] Those who have not faith or devotion adequate for the worship of the Divinity are instructed to practise karma-yōga; that is, to perform their duties, domestic, social, or humanitarian, dispassionately, caring for inner purification rather than secular gain, here or hereafter. Even this cannot be practised until the aspirant's mind discerns the futility of the temporal values and turns to the spiritual ideal.

Most men and women hanker after possessions and pleasures. They have to outgrow the inveterate worldly desires through legitimate experience before they can be interested in eternal verities. To get the most out of this life they are asked to fulfil their desires to the best of their ability, keeping firm on the path of virtue. The search for wealth, enjoyment, power, fame, or intellectual growth by unfair means is altogether forbidden. But nobody is to be rejected. Even for moral upliftment Vedānta provides a graduated course according to man's development. Its principle is to raise a person from where he is. This point is illustrated by a story in the *Bṛhadāraṇyaka Upaniṣad*:[89]

'Gods, men, demons (actually three types of men—godly, human, and ungodly), all descendants of Prajāpati, the progenitor Brahmā—went to him for instruction and lived austere life. On the completion of their term, the gods approached him for instruction. "Kindly instruct us, Sir", they said. Prajāpati uttered the syllable "Da", and said to them, "Have you understood?" They replied, "Yes, we have. You tell us: 'Damayata—be self-controlled'." "Yes, you have understood", said Prajāpati.
Next, the men approached him and said, "Kindly instruct us, Sir". Prajāpati uttered the same syllable "Da", and said to them, "Have you understood?" They replied, "Yes, we have. You tell us: 'Datta—be charitable'." "Yes, you have understood", said Prajāpati.
Then the demons approached him and said, "Kindly instruct us, Sir". Prajāpati uttered the same syllable "Da", and said to them,

[87] SB XI: 14.42–6. [88] *Vide* YS I: 28, 29. [89] *Vide* Br. U. V: 2.1–3.

"Have you understood?" They replied, "Yes, we have. You tell us: 'Dayadhvam—be compassionate'." "Yes, you have understood," said Prajāpati.
Even today the heavenly voice thunders from the cloud: "Da! Da! Da!—Be self-controlled! Be charitable! Be compassionate!"'

The three moral ideals of self-control, charity, and compassion are intended for three different grades of men. The cruel should practise non-injury and strive to be compassionate; the avaricious should overcome greediness by charity; and those who are free from other vices but still have sense-desires, should particularly practise inner control. In this context Śaṅkara remarks: 'Those among men who, though lacking in self-control, are possessed of other good qualities are the gods: those in whom greed prevails are men; while those who are cruel and violent are the demons (asuras, lit., the ungodly). So the same human species, according to the three drawbacks—lack of self-control, greediness, and cruelty, and according to the prevalence in them of the three guṇas—sattva, rajas, and tamas, are entitled gods, men, and demons. Therefore, it is men who should learn all the three lessons.'

The growth of an individual must be in conformity with his psychophysical constitution and his situation in life. The human mind is weak, but stubborn. It can grow only in the line of least resistance. The ultimate goal is one and the same for all. It is the realization of the self as Brahman, the Pure Being-Consciousness-Bliss that it really is. But many are the stairways to reach this peak. They go down to all levels of life. An individual can start climbing up the steps from where he stands.

12. *What becomes of the seekers of Brahman at death? Some reach the Goal immediately, some gradually. But none suffers. No spiritual gain is ever lost.*

By realizing Nirguṇa Brahman, even at the time of death, either through meditation with the symbol Ōm or through the worship of Saguṇa Brahman, the seeker attains 'immediate' Liberation (sadya mukti). His soul does not depart, but merges in Brahman like the soul of the one who realizes Brahman by the triple approach (śravaṇa, manana, and nididhyāsana). He reaches the Goal then and there. He traverses no path. 'Those who are eager to go beyond paths [the journey of life here and hereafter] tread no path', says the Upaniṣad.[90] 'Just as the footmarks of birds cannot be traced in the sky or of fish in water, so is the departure of the illumined', says the Mahābhārata (Śānti-parva, 239.24).[91]

[90] Quoted in S. com. on Mu. U. III: 2.6. [91] *Ibid.*

There is no difference whatsoever in final Liberation.[92] Whoever attains Brahman becomes the self-same Brahman. This is beautifully expressed in the *Muṇḍaka Upaniṣad* by an imagery. 'As rivers flowing down merge in the ocean, giving up their names and forms, even so does the illumined one, being free from name and form, attain the resplendent, all-transcendent Being. He who knows that Supreme Brahman verily becomes Brahman.'[93] There are exceptional cases of knowers of Brahman, who have a divine mission to fulfill in this world, such as the enlightenment of humanity. Their souls do not merge in Brahman. They are reborn as free souls for the fulfilment of their mission. They are called 'ādhikārika puruṣas (persons with special capacity to guide the world)'.[94]

In case the seeker cannot realize Nirguṇa Brahman but succeeds in realizing Saguṇa Brahman, he goes at death by the luminous path to Brahmalōka, which is the highest realm in the cosmic order, from where he does not return to the mortal plane.[95] After living there for aeons he realizes Nirguṇa Brahman and attains final Liberation with Hiraṇyagarbha, the Presiding Deity of Brahmalōka, at the cosmic dissolution.[96] This is called 'Gradual Liberation (krama-mukti)', as distinct from 'Immediate Liberation (sadya-mukti)' achieved by those who realize Nirguṇa Brahman in this very life. Whatever difference there may be in the way to reach it, final Liberation is the same in all cases. It is oneness with the same formless, featureless, attributeless Brahman. There is no variation in final emancipation, which is 'the cessation of all miseries and the attainment of the absolute bliss of Brahman'.[97]

If perchance a worshipper cannot reach Brahmalōka because of some latent desire for the temporal, he goes, as Śrī Kṛṣṇa has declared,[98] to the abode of the righteous, svarga-lōka (heaven or paradise), which is the highest plane of sense-fulfilment, the goal of the followers of pravṛtti-mārga—the path of desire regulated by moral ideal (dharma). After dwelling there an incalculably long period he is reborn on the human plane in a pure and well-to-do family. Or, a seeker who fails to realize Brahman is reborn soon in the family of wise yōgīs; a birth such as this is more difficult to attain in this world. There he recovers the knowledge he gained in his previous incarnation and strives for perfection more ardently than ever before. By his very past tendencies he is impelled involuntarily even. He who works for the Supreme Good never suffers, by no means can be retrogress, assures Śrī Kṛṣṇa.

[92] *Vide* BS III: 4.52. [93] Mu. U. III: 2.8.
[94] *Vide* BS III: 3.32.
[95] *Vide* BS IV: 4.22; Br. U. VI: 2.15.
[96] *Vide Kūrma Purāṇa* I: 12.269, quoted in VP VII.
[97] VP VIII, Conclusion. [98] BG VI: 40–44.

13. *The Yōgic and the Nondualistic view of self-realization and its methods*

According to both Nondualistic Vedānta and the Yōga system of Patañjali, the realization of the self is the direct means to Liberation and is attained in perfect tranquility of the mind, which is termed by the former 'nirvikalpa samādhi' and by the latter 'asamprajñāta samādhi'. But the two systems differ in their views of self-realization, of samādhi, and of Liberation, because of basic differences in their conceptions of fundamental reality.[99] The Yōgic self-realization is the complete withdrawal of the self from the not-self, which always exists in some form or other, being real in itself. It is the reinstatement of the self in its innate freedom and serenity as pure consciousness, on being dissociated from buddhi (the mind-stuff), which is then free from all its modes, contentless, and passive.[100] This is said to be the state of asamprajñāta samādhi, in which there is no cognition of any kind whatsoever in the mind, and the self shines by itself.

Finally, when the self is completely disconnected from buddhi (the mind-stuff), the yōgī attains Liberation. It is complete isolation of the self (kaivalya) from prakṛti (the entire objective universe), which exists as a fundamental principle. Released from all physical and psychical limitations, the self becomes aloof from the realm of mind and matter and shines as omnipresent spirit ever pure and free. According to Sāṁkhya-Yōga, the liberated soul is omnipresent; it is consciousness pure and simple, but not the sole reality; and there are countless souls. According to Vedānta, the Self in Liberation is the sole Reality; it is Consciousness that is all-Bliss. In Sāṁkhya-Yōga Liberation has a negative connotation; it is the cessation of all sufferings forever, but not a positive achievement. But in Vedānta Liberation is the cessation of all miseries and the attainment of absolute Bliss. The negative aspect is consequent on the positive. In this supreme state, prakṛti and all its transformations disappear altogether. Infinite Brahman shines in all Its glory and blissfulness. There is no other; the manifold with its root-cause māyā is altogether absent.

There is a marked difference in the nature of the Vedāntic nirvikalpa samādhi and the Yōgic asamprajñāta samādhi. In Vedānta the seeker of Self-knowledge does not dissociate the self from the mind (buddhi-sattva); on the contrary, he has to concentrate the mind on the innermost self and meditate on this as Brahman. Through intense practice of meditation with the thought 'I am Brahman', the mind conforms to Brahman. It becomes tranquil and transparent and absorbed in the all-pervading Self. By means of this mode of the mind corresponding to Brahman the self is realized as Nondual

[99] See Appendix C. [100] *Vide* YS I: 18.

Consciousness that Brahman is. This mental mode is called Brahmātmākārā vṛtti. It counteracts ajñāna that veils Brahman, but dissolves with the cessation of ajñāna. Then the mind, free from all modifications, blends with Brahman and the seeker enters into nirvikalpa samādhi, in which the Self shines as the sole Reality; not-self disappears altogether. As in asamprajñāta samādhi, so in nirvikalpa samādhi the mind is altogether modeless. But in the one case the mind is detached from the self, while in the other it is fused with the Self.

Both Yōga and Vedānta stress the practice of meditation as the means of Self-realization. In fact, Vedānta accepts the eightfold practical course of Yōga in spite of differences in their philosophical views. But their methods of meditation are not the same. The whole method of Yōga is based on the Sāmkhya system of Kapila, which Patañjali has adopted with a few divergences. In the realization of the Self, Sāṁkhya-Yōga has followed primarily the method of the withdrawal of the self from the not-self, particularly from the buddhi-sattva (the pure mind-stuff), with which it has the closest relation.[101] Vedānta also recommends the discrimination of the self from the not-self. But after being aware of the true nature of the self through discrimination, the aspirant has to fix the mind on the Self and the Self alone. Nothing else should be contemplated. So it is said: 'The Self alone is to be meditated upon, for all these [the limiting adjuncts] are unified in It [having no separate existence]. Of all these, this Self alone should be realized, for one knows all these through It, just as one may track [an animal] through its footprints.'[102] For the realization of Brahman, Saguṇa or Nirguṇa, the thoughts must be concentrated thereon. Says Śrī Kṛṣṇa: 'Fix thy mind on Me, be devoted to Me, sacirfice unto Me. Thus, having thy mind steadfast in Me, with Me as thy Supreme Goal, thou shalt reach Me [the Self of all beings].'[103] Again, 'Fix thy mind exclusively in Me, fasten thy intellect on Me; Thou shalt no doubt live in Me hereafter.'[104]

14. *The Vedas are of no use to a knower of Brahman*

The authority of the Vedas ends when Brahman is realized. A knower of Brahman has no use for them. He has nothing more to know, nothing more to gain. 'For him there is no rising or setting of the sun.'[105] He lives in perpetual sunshine, as it were, being identified with self-luminous Brahman. No lamp is needed in broad daylight. When Brahman becomes manifest then 'the Vedas are no Vedas.' All such distinctions as the means of knowledge, the object of knowledge,

[101] *Vide* YS II: 24–27; I: 51; IV: 34. For the Yogic method of meditation see Appendix D. [102] Br. U. I: 4.7.
[103] BG IX: 34. [104] *Ibid.* XII: 8. [105] Ch. U. III: 11.3.

the seeker of knowledge, hold good in the sphere of ajñāna (ignorance). All prescriptions and prohibitions are for the bound. So says Śaṅkara: 'The scriptures as well as other means of knowledge, including perception and the rest, are intended for the unillumined.'[106]

Further,

'So, in our view [the Nondualistic view] when the individual souls become united with the Supreme Being, the scriptures serve no purpose. They have, of course, a purpose to serve where there is avidyā. Just as, according to the Dualists of all classes, the scriptures have a purpose to serve only in the state of bondage, but not in the state of Liberation, so with us also.'[107]

As observed by Śrī Rāmakṛṣṇa:

'How long should one reason about the texts of the scriptures? So long as one does not have direct realization of God. How long does the bee buzz about? As long as it is not sitting on a flower. No sooner does it light on a flower and begin to sip honey than it keeps quiet.'[108]

'He whose knowledge is full depends on no book,' says he. Once Swāmī Vivekānanda was asked, 'What is the peculiarity of the Vedas?' He answered, 'One peculiarity of the Vedas is that they are the only scriptures that again and again declare that you must go beyond them.'[109]

The supreme purpose of the study of the Vedas is to realize Brahman, the Reality of realities, beyond the distinction of the knower, the knowable, and knowledge. Śaṅkara aptly remarks: 'If Brahman is not known, the study of the scriptures is to no purpose; if Brahman is known, then also the study of the scriptures is to no purpose.'[110]

So declares the Upaniṣad:

'Of what use are the Vedas to him who does not know the imperishable, all-pervading Supreme Being, the support of all the gods and the Vedas? But those who know That become perfect.'[111]

[106] BS, com., Intro. [107] BG XIII: 2, com.

[108] *The Gospel of Sri Ramakrishna*, p. 476.

[109] CW V, p. 235, Questions and Answers at the Twentieth Century Club, Boston, Mass., U.S. [110] VC 59. [111] Sv. U. IV: 8.

APPENDIX A

A SHORT ACCOUNT OF THE VEDIC TEXTS

The word 'Veda' (lit., knowledge, from the root *vid*, to know) signifies a body of sacred texts that is the foundation of Hinduism and is regarded by it as divine revelation of suprasensuous knowledge. The Vedic texts are said to have been collected and classified by an ancient sage Kṛṣṇa Dvaipāyana (lit., the island-born) better known as 'Veda-Vyāsa'—(The compiler of the Veda under four different heads: Ṛk, Yajuḥ, Sāma, and Atharva, each of which is called a Veda. Thus there are four Vedas.

Being transmitted orally from generation to generation each Veda had in course of time many versions (śākhās or recensions) with variations in reading. According to the Muktika Upaniṣad (I: 11–13), the Ṛg-Veda had twenty versions (śākhās), the Yajur-Veda one hundred and nine, the Sāma-Veda one thousand, and the Atharva-Veda fifty. But most of them are not available any more. One can hardly say when the Vedic hymns were first committed to writing.

Each Veda consists of two main parts: the Saṁhitā and the Brāhmaṇa. The Saṁhitā is the collection of the mantras, which are hymns, prayers, and sacrificial formulae. In the Saṁhitā part of each Veda there are, altogether, three different kinds of mantras: Ṛk, Yajuḥ, and Sāma. So the four Vedas are collectively called the *Trayī* (triad). Some think that the term *Trayī* refers to the first three Vedas, the fourth, the Atharva, being excluded, because it has no application in sacrificial rites, though it is acknowledged to be equally authoritative. In the Upaniṣads there are evidences of its authenticity.[1]

The Ṛk mantras are metrical. They are meant to be recited aloud for the invocation of the deities at the time of the fire-sacrifice. The Yajuḥ mantras are in prose. They are intended to be muttered while pouring oblation in sacrificial fire. The Sāma mantras are to be sung during the fire sacrifice. The Ṛk Saṁhitā consists mainly of the Ṛk mantras, the Yajuḥ Saṁhitā mainly of the Yajuḥ mantras, and the Sāma Saṁhitā mainly of the Sāma mantras. But the Atharva Saṁhitā has more Ṛk mantras than the other two kinds.

The Brāhmaṇa part is basically an explanatory treatise on the mantras and is mostly written in prose. What is the meaning of a particular mantra, in what ritual it has to be used and how to use it,

[1] Br. U. II: 4.10; IV: 1.2. Ch. U. III: 4.1. Tai. U. II: 3. Pr. U. II: 8. Mu. U. I: 1.5.

and what is the result of the use—all these are discussed therein. Almost each mantra has use for some rite or act of worship.

To the Brahmāṇa part proper are added the Āraṇyakas and the Upaniṣads. So in a wide sense the Brāhmaṇa includes both of these. The Āraṇyakas (Forest treatises) are meant to be studied by the Vānaprasthīs (anchorites), who in advanced age repair to forest retreats for contemplative life. They present the symbolic meanings of the fire-sacrifices and their accessories for the purpose of meditation. Evidently, their intention is to direct the aspirants' thoughts from ritualism to speculation and contemplation on spiritual truths. In the Taittirīya Āraṇyaka of the Kṛṣṇa Yajur-Veda (X: 48) there is the following prayer, in which devotional offering takes the place of the ritualistic:

'May Brahman be realized by me. May supreme Bliss be realized by me. May Brahman, who is supreme Bliss, be realized by me. O Thou, the all-knowing Being! Among Thy created beings I am like a child. O Thou, the dispeller of the dream of mortal life! Mayst Thou remove all distress. *To Thee I offer my mind, my senses, my life-functions, which are Thine.*'

In many cases the Āraṇyakas have been detached from the Brāhmaṇa proper and used as separate treatises. Thus, the two parts of the Ṛg-Veda Brāhmaṇa form two separate books: the Aitareya Brāhmaṇa and the Aitareya Āraṇyaka. The Kauṣītaki Brāhmaṇa and the Kauṣītaki Āraṇyaka are also parts of the Ṛg-Veda Brāhmaṇa.

The Yajur-Veda has two Saṁhitas: the Kṛṣṇa (black) and the Śukla (white), which have separate Brāhmaṇas. The Taittirīya Brāhmaṇa belongs to the Kṛṣṇa (black) Yajur-Veda and the Śatapatha Brāhmaṇa to the Śukla (white) Yajur-Veda. The Śukla Yajur-Veda Saṁhitā is also called the Vājasaneyī Saṁhitā and the Śatapatha Brāhmaṇa the Vājasaneyi Brāhmaṇa. The Śatapatha Brāhmaṇa has two Śākhās (recensions): the Kāṇva and the Mādhyandina.

The term 'Upaniṣad' denotes the knowledge of Brahman, which being duly received by a pupil, eradicates his ajñāna, the root-cause of all his bondages, and reinstates him in his intrinsic freedom. Those sections of the Brāhmaṇa that deal with this knowledge are figuratively called the Upaniṣads. Only one of the Upaniṣads, the Īśa, belongs to the Saṁhitā part, the rest belong to either the Brāhmaṇa proper or its Āraṇyaka section. The Īśa Upaniṣad forms the fortieth chapter of the Śukla (white) Yajur-Veda Saṁhitā. The Bṛhadāraṇyaka Upaniṣad is the last part of the Āraṇyaka that forms the concluding portion of the Śatapatha Brāhmaṇa of the Śukla (white) Yajur-Veda. It is included both in the Kāṇva and the Mādhyandina Śākhā (recension) with minor variations in reading. In his commentary on the Bṛhadāraṇyaka Upaniṣad Śaṅkara has followed the Kāṇva version.

In most cases the Upaniṣads have been separated from the rest of the Vedas and used as independent books, with the result that it is not always possible to ascertain to which of the Vedas, or to which recension or part of it, a particular Upaniṣad belongs. The difficulty is especially due to the fact that many Brāhmaṇas, Āraṇyakas, and their recensions have long been extinct. Of the extant Upaniṣads, numbering about 300, only one hundred and eight listed in the Muktika Upaniṣad (I: 30–40) are regarded as genuine. Among these the following twelve are counted primary: Īśa, Kena, Kaṭha, Praśna, Muṇḍaka, Māṇḍūkya, Aitareya, Taittirīya, Chāndōgya, Bṛhadāraṇyaka, Śvetāśvatara, and Kauṣītakī. Śaṅkara has written commentaries on the first ten of the group. He is also said to have written the commentary on the Nṛsiṁha-pūrva-tāpanīya Upaniṣad, which is included in the Memorial edition of his works, Vol. X (Vani Vilas Press, Sri Rangam). The commentary on the Śvetāśvatara that is generally attributed to him does not seem to be his. Except Īśa, Kena, and Māṇḍūkya, the rest of the above twelve Upaniṣads have been referred to in the Brahma-sūtras; but no one ever doubts the authenticity and the value of these three. In his commentary on the Brahma-sūtras Śaṅkara has referred to Jābāla, Paiṅgala, and Mahānārāyaṇa Upaniṣads besides the twelve.

The term 'Vedānta' (lit., the end of the Veda) signifies collectively the Upaniṣads, which form the crown of the Vedas (Śruti-śira), so to speak, inasmuch as they teach the supreme truth about the jīva and Brahman, which is the culmination of the Vedic knowledge. In a wide sense Vedānta includes all sacred texts that are based on the Upaniṣadic truth, including the commentaries on them. As defined by Vedānta-sāra (sec. 3): 'Vedānta means the Upaniṣads, the source of right knowledge, and the Śārīraka-sūtras, and other treatises that help to understand their meaning [such as the Bhagavad-gītā and the commentaries on the Upaniṣads, the Śārīraka-sūtras, and the Gītā].' The Upaniṣads, the Brahma-sūtras (also called the Śārīraka-sūtras), and the Bhagavad-gītā are the 'prasthāna-traya (the three standard works)' on Vedānta.

Another reason why the Upaniṣads are called 'Vedānta' (lit., the end of the Veda) is that they invariably form the concluding part (avasāna-bhāga) of their respective Saṁhitā, Brāhmaṇa, or Āraṇyaka (see Vidvanmanōrañjinī on Vedānta-sāra, sec. 3). As for instances: the Īśa Upaniṣad forms the last (fortieth) chapter of the Śukla (white) Yajur-Veda Saṃhitā; the Kena Upaniṣad forms the last (the ninth) chapter of the Talavakāra Brāhmaṇa of the Sāma-Veda; the Aitareya Upaniṣad consists of the last five chapters of the Aitareya Āraṇyaka of the Ṛg-Veda; the Taittirīya Upaniṣad the last three chapters of the Taittirīya Āraṇyaka of the Kṛṣṇa Yajur-Veda; the Bṛhadāraṇyaka Upaniṣad the last six chapters of the Śatapatha Brāhmaṇa of the Śukla Yajur-Veda; the Chāndōgya Upaniṣad the last eight chapters of the Chāndōgya Brāhmaṇa of the Sāma-Veda, and so on.

The modern scholars, Oriental as well as Occidental, widely differ in their opinion regarding the date of the Vedas. The Ṛg-Vedic hymns are considered by all to be the earliest. According to Bālagaṅgādhara Tilak and Hermann Georg Jacobi the Vedic hymns were composed about 4500 BC. From the different dates assigned to different parts of the Vedas—the Saṁhitā, the Brāhmaṇa, the Āraṇyaka, and the Upaniṣad, it can be assumed that the whole Vedic literature represents successive stages of development extending over a period of about two thousand years not later than 1500 BC. The intrinsic value of the Vedic literature does not, however, depend on its hoary antiquity; nevertheless its survival throughout the ages, with little or no interpolation, testifies to its lasting hold on the human mind.

In the orthodox Hindu view the Vedas are without beginning or end, and therefore ageless. The classical commentators on the Vedic texts recognize no chronological development of religious thought in them. The gradations of religious ideals noticeable in the Saṁhitā, the Brāhmaṇa, the Āraṇyaka, and the Upaniṣad are supposed to be due to the fact that the four sections were intended to be studied in the four successive stages of an individual's life, brahmacaryya (the student's life of study and celibacy), gārhasthya (the married life of a householder), vānaprastha (the life of retirement in the forest), and sannyāsa (the monastic life).

According to the subject-matter, the Vedic texts have two main divisions: the Work-section (karma-kāṇḍa) and the Knowledge-section (jñāna-kāṇḍa). The one paves the way to the other. By knowledge is meant the knowledge of Brahman, the Supreme Being. This is dealt with particularly in the Upaniṣads. The rest of the Vedas constitute the Work-section, which prescribes rites and duties and moral laws, by which man can attain welfare here and perpetual happiness hereafter. The Knowledge-section teaches the insignificance of all relative values, including the celestial, and the means to the attainment of the absolute good. There is a unity of purpose between the two sections: it is to lead human minds from the search of the temporal to the search of the eternal, which can be attained only by the knowledge of Truth and not by work.

In the Saṁhitā part of the Ṛg-Veda, which is the earliest according to the modern scholars, there are gradations of religious ideas from popular polytheism to highly philosophical monism. But this is not a sure indication of the gradual evolution of religious consciousness of the Indo-Aryans, as is generally assumed. In all probability higher and lower ideas suited to different grades of people prevailed simultaneously. Whatever might have been the popular conceptions of the deities mentioned in the Vedas, such as Indra (god of rain), Varuṇa (god of sky), Mitra (sun-god), Vāyu (god of wind), Agni (god of fire), etc., to the Vedic seers they were neither supernatural beings nor deified forces and phenomena of nature, but different manifestations of Nondual Brahman, the One without a second. Indeed, the prevailing note of the Saṁhitā part is not polytheism, henotheism, or even monotheism, but absolute monism or non-dualism.

In the first maṇḍala (one of the ten main divisions) of the Ṛg-Veda (I: 164.46) it is declared:

'Reality is One, the sages call It by various names: Agni (god of fire), Yama (god of death), Mātariśvan (god of wind).'

In the third maṇḍala also the unity of existence is recognized:

'The Infinite One is the Lord of the unmoving and the moving, of all that walk and all that fly, of this multiform creation.' (III: 54.8).

In the last (the tenth) maṇḍala again we find similar expressions:

'He who, though One, assumes the names of many gods.' (X: 82.3).
'The One existence is conceived as many.' (X: 114.5).

The human mind can conceive the Truth only according to its capacity.

We conclude with Max Muller's remarks on the monistic conception of the Vedic seers:

'Whatever is the age when the collection of the Ṛg-Veda Saṁhitā was finished, it was before that age that the conviction had been formed that there is but One, One Being, neither male nor female, a Being raised high above all the conditions and limitations of personality and of human nature, and nevertheless the Being that was really meant by all such names as Indra, Agni, Mātariśvan, nay, even by the name of Prajāpati, lord of creatures. In fact, the Vedic poets had arrived at a conception of the God-head which was reached once more by some of the Christian philosophers of Alexandria, but which even at present is beyond the reach of many who call themselves Christians.'[1]

A classified list of the Vedic texts which are considered authentic by the Vedic scholars in general.

I. Ṛg-Veda

Ṛk Saṁhitā	Brāhmaṇa	Āraṇyaka	Upaniṣad
	1. Aitareya	1. Aitareya	1. Aitareya
	2. Kauṣītaki (or Sāṁkhyāna)	2. Kauṣītaki	2. Kauṣītakī
	3. Paiṅgi		

II. Kṛṣṇa (Black) Yajur-Veda

Kṛṣṇa Yajuḥ Saṁhitā	Brāhmaṇa	Āraṇyaka	Upaniṣad
	1. Taittirīya	1. Taittirīya	1. Taittirīya
	2. Ballavi		2. Kaṭha
	3. Śāṭyāyani		3. Śvetāśvatara
	4. Maitrāyani		4. Mahānārāyaṇa
	5. Kaṭha		5. Maitrāyaṇīya

III. Śukla (White) Yajur-Veda

Śukla Yajuḥ Saṁhitā (or Vājasaneyī Saṁhitā)	Brāhmaṇa	Āraṇyaka	Upaniṣad
	1. Śatapatha	1. Śatapatha	1. Īśa
			2. Bṛhadāraṇyaka
			3. Jābāla
			4. Paiṅgala

[1] F. Max Muller, *The Six Systems of Indian Philosophy*, London, Longmans, 1899, p. 68.

IV. Sāma-Veda

Sāma-Saṁhitā	Brāhmaṇa	Āraṇyaka	Upaniṣad
	1. Tāṇḍya (or Pañcaviṁśa with the supplement Saḍviṁśa)		1. Chāndōgya
	2. Talavakāra		2. Kena
	3. Ārṣeya		
	4. Vaṁṣa		
	5. Daivatādhyāya		
	6. Mantra		
	7. Sāma-vidhāna		
	8. Saṁhitōpaniṣad Brāhmaṇa		

V. Atharva Veda

Atharva-Saṁhitā	Brāhmaṇa	Āraṇyaka	Upaniṣad
	1. Gōpatha		1. Muṇḍaka
			2. Māṇḍūkya
			3. Praśna

So there are five Saṁhitās, eighteen Brāhmaṇas, four Āraṇyakas, and sixteen Upaniṣads, which are the most important of the extant Vedic literature.

APPENDIX B

THE SIX VEDIC SCHOOLS OF PHILOSOPHY AND THEIR NOTABLE SANSKRIT WORKS

(with available English Translations)

SYNOPSIS

	page
1. The Classification of Indian Philosophy	311
2. Nyāya and Vaiśeṣika	312
3. Sāṁkhya and Yōga	314
4. Mīmāṁsā and Vedānta	316
5. The Vedānta Philosophy: its Triple Basis and Different Schools	318
6. The Living Hindu Religion is Vedānta	322
7. Notable Sanskrit Works of Advaita Vedānta and Available English Translations	324
8. Viśiṣṭādvaita of Rāmānuja (AD 1017–1137)	327
9. Dvaitādvaita of Nimbārka (eleventh century)	329
10. Dvaita of Madhvācārya (AD 1199–1276)	330
11. Śuddhādvaita of Vallabhācārya (AD 1479–1531)	331
12. Acintya-bhedābheda of Śrī Caitanya School (usually called Gauḍīya Vaiṣṇava School)	332

1. *The Classification of Indian Philosophy*

There are twelve major schools of Indian philosophy.[1] They form two main groups of six each:

I. The Vedic—those who accept the authority of the Vedas and are called 'āstika (orthodox)'

II. The Non-Vedic—those who deny the authority of the Vedas and are called 'nāstika (heterodox)'

The six Vedic systems can be arranged in three sets of two that are akin to each other:

1. Nyāya and Vaiśeṣika
2. Sāṁkhya and Yōga
3. Mīmāṁsā and Vedānta

[1] Mādhavācārya's *Sarvadarśana-saṁgraha* (fourteenth century AD), a compendium of sixteen different philosophical systems, includes some minor ones. (Trans. by E. B. Cowell and A. E. Gough, London, Kegan Paul, Trench, Trubner, 1904).

All Vedic schools have systematic text-books in aphorisms called Sūtras. The Sanskrit term for philosophy is 'darśana', lit., seeing, that is, vision, or view of Truth. The ultimate end of every school is man's deliverance from all sufferings and attainment of abiding peace by true knowledge; but each has its own conception of liberation. In India philosophy is not severed from religion. It is a way of life for complete self-fulfilment.

The six Non-Vedic systems come under the following three main heads:

1. Materialism known as Cārvāka or Lōkāyata darśana
2. Jainism
3. Buddhism, which has four subdivisions:
   (1) Vaibhāṣika (direct realism)
   (2) Sautrāntika (indirect realism)
   (3) Yōgācāra (idealism)
   (4) Mādhyamika (nihilism)

2. *Nyāya and Vaiśeṣika*

Nyāya means, primarily, logic, the process of inference. The system investigates into both physical and metaphysical subjects by the syllogistic method. Thus it includes metaphysics as well as the science of logic. It is based on the *Nyāya-sūtras* of Gautama (also called Gōtama), who lived not later than the third century BC. Its companion school, the Vaiśeṣika, is the earlier of the two and exercised considerable influence on the Nyāya. Both systems aim at a critical analysis of the universe by logical methods. In the opinion of Surendranath Dasgupta the Vaiśeṣika system is pre-Buddhistic (*A History of Indian Philosophy*, Vol. I, p. 282). Ulūka, the author of the *Vaiśeṣika-sūtras*, is its founder or the first known exponent. He is better known as Kaṇāda (lit., he who eats the particles of grains), because of his austere mode of living. So his philosophy is called after him 'Aulūka darśana' and 'Kaṇāda darśana'. The name 'Vaiśeṣika' derives from viśeṣa, which refers to the particularity or individual character of things, which the system emphasizes. In the first two aphorisms Kaṇāda states that the object of his philosophy is to expound dharma (virtue comprising true knowledge), which conduces to life's development and the attainment of the supreme Good. It is to be noted that all the Vedic systems uphold dharma and condemn adharma, its opposite. Each is a philosophy of life.

Though Nyāya and Vaiśeṣika are separate systems, they have more similarities than dissimilarities. It may be noted that the later Nyāya school called 'Navya-Nyāya (Neo-Logic)' developed as a result of a blending of the two. Both systems are realistic and pluralistic. In the view of both God is the efficient cause of the universe. Physical objects exist independently of the mind, although their perception depends on the mind aided by the sense-organs. Seven categories (padārthas) are ultimately real. These are substance (dravya), quality (guṇa), activity (karma), generality (sāmānya), particularity (viśeṣa), inherence (the relation of samavāya), and non-existence (abhāva). Of these substance is the only independent entity, the rest belong to it. The nine fundamental substances are—earth, water, fire, air, ether (ākāśa), time (kāla), space (dik), self (ātman), and mind (manas). The first seven compose the physical universe. Each of the elements—earth, water, fire, and air—is in its original state atomic. Four different types of atoms are the basic constituents of these elements. Ether (ākāśa), time (kāla), and space (dik) are infinite and pervasive.

While the self (ātman) is eternal and all-pervading, the mind is infinitesimal though eternal. Being associated with the mind, the organs, and the body through ignorance, the self is bound. When dissociated from all these adjuncts by the true knowledge of the self an individual attains liberation (apavarga). It is a state of complete release from all sufferings without any positive attainment. Righteous deeds and contemplation on truth conduce to true knowledge. There are innumerable selves ever distinct from one another. Consciousness is not an intrinsic quality of the self, nor its essence. In its disembodied state the self will have no knowledge or consciousness.

As noted by Swāmī Prabhavānanda, 'The two systems, in so far as they differ, do so mainly in their approach to the central problems of philosophy. The Vaiśeṣika begins with the conception of being and develops its ideas from that; the Nyāya begins with knowing.'[2] We have mentioned above that Vaiśeṣika acknowledges two pramāṇas—perception (pratyakṣa) and inference (anumāna); Nyāya adds two more—verbal testimony (śabda) and comparison (upamāna), which Vaiśeṣika includes in inference.

Texts and commentaries of the Vaiśeṣika school and English translations:

(1) *The Vaiśeṣika-Sūtras of Kaṇāda* with the com. *Upaskāra* of Śaṅkara Miśra (AD 1425) tr. by Nandalal Sinha, Sacred Books of the Hindus, Allahabad, The Panini Office, 2nd edn., 1923.
(2) *The Padārthadharma-saṁgraha of Praśastapāda* (fourth century AD with the com. *Nyāya-kandalī of Śrīdhara* (AD 990) tr. by Gaṅgānātha Jhā. Allahabad, E. J. Lazaras, 1916. Another com. available is Udayana's *Kiraṇāvalī*, AD 984. Praśastapāda's work is an exposition of the main topics of the *Sūtras* of Kaṇāda.

Texts and commentaries of the Nyāya school and English translations:

(1) *The Nyāya-Sūtras of Gōtama* tr. by S. C. Vidyābhūṣaṇa, Sacred Books of the Hindus. Allahabad, The Panini Office, 1930.
(2) *Gautama's Nyāya-Sūtras* with Vātsāyana's *Bhāṣya*, tr. by Gaṅgānātha Jhā. Poona, Oriental Book Agency, 1939. The *Vātsāyana-bhāṣya* (AD 300) is the earliest com. on the *Nyāya-Sūtras*. On this Udyōtakara wrote his *Vārttika* (AD 635), an expository treatise. The two sub-commentaries on the Vārttika are Vācaspati's *Nyāya-vārttika-tātparya-ṭīkā* and Udayana's *Nyāya-vārttika-tātparya-pariśuddhi*.

[2] Swāmī Prabhavānanda, *The Spiritual Heritage of India*, London, Allen and Unwin, 1962, p. 205.

(3) Udayana Ācārya's *Nyāya-Kusumāñjali* (tenth century AD), in which he tries to prove the existence of God. *The Kusumāñjali or Hindu Proof of the Existence of a Supreme Being*, with the com. of Hari Dasa Bhattacarya, tr. by E. B. Cowell. Calcutta, Baptist Mission Press, 1864.

(4) *Tattvacintāmaṇi* by Gaṅgeśa Upādhyāya (1200 AD), the founder of Navya-Nyāya (Neo-Logic) school. A number of commentaries and commentaries on commentaries have been written on its keen dialectics.

(5) *Tarka-saṁgraha*, an elementary treatise, by Annambhaṭṭa (AD 1559) with the com. *Nyāyanirṇaya.*

(6) Viśvanātha Nyāya-Pañcānana's *Bhāṣā-Pariccheda* with the com. *Siddhānta-Muktāvalī* (seventeenth century AD) tr. by Swāmī Mādhavānanda. Calcutta, Advaita Ashrama, 2nd edn., 1954.

3. *Sāṁkhya and Yōga*

The Sāṁkhya system of Kapila forms (with a few differences) the philosophical basis of Patañjali's yogic methods delineated in his *Yōga-sūtras* (aphorisms on Yōga). It is dualistic in that it maintains two ultimate principles: (1) puruṣa (the self-intelligent subject) and (2) prakṛti (the non-intelligent potential cause of the objective universe). Puruṣa is changeless, whereas prakṛti is changeful. There are numerous puruṣas, but prakṛti is one, though manifold. The whole objective universe—physical and psychical—has evolved from prakṛti. It comprises twenty-four categories including the subordinate ones. With puruṣa they constitute twenty-five categories or principles (tattvas) as enumerated in the table below:

1. Puruṣa

2. Prakṛti

3. Mahat (lit., the great principle, also called 'buddhi', the universal intellectual principle underlying self-consciousness)

4. Ahaṅkāra (egoism)

Sāttvika and Rājasika

5. Manas (mind)

6–10 Five sensory organs of hearing, sight, smell, taste, touch

11–15 Five motor organs of speech, prehension, movement, excretion, reproduction

Tāmasika

16–20 Five subtle elements: sound, touch, colour, taste, smell

21–25 Five gross elements: ākāśa, air, light, water, earth

Texts and commentaries of the Sāṁkhya school:

1. *Sāṁkhya-pravacana-sūtram* (527 aphorisms in six chapters) ascribed to the sage Kapila, the founder (sixth century BC), with commentaries by Aniruddha (fifteenth century AD) and Vijñāna Bhikṣu (sixteenth century AD).
2. *Sāṁkhya-kārikā* (seventy verses) by Īśvara Kṛṣṇa (third century AD) with commentaries by Gauḍapāda and Vācaspati Miśra (850 AD).

English translations:

(1) *The Sāṁkhya-pravacana-sūtram* (Text and trans.)—Nandalal Sinha, Sacred Books of the Hindus, Vol. XI, Allahabad, 1915.
(2) *Sāṁkhya-kārikā* with Gauḍapāda's com., ed. and trans. by H. T. Colebrooke and H. H. Wilson, Oxford 1837; Bombay, 1887.
(3) *Sāṁkhya-kārikā* of Īśvara Kṛṣṇa, ed. and tr. by Sūryanārāyaṇa Śāstrī (University of Madras, 1935).
(4) *The Tattvakaumudī* (Vācaspati Miśra's com. on *Sāṁkhya-kārikā*) tr. by Gaṅgānātha Jhā. Poona, Oriental Book Agency, 2nd edn., 1934.

The main difference between the Sāṁkhya and the Yōga views is briefly this: Sāṁkhya does not recognize an ever-free, eternal, Creator God, because His existence cannot be established by logical proof (SD I: 92–96). The only God it admits is 'Kalpa-niyāmaka-Īśvara,' a nearly perfected being temporarily in charge of a cycle of creation (SD III: 56, 57). But Patañjali admits a Personal God, a special Being untouched by any kind of misery whose knowledge is infinite and who, being unlimited by time, is the teacher of even the earliest teachers. (YS I: 24–26). For a further account of the two systems see Appendices C and D.

Reference to Yōga practice are to be found in the *Upaniṣads*, the *Mahābhārata* (of which the *Bhagavad-gītā* is a part), and also in Jaina and Buddhist literature. But the first systematic treatment of the subject as a method of self-realization is to be found in the *Yōga-sūtras* of Patañjali. Many commentaries have been written on the text. Of these the following are widely known.

1. Bhōjadeva's *Rāja-mārtaṇḍa.*
2. *Vyāsa-bhāṣya* (fourth century, AD).
3. Vācaspati Miśra's sub-commentary *Tattva-vaiśāradī* on Vyāsa's com. (ninth century, AD).

English translations of the Yōga texts and commentaries:

(1) *The Yōga-darśana, The Sūtras of Patañjali with the Bhāṣya of Vyāsa*—tr. by Gaṅgānāthā Jhā, R. T. Tatya for Bombay Theosophical Publication Fund, 1907.

(2) *The Yōga-sūtras of Patañjali* (with the *Yōga-bhāsya* of Vyāsa and the *Tattva-vaiśāradī* of Vācaspati Miśra) by Rama Prasada, Sacred Books of the Hindus. Allahabad, The Panini Office, 3rd edn., 1924.

(3) *The Yōga System of Patañjali* (The *Yōga-sūtras*, with Vyāsa's *Yōga-bhāṣya* and Vācaspati's *Tattva-vaiśāradī*) by Professor James Haughton Woods, Harvard Oriental Series. Cambridge, Harvard University Press, 2nd edn., 1927.

(4) *The Aphorisms of Patañjali*—Trans. and com. by Swāmī Vivekānanda —included in his *Rāja-Yōga*. Advaita Ashrama, Mayavati, Almora, 1930.

(5) *Aphorisms of Yōga* (by Patañjali)—Tr. by Shree Purohit Swami. London, Faber, 1938.

(6) *How to Know God*: *The Yōga Aphorisms of Patañjali* (Trans. and expl.) by Swāmī Prabhavānanda and Christopher Isherwood. New York, Harper, 1953.

4. *Mīmāṁsā and Vedānta*

Of the six orthodox schools Mīmāṁsā and Vedānta are primarily dependent on Vedic authority (Śruti-pradhāna) while the four others are primarily dependent on argument (yukti-pradhāna).[3] Mīmāṁsā is founded on Jaimini's *Pūrva-Mīmāṁsā-sūtras*, Vedānta on Bādarāyaṇa's *Uttara-Mīmāṁsā-sūtras*. The name Mīmāṁsā, common to the two treatises they originate from, usually means proper or rational investigation (pūjita-vicāra); in this context it means rational investigation into the meaning of the Vedic texts (Vedārtha-vicāra). The first treatise is called 'Pūrva-Mīmāṁsā (prior investigation),' since it dwells on the anterior portion of the Vedas, particularly the Brāhmaṇas; the second treatise is called 'Uttara-Mīmāṁsā (posterior investigation),' since it dwells on the subsequent portion of the Vedas, the Upaniṣads. Being mainly concerned with sacrificial rites and virtuous deeds prescribed by the earlier portion of the Vedas, 'Pūrva-Mīmāṁsā' is also called 'Karma-Mīmāṁsā.' Usually, the system of thought based on it is designated simply as 'Mīmāṁsā' or as 'Mīmāṁsā darśana (philosophy).' It investigates Vedic ritualism. 'Uttara-Mīmāṁsā', on the other hand, is mainly concerned with Vedic metaphysics, the subject-matter of the Upaniṣads. Being primarily an enquiry into Brahman, it is also called 'Brahma-Mīmāṁsā'.[4] The system founded on it is generally known as Vedānta or Vedānta darśana (philosophy).

The philosophy of Pūrva-Mīmāṁsā (shortly, Mīmāṁsā) is based on an attempt to uphold Vedic ritualism by a rational interpretation. According to it, the Vedas are the sole authority on religious and righteous deeds (dharma), being the only source of suprasensuous knowledge. A man must perform what is prescribed by the Vedas as conducive to his well-being here and hereafter.[5] The performance of sacrificial rites and other duties enjoined by the Vedas rests on the

[3] See ch. X, sec. 3.

[4] The book has other names. See ch. X, footnote 35.

[5] *Vide* PMS I: 1.2; Śabara's commentary.

recognition of suprasensuous truths such as the soul's survival of death, merit and demerit accruing from karma, retribution in heaven and hell, and the existence of ethical order in the universe. In order to establish the infallibility of the Vedic testimony Mīmāṁsā philosophers have dwelt at length on epistemological and other allied topics, such as the nature of knowledge, its different methods, its validity, its falsity, its criterion, and its objects (prameya). They have also discussed metaphysical questions regarding the nature of the universe, the nature of the soul, the law of karma and the final release from its bondage. So far as the epistemological views of Mīmāṁsā are concerned Advaita Vedānta agrees with it on many points, nevertheless the metaphysical views of the two schools differ markedly. We have mentioned above that the Kumārila school of Mīmāṁsā and Advaita Vedānta both acknowledge the same six pramāṇas; but there is difference of opinion between them regarding the self-manifestedness of knowledge (see ch. IV, sec. 1).

Like Nyāya and Vaiśeṣika, Mīmāṁsā is realistic and pluralistic in its view of the self and the universe. Unlike them, however, it avows no Īśvara as the efficient cause of the universe, though it does not deny Him. The law of karma is supposed to be adequate for maintaining the cosmic order. The realism of Mīmāṁsā is of course different from empiricism, which does not recognize suprasensible facts. It holds that the ultimate goal of life, which is freedom from all miseries and the attainment of the utmost happiness called heaven, is achieved not by Self-knowledge but by the performance of ceremonial and righteous deeds enjoined by the Vedas. But Advaita Vedānta affirms that no heaven attainable by karma can be final, for whatever is produced must come to an end; the eternal, the uncaused, cannot be the product of work.[6] While refuting the Mīmāṁsā view that the purpose of the entire Vedas, comprising the Karma-kāṇḍa (work-section) and the Jñāna-kāṇḍa (knowledge-section), is to advocate action and not knowledge, Advaita Vedānta maintains that the work-section of the Vedas prescribes karma for the unillumined as preparatory to Self-knowledge which is the direct means to Liberation (mōkṣa) and the purport of both the sections.[7]

Of the numerous works on Mīmāṁsā philosophy we shall mention a few that are prominent. Its primary source, as we have noted above, is the *Mīmāṁsā-sūtras* of Jaimini (*circ.* 300–200 BC). Later works consist mainly of commentaries on Jaimini's aphorisms and commentaries on commentaries. The earliest known commentary on *Mīmāṁsā-sūtras* is by Śabara Svāmin (second century AD). It is the basis of later Mīmāṁsā works. Two different interpretations of Śabara's commentary (Śabara-bhāṣya) by Kumārila Bhaṭṭa (AD 620–700) and his pupil, Prabhākara Miśra (AD 650–720), have led to the development of two main branches or schools of Mīmāṁsā philosophy, which we have mentioned above (ch. VI, footnote 1). Kumārila's explanatory treatises are known as *Ślōka-vārttika*, *Tantra-vārttika*, and *Ṭup-ṭīkā*; Prabhākara's as *Bṛhatī* and *Laghvī*. We have noted in the foregoing pages the main differences in the epistemological views of the two schools.

[6] *Vide* Tai. U., S. com. Intro.

[7] *Vide* BS I: 1.4, S. com.; PMS, Śabara's com., Intro.

The Prabhākara school generally acknowledges Īśvara. A few Mīmāṁsā writers, such as Murāri Miśra and Vedānta-deśika, have maintained their own views independently of the two schools. Kumārila's *Ślōka-vārttika* is remarkable for its contribution to epistemology. A well-known commentary on this work is *Nyāya-ratnākara* of Pārthasārathi Miśra. On Prabhākara's *Bṛhatī* and *Laghvī* Śālika-nātha Miśra wrote commentaties called *Ṛjuvimalā* and *Dīpaśikhā*.

Among other notable works on Mīmāṁsā, we mention the following:

1. Maṇḍana Miśra's *Vidhi-viveka* with Vācaspati's commentary *Nyāya-kaṇikā*
2. Śālika-nātha's *Prakaraṇa-pañcikā*
3. Pārtha-sārathi Miśra's *Śāstra-dīpikā*
4. Mādhavācārya's *Jaiminīya-nyāya-mālā*
5. Appaya-dīkṣita's *Vidhi-rasāyana*
6. Anantadeva's *Mīmāṁsā-nyāya-prakāśa* }
7. Laugākṣi Bhāskara's *Artha-saṁgraha* } Mīmāṁsā manuals
8. *Mīmāṁsā-paribhāṣā* of Kṛṣṇa Yajvan }

Available English translations:

(1) Jaimini's *Mīmāṁsā-sūtras* with *Śabara-bhāṣya*, by Gaṅgānātha Jhā, Gaekwad's Oriental Series, Vols. LXVI, LXX, LXXIII, Baroda, Oriental Institute, 1933, 1934, 1936.
(2) Kumārila Bhaṭṭa's *Ślōka-vārttika* by Gaṅgānātha Jhā, Asiatic Society of Bengal, Calcutta, 1909.
(3) *Mīmāṁsā-paribhāṣā* of Kṛṣṇa Yajvan by Swāmī Mādhavānanda. Belur Math, Howrah, The Ramakrishna Mission Sarada Pitha, 1948.

On the influence of the Mīmāṁsā tenets on Hindu Society Dasgupta remarks:

'The importance of Mīmāṁsā literature for a Hindu is indeed great. For not only are all Vedic duties to be performed according to its maxims, but even the smṛti literatures which regulate the daily duties, ceremonials and rituals of Hindus even at the present day are all guided and explained by them. The legal side of the smṛtis consisting of inheritance, proprietory rights, adoption, etc., which guide Hindu civil life even under the British administration is explained according to the Mīmāṁsā maxims.'[8]

5. *The Vedānta Philosophy; its Triple Basis and Different Schools*

Broadly speaking, the Vedānta philosophy has two main divisions: (1) Monistic (Nondualistic) and (2) Monotheistic. Their classification into different schools is shown below:

[8] Surendranath Dasgupta, *A History of Indian Philosophy*, Vol. I, p. 371.

The Vedānta Philosophy

I. Monistic (Nondualistic) — II. Monotheistic

I. Monistic (Nondualistic)		II. Monotheistic
(1) Vivaraṇa School	(2) Vācaspati School	The five Vaiṣṇava Schools of (1) Rāmānuja (2) Nimbārka (3) Madhva (4) Vallabha (5) Śri Caitanya

According to the Monistic or Nondualistic (Advaita) Vedānta, Nirguṇa (attributeless) Brahman, Pure Being-Consciousness-Bliss, the One without a second, where there is not the least differentiation of any kind whatsoever, not even the distinction between substance and attribute, is the sole Reality. According to the Monotheistic Vedānta, Saguṇa Brahman, the repository of all blessed qualities, the Omniscient, Omnipotent, Omnipresent Supreme Being, is the fundamental Reality; the individual selves (the jīvas) and the inanimate world (jagat), though ever distinct from the Supreme Ruler (Īśvara), have no existence apart from Him. Thus, in the Vedānta philosophy there is no absolute dualism as in the Sāṁkhya. Even the monotheistic school of Madhva, which is usually characterized as dualistic, is not so in the sense in which the Sāṁkhya is. The Nondualistic (Advaita) Vedānta recognizes the monotheistic position, but does not view it as ultimate. According to both schools, the individual self (the jīva) is intrinsically conscious. While the monotheistic Vedānta holds that the jīva is akin to Brahman (Saguṇa), though distinct, and emphasizes their relationship, the Advaita Vedānta maintains their essential identity, the distinction between the two being adventitious and not absolute.

The principal tenets of Advaita Vedānta are briefly these:

1. The fundamental Reality (Nirguṇa Brahman) is Pure Being-Consciousness-Bliss (Sat-Cit-Ānanda). That alone exists in the absolute sense. The manifold has no ultimate reality. It has an apparent existence, being due to māyā, a mysterious principle that seemingly diversifies the undiversified Reality.
2. Transcendentally the One without a second, Brahman is immanent in the world of phenomena as its all-pervading Self. As such, Brahman is the Internal Ruler—the Creator, Preserver, and Destroyer of the universe, the Adorable God of love and grace, and also the indwelling conscious self in every living being. Thus, the same Nondual Brahman has different aspects in relation to the apparent manifold.
3. Man's inmost self is identical with Brahman.
4. To realize Brahman, Saguṇa or Nirguṇa, is the goal of human life. It means Liberation from the round of births and deaths and the attainment of complete blessedness. All life-values should subserve this supreme end.
5. The experience of the manifold persists for the jīva as long as he is subject to māyā and does not realize his essential oneness with Brahman.

6. The methods of God-realization vary, within the framework of the fundamental principles, according to the aspirants' tendencies, capacities, and conditions of life.
7. Universal spiritual truths underlie the different religions despite the differences of dogmas and practices.

According to Vedānta, there are two main approaches to the ultimate goal of life: (1) the path of knowledge (jñāna-yōga) and (2) the path of devotion (bhakti-yōga). The path of selfless work (karma-yōga) is preparatory to either of them. The path of knowledge is, strictly speaking, the search for Nirguṇa Brahman. It is characterized by the aspirant's awareness of the identity of the self with Brahman. The path of devotion is the approach to Saguṇa Brahman. It is characterized by the aspirant's awareness of his relationship with Brahman. Both Nondualistic and Monotheistic Vedānta recognize the path of devotion as the direct way to the realization of Saguṇa Brahman. According to Monotheistic Vedānta it is the final spiritual course. But Nondualistic Vedānta holds that the path of devotion leads to the path of knowledge, which is the only direct way to the realization of Nirguṇa Brahman. Most spiritual aspirants must attain Saguṇa Brahman through devotion before they can reach the Nirguṇa.

The Upaniṣads, embodying the revealed truths, are the primary source of the Vedānta philosophy. The Vedic seers declare the suprasensuous truths revealed to their mystic vision. They do not, as a rule, reason or argue. They say what they see. Speculation is not their way. In course of time there arose the need to systematize the Upaniṣadic teachings. Several attempts were made in this direction, but none of these works is available now except Bādarāyaṇa Vyāsa's *Brahma-sūtras* (Aphorisms on Brahman, circ. 550 BC) which is highly esteemed as authoritative by all schools of Vedānta. In fact, every school of Vedānta nondualistic or monotheistic, has a commentary on the *Brahma-sūtras* to corroborate its views. Thus, from the state of the revealed truths Vedānta reached the stage of rationalized truths. Properly speaking, the *Brahma-sūtras* forms the basis of Vedānta as rational philosophy. The term 'Uttara-Mīmāṁsā' strictly applies to this treatise.

The *Bhagavad-gītā*, which dwells particularly on the application of the Upaniṣadic teachings to the practical life, marks the third stage of Vedānta—that of 'applied' truths. It enunciates spiritual and moral disciplines for different types and grades of seekers and points out the way to conform normal life to the highest ideal. Thus, the *Upaniṣads*, the *Brahma-sūtras*, and the *Bhagavad-gītā* are the three norms or standard works of Vedānta, forming its triple basis (prasthāna-traya). They are respectively called the Śruti-prasthāna, the Nyāya-prasthāna, and the Smṛti-prasthāna Vedānta in view of the fact that they follow the course of the Revelation (Śruti), reason (nyāya), and the regulation of life (smṛti). The term Vedānta (Veda+anta) denotes the end or the culmination (anta) of knowledge (veda), specifically, suprasensuous knowledge (the Veda). Secondarily, it refers to the concluding portions of the Vedas, which embody that knowledge and are called the Upaniṣads. In a wide sense, Vedānta signifies the three aforesaid Sanskrit religious classics and all authentic explanatory treatises on them.

Each system of the Vedānta philosophy is primarily an interpretation of the *Brahma-sūtras*. It is also supported by the commentaries on the *Upaniṣads* and the *Bhagavad-gītā*. Besides, each school has original writings elaborating on the teachings of the three primary works to confirm its views. It is to be noted that both the schools of Advaita Vedānta are based on Śaṅkara's commentary on the *Brahma-sūtras*; but each of the five monotheistic schools has its own commentary on the treatise.

The earliest known Vedānta philosopher who reconciled authority with logic and established Nondualism on a rational basis is Gauḍapāda (circ. seventh century AD). His *Māṇḍūkya-kārikā* (an elaborate versified exposition of the *Māṇḍūkya Upaniṣad*) is the first available systematic presentation of the cardinal truths of Advaita philosophy. He was the parama-guru, (the grand-preceptor) of the seer-philosopher, Śaṅkarācārya, the greatest exponent of Advaita Vedānta, who reinstated the Vedic religion in its pristine purity and glory after its decline during the Buddhistic period. According to modern historians, Śaṅkara lived between 788 and 820 AD, but according to the orthodox view, he lived about a century earlier. His commentaries or explanatory treatises on the principal Upaniṣads (including *Māṇḍūkya-kārikā*), the *Brahma-sūtras*, and the *Bhagavad-gītā* are the pillars of Advaita philosophy. Besides, he wrote numerous other works in prose and poetry for the enlightenment and guidance of the seekers of Truth. Apart from his other great achievements as a reviver of the Vedic religion, his literary output within a short life of thirty-two years is amazing. The two main schools of Advaita Vedānta founded on his commentary on the *Brahma-sūtras* are (1) the Vivaraṇa school and (2) the Vācaspati school, which we have mentioned in the foregoing pages (ch. XI, sec. 5, 6). In order to explain the nature of the jīva and its relation to ajñāna different theories have been propounded by the later Advaita philosophers. These are all based on the authority of Śaṅkara.

Among the founders of the monotheistic schools of Vedānta (better known as the schools of Vaiṣṇavism) five are prominent: Rāmānuja (1017–1137 AD), Nimbārka (eleventh century, AD), Madhva (1199–1276 AD), Vallabha (1479–1531 AD), Śrī Caitanya (1485–1533 AD). Their systems, as previously indicated (ch. X, sec. 3), are known respectively as Viśiṣṭādvaita, Dvaitādvaita, Dvaita, Śuddhādvaita, Acintya-bhedābheda. Except for Śrī Caitanya, all the other founders wrote commentaries on the *Brahma-sūtras* to corroborate their views. Śrī Jīva Gosvāmī, a grand-disciple of Śrī Caitanya, systematized his views, which were later confirmed by a commentary on the *Brahma-sūtras* by Baladeva Vidyābhūṣaṇa who lived in the eighteenth century AD.

The metaphysical distinctions among the five monotheistic systems consist of subtle differences in their conceptions of the relation between the jīva (the individual self) and Brahman, the Supreme Self. All recognize the difference between the individual self and the Supreme Self, but the difference does not mean that the two are separate or altogether dissimilar. It is difference in the presence of non-difference. Rāmānuja, Vallabha, and Jīva Gosvāmī (Śrī Caitanya's follower) have emphasized the non-difference, Madhva the difference. Rāmānuja's system is known as Viśiṣṭādvaita (lit., qualified nondualism), and Madhva's as Dvaita (dualism), but not in the sense in which Sāṁkhya system is, as we shall see later. In Nimbārka's system, Dvaitādvaita (dualism in nondualism) difference and non-difference balance. Though different, the jīva is one with Brahman. It is Brahman that is manifest as the jīvas without losing His fullness and perfection. The relation is somewhat like the relation between the sun and its radiance (prakāśa).

According to Vallabha, Brahman, the Supreme Being, is unassociated with māyā and therefore pure (śuddha). He creates the manifold out of Himself by His inherent knowledge and power of action without undergoing any change whatsoever. The individual selves and the world are consequently non-different from Brahman. Vallabha's system is called Śuddha-advaita (pure nondualism) in contrast with Kevala-advaita (simple nondualism) of Śaṅkara. According to Saṅkara, Brahman is Nirguṇa and Nirviśeṣa, without any attribute and distinction whatsoever; according to Vallabha and other monotheistic philosophers, Brahman is Saguṇa and Saviśeṣa, possessed of attributes and distinctive features.

The system of Śrī Caitanya school is called Acintya-bheda-abheda, incomprehensible difference in nondifference. The relation between the jīva and Brahman (God) is like that between power (śakti) and the possessor of power (śaktimān); they are distinct yet inseparable. The world as well as the jīvas are the manifestations of God's powers. Being the manifestation of His power, the jīva is neither one with Him nor different from Him, even as heat is neither identical with, nor different from the fire that radiates it. The relation is inexplicable. We shall dwell on this later.

6. *The Living Hindu Religion is Vedānta*

Besides the schools of Vaiṣṇavism there are in Hinduism other monotheistic schools, e.g., those of Śaivism and Śāktism. The same Supreme Being is worshipped in three different aspects: as (1) Viṣṇu (the Omnipresent Preserver) by the Vaiṣṇavas, as (2) Śiva (the All-good and transcendent Being) by the Śaivas, and as (3) Śakti (Śiva's power, the Mother of the universe) by the Śāktas. All these schools owe their o .gin to the Vedic hymns and the Upaniṣads, though their later developments are due mainly to the Purāṇas, the Āgamas, and the Tantras, which elaborate on the Vedic teachings.

There are three main schools of Śaivism: (1) Southern Śaivism, (2) Vīra-Śaivism, and (3) Kāśmīra-Śaivism. The monotheistic systems of the Śaivas and the Śāktas, though in many respects similar to those of the Vaiṣṇava schools, are not usually included in the Vedānta philosophy, but are regarded as non-Vedantic, since they are not directly based on the *Brahma-sūtras* (also called the *Vedānta-sūtras*) in the way Advaitism and Vaiṣṇavism are. Nevertheless, a few Śaiva philosophers have written commentaries on the *Brahma-sūtras* in order to reconcile the teachings of the Śaiva Āgamas with the teachings of the Upaniṣads. In fact, the Śaiva and the Śākta schools accept the authority of, and are sustained by, the triple Vedānta—the *Upaniṣads*, the *Brahma-sūtras*, and the *Bhagavad-gītā*. One and the same Upaniṣadic Brahman is conceived by the Vaiṣṇavas as Sat-cid-ānanda Viṣṇu and by the Śaivas as Sat-cid-ānanda Śiva. It is the dynamic aspect of Śiva that the Śāktas worship as Śakti (power). Thus, in a wide sense, all the three monotheistic schools are Vedāntic. Kāśmīra-Śaivism and Śāktism, though very close to Advaita Vedānta, are not strictly nondualistic, because the ultimate Reality as conceived by them is not the attributeless nondual Brahman declared by the Upaniṣads and advocated by Śaṅkara. So they belong to the monotheistic group rather than the monistic.

The Vedās are the perennial source of all the outflow of Hindu religion and philosophy. So the true name of Hinduism is 'Vaidika Dharma (the religion of the Vedas).' It is also called 'Sanātana Dharma (the eternal religion),' since it holds fast throughout the ages to the eternal and universal truths declared by the Vedas, such as (1) the fundamental Reality is one, the sages call it by different names, (2) this self is Brahman, (3) the knower of Brahman attains the Highest. What is non-Vedic is non-Hindu, in other words, heretical. Present-day Hinduism is, truly speaking, the religion and philosophy of Vedānta. Hinduism is a misnomer.[9] Of the six Vedic systems, only Vedānta has a religious following in modern India. There are however solitary instances of spiritual aspirants who follow the purely Sāṁkhya or the Yōgic method of self-realization. The practical courses of Sāṁkhya and Yōga and some of their psychological and philosophical views, excluding the divergent elements, have been adapted to the religion and philosophy of Vedānta.

The six Vedic schools do not contradict each other, but serve as grades of philosophic knowledge leading to the highest. In the words of Dr Radhakrishnan:

'The Nyāya-Vaiśeṣika realism, the Sāṁkhya-Yōga dualism and the Vedānta monism, do not differ as true and false but as more or less true. They are adapted to the needs of the slow-witted (mandādhikārī), the average intellect (madhyamādhikār) and the strong-minded (uttamādhikārī) respectively. The different views are hewn out of one stone and belong to one whole, integral, entire and self-contained. No scheme of the universe can be regarded as complete, if it has not the different sides of logic and physics, psychology and ethics, metaphysics and religion.'[10]

9 The word is derived from 'Sindhu', Sanskrit name of the river Indus, which the ancient Persians mis-spelt as 'Hindu'. Gradually the term was applied to the inhabitants of ancient India, and their religion became known as Hinduism. Similarly, 'India' is a foreign appellation, derived from the same word 'Sindhu', which the Greeks mispronounced as 'Indus' and called the adjoining country 'India' and her people 'the Indians'. The original name of the country is 'Bhārata' or 'Bhārata-varṣa'.

10 S. Radhakrishnan, *Indian Philosophy*, Vol. II, p. 770.

All the Vedic systems agree on these points that the real self of man is distinct from the psychophysical system, that being identified with it through ignorance he is bound and that being dissociated from it through right knowledge he attains liberation. Nyāya-Vaiśeṣika points out the distinctness of the self from the psychophysical system; Sāṁkhya-Yōga maintains its self-luminosity as pure intelligence and its unrelatedness; monotheistic Vedānta stresses its kinship with the Supreme Self, the sole Controller of the knower and the known. Advaita Vedānta refutes the plurality of the self and affirms its sole reality as Nondual Pure Consciousness.

7. *Notable Sanskrit Works of Advaita Vedānta and Available English Translations*

The Vedāntic literature is very vast. In addition to the numerous original works each school has commentaries and sub-commentaries on the important texts. In this section we shall mention the leading treatises of the Advaita school.

Gauḍapāda (seventh century AD)—*Māṇḍūkya-kārikā* (a versified exposition of the Māṇḍūkya Upaniṣad).

Śaṅkarācārya (AD 686–718)—Commentaries on ten Upaniṣads (Īśa, Kena, Kaṭha, Praśna, Muṇḍaka, Māṇḍūkya including Gauḍapāda's Kārikā, Chāndōgya, Bṛhadāraṇyaka, Aitareya, and Taittirīya), the Brahma-sūtras, the Bhagavad-gītā, and other texts; about fifty original works (prose and poetry)—*Viveka-cūḍāmaṇi, Upadeśa-sāhasrī, Aparōkṣānubhūti, Ātma-bōdha, Ātma-jñānōpadeśa-vidhi, Atmānātma-viveka, Vākya-vṛtti, Laghu-vākya-vṛtti, Pañcīkaraṇa, Nirvāṇa-daṣaka,* etc.; and more than sixty hymns including *Dakṣiṇāmūrti-stōtra.*

Padmapāda (one of the four chief disciples of Śaṅkarācārya)—*Pañca-pādikā,* an exposition of Śaṅkara's commentary on the first four aphorisms of the Brahma-sūtras (see footnote 46 on the Vivaraṇa school, ch. XI, sec. 6).

Suresvarācārya (AD 675–773)—*Bṛhadāraṇyaka-bhāṣya-vārttika, Taitti-rīya-bhāṣya-vārttika, Pañcīkaraṇa-vārttika,* and other explanatory treatises. Original writings—*Brahma-siddhi, Naiṣkarmya-siddhi,* and *Svārājya-siddhi* (or *Iṣṭa-siddhi*).

Sarvajñātma-muni (approx. AD 710–810), a disciple of Sureśvarācārya —*Saṁkṣepa-śārīraka,* an exposition in verse of the Brahma-sūtras in accordance with Śaṅkara.

Vācaspati Miśra (AD 801–881)—*Bhāmatī,* an interpretation of Śaṅkara's commentary on the Brahma-sūtras (see footnote 42 on the Vācaspati school, ch. XI, sec. 5).

Prakāśātma-yati (twelfth century AD)—*Pañcapādikā-vivaraṇa,* an elucidation of Padmapāda's work (see footnote 46 on the Vivaraṇa school, ch. XI, sec. 6).

Śrīharṣācārya (twelfth century AD)—*Khaṇḍana-khaṇḍa-khādya,* lit., the refutation [of the views of the opponent schools] as a dainty delicacy.

Citsukhācārya (thirteenth century AD)—*Pratyak-tattva-pradīpikā*, usually called 'Tattva-pradīpikā' or 'Citsukhī', which established nondualism by disproving Nyāya-Vaiśeṣika and other divergent systems.

Śaṅkarānanda (AD 1228–1333)—Commentaries on 108 Upaniṣads and other works.

Amalānanda-yati (thirteenth and fourteenth century AD)—*Vedānta-kalpa-taru*, a commentary on Vācaspati's commentary 'Bhāmatī' (see footnote 42 on the Vācaspati school, ch. XI, sec. 5).

Śrīdhara Swāmī (thirteenth century AD)—well-known for his lucid commentaries on the Śrīmad-Bhāgavata, the Bhagavad-gītā, and the Viṣṇupurāṇa.

Sāyaṇācārya (fourteenth century AD)—well-known for his commentaries on the Vedic texts.

Vidyāraṇya (Sāyaṇa's brother)—*Pañcadaśī*, *Sarvadarśana-saṁgraha*, *Vivaraṇa-prameya-saṁgraha*, *Jīvanmukti-viveka*, and a number of commentaries.

Ānanda-jñāna or Ānanda-giri (fourteenth century AD)—well-known for his commentaries on Śaṅkara's commentaries and other works.

Prakāśananda Sarasvatī (fifteenth century AD)—*Vedānta-siddhānta-muktāvalī*.

Appayadīkṣita (AD 1550–1622)—a great scholar, author of 104 treatises on different subjects. His famous works on Advaita Vedānta are *Siddhānta-leśa-saṁgraha*, *Nyāya-rakṣā-maṇi*, *Nyāya-mañjarī*, and *Vedānta-kalpa-taru-parimala* (a commentary on Amalānanda-yati's 'Vedānta-kalpa-taru').

Sadānanda Yōgīndra (sixteenth century)—*Vedānta-sāra* (lit., the essence of Vedānta), a primer of Advaita Vedānta.

Rāmatīrtha Swāmī (bet. 1475 and 1575 AD)—Commentaries on Vedānta-sāra, Saṁkṣepa-śārīraka, Upadeśa-sāhasrī, etc. His com. on Vedānta-sāra is called *Vidvanmanōrañjinī*.

Madhusūdana Sarasvatī (AD 1525–1632)—*Advaita-siddhi*, a monumental work on Advaita philosophy, establishes Śaṅkara's nondualism on a secure foundation by thoroughly refuting all the charges levelled against it by Vyāsācārya (a follower of Madhvācārya) in his 'Nyāyāmṛta.' Besides, he wrote commentaries on the Bhagavad-gītā, Saṁkṣepa-śārīraka, Śrīmad-Bhagavatam, Nirvāṇa-daśakam, Ātma-bōdha, Śiva-mahimna-stōtra, etc. His original works are *Bhakti-rasāyana*, *Prasthāna-bheda*, *Advaita-ratna-rakṣaṇa*, *Vedānta-kalpalatikā*, etc.

Dharmarāja Adhvarīndra (bet. 1575–1675 AD)—*Vedānta-paribhāṣā*, a manual of Advaita Vedānta, dwelling on its epistemology, metaphysics, and purpose.

Available English translations:

The Upaniṣads (eleven), Vols. I–IV with introduction and explanatory notes based on Śaṅkara's commentary. Swāmī Nikhilānanda (tr.). New York, Harper and Brothers, 1949–1959.

The Thirteen Principal Upaniṣads—R. E. Hume, Madras, Oxford University Press, 1951.

Principal Upaniṣads—with introduction, transliterated text and notes —S. Radhakrishnan. London, Allen and Unwin; New York, Harper and Brothers, 1953.

Eight Upaniṣads (including texts), with the commentary of Śaṅkarācārya, Vols. I, II, Swāmī Gambhīrānanda (tr.). Mayavati, Almora, Advaita Ashrama, 1957, 1958.

The Upaniṣads (selections from twelve), Swāmī Prabhavānanda and Frederick Manchester (trs.). Hollywood, Vedānta Press, 1947.

The Upaniṣad Series (eight) with text, Swāmī Sharvānanda (tr.), Madras, Sri Ramakrishna Math.

Bṛhadāraṇyaka Upaniṣad (including text) with the commentary of Śaṅkarācārya, Swāmī Mādhavānanda (tr.). Almora, Advaita Ashrama, 1934. The first complete translation of this commentary, Śaṅkara's masterpiece according to some.

The Māṇḍūkyōpaniṣad with Gauḍapāda's Kārikā (including text) and Śaṅkara's commentary (annotated), Swāmī Nikhilānanda (tr.). Mysore, Sri Ramakrishna Ashrama, 1936.

Śvetāśvatara Upaniṣad (including text) with copious notes, Swāmī Thyāgīśānanda (tr.). Madras, Sri Ramakrishna Math, 1937.

The Chāndōgya Upaniṣad (including text) with copious notes, Swāmī Swāhānanda (tr.). Madras, Sri Ramakrishna Math, 1956.

Mahānārāyaṇōpaniṣad (including accented text) with a Sanskrit commentary on the text and explanatory notes, Swāmī Vimalānanda (tr.). Madras, Sri Ramakrishna Math, 1957.

The Vedānta-sūtras with the commentary of Śaṅkarācārya, George Thibaut (tr.), Sacred Books of the East, Vols. XXXIV and XXXVIII. Oxford, The Clarendon Press, 1890, 1896.

Brahma-sūtras (including text) with an introduction and explanation based on Śaṅkara's commentary, Swāmī Vīreśwarānanda (tr.). Almora, Advaita Ashrama, 1936.

The Pañcapādikā of Padmapāda with an introduction and a conspectus, D. Venkataramiah (tr.), Gaekwad's Oriental Series, CVII. Baroda, Oriental Institute, 1948.

The Bhagavad-gītā—The Song Celestial. Trans. in verse by Edwin Arnold. Bombay, Jaico Publishing House, 1957.

——(including text) with the commentary of Śaṅkarācārya and notes from Ānandagiri's gloss, A. Mahādeva Śāstrī (tr.). Madras, V. Ramaswamy Sastrulu, 1929.

——with text, notes, and index to first lines, Swāmī Swarūpānanda (tr.). Almora, Advaita Ashrama, 1933.

——with an introduction and explanatory notes based on Śaṅkara's commentary, Swāmī Nikhilānanda (tr.). New York, Ramakrishna-Vivekananda Center, 1944.

——with an introduction by Aldous Huxley, Swāmī Prabhavānanda and Christopher Isherwood (trs.). Hollywood, Vedanta Press, 1951.

——with transliterated text, an introductory essay, and notes, S. Radhakrishnan (tr.). London, Allen and Unwin; New York, Harper.

——(including text) with Śrīdhara Swāmī's commentary, Swāmī Vīreśwarānanda (tr.). Madras, Sri Ramakrishna Math, 1949.

Aṣṭāvakra-Saṁhitā—with text, an introduction, and notes, Swāmī Nityaswarūpānanda (tr.). Calcutta, The Ramakrishna Mission Institute of Culture, 1940.

Siddhānta-leśa-saṁgraha—S. S. Sūryanārayaṇa Śāstrī, University of Madras, India.

Vedānta-sāra (the essence of Vedānta) of Sadānanda Yōgīndra, with text and copious notes, Swāmī Nikhilānanda (tr.). Almora, Advaita Ashrama, 1931.

Vedānta-paribhāṣā of Dharmarāja Adhvarīndra, with text, notes, glossary, and index, Swāmī Mādhavānanda (tr.). Belur Math, Howrah, The Ramakrishna Mission Sarada Pitha, 1942.

Dṛg-dṛśya-viveka (Discrimination of the 'seer' from 'the seen') by Bhāratī Tīrtha. Also called 'Vākya-sudhā' and ascribed to Śaṅkara.—with text and copious notes, Swāmī Nikhilānanda (tr.). Mysore, Sri Ramakrishna Ashrama, 1931.

Of Śaṅkarācārya's original works:

Viveka-cūḍāmaṇi (The Crest-Jewel of Discrimination)—with text and notes, Swāmī Mādhavānanda (tr.). Almora, Advaita Ashrama, 1921.

——with an introduction to Śaṅkara's philosophy, Swāmī Prabhavānanda and Christopher Isherwood (trs.). Hollywood, Vedanta Press, 1947.

Aparōkṣānubhūti (Self-realization)—with text and notes, Swāmī Vimuktānanda. Almora, Advaita Ashrama, 1938.

Ātma-bōdha (Self-knowledge) and 14 hymns—with an introduction and notes, Swāmī Nikhilānanda. New York, Ramakrishna-Vivekananda Center, 1946.

Upadeśa-sāhasrī (A thousand teachings)—with text and explanatory notes, Swāmī Jagadānanda. Madras, Sri Ramakrishna Math, 1949.

Vākya-vṛtti (An exposition of the sentence, 'Thou art That') and *Ātmajñānōpadeśa-vidhi* (The way of instruction on Self-knowledge) with texts and notes. Deoghar (S.P.), Swami J., Ramakrishna Mission Vidyapith, 1941.

Pañcīkaraṇam (the process of quintuplication) with Sureśvarācārya's Vārttikam. Vrindavan, Mathura, Ramakrishna Mission Sevashrama, 1962.

8. *Viśiṣṭādvaita of Rāmānuja*

The first great exponent of the monotheistic Vedānta is Rāmānuja, the founder of the Śrī-Vaiṣṇava school, who lived from AD 1017 to 1137. His system is known as Viśiṣṭādvaita, which signifies *qualified* nondualism or unity of Reality. According to both Śaṅkara and Rāmānuja, the ultimate Reality is the unity of Brahman. While in Śaṅkara's view Brahman is undifferentiated (nirviśeṣa), being absolutely free from all distinctions, in Rāmānuja's view Brahman is differentiated (saviśeṣa), being characterized by internal distinctions. Conscious selves and non-conscious nature belong to Him as integral parts. He is the sole Reality inclusive of them all, being their innermost Self and Ruler.

But Rāmānuja is not the originator of the system. In his commentary, *Śrī-bhāṣya*, on the Brahma-sūtras, he states that he has followed an earlier commentator (vṛtti-kāra), Bōdhāyana (whose work is not available now). He was directly influenced by the Tāmil ācāryas (spiritual teachers), Nātha Muni and Yāmuna Muni (AD 916–1042), the precursors of the system. The chief writings of Yāmuna Muni (also called Yāmunācārya) are *Āgama-prāmāṇya, Siddhitraya, Mahāpuruṣa-nirṇaya,* and *Gītārtha-saṁgraha.* Rāmānuja has based his teachings particularly on the Upaniṣads, the Brahma-sūtras, and the Bhagavad-gītā. Besides the commentaries on the Brahma-sūtras and the Bhagavad-gītā his other works are *Vedārtha-saṁgraha, Vedānta-sāra, Vedānta-dīpa,* and *Bhagavad-ārādhanā-krama.* He did not write any commentary on the Upaniṣads. Out of the many sub-commentaries on his *Śrībhāṣya* (commentary on the Brahma-sūtras) we may mention particularly Sudarśana Sūri's *Śruta-prakāśikā,* Meghanādāri's *Naya-prakāśikā,* and Veṅkaṭanātha's *Tattva-ṭīkā.* Veṅkaṭanātha also wrote a sub-commentary called *Tātparya-candrikā,* on Rāmānuja's commentary on the Bhagavad-gītā.

After Rāmānuja there was a long succession of writers on his system. Two of them can be specially mentioned—Meghanādāri (between AD 1150 and 1250) and Veṅkaṭanātha (AD 1267–1389). The latter was the most remarkable of them all. Besides *Naya-prakāśikā* (a commentary on Rāmānuja's Śrī-bhāṣya) Meghanādāri wrote *Bhāva-prabōdha, Mumukṣūpāya-saṁgraha,* and *Naya-dyumaṇi.* Veṅkaṭanātha, better known as Vedānta-deśika, was a prolific writer on various subjects and also a gifted poet. His principal works on Rāmānuja doctrines (besides the two sub-commentaries *Tattva-ṭīkā* and *Tātparya-candrikā*) are *Nyāya-pariṣuddhi, Nyāya-siddhañjana, Tattva-muktā-kalāpa* (in verse) with his own commentary upon it called *Sarvārtha-siddhi,* and the *Śata-dūṣaṇī* (a hundred objections to Advaita Vedānta). A later noteworthy book, though a short manual for the beginners, is *Yatīndra-mata-dīpikā* of Śrīnivāsācārya (AD 1700).

Comparing the philosophical acumen and logical subtlety of Rāmānuja school with those of the schools of Śaṅkara and Madhva Dasgupta remarks:

'It seems, however, that the Viśiṣṭādvaita philosophy was not a source of perennial inspiration for the development of ever newer shades of thought, and that the logical and dialectical thinkers of this school were decidedly inferior to the prominent thinkers of the Śaṅkara and the Madhva school. There is hardly anyone in the whole history of the development of the school of Rāmānuja whose logical acuteness can be compared with that of Śrīharṣa or Citsukha, or with that of Jayatīrtha or Vyāsatīrtha. Veṅkaṭanātha, Meghanādāri, or Rāmānujācārya called also Vādihaṁsa, were some of the most prominent writers of this school; but even with them philosophic criticism does not always reach the highest level. It was customary for the thinkers of the Śaṅkara and the Madhva schools in the fourteenth, fifteenth, and sixteenth centuries to accept the concepts of the new School of Logic of Mithila and Bengal and introduce keen dialectical analysis and criticism. But for some reason or other this method was not adopted to any large extent by the thinkers of the Śrī-Vaiṣṇava school. Yet this was the principal way in which philosophical concepts developed in later times.'[11]

English translations:

1. *The Vedānta-sūtras* with the commentary of Rāmānuja by George Thibaut, Sacred Books of the East, Vol. XLVIII. Oxford: Clarendon Press, 1904.
2. *The Vedānta-tattva-sāra* ascribed to Rāmānuja, tr. by J. Johnson. Banaras, E. J. Lazarus, 1898.
3. *Yatīndra-mata-dīpikā* by Śrīnivāsadāsa, text and tr. with notes by Swāmī Ādidevānanda. Madras, Sri Ramakrishna Math, 1950.

9. *Dvaitādvaita of Nimbārka*

Nimbārka, a Telegu Brāhmana, lived in the eleventh century, A.D. In all probability he was a junior contemporary of Rāmānuja. The literature of this school is scanty compared with that of other Vaiṣṇava schools. Nimbārka (also known as Nimbāditya) wrote a short commentary on the Brahma-sūtras called *Vedānta-pārijāta-saurabha*, lit., the fragrance of the heavenly flower-plant of Vedānta. To elaborate Nimbārka's views his direct disciple Śrīnivāsa wrote a commentary on the Brahma-sūtras, called *Vedānta-kaustubha*. On this a sub-commentary called *Vedānta-kaustubha-prabhā*, lit., the lustre of the gem of Vedānta, was written by Keśava Kāśmīrī Bhaṭṭa, who also wrote commentaries on the Bhagavad-gītā, Śrīmad-Bhāgavatam (sec. X), and the Taittirīya Upaniṣad.

As explained by *Vedānta-kaustubha* (iii: 2.29):

'The relation of God and the world is like that of a snake and its coiled existence. The coiled (kuṇḍala) condition of a snake is neither different from it nor absolutely identical with it. So God's relation with the individuals also is like that of a lamp and its light (prabhā-tadvatōriva) or like the sun and the illumination (prakāśa). God remains unchanged in Himself and only undergoes transformation through His energies as conscious (cic-chakti) and unconscious (acic-chakti).'[12]

Nimbārka also wrote a poem of ten stanzas called *Daśaślōkī* and a hymn to Śrī Kṛṣṇa called *Śrī Kṛṣṇa-stava-rāja*. Other works attributed to him are not available. In *Daśaślōkī* (also called *Siddhānta-ratna*), he dwells on the triple reality (tri-tattva): Brahman, soul (cit), and matter

[11] Surendranath Dasgupta, *A History of Indian Philosophy*, Vol. III, pp. 111–12.

[12] *Ibid.* p. 416.

(acit). These are held to be three ultimate reals and co-eternal. The poem sums up his views. There are several commentaries on this. A notable commentary is *Vedānta-ratna-mañjūṣā* by Puruṣōttama Prasāda, who also wrote a commentary on *Śrī Kṛṣṇa-stava-rāja*.

English translations:

Vedānta-pārijāta-saurabha with Vedānta-kaustubha of Śrīnivāsa, commentaries on the Brahma-sūtras. Text and translation with notes by Mrs Roma Chaudhuri, Bibliotheca Indica, Work No. 259. Calcutta, Royal Asiatic Society of Bengal, 1940–1943, 3 vols.

10. *Dvaita of Madhvācārya* (AD 1199–1276)

According to Madhvācārya, God (Paramātman), the individual selves, and prakṛti (the potential cause of the physical and the psychical universe), with their fivefold differences, are ultimately real. The differences between God and the individual self, between God and prakṛti, between the individual self and prakṛti, between one individual self and another, between one category of prakṛti and another endure forever. But the sole *independent* entity is God (Paramātman). Individual selves and prakṛti (manifest or unmanifest) have no existence apart from Him. Thus Madhva's view is different from the pluralism of Nyāya-Vaiśeṣika on the one hand and from the dualism of Sāṁkhya-Yōga on the other. It is dualism as opposed to nondualism of Śaṅkara. Professor Hiriyanna thus differentiates the dualism of Madhva from the non-dualism of Śaṅkara:

'If the Advaita explains the prevailingly absolutistic standpoint of Upaniṣadic teaching by postulating only one reality and explaining the rest of the universe as its appearance, the Dvaita [of Madhva] does the same by postulating God as the only supreme entity and explaining the rest as altogether dependent upon him.'[13]

Madhva's system is called *Sad*-Vaiṣṇavism as distinguished from *Śrī*-Vaiṣṇavism of Rāmānuja. The seat of the one is Udipi near Mangalore on the West coast and of the other Conjeeverum near Madras on the East coast of South India.

Madhva is the reputed author of thirty-seven books (prose and verse). In his writings he calls himself 'Ānanda-tīrtha.' These include commentaries on the ten principal Upaniṣads (Īśa, Kena, Kaṭha, Praśna, Muṇḍaka, Māṇḍūkya, Aitareya, Taittirīya, Chāndōgya, Bṛhadāraṇyaka), the Brahma-sūtras, and the Bhagavad-gītā. Besides *Brahma-sūtra-bhāṣya*, he wrote other interpretations of the Brahma-sūtras, namely, *Brahma-sūtrānubhāṣya*, *Brahma-sūtrānuvyākhyāna*, *Brahma-sūtrānuvyākhyāna-nirṇaya*. His *Mahābhārata-tātparya-nirṇaya*, *Bhāgavata-tātparya-nirṇaya*, and *Bhagavad-gītā-tātparya-nirṇaya* are compendiums of the three great books. The ten important manuals among his original works are: *Pramāna-lakṣaṇa*, *Kathā-lakṣaṇa*, *Mithyānumāna-khaṇḍana*,

[13] M. Hiriyanna, *The Essentials of Indian Philosophy*, p. 195.

Upādhi-khaṇḍana, Māyā-vāda-khaṇḍana (refutation of the doctrine of Māyā), *Tatva-saṁkhyāna* (a brief statement of his principles), *Tattvōd-dyōta, Tattva-viveka, Viṣṇu-tattva-nirṇaya, Karma-nirṇaya.*

On most of his works there are commentaries and sub-commentaries by different writers. On some there are a number of commentaries and explanatory treatises. The most distinguished of the commentators is Jayatīrtha (AD 1217–1280) who wrote commentaries on the major part of Madhva's works. His *Nyāya-sudhā* is a masterly exposition of Madhva's *Brahma-sūtrānuvyākhyāna*. It is 'the principal source-book of most of the writers of the Madhva school.' On this Rāghavendra Yati wrote a commentary called *Nyāya-sudhā-parimala*. The writers of Madhva school, like many other Vedic and non-Vedic philosophers, have directed their criticism against the nondualism of Śaṅkara. As we have noted above, it is in refutation of Vyāsācārya's (AD 1446–1539) counter-arguments put forward in *Nyāyāmṛta* that Madhusūdana Sarasvatī wrote his celebrated work *Advaita-siddhi* (Establishment of Non-dualism).

English translations:

1. *Pūrṇa-Prajñā-darśana* (Brahma-sūtra-bhāṣya of Madhvācārya), tr. by S. Subba Rau. Tirupati, Sri Vyasa Press, 2nd edn. (rev. 1936).
2. *The Bṛhadāraṇyaka Upaniṣad with the Commentary of Śrī Madhvā-cārya called also Ānanda-tīrtha*, tr. by Rai Bahadur Srischandra Vidyarnava with the assistance of Pandit Ramaksaya Bhatta-carya Vidyabhusana, 2nd edn., Sacred Books of the Hindus, XIV, 1923.

11. *Śuddhādvaita of Vallabhācārya* (AD 1479–1531)

We have briefly noted Vallabha's metaphysical views. He was a contemporary of Śrī Caitanya, who lived from 1485 to 1533 AD. The Vaiṣṇava philosophers, particularly, Madhva, Vallabha, and Śrī Jīva Gōsvāmī, an adherent of Śrī Caitanya, rely on the authority of the Bhāgavatam as much as on the Upaniṣads, the Brahma-sūtras, and the Bhagavad-gītā. According to Vallabha, the supreme end of human life is the ardent love for the Divine Lord Śrī Kṛṣṇa which (as depicted in the Bhāgavatam) the gōpis (the pastoral women) of Vrindāvana had for Him when He was incarnate in human form. It is through this love alone that the individual self (the jīva) can relish the transcendent bliss of God and even give up the desire for emancipation (mukti).

Vallabha is said to have written eighty-four books (including sixteen small tracts). His principal writings are the commentaries on the Brahma-sūtras, the Bhāgavatam, and the Bhagavad-gītā. The commentary on the Brahma-sūtras called *Brahma-sūtrānu-bhāṣya* has a number of sub-commentaries among which *Bhāṣya-prakāśa* of Puruṣōttama (who lived late in the seventeenth century AD) ranks very high. There are several sub-commentaries on Vallabha's commentary *Subōdhinī* on the Bhāgavatam. He also wrote some treatises expounding the teachings of the Bhāgavatam, such as *Bhāgavata-tattvadīpa*, with his own commentary on it called *Prakāśa*. One of his small tracts, *Sannyāsa-nirṇaya*, in which he discusses three ways of renunciation—through karma (work), through jñāna (knowledge), and through bhakti (devotion)—has no less than seven commentaries on it.

Vallabha's son Viṭṭhala (AD 1518–1588) was also a great writer. The most important of his works is *Vidvan-maṇḍana* on which Puruṣōttama wrote a commentary called *Suvarṇa-sūtra*. Viṭṭhala's sons, Gōkulanātha and others, and his pupil, Muralīdharā, wrote mostly commentaries on Vallabha's works and some original books as well. Thus, theological and philosophical writings by the followers of Vallabha flowed on close to the end of the eighteenth century.

English version:

The Vedānta: *A Study of the Brahma-Sūtras with the Bhāṣyas of Śaṅkara, Rāmānuja, Nimbārka, Madhva, and Vallabha*. Poona, Bhandarkar Oriental Research Institute, 1926 (trans. in slightly different form of V. S. Ghate's *Le Vedanta*: *Etude sur les Brahmasutras et leur cinq Commentaries*, Tours, Imp. E. Arrault, 1918).

12. *Acintya-bhedābheda of Śrī Caitanya School (usually called Gauḍīya Vaiṣṇava School)*

This system is based on the teachings of Śrī Caitanya, who lived from 1485 to 1533 AD. His life demonstrates the consummation of the love for God, the Supreme object of all love. Loving God for love's sake is supreme bliss. It is an end in itself. The followers of Nimbārka, Vallabha, and Śrī Caitanya worship Śrī Kṛṣṇa and His eternal consort Śrī Rādhā as the embodiment of the infinite bliss and love of God, which, though distinct, are inseparable. It is through whole-souled loving devotion that an adorer realizes God as such.

Unlike the founders of other Vaiṣṇava schools, Śrī Caitanya wrote no commentary on the Brahma-sūtras. The philosophical view of acintya-bhedābheda was set forth by his grand-disciple, Śrī Jīva Gosvāmī, in a well-known book called *Ṣaṭ-sandarbha* (a group of six treatises). It was later confirmed by Baladeva Vidyābhūṣaṇa (eighteenth century) in his commentary, *Gōvinda-bhāṣya*, on the Brahma-sūtras. Jīva Gōsvāmī followed his predecessors, Sanātana Gōsvāmī and Rūpa Gōsvāmī, the two brothers who were intimate disciples of Śrī Caitanya and wrote important books on the philosophy and psychology of spiritual love based on the master's teachings. Jīva Gōsvāmī was their nephew and a disciple of Rūpa Gōsvāmī.

The system is called 'acintya-bhedābheda' (incomprehensible difference–nondifference), because the relation between the jīva and Brahman, like the relation between power and the possessor of power, is an inexplicable case of difference and nondifference. It recognizes triple power of God: (1) interior, (2) exterior, and (3) intermediate. The manifestation of God's abode and all that pertains to it is due to the interior power (antaraṅgā śakti), which belongs to His inner being, and is also called essential power (svarūpa-śakti). The phenomenal world is the manifestation of His exterior power (bahiraṅgā māyā-śakti), which is constituted of the three guṇas, sattva, rajas, and tamas, and creates all temporal objects. The individual selves (the jīvas) are the manifestation of His intermediate power (taṭasthā śakti) which is neutral. Consequently, they can turn either way—towards God, the Supreme Self, as well as towards the world of phenomena.

The internal or the essential power of God is threefold: (1) sandhinī, (2) sambit, and (3) hladinī, associated respectively with the three aspects of His being—sat (Existence absolute), cit (Knowledge or Consciousness absolute), and ānanda (Bliss absolute). By sandhinī śakti (the power of existence) God maintains His own existence and endows all else with existence. By sambit śakti (power of knowledge) God is all-knowing and endows others with knowledge. By hlādinī śakti (power of delight) God enjoys and enables others to enjoy His bliss by drawing them towards Himself. It is to be noted that in the view of all schools of Vedānta, the Supreme Being is Existence-Knowledge-Bliss (sat-cid-ānanda). According to nondualistic Vedānta these three refer to one and the same undiversified attributeless Brahman, because they are identical in essence (Existence = Knowledge = Bliss). According to monotheistic Vedānta these are the three essential features of Brahman who is saguṇa and saviśeṣa, possessed of attributes and distinctions.

We conclude the article as we note below the important works of five great acāryas (spiritual teachers) of the Gauḍīya Vaiṣṇava school, the latest of the monotheistic schools of Vedānta:

Śrī Sanātana Gōsvāmī—*Hari-bhakti-vilāsa* (the pastime of divine love) with the commentary *dikdarśanī*.
Bṛhad-bhāgavatāmṛtam—dwells on the Divinity of Śrī Kṛṣṇa, the meaning of devotion (bhakti), and other topics.
Commentary *Vaiṣṇava-tōṣiṇī* on the Bhāgavatam, sec. X.

Śrī Rūpa Gōsvāmī—*Bhakti-rasāmṛta-sindhu* (the ocean of the nectar of devotion to God).
Ujjvala-nīlamaṇi—the philosophy of divine love.
Laghubhāgavatāmṛta—dwells on the meaning of the Divine Incarnation.
Besides, two religious dramas viz: *Vidagdha-Mādhava*, *Lalita-Mādhava*, and many poems and hymns.

Śrī Jīva Gōsvāmī—(Appr. 1512–1592 AD) *Ṣaṭ-sandarbha* (Six-treatises) namely, (1) Tattva-sandarbha, (2) Śrī Kṛṣṇa-sandarbha, (3) Bhagavat-sandarbha, (4) Paramātma-sandarbha, (5) Bhakti-sandarbha, (6) Prīti-sandarbha.
Krama-sandarbha—Running commentary on the Bhāgavatam.
Sarva-samvādinī—Commentary on Ṣaṭ-sandarbha.
Commentaries on Śrī Rūpa Gōsvāmī's Bhakti-rasāmṛta-sindhu, Ujjvala-nīlamaṇi, Laghu-bhāgavatāmṛta.
Besides, many other commentaries and books.

Viśvanātha Cakravarttī—(Circ. 1654–1754 AD)—wrote many books, commentaries, poems, and hymns, altogether about thirty-five works. Among them commentaries on Brahma-saṁhitā, Bhagavad-gītā, Bhāgavatam, Bhakti-rasāmṛta-sindhu, Ujjvala-nīlamaṇi are especially noteworthy.

Baladeva Vidyābhūṣaṇa (a pupil of Viśvanātha Cakravarttī)—Commentary *Gōvinda-bhāṣya* on the Brahma-sūtras, commentaries on the ten Upaniṣads, the Bhagavad-gītā, Viṣṇu-sahasranāma, Tattva-sandarbha, etc., and some original works including *Prameya-ratnāvalī*.

English Translation:

The Vedānta-Sūtras of Bādarāyaṇa with the commentary of Baladeva (including Baladeva's *Prameya-ratnāvalī*) tr. by Srischandra Basu, Allahabad, Panini Office.

APPENDIX C

THE YŌGIC DUALISM AND THE VEDĀNTIC NONDUALISM

According to the dualistic Sāṁkhya system of Kapila, which Patañjali has adopted with some differences in delineating the method of Yōga, the self-intelligent puruṣa and the non-intelligent prakṛti[1] are the two distinct fundamental principles. Puruṣa is of the nature of consciousness, pure and simple, and is changeless; whereas prakṛti, the origin of all psychical and physical elements, is altogether devoid of consciousness and subject to change in proximity to puruṣa, like iron moving near a magnet. While prakṛti is one, puruṣas are many. Unlike Sāṁkhya, Vedānta maintains that puruṣa (the individual self) and prakṛti (the world of objects—physical and psychical) are both subordinate to Īśvara, the Supreme Lord. Further, it holds that puruṣa, prakṛti, and Īśvara are basically Nondual Brahman, the ultimate Reality. All objects, physical and psychical, are apparent modification (vivarta) of Brahman through transformations of māyā.

In the Sāṁkhya-Yōga view, all objects, psychical and physical, are transformations (pariṇāma) of prakṛti.[2] These are mahat (the pure mind-stuff), egoism, the internal organ or the mind, the five organs of perception, the five organs of action, the five subtle elements, and the five gross elements, all of which have successively evolved from prakṛti. Thus, there are twenty-four categories of objects, including prakṛti. The first and finest product of prakṛti is mahat, also called "buddhi-sattva", the pure mind-stuff in which the principle of sattva is predominant. It is transparent and pervasive by nature. Being reflected in mahat or buddhi-sattva, puruṣa is identified with it. Because of this association they seemingly partake of each other's characteristics, somewhat like the sun and the mirror on which it is reflected. Buddhi-sattva, which is intrinsically non-intelligent, appears to be intelligent or conscious; and puruṣa, which is changeless consciousness, ever pure, free, and luminous, appears to undergo such changing states as knowledge and ignorance, pain and pleasure, virtue and vice, bondage and freedom, which are the modes of

[1] Also called 'pradhāna (the basis)' and 'avyakta (the unmanifest).'

[2] The primal constituents of prakṛti are the three guṇas (strands)—sattva, rajas, and tamas, which form a triad, and are inseparable. It is the predominance of one or the other in varying degrees that causes all changes. Sattva is the principle of poise conducive to purity, knowledge, joy. Rajas is the principle of motivity leading to activity, desire, restlessness. Tamas is the principle of inertia, resulting in inaction, dullness, delusion. (See footnote 48, chap.I).

buddhi-sattva.[3] Due to its association with buddhi-sattva, puruṣa turns out to be 'the seer' or the experiencer, and prakṛti to be 'the seen' or the experienced. All transformation of prakṛti is for the experience and the liberation of 'the seer'.[4]

Thus begins the erroneous identification of the self with the not-self.[5] This is the primary cause of the jīva's miseries, according to both Sāṁkhya-Yōga and Vedānta. 'The union of the seer and the seen is the cause of suffering to be prevented,' says Patañjali, 'Ignorance is its root.'[6] Like a pure crystal appearing red in proximity to a red flower, 'the seer' appears to be bound to prakṛti and its modifications in association with them.[7] Its closest association is, of course, with buddhi-sattva. The freedom of the self consequently means its complete withdrawal and aloofness from prakṛti and its transformations, gross and subtle. This is achieved through sharp discrimination of the self from the not-self, particularly from buddhi-sattva. Keen introspection and intense meditation, with preparatory steps, are essential requisites for such an end. So far as the practice of the discrimination of the self from the not-self is concerned Vedānta agrees with Sāṁkhya-Yōga and prescribes it for the seekers of liberation. But the Vedāntic view of liberation and the proximate method of its attainment is very different.

3 *Vide* Vijñānabhikṣu's com. on SD I: 1, 19; II: 35. See also YS II: 20.
4 YS II: 21. 5 *Vide* SK 20. 6 YS II: 17, 24.
7 *Vide* SD I: 19; II: 35.

APPENDIX D

THE YŌGIC METHOD OF MEDITATION LEADING TO SELF-REALIZATION

Starting the practice of concentration on the gross physical objects, the yōgī succeeds in fixing the mind on finer and finer entities. The finest of all objects is, of course, prakṛti, their origin. The three main stages of meditation mentioned by Patañjali are:

(1) Meditation on the grāhya (the sensible objects).

(2) Meditation on the grahaṇa (the sense-organs and the mind, the instruments of knowledge).

(3) Meditation on the grahītā (the knowing self, the experiencer).

Through the practice of concentration on any single object of the triad, when all other thoughts are eliminated, the mind-stuff becomes absorbed in it and imbued with it like a pure crystal that assumes the colour of whatever object it is set on.[1]

Thus, the yōgī enters into different states of 'samprajñāta samādhi' in which the object of meditation is definitely known, free from doubts and misconceptions. In this samādhi a single mode prevails in the mind, which is not therefore contentless like the asamprajñāta samādhi.

Patañjali thus distinguishes between meditation (dhyāna) and samādhi:

'Meditation is the uninterrupted concentration of thought on its object. This itself turns into samādhi when the object alone shines and the thought of meditation [and of the meditator] is lost, as it were.'[2]

As a result of intense meditation on the subtle entities,[3] when the mind goes beyond contemplation (vicāra) and becomes refined and transparent the yōgī develops intuitive knowledge which unveils what inference and scriptural study cannot. Says Patañjali:

'In that state knowledge is said to be "truth-bearing".
This knowledge is of a different order than the knowledge gained from inference and the scriptures. For, it is definite in nature [being superconscious experience].'[4]

[1] YS I: 41.

[2] YS III: 2, 3.

[3] Prakṛti and all its fine and finer products excepting the five gross elements (*Vide* YS I: 45).

[4] YS I: 48, 49.

In deep meditation on the grahītā, the experiencer, which is the self identified with buddhi-sattva, the yōgī discerns the two, and realizes the self as distinct from the other. A clear and steady perception of the self as other than buddhi-sattva is called 'viveka-khyāti' (lit., discriminating knowledge). It counteracts avidyā (wrong knowledge), the primal cause of the identification of the self with the not-self. As stated by Patañjali:

'The cause of this [the identification of the self with buddhi-sattva] is avidyā [wrong knowledge].
When avidyā has been eradicated, the identification ceases. Then bondage drops, as the experiencer becomes aloof [that is, reinstated in its innate freedom].
The way to eradicate avidyā and sever bondage is the constant apprehension of the self as other than buddhi-sattva.
At the seventh stage of this [discriminating] knowledge the yōgī reaches its highest level.'[5]

Even then the self is not realized. Being firmly established in samprajñāta samādhi, the yōgī develops the power to enter into asamprajñāta samādhi, which is the complete withdrawal of the self from buddhi-sattva. By supreme detachment he foregoes even the knowledge that the self is altogether different from buddhi-sattva. For he realizes that this discriminating knowledge, howsoever high it may be, is a mode of buddhi-sattva to which the self has no relation at all. So he becomes completely withdrawn from buddhi-sattva, and the knowledge that is manifest in it. Then buddhi-sattva being absolutely free from all modes and contentless, becomes perfectly calm and restored to its pristine purity. This is the state of asamprajñāta samādhi, in which there is no cognition of any kind whatsoever. The self, being detached from buddhi-sattva, is no longer 'the seer (draṣṭā).' Finally, the self is wholly dissociated from buddhi-sattva, which, being 'seedless (unproductive)' forthwith resolves itself back into prakṛti, its origin. This means that the entire subtle body of the yōgī, of which buddhi-sattva is the mainstay, merges in basic prakṛti, while the physical body drops and in due course resolves into its constituent elements. Thus, the yōgī attains final liberation, which is complete aloofness or isolation of puruṣa (the luminous self) from prakṛti, as we have stated above.[6]

[5] YS II: 24–27. [6] *Vide* YS I: 51; IV: 34.

BIBLIOGRAPHY I

ENGLISH WORKS QUOTED FROM IN THIS BOOK

Alexander, S. *Space, Time, and Deity*. The University of Manchester. London: Macmillan and Co., Ltd., 1920.

Aquinas, Saint Thomas. *Summa de Veritate*, Qu. 21. Eng. Trans. by Robert W. Schmidt, S.J., *Truth*, Vol. III (qu. XXI–XXIX). Chicago: Henry Regnery Co., 1954.

Berkeley, George. *The Principles of Human Knowledge*. LaSalle, Ill.: Open Court Publishing Co., 1920.

Brightman, Edgar Sheffield. *An Introduction to Philosophy*. New York: Holt, Rinehart and Winston, Inc. 1953.

Chatterjee, Satischandra. *The Problems of Philosophy*. Calcutta: Das Gupta and Co., Ltd., 1949.

Chatterjee, Satischandra and Datta, Dhirendramohan. *An Introduction to Indian Philosophy*. Calcutta: University of Calcutta, 1950.

Creighton, James Edwin. *An Introductory Logic*. New York: The Macmillan Company, 1937.

Dasgupta, Surendranath. *A History of Indian Philosophy*, Vols. I–V. London: Cambridge University Press, 1957, 1952, 1952, 1955, 1955.

Datta, D. M. *The Six Ways of Knowing*. London: George Allen and Unwin Ltd., 1932.

Davids, T. W. Rhys. *The Questions of King Milinda* (Trans. from Pali). Sacred Books of the East, Vol. XXXV. Oxford University Press. London: Humphrey Milford, 1925.

Deussen, Dr Paul. *The System of the Vedānta*. Trans. by Charles Johnston. LaSalle, Ill.: Open Court Publishing Co., 1912.

——*The Philosophy of Vedānta*. Madras: Theosophical Publishing House.

Eckhart, Meister. *The Works*, Vols. I, II. Trans. by C. de B. Evans. London: John M. Watkins, 1956, 1952.

Eddington, Arthur Stanley. *Science and the Unseen World*. London: George Allen and Unwin Ltd., 1949.

Goulden, Charles Bernard. *Vision or Sight* (an article). The University of Chicago. Encyclopaedia Brittanica, Inc., 1948.

Gupta, Nagendranath. *Ramakrishna-Vivekananda*. Bombay: Sri Ramakrishna Math, 1933.

Hamilton, Sir William. *Lectures on Metaphysics*. Boston, Mass.: Gould and Lincoln, 1859.

Hicks, George D. *Theory of Knowledge* (an article). The University of Chicago: Encyclopaedia Brittanica, Inc., 1948.

Hill, Thomas English. *Contemporary Theories of Knowledge*. New York: The Ronald Press Company, 1961.

Hiriyanna, M. *The Essentials of Indian Philosophy*. London: George Allen and Unwin Ltd., 1949.

Hobhouse, L. T. *The Theory of Knowledge*. London: Methuen and Co., 1905.

Hume, David. *A Treatise of Human Nature*. Oxford: The Clarendon Press, 1896.

Huxley, Aldous. *The Perennial Philosophy*. New York: Harper and Row, Publishers, Inc., 1945.

James, William. *Pragmatism*. Harlow, Essex: Longmans, Green and Co. Ltd., 1949.

——*Principles of Psychology*. New York: Holt, Rinehart and Winston, Inc., 1920.

Jeans, Sir James. *Physics and Philosophy*. London: Cambridge University Press, 1946.

Joachim, Harold H. *The Nature of Truth*. Oxford: The Clarendon Press, 1906.

Joad, C. E. M. *Guide to Modern Thought*. London: Faber and Faber Limited, 1933.

Locke, John. *An Essay Concerning Human Understanding*, Vols. I, II (Fraser). Oxford: The Clarendon Press, 1894.

Mahadevan, T. M. P. *Gauḍapāda: A Study in Early Advaita*. Madras: University of Madras, 1952.

M. (Mahendranath Gupta). *The Gospel of Sri Ramakrishna*. Trans. with an Introduction by Swāmī Nikhilānanda. New York: Ramakrishna-Vivekananda Center, 1942.

McDougall, William. *Outline of Psychology*. New York: Charles Scribner's Sons, 1924.

Montague, William Pepperell. *The Ways of Knowing*. London: George Allen and Unwin Ltd., 1925.

Muller, Professor F. Max. *Three Lectures on Vedānta Philosophy* (Reprinted). Calcutta: Susil Gupta Ltd., 1950.

——*The Six Systems of Indian Philosophy*. London: Longmans, Green and Co. Ltd., 1899.

Planck, Max. *The New Science*. Cleveland, Meridian Books, Inc., 1959.

Plato—*The Republic* (Bks. I–X). Trans. by B. Jowett. New York: The Modern Library, 1941.

Plotinus—*The Ethical Treatises* (The Enneads). Trans. by Stephen MacKenna, Vols. I, II. Boston: Charles T. Branford Company, 1916.

Radhakrishnan, Sarvepalli. *Indian Philosophy*, Vols. I, II. London: George Allen and Unwin Ltd., 1931, 1940.

——*An Idealist View of Life*. London: George Allen and Unwin Ltd., 1957.

Radhakrishnan, Sarvepalli and Moore, Charles A. *A Source Book in Indian Philosophy*. Princeton, New Jersey: Princeton University Press, 1957.

Reid, Louis Arnaud. *Knowledge and Truth*. London: Macmillan and Co. Ltd., 1923.

Rhine, J. B. *The Reach of the Mind*. New York: William Sloane Associates, Inc., 1947.

Runes, Dagobert D. *Dictionary of Philosophy*. New York: Philosophical Library, Inc., 1960.

Russell, Bertrand. *History of Western Philosophy*. London: George Allen and Unwin, Ltd., 2nd ed., 8th imp., 1963; New York: Simon and Schuster, Inc., 1945.

St John, St Luke, St Matthew, St Paul—*The Holy Bible*. Ed. by Rev. C. I. Scofield, D.D., New York: Oxford University Press, 1917.

Seal, Dr Brajendranath. *The Positive Sciences of the Ancient Hindus*. Harlow, Essex: Longmans, Green and Co. Ltd., 1915.

Sinha, Jadunath. *Indian Psychology—Perception*. London: Routledge and Kegan Paul Ltd., 1934.

——*Indian Realism*. London: Routledge and Kegan Paul Ltd., 1938.

Sircar, Dr Mahendranath. *Comparative Studies in Vedantism*. Calcutta: Humphrey Milford, Oxford University Press, 1927.

Stout, G. F. *Studies in Philosophy and Psychology*. London: Macmillan and Co. Ltd., 1930.

Swāmī Brahmānanda. *Words of the Master* (Select Precepts of Śrī Rāmakṛṣṇa). Calcutta: Udbodhan Office, 8th edn., 1938.

Swāmī Prabhavānanda. *The Spiritual Heritage of India*. London: George Allen and Unwin Ltd., 1962.

Swāmī Sāradānanda. *Sri Ramakrishna, The Great Master*. Trans. by Swāmī Jagadānanda. Madras: Sri Ramakrishna Math, 1952.

Swāmī Vivekānanda. *The Complete Works*, Vols. I–VIII. Mayavati, Almora: Advaita Ashrama, 1922–1951.

Ward, James. *Psychological Principles*. Cambridge: Cambridge University Press, 1933.

Weber, Alfred. *History of Philosophy*. Trans. by Frank Thilly. New York: Charles Scribner's Sons, 1925.

BIBLIOGRAPHY II

SANSKRIT WORKS QUOTED FROM IN THIS BOOK

Advaita-siddhi by Madhusūdana Sarasvatī. With 'Gauḍa-Brahmānandī (Laghucandrikā),' 'Siddhi-Vyākhyā,' and other commentaries. Ed. with critical notes by Mm. Ananta-kṛṣṇa Śāstrī. NSP, 2nd edn., 1937.

**Ajñāna-bōdhinī*, **Ātma-bōdha*, **Ātmajñānōpadeśa-vidhi*, *Ātmānātma-viveka*, *Ātma-ṣaṭkam* (or Nirvāṇa-ṣaṭkam) by Śaṅkarācārya. Memorial Edition of his Works, Vols. XV, XVI; VVP, 1910 ff. Also included in 'Śaṅkara-grantha-ratnāvalī,' a compilation of Śaṅkara's forty-three poems and prose-writings with text and Beng. trans. in 2 pts. Ed. by Rajendranatha Ghose, Calcutta, 1928.

**Aṣṭāvakra-Gītā* (or *Aṣṭāvakra-Saṁhitā*)—Text and explanation in Hindi by Zalim Singh, Lucknow, 1935.

**Bhagavad-gītā*—with the commentaries of Śaṅkara, Ānanda-giri, Śrīdhara, Madhusūdana and three others. NSP, 2nd edn., 1936.

†*Bhāṣā-pariccheda* (*Kārikāvalī*) and com. 'Siddhānta-muktāvalī' by Viśvanātha Nyāya-pañcānana. With explanatory notes 'Dinakarī' and 'Rāmarudrī'. NSP, Revised Edn., 1928.

**Brahma-sūtras* of Bādarāyaṇa—with Śaṅkara's commentary and sub-commentaries—Gōvindananda's 'Ratnaprabhā,' Vācaspati's 'Bhāmatī,' and Ānanda-giri's 'Nyāya-nirṇaya.' NSP, 3rd edn., 1934.

Bṛhadāraṇyakōpaniṣad-bhāṣya-vārttika by Sureśvarācārya with Ānandagiri's com. 'Śāstraprakāśikā'; in 3 pts.; ASS, 2nd edn., 1937.

Laghuvākya-vṛtti (a short exposition of Mahāvākya 'I am Brahman') by Śaṅkarācārya—(1) Included in Calcutta edition of his Works, Pt. I. (2) Text and com. 'Puṣpāñjali' with Eng. trans. and notes. Almora, Sri Ramakrishna Kutir, 2nd edn., 1963.

Majjhima Nikāya (Pali book)—Ed. by Trenckner and Chalmers, 3 vols. London, Pali Text Society, 1888–99.

Mahābhārata of Kṛṣṇa-dvaipāyana Veda-vyāsa—Calcutta, Bangavasī Press, 2nd ed., 1908.

**Māṇḍūkyōpaniṣad-kārikā* by Gauḍapāda—with Śaṅkara's com. and Ānanda-giri's gloss. ASS, 1928.

Manu-smṛti (or *Manu-saṁhitā*)—with Kullūka Bhaṭṭa's com. 'Manvartha-muktāvalī' and alphabetical index to first lines of the couplets. NSP, 1929.

N.B.—Eng. versions of books marked with †, ⊗, ○, * are noted in sec. 2, 3, 4, 7 respectively of Appendix B.

○*Mīmāṁsā-darśana* (*Pūrva-Mīmāṁsā-sūtras*) of Jaimini—(1) with Sabara's commentary. CSS, in 2 pts. (2) with Sabara's com., ASS, no. 97, in 6 vols., 1933 ff. (3) with text, Beng. trans. and expl. of Sabara's com. by Bhūtanātha Saptatīrtha, in 2 pts., Calcutta, Vasumatī Press, 1938.

(*Mīmāṁsā*) *Ślōka-vārttika* by Kumārila Bhaṭṭa—with Sucarita Miśra's com. 'Kāśikā'. (1) Pts. I, II, Government Press, Trivandrum (1926–29). (2) CSS, 1943. (3) with com. 'Nyāyaratnākara' of Pārthasārathi Miśra. Ed. by Mm. Pt. Rāma Shastri Tailanga, 1898 (CSS).

Naiṣkarmya-siddhi by Sureśvarācārya—(1) with Jñānōttama's com. 'Candrikā'. Revised edn. by M. Hiriyanna, Bombay Sanskrit and Prakrit Series, 38, 1925. (2) Text and Beng. trans. with notes by Swāmī Jagadānanda, Calcutta, Udbodhana Office, 1953.

Nirvāṇa-daśakam (or *Daśa-ślōkī*)—Ten stanzas on Nirvāṇa by Śaṅkarācārya. With Madhusūdana Sarasvatī's com. *Siddhānta-bindu* (which is like a treatise in itself) and Brahmānanda Sarasvatī's supercommentary *Nyāyaratnāvalī*. Included in Śaṅkara's Works, Pt. I, ed. by Rajendranatha Ghose, Calcutta, 1928.

†*Nyāya-darśana* (Sūtras of Gautama)—(1) with Vātsāyana's com., Udyōtakara's 'Nyāya-vārttika,' and Vācaspati Miśra's 'Nyāya-vārttika-tātparya-ṭīkā.' Ed. by Gaṅgānātha Jhā (CSS). (2) with Vātsāyana's com., Beng. trans., expl., notes, etc., by Pt. Phaṇibhūṣaṇa Tarkavāgīśa, 5 pts., Bangiya Sahitya Parisad, Calcutta, 1923–24 approx. (3) with 'Nyāya-mañjari' of Jayanta Bhaṭṭa, exposition, notes, etc., University of Calcutta.

Nyāya-bindu by Dharmōttara—(1) with 'Nyāya-bindu-ṭīkā' of Dharmakīrti. Calcutta, Bibliotheca Indica, 1889. (2) Eng. trans. with notes by F. Th. Stcherbatsky, *Buddhist Logic*, Vol. II, New York, Dover Publications, Inc., 1962.

Pañcadaśī by Bhāratī-tīrtha Vidyāraṇya—with the commentary of Rāmakṛṣṇa, NSP, 1935.

**Pañcapādikā* of Padmapāda and *Pañcapādikā-vivaraṇa* of Prakāśātmayati (each with two commentaries)—Madras Government Oriental Series, No. CLV, 1958.

Prakaraṇa-pañcikā of Śālikanātha Miśra—with com. 'Nyāya-siddhi' of Jayapuri Nārāyaṇa Bhaṭṭa. Ed. by Pt. A. Subrahmaṇya Śāstrī, Motilal Banarasidass, Varanasi.

Puruṣa-sūktam (*Ṛg-Veda* X: 90) with Sāyaṇa's com., ASS, no. 3.

Ṛg-Veda-bhāṣya-bhūmikā of Sāyaṇa—Poona, Tilakmandir, 1933.

Ṛg-Veda Saṁhitā with Sāyaṇa's commentary —(1) Ed. by F. Max Muller, 4 vols. London, Oxford University Press, 1890. (2) Ed. by Sontakke, Kashikar, and others, with exhaustive Index, 5 vols. Poona, Vaidika Saṁśōdhana Maṇḍala, 1933–51.

⊗*Sāṁkhya-darśana* (*Sāṁkhya-sūtras*) of Kapila—with Vijñāna-bhikṣu's com. 'Pravacana-bhāṣya.' Calcutta, Vācaspatya Press, 1936.

⊗*Sāṁkhya-kārikā* of Īśvarakṛṣṇa—with Vācaspati Miśra's com. 'Tattvakaumudī' and explanatory notes by Pt. Rājeśvara Śāstrī Drāviḍa. CSS, 2nd edn., 1932.

Saṁkṣepa-śārīraka by Sarvajñātma-muni—with Rāmatīrtha Swāmī's com. 'Anvayārtha-prakāśikā.' CSS, 1913.

Sarvadarśana-saṁgraha by Mādhavācārya—(together with Madhusūdana Sarasvatī's *Prasthāna-bheda*), ASS, 1950.

Śāstra-dīpikā by Pārtha-sārathi Miśra—with Sōmanātha's com. 'Mayūkha-mālikā,' NSP, 1928.

Śatapatha Brāhmaṇa (Mādhyandina recension)—(1) with Sāyaṇa's commentary. In five parts. Asiatic Society of Bengal, Calcutta, 1906–1910. (2) with Sāyaṇa's commentary and gloss. In five parts. Bombay, Sri Venkatesvara Steam Press, (3) Text only in two parts. Acyuta-granthamālā, Varanasi. (4) Eng. Trans. by Julius Eggeling, Sacred Books of the East, Vols. XII, XXVI, XLI, XLIII, XLIV, Oxford, 1882–1900.

Siddhānta-leśa-saṁgraha by Appaya-dīkṣita—Introduction, translation, and copious notes in Hindi. Acyuta-granthamālā, Varanasi, 1954.

Śrīmad-Bhāgavatam by Kṛṣṇa-dvaipāyana Veda-vyāsa—with Śrīdhara Swamī's com. 'Bhāvārtha-dīpikā,' Calcutta, Bangavasi Press, 1927.

Taittirīya Āraṇyaka—with Sāyaṇa's com., in 2 pts. ASS, no. 36.

Taittirīya Brāhmaṇa—with Sāyaṇa's com., in 3 pts. ASS, no. 37.

Tarka-saṁgraha by Annam-bhaṭṭa—with 'Dīpikā' and 'Nyayabōdhinī.' Text and Eng. trans. with notes. Bombay Sanskrit Series, 1918. (2) with Beng. trans. and expl. by Rajendranath Ghose, Calcutta, 1932.

Tattva-cintāmaṇi by Gaṅgeśa Upādhyāya—Ed. by Paṇḍit Kāmākhyānātha Tarkavāgīśa. Calcutta, Bibliotheca Indica.

Tattva-pradīpikā (or *Citsukhī*) by Citsukhācārya with com. 'Nayana-prasādinī' of Pratyagrupa Bhagavan. NSP, 1931.

**Ten Upaniṣads—with Śaṅkara's commentary* (*Daśōpaniṣad-bhāṣya*), Pt. I—Iśa, Aitareya, Kaṭha, Kena, Chāndōgya, Taittirīya, Praśna, Māṇḍūkya, and Muṇḍaka. Pt. II—Bṛhadāraṇyaka. Poona, Ashtekar and Co., 1927–28.

Each a separate book with S. com. and Ānandagiri's gloss, ASS.

Twenty-eight Upaniṣads—Text only. Besides the above ten includes Śvetāśvatara, Jābāla, Kaivalya, Kauṣītakī, Muktika, Nārāyaṇa (Mahānārāyaṇa), and others.

Upaniṣads—Text of 108 Upaniṣads (*Aṣṭōttara-śatōpaniṣad*), NSP, 1930.

Brahma-bindu, one of the minor among the one hundred and eight enumerated by Muktikōpaniṣad; differs very little from 'Amṛtabindu' included in *Minor Upaniṣads*. Eng. rendering of eight with notes, Almora, Advaita Ashrama, 1956.

——*Nṛsiṁha-pūrva-tāpanīya*—with Śaṅkara's commentary. Memorial Edn. of his Works, Vol. X; VVP, 1910.

——*Nṛsiṁha-pūrvottara-tāpanīya*—with commentaries, ASS, no. 30.

*——*Śvetāśvatara* with commentary and gloss—(1) ASS, no. 17. (2) Beng. trans. of text and commentary (attributed to Śaṅkara) by Paṇḍit Durgācaraṇa Sāṁkhya-Vedānta-tīrtha, Calcutta, 1931.

**Upadeśa-sāhasrī* by Śaṅkarācārya—(1) Memorial Edn. Vol. XIV; VVP. (2) with Rāmatīrtha's com. 'Pada-yōjanā,' NSP, 1930.

Vaiśeṣika-darśana (Sūtras of Kaṇāda)—(1) with Śaṅkara Miśra's com. 'Upaskāra' and Praśastapāda's exposition 'Padārthadharma-saṁgraha,' in 2 pts, CSS, 1924–1931. (2) with Udayanācārya's gloss 'Kiraṇāvalī' on Praśatapāda and other commentaries. Calcutta, Sanskrit Book Depot.

Vākya-padīya (Brahma-kāṇḍa) by Bhartṛhari. Ed. with com. and notes by Paṇḍit Sūryanārayaṇa Śukla. CSS, 1937.

* *Vākya-vṛtti* (Exposition of Mahāvākya 'Thou art That') by Śaṅkarācārya; with commentary, ASS, no. 80.

Vāśiṣtha Dharma-śāstra—(1) Bombay Sanskrit Series, 23; 1916. (2) Trans., Sacred Books of the East, Vol. XIV, Oxford.

Vedānta-kalpataru by Amalānanda Yati and *Vedānta-kalpataru-parimala* by Appayadīkṣita with Vācaspati's com. 'Bhāmatī' on Brahma-sūtra-Śāṅkara-bhāṣya. In one volume, NSP.

* *Vedānta-paribhāṣā* by Dharmarājā Adhvarīndra—(1) Ed. by Mm. Anantakṛṣṇa Śāstrī with introduction and com. 'Paribhāsā-prakāśikā,' University of Calcutta. (2) with Rāmakṛṣṇa Adhvarīndra's com. 'Śikhāmaṇi' and Amaradās's gloss 'Maṇiprabhā,' Sri Venkatesvara Press, Bombay, 1911.

* *Vedānta-sāra* by Sadānanda Yōgīndra—with commentaries 'Subōdhinī' of Nṛsiṁha Sarasvatī and 'Vidvanmanōrañjinī' of Rāmatīrtha. Ed. by Col. G. A. Jacob; NSP, 1925.

Vivaraṇa-prameya-saṁgraha by Bhāratī-tīrtha Vidyāraṇya—(1) Ed. by Rama Shastri Tailanga; Vizianagram Sanskrit Series, no. 7; Benaras, E. J. Lazarus and Co., 1893. (2) Text and Beng. trans. by Mm. Pramathanātha Tarka-bhūṣaṇa; Calcutta, Vasumati Press, 1927.

* *Vivekacūḍāmaṇi* by Śaṅkarācārya—(1) Memorial Edn. Vol. XIV; VVP. (2) with Sanskrit com. of Swāmī Keśavācārya and Hindi trans., Munimandal, Kankhal, India.

Yājñavalkya-Smṛti—with Vijñāneśvara's com. 'Mitākṣarā,' Bombay, 1882. (2) with the com. of Aparārka, in 2 pts. ASS, no. 46.

⊕ *Yōga-sūtras* of Patañjali—with Vyāsa-bhāṣya, Vācaspati's 'Tattva-vaiśāradī' and Bhōjadevā's 'Rājamārtaṇḍa'. ASS, 3rd edn., 1932.

Yōga-vāśiṣtha Rāmāyaṇa of Vālmikī—with com. 'Vāśiṣṭha-mahārāmāyaṇa-tātparya-prakāśa' of Ānandabodhendu Bhikṣu. (1) NSP, 2nd edn., 1918. (2) Ed. with Beng. trans. of the text by Kālivara Vedānta-vāgīśa. Calcutta, Vasumatī Press.

INDEX

Abādhitatvam (*see* non-contradictedness)
Abhāva (*see* non-existence)
Abhedābhivyakti, 97, 98, 104–5
Absolute, the, 70, 76–7, 118, 213 n, 251, 252–4, 286, 289, 289 n, 290
Absolute monism (non-dualism), 308; *see* Advaita Vedānta
Absolute (pāramārthika), 63, 118, 127, 153
Acintya-bhedābheda, 107 n, 227, 321–2, 332
Adhikāri-bheda, 206; (*see* spiritual aspirants, their gradation)
Ādhikārika puruṣas, 300
Adhvarīndra, Dharmarāja, 104
Adhyārōpa (*see* superimposition)
Adhyāsa (illusion), 121, 124, 125 n, 125–6; two kinds of, 124, 124 n theories of, 126; (*see also* illusion)
Advaita (nondualistic) Vedānta, its views, etc., 15, 17, 35–7, 39, 62–4, 67, 69, 72, 89, 91, 94, 96–7, 99, 102, 106, 110, 117–18, 120–21, 127, 128 n 130–31, 132–33, 141, 141 n, 142, 150, 152–3, 155–6, 159, 163, 165, 169, 170, 183, 190, 216, 218, 229, 247, 250, 270, 290, 301, 317, 319–20; its two schools, 257 n, 259 n, 319; its principal tenets, 319; its leading treatises, 324
Advaita-ratna-rakṣaṇa, 325
Advaita-siddhi, 97 n, 100 n, 101, 103, 103 n, 220, 220 n, 283, 283 n, 325, 331, 342
Advaitins (nondualists), 42 n, 48 n, 70, 95–8, 104, 108, 116–18, 130, 132, 140, 144–6, 149–51, 154, 169
Affirmation, negation, 164
Āgama (sacred text), 35, 173, 190, 195, 220, 239; (*see also* verbal testimony)
Agnostic, 109
Agreement, in presence (anvaya-vyāpti), 144, 149–50, 159; in absence (vyatireka-vyāpti), 144, 149–50, 159–60
Ahaṁ-graha upāsanā, 296
Ahaṅkāra ('I-ness'), 53, 234, 314
Ajñāna (anti-knowledge), 49, 70, 76–9, 83, 85, 98, 99 n, 100–1, 127, 134 n, 134–7, 139–40, 170, 192, 219, 221, 225, 232–3, 236, 236 n, 237, 240, 249, 256, 258, 263, 270, 272, 274, 276–8, 280, 282–3, 289, 302–3, 306, 321; primal (mūla), subsidiary (tula), 99, 134, 260, 274, 279; its twofold power, 280; its twofold veil, 109, 280; (*see also* avidyā)
Ajñānabōdhinī, 283 n, 342
Ākāśa, 38, 50 n, 53, 105, 156
Akhaṇḍārtha-bōdhaka, 200
Akhaṇḍa Saccidānanda, 279; (*see* Being-Consciousness-Bliss)
Akhyāti, a theory of illusion, 126, 130, 138
Ākṛti (generic nature), 183, 183 n
Alaukika jñāna-lakṣaṇa-sannikarṣa, 95, 130–31, 133
Ālaya-vijñāna, 129
Alexander, S., 137, 138 n
Amalānanda-yati, 257 n, 325
Analogical argument, 228
Ānandagiri (or Ānandajñāna), 68 n, 205, 238 n, 325
Aniruddha, 131, 315
Anirvacanīya (indefinable), 122, 127, 134, 136
Anirvacanīya-khyāti, Advaita theory of illusion, 121, 126, 131
Annam-bhaṭṭa, 121–2, 314
Antaḥkaraṇa (*see* mind)
Antaḥkaraṇa-pariṇāma, 91
Antaḥkaraṇa-vṛtti, 62, 88–9, 91–2, 97, 101, 104, 111
Antarindriya, 42 n, 48 n
Anumāna, 35–6, 92, 143, 147, 152, 203, 229; (*see also* inference)
Anumiti (inferential knowledge), 143
Anupalabdhi (*see* non-apprehension)
Anuśravaḥ (the Vedas), 203
Anuvyavasāya, 112, 155; (*see also* apperception)
Anvayārtha-prakāśikā, 135 n, 260 n
Anyathā-khyāti, theory of illusion, 126, 130, 138
Aparōkṣa-Brahmānubhūti (realization of Brahman), 41, 278, 288; triple way to, 153, 222–3, 256–62, 264–5, 273, 288–90, 299
Aparōkṣa-jñāna, 142, 191, 260; (*see also* knowledge)
Aparōkṣānubhūti, 324, Eng. trans., 327
Āpastamba, 204 n
Apauruṣeya, 217
A posteriori, 152, 229
Appayadīkṣit, 257 n
Apperception, 40, 155, 160; (*see also* anuvyavasāya)
Apprehension, immediate, 55, 90
Apramā, 89, 119 n, 120, 122
A priori, 149, 152, 229
Āpta-vacana, āpta-vākya (authentic word), 38, 173, 189

Apūrva, 157
Aquinas, Saint Thomas, 63, 63 n, 339
Āraṇyaka(s), 306–7, 309–10; Aitareya, 306–7, 309; Kauṣītaki, 306, 309; Taittirīya, 207 n, 306–7, 309, 344
Argument (tarka), 119, 122, 122 n, 229–30; fallacious, 66
Aristotle, 148
Artha-kriyā-kāritva, pragmatic test of knowledge, 115, 117
Arthāpatti, 35, 92, 142, 151, 158, 160–61; (*see also* postulation)
Artha-saṁgraha, 318
Asat-khyāti (a theory of illusion), 126–7
Assumption, 211
Aṣṭāvakra-saṁhitā (or *Aṣṭāvakra-gītā*), 284 n, 342; Eng. trans., 327
Āśubōdhinī, 183 n
Ātma-bōdha, 276 n, 324, 342; Eng. trāns, 327
Ātma-gītā, 290
Ātmajñānōpadeśa-vidhi, 238 n, 239 n, 324, 342; Eng. trans., 327
Ātma-khyāti (a theory of illusion), 126, 129
Ātman (self), 46, 67, 69, 81, 86–7, 89, 140, 155, 200, 203, 224, 236, 239, 246, 256, 263–4, 272, 274, 278, 291, 295, 313; knowledge of, 264; (*see also* self)
Ātmānātma-viveka, 50 n, 223 n, 262 n, 264 n, 324, 342
Attribute, in relation to substance, 48 n, 49 n, 63, 182; generic, specific, 107
Authority, 173, 175, 189–90, 203, 211, 216, 218, 223–4, 226; scriptural, 216, 226, 257; (*see also* verbal testimony)
Āvaraṇa-bhaṅga, 97–9
Āvaraṇābhibhava, 97, 99
Avidyā, 76, 78, 98, 123, 139–40, 258, 265, 303, 338; (*see also* ajñāna)
Avidyā-leśa, 280
Avyakta, 335 n
Awareness, 60, 62, 90; intuitive or mystical, 213, 216; blissful, 249

Bādarāyaṇa, 225, 227, 261, 320; (*see* also Vyāsa)
Behaviour, purposive, 237
Behaviourists, 40
Being, 63, 199; cosmic, 69; omnipresent, 250; oneness of, 219; pure, 246; supreme, 200–1, 203, 206, 214, 218, 293–5, 303; all-transcendent, 251, 300
Being-Consciousness-Bliss, 65, 73, 199, 212, 246, 256, 258, 265, 269, 271–2, 274, 277–9 288–9, 299
Belief, 189–90
Berkeley, George, 68–9, 69 n, 71, 339
Bhagavad-ārādhanā-krama, 328
Bhagavad-gītā, 43, 43 n, 46 n, 128 n, 203, 208, 214 n, 217, 220 n, 254 n, 266 n, 267 n, 284 n, 289, 289 n, 294 n, 300 n, 302 n, 303 n, 307, 320, 342; Eng. trans., 326
Bhagavad-gītā-tātparya-nirṇaya, 330
Bhāgavata-tātparya-nirṇaya, 330
Bhāgavata-tattvadīpa, 332
Bhakti-mārga, 204; -yōga, 320; (*see also* devotion)
Bhakti-rasāmṛta-sindhu, 333
Bhakti-rasāyana, 325
Bhāmatī, 125 n, 130 n, 206 n, 257 n, 261 n, 324, 342; (*see also* Vācaspati Miśra)
Bhartṛhari, 107, 107 n, 186 n, 345
Bhāṣā-pariccheda, 37 n, 38 n, 95 n, 106 n, 107 n, 108 n, 115 n, 119 n, 120 n, 121 n, 122 n, 131 n, 150 n, 154 n, 159 n, 166 n, 169 n, 170 n, 173 n, 176 n, 178 n, 180 n, 181 n, 183 n, 229 n, 342
Bhāṣya-prakāśa, 331
Bhaṭṭa, Kumārila, 107, 112, 141 n, 156 n, 158 n, 163, 165, 167, 180, 257 n, 317–18, 343
Bhāva-mukha, 286
Bhāva-prabōdha, 328
Bhōjadeva, 45, 315
Bhōktā (experiencer), 79, 234, 238
Bōdhāyana, 328
Bodies, three, 236, 236 n
Body, 47, 67, 156; gross, 79, 236, 277, 280, 283; causal, 49, 51, 79, 232–3, 236, 236 n, 277; subtle, 44–5, 49–51, 79, 233, 236, 271–2, 277, 280, 282–3, 338
Bossuet, 194
Brahmā, 52, 217, 250, 263, 291, 298; (*see also* cosmic soul)
Brahma-caitanya, 102–3, 279; Brahma-jijñāsā, 262; Brahma-jñāna, 264; Brahma-niṣṭha, 265–6; Brahma-vidyā, 263
Brahmacaryya, 308
Brahmalōka, 300
Brahma-Mīmāṁsā, 316
Brahman, 17, 41, 52, 61–2, 64–5, 67–9, 72, 75–9, 82, 87, 118, 140, 151, 155–6, 169, 187, 196–206, 213, 221–2, 228, 239, 246–8, 250, 253–4, 256–7, 258 n, 260–9, 273–4, 276–8, 281–8, 291, 295–6, 299–300, 302–3, 307; knowledge (anubhūti) of, 41, 118. 123, 264, 266, 275, 278, 288; self of all, 78
— Conditioned and unconditioned, 205, 291–2

Brahman, Immanent and transcendent, 254, 293; impersonal, 297
— Nirguṇa (attributeless), 198–9, 204–6, 222, 246, 253–5, 265, 276, 280, 282, 286–8, 289 n, 290–3, 295, 296–7, 299–300, 302, 319–20
— Nondual, 66, 151, 153, 169–70, 196–8, 204, 212, 217, 219, 223, 248, 250, 254, 256–7, 262, 269, 277, 296, 308
— Saguṇa, 107, 198, 204–5, 222, 250, 255, 276, 286, 291–3, 295, 297, 299–300, 302, 319–20; worship of, 270, 297, 299–300; meditation on, 297–8
Brāhmaṇa(s) (Vedic texts), 70, 204 n, 305–10; of diff. Vedas, 309–10; Aitareya, 306, 309; Kauṣītaki, 306, 309; Pañca-viṁśa, 292 n, 310; Śatapatha, 292 n, 307, 309, 344; Taittirīya, 17 n, 293 n, 306, 309, 344; Talavakāra, 307, 310
Brahma-siddhi, 283, 324
Brahma-sūtra-bhāṣya, 330–1
Brahma-sūtrānubhaṣya 330–1
Brahma-sūtrānuvyākhyāna, 330–1
Brahma-sūtrānuvyākhyāna-nirnaya, 330
Brahma-sūtras, 48 n, 65, 65 n, 76, 76 n, 77 n, 78 n, 79 n, 82 n, 127 n, 128 n, 182 n, 193 n, 199 n, 205 n, 219 n, 226 n, 227, 227 n, 230 n, 231 n, 244, 255 n, 257 n, 258 n, 259 n, 261 n, 262 n, 276 n, 282 n, 288 n, 290 n, 293 n, 296 n, 297 n, 300 n, 307, 317 n, 320–1, 332, 342; its different names, 227 n; (*see also* Śaṅkara's commentary on)
Brahmātmākārā vṛtti, 278–9, 281, 302
Brain, 52, 55; its processes, 61
Bṛhadāraṇyaka-Upaniṣad-bhāṣya-vārttika, 103, 260, 288, 288 n, 324, 342
Bṛhad-bhāgavatāmṛtam, 333
Bṛhatī, 317–18
Bṛhatsaṁhitā, 197 n
Brightman, Edgar Sheffield, 116, 116 n, 339
Buddha, The, 72, 211, 211 n, 242 n
Buddhi, 51, 101, 108, 235, 240, 248 n, 253, 261, 264, 278, 301; (*see also* cognitive mind)
Buddhīndriyas, 45, 48 n, 53
Buddhi-sattva (pure mind-stuff), 301, 336, 338
Buddhism, 68 n, 72 n, 225 n, 242 n; its two branches and four schools, 64 n, 312
Buddhist(s), 38–9, 49, 54, 90, 115, 143–4, 149, 154, 167, 175
Cakravarttī, Viśvanātha, 334
Cārvāka(s), 38, 142, 175, 225 n, 312
Causality, 149, 211; cause and effect, 128, 144, 149, 211, 250; law of causation, 209
Cause, efficient, 229; of the universe (efficient and material), 228, 293
Central nervous system, 52
Chatterjee, Dr Satischandra, 57, 57 n, 68 n, 74–5, 75 n, 96 n, 115, 115 n, 119, 119 n, 161, 161 n, 339
Cidābhāsa (reflected self), 83, 103, 110, 233, 235
Ciduparāga, 97–8
Citsukhācārya (or Citsukhī), 110–11, 113 n, 117 n, 328
Citta, 53, 93; citta-vṛtti, 93; (*see also* antaḥkaraṇa-vṛtti)
Clairvoyance, 42 n, 43–5, 45 n; clairvoyant perception, 42
Cogitation, 17, 42 n
Cogito ergo sum, 83, 231, 231 n
Cognition, 15, 43, 53, 56, 60, 62, 68, 82–4, 86, 89 n, 89–91, 93, 103, 107–8, 111, 119, 125, 128–9, 164, 235, 237; complex, 94, 95 n, 95–6; direct or immediate, 36, 55, 90, 96, 98; doubtful, 190; erroneous, 126; illusory, 133; inner, internal, 15, 68, 92–3, 129; instrument of, 52; invalid, 89 n, 114, 119, 119 n; non-perceptual, 17; non-valid, 119, 119 n, 120–21; object of, 46, 68; perceptual, 37, 136; valid, 66, 89 n, 114, 119, 119 n; verbal, 178; its relation to emotion and volition, 90
Cognition of cognition, 235
Cognitive, mind, 52, 88, 101, 233, 240, 248 n; mode, 92–4, 111; process(es), 16, 83–4, 98, 101; (*see also* buddhi)
Cognizer (pramātā), 16, 46, 52, 84, 111, 235, 238; distinct from cognizable (prameya), 46
Coherence theory, of East and West, 116–18
Comparison (upamāna), 17, 35, 39, 92, 142, 153–6, 164, 189
Comparative Studies in Vedāntism, 228 n, 341
Concomitance, invariable (vyāpti), 92, 142–51, 159, 175–6, 188, 228; two kinds of, 143–4; how ascertained, 148–9
Consciousness (cit or caitanya), 15–16, 36, 40–41, 46, 52, 56, 58, 60–3, 80–83, 85–6, 98–9, 101–2, 128–9, 138, 199, 234, 236–40, 244, 244 n; 246, 248–9, 252–3, 255, 276, 313, acosmic, 76; cosmic, 282, 293; finite, 76; immutable, 91; indi-

vidual, 185, 200, 250, 282; inner, 129; modal, 63, 88, 111; momentary, 244; moral, 208; percipient, 99; self-effulgent, 248, 255; unvaried, 271; its distinction from physical light, 15, 85–6; its source and nature, 60–3
Consciousness, Pure, 15, 17, 61, 63–4, 66, 70, 81, 83–4, 86, 88–91, 93, 99, 103, 106, 110–11, 134, 174, 185, 200, 246, 249, 255, 272, 285, 293, 296; nondual, 252, 254, 272; nonrelational, 212; unitary, 249; universal, 185, 200
Conscious state, 82
Consequents, 161
Consilience, 118
Consistency (yōgyatā), 179–80
Contemplation, 90, 252
Contemporary Theories of Knowledge (Hill), 59 n, 340
Contiguity (āsatti), 179–80
Continence, 263, 291
Co-presence (sahacāra), 149
Corinthians II, 222 n
Correlativity of subject and object, 66
Correspondence, Eastern and Western theory of, 115–18
Cosmic, being, 294; law, 209; māyā, 73, 77; order, 292, 300; process, 76–7
Cosmic soul, self, 52, 203, 217, 250, 263, 295; (*see also* Brahmā)
Cosmological view, 132
Counter-positive (pratiyōgī), 151, 165
Creation, 253; Divine Idea of, 217
Creative idea of God, 293; creative process, 76
Creator, 151, 250; Omniscient and Omnipotent, 161, 229
Creator God, Sāṁkhya view of, 315
Creighton, James Edwin, 41 n, 339

Dakṣiṇāmūrti-stōtra, 324
Darkness, Vedāntic view of, 88
Dasgupta, Surendranath, 128 n, 186 n, 189, 189 n, 329 n, 339
Datta, D. M., 49 n, 57, 63, 64 n, 89, 89 n, 96 n, 148, 155, 158, 158 n, 160 n, 160–61, 161 n, 188, 212 n
Datum of sensation, 75
Davids, T. W. Rhys, 242 n, 339
Deduction, 148, 160–61
Deductive, inductive, 147–8
Deity, chosen, 297
Deliberation (manas), 53
Delusion, 125
Demerit (pāpa), 49, 250
Departure of the illumined, 300
Descartes, René, 63, 231
Desire(s), 123; latent, 300; worldly, 298
Determination (buddhi), 53
Deussen, Dr Paul, 61 n, 214
Devotion, 252; path of, 250; devotional attitudes, 253, 253 n; (*see also* bhakti)
Dharma (*see* moral ideal)
Dharmakīrti, 115, 167
Dharma-prasaṅge Swāmī Brahmānanda, 252 n, 286 n
Dharma-śāstras (Smṛtis), 202
Dharmōttara, 115 n, 167 n
Dhyāna (meditation), 288–91
Dictionary of Philosophy, 126 n, 341
Dikdarśanī, 333
Dīpaśikhā, 318
Disciple(s), 265; Śaṅkara's chosen four, 125 n, 260 n
Discrimination, 253, 336
Dissolution, 253, 255; cosmic, 300; of the universe, 199
Doubt(s), 39–40, 119 n, 119–22, 190, 245
Draṣṭā, dṛk (seer, perceiver), 238–9
Dream, 51–2, 65–6, 82, 88, 119–20, 122–3, 125, 129, 133, 236–7, 241, 249, 255, 270, 295; experience, 114, 129, 191, 219, 242; imagery, 122; objects, 68, 123; its distinction from memory and illusion, 122–3
Dṛgdṛśya-viveka Eng. trans., 327
Dṛśya (seen, perceived), 239
Dualism, epistemic, 65, 72; of Sāṁkhya-yōga, 330
Duality, 249, 251, 256, 277
Dvaita (Dualism) of Madhvācārya, 107 n, 227, 321–2, 330
Dvaitādvaita of Nimbārka, 107 n, 227, 321–2, 329

Eckhart, Meister, 214, 252
Eddington, Sir Arthur Stanley, 41 n
Ego, 15, 41, 79, 82–3, 91, 203, 214, 232, 234, 236–7, 249, 253, 271, 279, 281; -consciousness, 82, 92, 250, 296; -idea, 62, 83, 244, 257, 271, 279–82
Egoism, 51, 138–9
Eight Upaniṣads, 326
Elements (five), gross, subtle, 50, 50 n, 51 n, 314
Emancipation, final, 300
Emotion, its relation to cognition, 90; (*see also* feeling)
Empirical (vyavahārika), distinct from illusory (prātibhāsika), 67, 118, 127, 153; experience, 219, 222, 254; facts, 197; investigation, 61 n; object, 133; order, 72, 127; reality,

66; realm, 66; validity, 219–20; view, 61 n; (*see also* existence)
Empiricism, 59; empiricists, 40
Encyclopaedia Britannica, 16 n, 55 n, 339
End organs, 45
Energy, cosmic, 255
Eng. trans. of Sanskrit works of diff. systems: Vaiśeṣika, 313; Nyāya, 313–14; Sāṁkhya, 315; Yōga, 315–16; Mīmāṁsā, 318; Advaita, 325–7; Viśiṣṭādvaita, 329; Dvaitādvaita, 330; Dvaita of Madhva, 331; Śuddhādvaita, 332, Acintya bhedābheda, 334
Enlightenment of humanity, 300
Entity, positive (beyond negations), 251
Environment, 50
Epistemological, conclusions, 64; enquiry (in East and West), 16, 63, 84; principles, 63; problems, 15; theories, modern, 64; truths, 15; views, 126, 317
Epistemologists, 64
Epistemology, 15, 61, 63–4, 141 n; its relation to metaphysics, 61–4
Equipollent concomitance (samavyāpti), 144
Erigena, Johannes Scotus, 216
Error, 119, 119 n, 120–22; perceptual, non-perceptual, 121, 124
Essay Concerning Human Understanding, An, 40 n, 71 n, 340
Essentials of Indian Philosophy, The, 70 n, 115 n, 147 n, 155 n, 330 n, 340
Ethical, principles, 198, 205, 208, 212; conduct (dharma), 224; (*see also* moral ideal)
Ethical Treatises, The (The Enneads), 251 n, 340
Ethics, 198; of enlightened self-interest, 208; Hindu, 224
Evans, C. de B., 252 n, 339
Ex hypothesi, 148
Existence, pure, 67, 128, 204, 246; and non-existence, their distinction, 128; apparent, 65; empirical, 67, 118, 123, 133, 153; three orders of, 67, 118, 127, 153; triple, 65–6
Expectancy (ākāṅkṣā), 179–80
Experience(s), 74; beatific, 248; cognitive, 59; common, 247; direct, 56; dual, 255; empirical, 219, 222, 254; erroneous, 138; gustatory, tactile, 97; immediate, 274; inner, 47; internal, 40; intuitive (aparōkṣānubhūti), 153, 258; mystical, 251–2; negative, positive, 163; normal, 127, 133; sensory, 44; spiritual, 250–51; superconscious, 203; transcendental, 18, 170, 248–9, 252, 278; world of, 75, 219, 256
Experiencer, 75, 250, 256–7
Extraordinary powers, 43
Extra-sensory experience, 43, 45; perception, 42, 44, 50
Extra-sensory Perception after Sixty Years, 42 n

Facts, empirical, 197; suprasensuous, 203
Faith (śraddhā), 190, 216, 223, 252, 266, 290
Fancy, its distinction from illusion, 137
Feeling (its distinction from cognition), 52, 62, 108
First Cause, 228
Formal-deductive process, 148
Fourfold means (sādhana-catuṣṭaya), 262, 264 n, 266

Gaṅgeśa Upādhyāya, 37, 344
Gārhasthya (the married life), 308
Gauḍapāda, 77, 215, 224–5, 321, 324, 342
Gauḍapāda, A Study in Early Advaita, 153 n, 224 n, 340
Gauḍīya Vaiṣṇava School, 332–4; works of, 333–4
Gautama (or Gōtama), author of *Nyāya-sūtras*, 152, 225, 228, 257 n, 313
Generalization(s), 147, 149, 247
Generic attributes, 49
Gītārtha-saṁgraha, 328
Goal, highest, 205; supreme, 208, 277, 302; ultimate, 206–7
God, 68, 68 n, 70–72, 76, 109, 151, 161–2, 193–6, 201, 205, 214, 217, 226, 228–9, 231, 251 n, 253–4, 275–6, 293–4, 297; His existence beyond reasoning, 161, 228–30; Sāṁkhya and Yōga views of, 315
God-realization, 205, 269
Goddess Kālī, 287
God-head, 309
Good and evil, 283
Good, Highest, 213, 268; ineffable, 252; Supreme, 300
Gospel of Sri Ramakrishna, The, 253 n, 254 n, 275 n, 303 n, 340
Gōsvāmī, Jīva, 107 n
Goulden, Charles Bernard, M.D., 55 n
Gōvinda-bhāṣya, 332
Gōvindapāda, 250
Grammarians (philsophers of language), 185, 185 n, 186 n, 187
Greek philosophy, 61 n
Guide to Modern Thought, 237 n, 340

Guṇas, three, 50 n, 251, 255, 257, 273, 281, 299, 335 n
Gupta, Mahendranath, 252, 253 n, 340
Gupta, Nagendranath, 287, 287 n, 339
Guru, 269, 275; (*see also* Teacher)

Hallucination, 65, 71, 119, 125, 126 n, 129
Hamilton, Sir William, 62, 62 n, 339
Hari-bhakti-vilāsa, 333
Hearing (śravaṇa); (*see* Self-realization, its threefold way)
Heart, 51–2, 82, 88
Hegel, G. W. F., 63
Henotheism, 308
Hereditary transmission, 50
Hetu (the middle term), 145–6, 148, 153, 228
Hicks, George, 16
Hill, Thomas English, 59, 59 n
Hīnayāna, 68 n
Hinduism, of present day, 323; its true name, 323, 323 n
Hindu philosophers, 46, 48 n, 312–16, 324–5, 327–34
Hindu Psychology: Its Meaning for the West, 42 n
Hiraṇyagarbha, 203, 300
Hiriyanna, Prof. M., 70, 70 n, 115, 115 n, 147, 155 n, 330 n, 340
History of Indian Philosophy, A (Dasgupta), 186 n, 187 n, 189 n, 329 n, 339
History of Philosophy (Weber), 231 n, 341
History of Western Philosophy, A (Russell), 59 n, 341
Hobhouse, L. T., 36 n, 58, 58 n, 73, 73 n, 340
Holy Bible, The, 341
Horns of a hare, 68, 77
How to know God: The Yōga Aphorisms of Patañjali, 316
Human Plane, its distinction from subhuman, 212
Hume, David, 243, 243 n, 340
Huxley, Aldous, 213 n, 340
Hypnotized subject, 50
Hypothesis, 160–61

'I am Brahman', 200, 204, 221, 221 n, 259, 261, 273, 277–8, 301
I-consciousness, 286
Idea(s), 68 n, 69, 70; absolute, 187; apprehending, 71; God's, 72; internal, 66, 71–3, 129; mental, 70, 72; of ideas, 217, 293; of reflection, of sensation, 36, 71; subjective, 68 n; and word, 293
Ideal, 246; highest, 277; spiritual, 298; supreme, 269
Idealism, 17, 59, 66, 68, 68 n; metaphysical or absolute, 64, 66; subjective, 64–6, 68
Idealist(s), 59, 68 n, 72, 129; Buddhist, 244; (*see* Yōgācāra school)
Idealistic, position, 71; theories, 59; view, 70
Idealist View of Life, An, 278 n, 340
Ideation(s), 250, 253; cosmic, 293
Identity of essence (tādāmya), 67, 144, 149; (*see also* relation of identity)
Ignorance, 62; primal (mūlājñāna), 99, 134, 260, 274, 279; veil of, 97
Illumination, 195, 276, 282
Illumined one(s), 283, 300; persons, 280–81, 284; souls, 216, 254
Illusion, 66, 119, 121, 124, 124 n, 125–6, 126 n, 131–3, 135–8; its distinction from dream, 122; without delusion, 125; object of, 127; optical, 115; nacre-silver, 127, 129–36; rope-snake, 118, 127, 136; theories of, 126–7
Illusionism, 67, 69
Illusory (prātibhāsika), appearance, 134–8; object, 124, 127, 134; perception, 91, 124, 125 n, 127, 129–31, 133, 136, 258
Imagination, 62, 119
Immanence, 69–70; immanent, 254
Implication (lakṣanā), 185
Impressions, 58; mental, 123; subtle (saṁskāra), 210; subconscious, 108
Inborn capacities, the reason for, 50
Incarnation(s), Divine, 254, 297; past 264 n
Indefinable (anirvacanīya), 127, 134
India, its original name, 323 n
Indian Philosophy (Radhakrishnan), 66 n, 70 n, 186 n, 195 n, 323 n, 340
Indian Psychology-Perception, 95 n, 107 n, 341
Indian Realism, 69 n, 341
Indian thinkers, 49; (*see also* philosophers, philosophy)
Individual, correlated to cosmic, 294
Individual characteristics, 49
Indriya(s), organs, 42 n, 45, 48 n, 49; two kinds of, 44–5, 48 n; (*see also* organs)
Induction, deduction, 148
Induction, Mill's, 148
Inductive generalization, 148
I-ness, 62, 105, 111, 234, 238
Inference (anumāna), 17, 35–6, 38, 44, 57, 66, 92, 94, 112, 119, 142–4, 146–8, 150–2, 154, 158–9,

159 n, 160, 164, 175–6, 188–9, 194, 207, 210–11, 219, 222, 226, 228–9, 231 n, 312; different types of, 150–52, 228–9; from analogy, 229–30; Hindu method of, 147–8; immediate, 155; syllogistic, 155, 161, 222 n, 228; and suprasensuous knowledge, 152–3, 229; (*see also* syllogism)
Infinite, 140; infinite, finite, 247
Inner Controller, 199; (Internal) Ruler, 78
Insight, 65, 247
Instinct; instinctive behaviour, 80
Instruction of Brahman, direct, indirect, 201–2
Intellect, 195; its relation to virtue, 208
Introduction to Indian Philosophy, An, 96 n, 161 n, 339
Introduction to Philosophy, An, 116 n, 339
Introductory Logic, An, 41 n, 339
Introspection, 41, 65
Intuition, 39, 58–9, 190, 194–5, 225; immediate, 251; mystic, 195; mystical, 203
Intuitive, awareness, 213; experience, 153, 258; perception, 41, 193, 195, 211, 216, 225; vision, 43
Invariable concomitance (vyāpti), 142–4, 147–51, 159–60, 164, 175–6, 188, 228; different kinds of, 143–4, 150–51; knowledge of, 143, 146–50;
Īśvara, 43, 73–8, 106, 181–2, 209, 216, 226, 254, 269, 335; Mīmāṁsā view of, 226, 317–18
'Īśvara and His Māyā', 76 n
Īśvarahood, 77, 269
Īśvarakṛṣṇa, 257 n, 315, 343

Jacobi, Hermann Georg, 307
Jaimini, 225
Jaiminīya-nyāya-mālā, 318
Jaina(s), 38–9, 225 n
Jainism, 43, 128, 183, 312
James, William, 115, 115 n, 244, 244 n, 340
Janaka, 87–8
Jāti (genus), 183, 183 n; (*see also* universal)
Jayatīrtha, 328
Jeans, Sir James, 221 n, 340
Jesus Christ, 195
Jhā, Gaṅgānātha, 313, 318
Jīva, 67, 74–5, 77–9, 97, 106, 110, 118, 201, 209, 219, 222, 233–5, 248–9, 260, 269, 271–2, 307, 319; (*see also* individual self)
Jīva-caitanya, 83
Jīvahood, 77, 269
Jīvanmukta (liberated-in-life), 280, 282–3; their ways, 283–4
Jīvanmukti-viveka, 225 n, 325
Jīva-sākṣī, 82; (*see* self as witness)
Jīvātmā, 83
Jñāna, 88, 89 n, 112–13, 119, 119 n, 288; its distinction from dhyāna (meditation), 288; from vijñāna (realization), 284, 284 n; (*see also* knowledge and cognition)
Jñānādhyāsa, 124 n
Jñāna-kāṇḍa (knowledge-section of the Vedas), 141 n, 206, 227, 308, 317
Jñāna-mārga (path of knowledge), 204
Jñāna-virōdhi (antiknowledge), 134 n; (*see* ajñāna)
Jñānendriyas, 45, 48 n; (*see also* organs of sense)
Joachim, Harold H., 115, 116 n, 122, 122 n, 340
Joad, C. E. M., 237 n, 340
John, Saint, 293, 341

Kaivalya, 301
Kalpa-niyāmaka Īśvara, 315
Kaṇāda (Ulūka), 225, 312, 345
Kant, Immanuel, 61 n, 63; Kantian school, 63
Kant's transcendental proof, 161
Kāṇva (one of the two recensions of Br. U), 306; *see* Mādhyandina
Kapila, 131, 225, 302, 314, 343
Karaṇa (special cause), 35
Karma, 123, 209–12, 271, 282, 317; impressions of, 100, 123, 280, 282–3; law of, 70, 209–12, 317
Karma-kāṇḍa (work-section of the Vedas), 141 n, 206, 227, 308, 317
Karma-Mīmāṁsā, 316
Karma-nirṇaya, 331
Karma-yōga, 298, 320
Karmendriyas (motor organs), 45, 48 n, 52; (*see also* organs)
Kartā (doer), 79, 234, 238
Kathā-lakṣaṇa, 330
Kevala-Advaita (Śaṅkara's non-dualism), 322
Khaṇḍana-khaṇḍa-khādya, 122, 324
Khyāti (cognition), 126
Kiraṇāvalī, 313
Knower (jñātā, vijñātā), 16, 42, 46, 60, 85, 102, 236, 238–42, 248–50, 255, 276; of Brahman, 262, 265, 281–2, 284, 291, 300; 302; distinct from the known, 239
Knowledge, 15, 41, 52, 62, 66, 83–8, 89, 89 n, 90, 108, 110, 236, 246–7, 266, 269, 283–4, 284 n; criteria of, 114–18; direct, 17, 55, 92, 164;

direct and indirect, 17; empirical, 61 n, 266; extraordinary cases of, 45–6; function of, 17; ideal or goal of, 212, 246, 258–60; immediate, 92, 109, 191; inferential, 73, 97, 143, 146, 159, 187, 215, 229, 231; instruments of, 43, 52; intuitive (prajñā), 274, 278, 278 n, 337; mediate, 42 n, 44, 73, 92, 109, 142, 164, 257–60, 266; nature of, 62–3, 88–90; non-perceptual, 90, 92, 94, 97, 109, 141; perceptual, 36, 44, 61–3, 73, 85, 90–92, 94, 97, 109, 141, 188, 211, 215, 219–20; relational (its four factors), 16, 102; scriptural, 219, 222, 225; self-manifestedness of, 110–11, 114; self-validity of, 112–14; speculative, 225; suprasensuous, 152, 193, 215, 227, 266, 305, 316, 320; its triple distinction, 85, 111, 223, 248; valid, 108, 111, 115–20, 174; validity of, 110, 112–15; invalidity of, 113–14; (*see also* verbal knowledge)

Knowledge, methods or sources of (pramāṇas), 39, 43, 66, 84, 302–3

Knowledge of the Self, direct and indirect, 283

Knowledge and Truth, 89 n, 340

Knownness (jñātatā), 112

Krama-sandarbha, 333

Kṛṣṇa Dvaipāyana, 305; (*see also* Veda-Vyāsa)

Kullūka, 37 n, 342

Kūrma Purāṇa, 300 n

Kūṭastha (immutable self), 78, 83, 91, 233–8, 260, 272, 277, 280, 296

Kūṭastha caitanya, 111, 272

Laghubhāgavatamṛta, 333

Laghu-vākya-vṛtti, 235 n, 236 n, 238 n, 324, 342

Laghvī, 318

Lalita-Mādhava, 333

Lectures on Metaphysics (Hamilton), 62 n, 339

Leibniz, Gottfried William Von, 40, 93

Liberation, gradual (krama-mukti), 300; final (videha-mukti), 282, 300

Liberation, immediate (sadya mukti), 279, 299–300

Liberation (mōkṣa), 77, 77 n, 78, 118, 197, 203, 206–7, 256, 258, 262, 269, 275, 281–3, 290, 295, 299–301, 303, 313, 338; definition of, 258 n

Liberation-in-life (jīvanmukti), 283

Life, four stages (āśrama) of, 263, 308

Life-principle (prāṇa), 51 n

Light of lights, 87, 248

Limiting adjunct(s) (upādhi), 47, 76–7, 79, 83, 98, 185, 221, 236, 248, 255, 271–2, 277, 282, 289

Liṅga (mark, the middle term), 146; liṅga śarīra (the index body), 271; (*see also* body, subtle)

Locke, John, 40, 63, 71, 71 n, 72, 340

Locus (adhikarana), 165–6, 169

Logic, 119, 147–8, 216, 312; Indian, 147, 222 n

Logician(s), Indian, 148, 155, 228; Buddhist, 115, 167

Logos, 292

Lōkāyata darśana, 312; (*see* Cārvāka)

Luke, Saint, 195 n, 341

MacKenna, Stephen, 251 n, 340

Macrocosm, Microcosm, 294

Mādhavācārya, 186 n, 225 n, 311 n, 344

Madhva (Madhvācārya, also called Ānanda-tīrtha), 107 n, 319, 330–31; school of, 328–30; dualism of, 330

Mādhyamika(s), 68 n, 127–9, 312

Mādhyamika-kārikā, 128 n

Mādhyandina, 306; (*see* Kāṇva)

Mahābhārata, 16, 217, 299, 342

Mahābhārata-tātparya-nirṇaya, 330

Mahābhāṣya, 186 n

Mahābhūtas (gross elements), 38, 51 n, 132

Mahādevan, Dr T. M. P., 152, 153 n, 224, 340

Mahāpuruṣa-nirṇaya, 328

Mahat, 314, 335

Mahāvākya(s), 106, 200–1, 204, 221, 242 n, 246, 256, 258–9, 261–2, 269–70, 273; Monotheistic interpretation of, 269

Mahāyāna, 68 n

Maitreyī, 249, 256

Majjhima Nikāya, 211 n, 342

Major premise, 145, 145 n, 150, 154, 158, 160, 231 n

Major term (sādhya), 143–5, 205, 147–8, 154

Man of realization, 258, 284

Manana (reflection); *see* Self-realization, its threefold way)

Manas, 53

Māṇḍūkya (*Upaniṣad*) *Kārikā*, 68 n, 77 n, 125 n, 133 n, 215 n, 224 n, 225 n, 321, 324, 342

Manifold, 72–3, 77, 81, 219, 247, 249, 253–4, 262, 281, 293, 295, 298, 301

Mantras (Vedic text), 70, 204, 204 n, 305; (*see also* Saṁhitā)

Manu, 37, 203, 224

Manu-saṁhitā or *Manu-smṛti*, 37 n, 224 n, 342

Mark (middle term), 146–50, 154

Materialism, Materialists, 38, 312; (*see also* Cārvākas)
Matthew, Saint, 195 n
Māyā, 73–4, 76–8, 81, 98, 99 n, 271–2, 277, 301; cosmic, 73; individual, 76; (*see also* ajñāna, avidyā)
Māyā-vāda-khaṇḍana, 331
McDougall, Dr William, 80, 81 n, 340
Meanings, primary, 176, 184–5, 184 n, 199, 215, 222; implied, 184–5, 215, 224
Meditation (dhyāna, nididhyāsana), 43, 153, 195, 201, 205–6, 256–62, 265, 273–76, 281, 288–91, 295–6, 299, 302, 337; Nirguṇa Brahman, 277–8; on Saguṇa Brahman, 297; its distinction from knowledge, 90; its distinction from samādhi, 276
Meghanādāri, 328–9
Meister Eckhart (The Works of), Vol. I, II, 214, 214 n, 252, 252 n, 339
Memory (smṛti), 44, 62, 94, 96, 107–8, 118–20, 119 n, 122, 125–6, 130, 133, 176–8, 244; memory-image, 127, 130; memory-synthesis, 177
Men, three grades of, 299
Mental, ailments (distinct from the physical), 47; ideas, 66, 71; impressions, 122–3; mode, 17, 84, 88–9, 91–4, 105, 235, 278–9, 301–2; mode as a means to external perception, 96–102; modifications, 49, 62, 86, 91, 93–4, 104; phenomena, 119; process, 61–2; states, 46, 72, 74, 91, 93
Metaphysical assumptions, truths, etc., 63–4; basis, 60; concepts, conceptions, 63, 198; speculations, 63, 215; views of Advaita and Mīmāṁsā, 317
Metaphysics, 15, 61, 61 n, 63–4, 312; its relation with epistemology, 61–4
Middle term (hetu), 143–7, 154
Mīmāṁsā (Pūrva or Karma) of Jaimini, 106–7, 141, 141 n, 156, 158, 185 n, 190, 225–7, 257 n, 311, 316–18; Kumārila School of, 39, 112–15, 141–2, 163, 165–6, 170, 183, 226, 317; Prabhākara School of, 36, 38, 111, 113–14, 130, 138, 141 n, 142, 150, 165–6, 226, 318; notable works on, 318
Mīmāṁsā-darśana, 343
Mīmāṁsakas, 49–50, 90, 118, 151, 154, 157, 160, 184, 218
Mīmāṁsā-nyāya-prakāśa, 318
Mīmāṁsā-paribhāṣā, 318
(*Mīmāṁsā*) *Ślōka-vārttika*, 107 n, 141 n, 156 n, 158 n, 166 n, 317–18, 343
Mīmāṁsā-sūtras of Jaimini and *Śabara-bhāṣya*, 14 n, 181, 316, 316 n, 317, 317 n, 318, 343
Mīmāṁsā (Uttara or Brahma-Mīmāṁsā) of Bādarāyaṇa, 141 n, 227, 316, 326; (*see Brahma-sūtras*)
Mind (antaḥkaraṇa), 17, 35, 37, 40–42, 42 n, 44–8, 48 n, 49, 51–7, 59–62, 64, 67, 68 n, 69, 70–71, 73–4, 78–9, 82–4, 86–93, 96–8, 100–1, 108, 110–11, 233–7, 240–41, 243, 249–50, 252–3, 261, 271, 273, 276, 278 n, 278–9, 296–7, 299, 301–2, 312–13; its three aspects, 52–3, 90–91, 93–4; cosmic, 52; four functions of, 53; modes of, 47; purification of, 263; universal, 43; as an instrument of knowledge, 17, 52, 88
Minor premise, 145, 145 n
Minor term (pakṣa), 145, 148, 154
Mirage, 66–7, 91, 115, 118, 125, 136, 248, 258
Miśra, Maṇḍana, 259, 283, 318
Miśra, Murāri, 318
Miśra, Pārthasārathi, 141 n, 158 n, 318
Miśra, Prabhākara, 141 n, 317–18; (*see* Mīmāṁsā)
Miśra, Śālikanātha, 36 n, 141 n, 318, 343
Miśra, Śaṅkara, 313
Miśra, Vācaspati, 38, 120, 125, 158, 165, 187 n, 229 n, 257, 259–60, 313, 315, 342–3, 345; commentaries of, 257 n; school of, 257, 257 n, 258, 319, 321
Mithyānumāna-khaṇḍana, 330
Mōkṣa, 118, 197, 207; (*see also* liberation)
Momentariness, theory of, 244
Monism, 70, 308
Monotheism, 308
Monotheistic systems and their founders, 227, 318–19, 321–2, 327–34
Montague, William Pepperell, 39, 40 n, 121, 190, 190 n, 340
Moore, Charles A., 211 n, 226 n, 340
Morae (mātrās), 294
Moral, ideal, conduct (dharma), 207–9, 222, 299, 300, 312; evolution, 207–8; upliftment, a graded course, 298–9; (*see also* ethical principles, conduct)
Morality, 198, 208; definition of, 208
Mother, of the universe, 285; Divine, 285
Motor-organs, 45, 48 n, 52; (*see also* organs)
Muller, Prof. F. Max, 227 n, 293 n, 309, 309 n, 340

Multiplicity, 213, 247
Mumukṣu, 262; (*see* seeker of liberation)
Mumukṣūpāya-saṁgraha, 328
Muir, John (*Original Sanskrit Texts*), 292 n
Muni, Sarvajñātma, 260, 344
Muni, Yāmuna, 328
Mystical perception, 203; intuition, 203
Mysticism, mystics, 212, 252

Nāgārjuna, 128 n
Nāgasena, 242, 242 n
Naiṣkarmya-siddhi, 111 n, 219 n, 221 n, 231 n, 233 n, 235 n, 238 n, 242 n, 260 n, 282 n, 289, 289 n, 324, 343
Naiyāyikas (Nyāya philosophers), their views, etc., 38, 38 n, 54, 89, 95, 118, 130–31, 138, 143–6, 149, 150–51, 154–5, 169, 182, 230; (*see also* Nyāya and Nyāya school)
Naturalists, 65
Nature of Truth, The, 116 n, 122 n, 340
Navya-Nyāya school (Neo-logicians), 37, 106, 159, 159 n, 183, 312
Naya-dyumaṇi, 328
Naya-prakāśikā, 328
Neoplatonist, 216
Neo-realists, 56, 64
Nescience, 15, 70, 77 n
New Frontiers of the Mind, 42 n, 44 n
New Science, The, 213 n, 340
New Testament, The, 293
Nididhyāsana (vijñāna or right apprehension), 288–91; (*see also* threefold means of Self-realization)
Nihilism, 128–9, 128 n; nihilists, 68 n
Nimbārka (Nimbāditya), 107 n, 319, 321, 329
Nirvāṇa-daśakam or *Daśa-ślōkī*, 97 n, 102 n, 324, 329, 343
Nirvāṇa-ṣaṭkam or *Ātma-ṣaṭkam*, 289
Non-apprehension (anupalabdhi), 17, 35, 141 n, 142, 163, 166–8; appropriate (yōgya), 167–8, 170
Non-cognition, 120, 167
Non-consciousness, 99–100
Non-contradictedness (abādhitatvam 116–18
Nondualism, 308; nonduality, 252; (*see* Advaita Vedānta and Advaitins)
Non-equipollent concomitance (asama-vyāpti), 144
Non-existence, 17, 128; how known, 163 ff; its four kinds, 168–70; different views on, 164–6
Non-perception, 163, 167
Non-sensory, 45
Non-Vedic schools, 311–12
Not-self, 139, 208, 239, 290, 301–2
Nyāya School, 37–9, 42 n, 51, 112–13, 119–22, 132–3, 142, 149–50, 159, 166. 180, 182–3, 217, 226, 228–9; early, 149; works of, 313–14; (*see also* Naiyāyikas and Nyāya)
Nyāya (system), 144, 152, 166, 169 n, 181, 183, 189, 225, 228–9, 257 n, 311–13; syllogism, 146–7, 147 n; (*see also* Naiyāyikas and Nyāya school)
Nyāya-bindu, 115 n, 167, 343
Nyāya-bindu-ṭīkā, 115 n
Nyāya-kandalī, 313
Nyāya-kaṇikā, 318
Nyāya-kusumāñjali, 314
Nyāya-mañjari, 189 n, 325
Nyāyāmṛta, 325, 331
Nyāyanirṇaya, 314
Nyāyapañcānana, Kṛṣṇanātha, 183 n
Nyāyapañcānana, Viśvanātha, 106, 121–2, 159
Nyāya-pariśuddhi, 328
Nyāya-prasthāna, 320
Nyāya-rakṣā-maṇi, 325
Nyāya-ratnākara, 318
Nyāya-ratnāvalī, 102 n, 104 n
Nyāya-siddhañjana, 328
Nyāya-sudhā, 331
Nyāya-sudhā-parimala, 331
Nyāya-sūtras or *Nyāya-darśana* of Gautama, 35 n, 37 n, 152 n, 228 n, 312–13, 343
Nyāya theory, 89, 130
Nyāya-Vaiśeṣika, 48 n, 106, 108, 113, 115, 141 n, 147, 150; pluralism of, 330
Nyāya-vārttika-tātparya-pariśuddhi, 313
Nyāya-vārttika-tātparya-ṭīkā, 313

Object(s) (in relation to the subject), 62, 65, 81–2, 85–6, 94, 129, 255; external, 57–8, 68, 70–73, 84; of perception, 47–50
Object-consciousness, 101, 104–5
Om, 181, 217, 274, 291–8
Oneness (absolute), 212, 213 n, 246–8
Oṅkāra, 294
Oṅkāranātha, 250
Ontological enquiry, 84
Ontology, 63
Organ(s), bodily, 44–5, 53–4; external, internal, 47–8; of action, 45, 48 n, 51 n, 52, 74, 237, 249, 314; of perception, 35, 48–9, 48 n, 52, 54, 74; of sense, 44–5, 51, 54, 56, 84; sensory, 35–6, 237, 314; (*see also* perception and sense-organ)
Organism, living, 80–81

Origination, dependent (pratītya-samutpāda), 211 n
Outline of Psychology, 81 n, 340

Padārtha-dharma-saṁgraha of Praśastapāda, 175 n, 313, 345
Padārthas, 312
Padmapāda, 97, 125, 125 n, 131, 142, 259 n, 260 n
Pakṣa (the minor term), 145
Pañcadaśī, 45 n, 48 n, 52 n, 73, 74 n, 83 n, 93 n, 103, 103 n, 117 n, 215, 225 n, 233, 233 n, 235 n, 238 n, 259 n, 262 n, 269 n, 271 n, 278 n, 281 n, 289 n, 290 n, 325, 343
Pañca-pādikā, 125, 127 n, 131 n, 259 n, 324, 343; Eng. trans., 326
Pañcapādikā-vivaraṇa, 48 n, 82 n, 259, 259 n, 324, 343
Pañcīkaraṇa (quintuplication), 51 n
Pañcīkaraṇa-vārttika, 324
Pañcīkarṇam, 324; Eng. trans., 327
Pāṇini, 185 n
Pāṇini sūtras, 186 n
Pantheism, 67, 69–70
Pāpa, 210, 282
Paramahaṁsa, 287, 287 n
Pariṇāma, 93, 335
Parinirvāṇa, 72, 72 n
Parmenides, 61 n
Parōkṣa - bhrama (non - perceptual error), 121
Parōkṣa-jñānam, 260; (*see* knowledge, mediate)
Particular(s) (vyakti), 182–4, 246; (*see also* universal)
Pascal, 194
Patañjali, 42–3, 46, 60, 82, 93, 20, 181, 186 n, 187, 194, 196 225, 240–41, 297 n, 298, 301–2, 337–8, 345
Paul, Saint, 222 n, 341
Pauruṣeya, 217
Perceiver, 100, 243
Percept, 41, 58, 71, 102, 130; complex, 58
Perception, 17, 35–8, 40, 54–60, 65, 68 n, 71, 75, 94, 119, 130, 152, 154, 163–4, 175, 188–9, 193, 207, 210, 219, 243, 256; auditory, 54, 97, 100, 101 n; clairvoyant, 42–3; complex, 95; definition of, 36–7; determinate, indeterminate, 106–7; distinctive character of, 75; its distinction from inference, 36; external, 17, 35–6, 40, 42, 42 n, 45, 52–3, 56–7, 59, 73, 86, 92, 96–104 (process), 103–4, 278; extrasensory, 42, 44, 50; internal, 17, 35–7, 40–42, 60, 65, 86, 92, 96–7, 109, 175, 235; luminous, 55–6; supernormal, 43, 45; visual, 53–5, 57, 86, 95, 97, 100, 102; (*see also* sense-perception)
Perception of movement, weight, time, etc., 48–9
Perceptual process, 55–6, 61, 103
Percipient, 71, 91, 98, 101–2, 110
Perennial Philosophy, 213 n, 340
Perfection, path of, 205
Personal identity, 244
Petitio principii, 158–60, 167
Phala (lit. fruit, resultant knowledge), 102–3
Phala-catanya, 103, 278
Phantom, 137
Phenomena, world of, 62, 77, 81, 132, 153, 156, 219, 262, 282–3; order of 66, 215, 278
Phenomenalists, 56
Philosophers, 73, 90, 110, 221; Eastern, 93, 97, 194, 225; Indian, 90, 108, 114, 118, 120, 142, 148, 154, 175; modern, 90, 245; of East and West, 97, 114–15, 142, 225; nondualistic, 205, 216, 283; (*see also* Western)
Philosophy, 213, 213 n, 246; modern, 61 n; of the West, 61 n; schools of Indian, 126, 187, 225 n, 226, 311; Vedic systems of, 225; (*see also* Western)
Philosophy, science, and religion, 213, 246
Philosophy of Vedānta, The, 215 n, 339
Physics, 61 n
Physics and Philosophy, 221 n, 340
Physiological, function, 55; operation, 61; process, 55–6, 62
Physiology, 61
Pippalāda, The sage, 292
Planck, Max Karl Ernst Ludwig, 213 n, 237 n, 340
Plato, 187
Plotinus, 251, 251 n
Polytheism, 308
Porphyry, 251, 251 n
Positive Sciences of the Ancient Hindus, The, 148 n, 341
Postulation (arthāpatti), 17, 35, 92, 142, 144, 151, 156–61, 164
Pradhāna, 335 n
Pragmatic, test, 115, 117; theory of East and West, 115; view of truth, 118
Pragmatism, 115 n, 340
Prajāpati, 292, 298, 309
Prajñā (intuitive cognition), 274, 278
Prakaraṇa-pañcikā, 36 n, 141 n, 318, 343

Prakatārtha-vivaraṇa, 259 n
Prakṛti, 50 n, 99 n, 181, 217, 301, 314, 335; undifferentiated, 49, 76
Pramā, 15, 35, 62, 89, 108, 111–12, 118, 119 n, 120
Pramāṇa(s), 15, 18, 35, 38–9, 104, 120, 161, 163, 165, 189, 196, 219, 222 n, 258, 313; necessary for the unillumined, 303; their validity, 219
Pramāṇa-caitanya, 104
Pramāṇa-lakṣaṇa, 330
Pramāṇa-phalam, 103
Pramātā, 83–4, 91, 98, 102, 104, 110–11, 163, 234–5, 238; (*see also* perceiver, percipient)
Pramātṛ-caitanya, 99, 104, 278
Prameya, 84, 102–4, 111
Prameya-caitanya, 104
Prameya-ratnāvalī, 334
Pramiti, 84, 102–4, 111
Prāṇa (vital principle), 51 n, 234, 249
Praṇava, 291, 293, 295–6; (*see also* Ōm)
Prārabdha-karma, 280, 283
Prasaṁkhyāna, 289–90
Praśastapāda, 38 n, 175 n, 313, 345
Prasthāna-bheda, 325
Prasthāna-traya (the triple basis of Vedānta), 307
Prātibhāsika (apparent, illusory), 118, 133
Pratijñā (proposition), 145–6, 153
Pratīka (symbol), 297
Pratītya-samutpāda (dependent origination), 211 n
Pratiyōgī, 151, 165
Pratyakṣa, 35, 35 n, 141, 170, 203
Pratyak-tattva-pradīpikā (also called 'Tattva-pradīpikā' or 'Citsukhī'), 110 n, 113 n, 117 n, 325, 344
Pravṛtti-mārga, 300
Pravṛtti-vijñāna, 129
Preceptor, 258, 277; (*see also* teacher)
Presentation, representation, 75, 130
Presentative, representative, 94–5, 122
Preservation (of the universe), 199, 253
Principal Upaniṣads, 326
Principle of becoming, 73
Principles of Human Knowledge (Berkeley), 69 n, 339
Principles of Psychology, 244 n, 340
Problems of Philosophy, The, 57 n, 68 n, 75 n, 115 n, 119 n, 339
Projection (of the Universe), 199
Proposition, universal, 149, 150
Psychiatry, 47
Psychical, functions, 61; processes, 62
Psychological Principles, 59 n, 95 n, 341
Psychological process, 62
Psychologists, modern, 46, 90, 95, 119, 245
Psychology, 61, 119
Psychophysical, adjunct, 232; constitution, 299; organism, 74; process, 62; realm, 60
Puṇya, 210, 282
Pupil, 258, 266–69, 273, 277; (*see also* teacher)
Pūrṇa-Prajñā-darśana Eng. trans., 331
Purposive behaviour, 237
Purposiveness, 80
Puruṣa (the luminous self), 93, 111, 314, 335, 338
Puruṣa-Sūktam, 70 n, 343
Pūrva-Mīmāṁsā-sūtra, see *Mīmāṁsā-sūtras*
Puṣpāñjali, 235 n

Qualification(s), of a seeker of liberation, 262–3; of the pupil and the preceptor, 266
Qualities conducive to right knowledge, 267
Questions of King Milindā, The, 242 n, 339
Quietism, 252
Quintuplication (pañcīkaraṇa), 51 n

Radhakrishnan, S., 66, 66 n, 70, 70 n, 186, 194, 211 n, 226 n, 278 n
Rāja-mārtaṇḍa, 45 n, 315
Rajas, 51, 51 n, 257, 273; (*see also* guṇas)
Rāma, 297
Ramakrishna-Vivekananda, 287 n, 339
Rāmakṛṣṇa (commentator on *Pañcadaśī*), 83 n, 103 n
Rāmānuja, 107 n, 319, 321–2, 327–9; Works of Rāmānuja School, 328–9; *see also* Viśiṣṭādvaita)
Rāmatīrtha Swāmī (commentator), 135 n, 325, 344–5
Reach of the Mind, The, 43 n, 45 n, 341
Real, 246, 263
Realism, 17, 64; and Vedānta, 64–6
Realist(s), 57, 59, 64, 68 n, 72; dualistic, 59; monistic, 59
Realistic, thinkers, 56; school of, 115
Reality, 15, 63–4, 66, 70, 73–4, 194, 196–7, 201, 204, 207, 246–9, 251, 254–5, 278 n, 303; absolute, 196, 217; criteria of, 40; fundamental, 60–61, 63–6, 81, 93, 134, 196, 215, 219, 221, 247, 301; nondual, 106, 224; of realities, 251, 303; spiritual, 64; transcendent, 66, 207; ultimate,

64, 66, 73, 107, 118, 196, 199, 212, 221, 227, 230; underlying, 84
Realization of (Absolute) Brahman, 262–3, 270, 274, 278; its triple means, 216, 225, 256; (*see also* aparōkṣa-Brahmānubhūti)
Reason, 39, 152, 190, 194–6, 207–8, 212, 215–16, 219, 222–6, 228, 290
Reasoning, 153, 220, 222–4, 228, 236, 239, 241, 242 n, 245, 252–3, 256, 258, 264, 273, 275; disjunctive, 158; hypothetical (tarka), 222 n; syllogistic, 155
Recognition (pratyabhijñā), 39, 107, 107 n, 108, 125–6, 129, 133
Recollection (smṛti), 53, 95, 107–8, 129, 177
Reductio ad absurdum, 122
Reflection, 36, 223, 256–7, 261–2, 289
Reflex action, 80
Regressus ad infinitum, 48 n, 113, 166
Reid, Louis Arnaud, 89, 89 n, 340
Relation(s), 49 n, 63, 89–90, 270; apparent, seeming, 137; between the jīva and Īśvara, 270; between the preceptor and the pupil, 267–9; universal, 149
Relational, 107
Relation, of cause and effect, 144, 149, 250; of conjunction (saṁyōga), 49 n, 166; of identity (tādātmya), 48 n, 139, 144, 149; or inherence (samavāya), 48 n, 166, 182–3
Relationship (with God, its diff. types), 253, 253 n
Relative (order), tripartite, 64, 75–6, 202
Relativity, 68
Religion, 198, 213, 224, 246
Religious observances, 205
Repetition, 298
Representation, 75, 130
Representationism, 57, 72
Representative, dream, 122; realism, 72; theory of perception, 94–5
Republic, The, 187 n, 340
Retina, 55
Retinal pictures, 57
Revelation (scriptural), 215–16, 225, 227 n, 256, 320; Divine, 196, 203, 215, 217; and intuition, 225; and reason, 225
Ṛg-Veda-bhāṣya-bhūmikā (Sāyaṇācarya), 193 n, 207 n, 219 n, 343
Rhine, J. B., 42, 42 n, 43 n, 44, 44 n, 45 n
Righteousness, 206; practice of, 208
Rites and ceremonials, 218; their efficacy, 206
Ṛjuvimala, 318
Ṛta (the cosmic moral principle), 209
Ruler, Internal, 78, 296
Runes, Dagobert D., 126 n
Russell, Bertrand, 56, 59, 59 n

Śabara Svāmin, commentator on Pūrva-Mīmāṁsā-sūtras, 141 n, 317, 317 n, 343
Śabda (word), 35, 173, 175–6, 178, 188–9, 293
Śābda-bōdha (verbal comprehension), 174, 178
Śabda-pramā, 174, 178, 191; *see* verbal knowledge
Śabda-pramāṇa (verbal testimony), 173–6, 178, 191–3
Śabda-tattva, 187
Sacred Books of the East, The, 242 n
Sacrificial rites, their efficacy, 206, 316–17
Sadasat-khyāti (theory of illusion), 126, 131
Sādhya (the major term), 145, 147–8, 150, 228
Sad-Vaiṣṇavism, 330
Śaivism, three main schools of, 322
Sākṣī (*see* self as witness)
Sākṣi-caitanya, 83–4, 89, 272
Śakti, Śaktism, 297, 322
Samādhi, 194, 250–52, 258, 262, 276, 287, 337; savikalpa, 248, 250, 273, 276, 286; nirvikalpa, 223, 248, 250, 252, 254, 273, 277–81, 284–6, 296–7, 301; asamprajñāta, 301–2, 337–8; samprajñāta, 337–8; nirvikalpa as described by Śaṅkara, 250; its distinction from savikalpa, 276; its distinction from asamprajñāta, 301–2
Sāmānyatō-dṛṣṭam (inference from analogy), 152, 229
Samartha-pravṛtti-janakatva (practical efficacy, a test of knowledge), 115
Samavāya-sambandha (*see* relation of inherence)
Saṁhitā (compilation of the Vedic mantras), 305, 307–9; five saṁhitās, 309–10
Sāṁkhya (philosophy, school), 38–9, 43, 52, 80, 106, 111, 118, 126, 131–2, 141 n, 154, 165–6, 183, 225–6, 228–9, 302, 311, 314–15; theory of illusion, 126–7, 131–2
Sāṁkhya categories, 314
Sāṁkhya-darśana, 43 n, 80 n, 127 n, 131 n, 343
Sāṁkhya-kārikā, 38 n, 106 n, 111 n, 154 n, 158, 158 n, 165, 165 n, 229 n, 257 n, 315, 343
Sāṁkhya-pravacana-sūtram, 315

Sāṁkhya and Yōga, 141 n, 314; difference between, 315
Sāṁkhya-Yōga, 113–14, 301–2; dualism of, 330
Saṁkṣepa-śārīraka, 135 n, 260 n, 269 n, 283, 324, 344
Saṁsarga (connection), 269 n
Saṁśaya (doubt), 119
Saṁskāra(s), 94, 210
Samvit (consciousness), 103
Sanātana dharma, 323
Śaṅkara, school of, 328; nondualism 330
Śaṅkarācārya (Śaṅkara), 46, 66–7, 69, 71, 74, 76, 87–8, 90, 97, 101, 103, 123–5, 125 n, 129, 183, 187–8, 191, 192 n, 193, 196, 203, 205–6, 209, 218–19, 222–3, 225, 227–8, 231, 233, 238, 238 n, 240–41, 242 n, 244, 248, 250–51, 255, 257 n, 258–62, 264–5, 268, 271, 273–5, 278, 281–3, 283 n, 288–9, 289 n, 291, 293, 296, 299, 303, 306, 322–4, 327
Śaṅkara's commentaries on:
Brahma-sūtras, 48 n, 67 n, 68, 68 n, 74, 74 n, 76, 76 n, 79 n, 81 n, 90 n, 124, 124 n, 125, 125 n, 128 n, 129, 129 n, 181 n, 182 n, 183 n, 187 n, 193, 193 n, 196, 196 n, 197 n, 203, 203 n, 205, 205 n, 206, 206 n, 215 n, 219 n, 226 n, 228 n, 230 n, 231 n, 244, 255, 255 n, 258 n, 262 n, 282 n, 288 n, 291 n, 293 n, 303, 303 n
Bṛhadāraṇyaka Upaniṣad, 47 n, 47–8, 50 n, 87, 87 n, 88, 101, 101 n, 188 n, 192 n, 203, 203 n, 206 n, 218, 218 n, 220 n, 222 n, 241 n, 251 n, 260 n, 261 n, 265 n, 274, 274 n, 281, 281 n, 282, 282 n, 291, 291 n, 299
Bhagavad-gītā, 43 n, 46, 46 n, 128 n, 205, 220 n, 303, 303 n
Chāndōgya Upaniṣad, 67 n
Māṇḍūkya Upaniṣad, 123, 123 n
Māṇḍūkya-Upaniṣad-kārikā, 125, 125 n
Muṇḍaka Upaniṣad, 265, 299 n
Praśna Upaniṣad, 291 n
Taittirīya Upaniṣad, 67, 67 n, 209, 209 n, 317 n
Śaṅkarānanda, 325
Sannyāsa-nirṇaya, 332
Sannyāsin(s), 263, 308
Sarasvatī, Brahmānanda, 102 n, 343
Sarasvatī, Madhusūdana, 98, 101, 102, 102 n, 103, 103 n, 220, 283, 289, 325, 342, 343
Sarasvatī, Rāmānanda, 259 n
Śārīraka-Mīmāṁsā, 227 n
Śārīraka-sūtras, 227 n, 307
Sarkar, Mahendralal, 286
Sarvadarśana-saṁgraha, 186 n, 187 n, 197 n, 225 n, 311 n, 344
Sarvajñātma-muni, 260, 283, 344
Sarvārtha-siddhi, 328
Sarva-samvādinī, 333
Śāstradīpikā, 141 n, 158 n, 318, 344
Śata-dūṣaṇī, 328
Sat-cid-ānanda, 323; (*see also* Being-Consciousness-Bliss)
Sat-khyāti (theory of illusion), 126, 132
Ṣaṭ-sandarbha, 332–3
Sattva, 50–51, 51 n, 52, 64, 104, 257, 273; (*see* guṇas)
Satyakāma, 292
'Satyatvam bādharāhityam', 116
Sautrāntika, 68 n, 72, 312
Sāyaṇācārya, 193; his com. on Ṛg.V., 193 n, 207 n, 219 n
Scholasticism, Medieval, 216
Schoolmen, 216
Schopenhauer, 238
Science, 213, 213 n, 246
Science and the Unseen World (Eddington), 41 n, 339
Scientists, 73, 221
Scriptural study, 274–5, 303; testimony, 177, 257
Scripture(s) (śāstras), 193, 195–8, 208, 258; scriptural truths, 216
Seal, Dr Brajendranath, 147, 341
Seeker(s) of Brahman, 263, 265, 274, 276–8, 295, 299; what becomes of him, 299–300
Seeker(s) of liberation, 256, 262, 264, 273, 279, 283, 288, 290–91, 297; of self-knowledge, 266, 301, 303; of truth, 264; (*see also* spiritual aspirants)
Seer(s), 43, 63, 254, 263, 281, 284; Vedic, 282
Self (ātman), 41, 52, 62, 65, 68 n, 78–9, 81, 86, 88, 138–9, 153, 197–8, 201, 203–4, 208, 213, 221–2, 230–34, 238–9, 241–4, 246–7, 249, 256–8, 264–5, 270–72, 274, 282, 290, 301–2; all-pervading, 73; continuity of, 244; empirical or apparent, 36, 41, 83, 91, 111, 214, 221, 230, 234, 237, 272; individual, 16–17, 62, 66, 81–3, 86, 88–9, 106, 110, 138–9, 200, 212, 269, 295–6; inmost, innermost, (pratyak ātmā), 60, 200, 208, 231–3, 236, 238, 240, 252, 255; knowing, 15–16, 42, 46, 55, 60, 82, 97, 245; luminous, 46, 65, 69, 81, 86, 90; transcendental, 36, 82, 111, 230, 234, 272; of the universe, 81, 106, 269
Self as witness (sākṣī), 41–2, 49, 62,

79, 82–4, 89, 91, 93–4, 110–11, 113–14, 230, 232–7, 240, 255, 272, 277
Self, its distinction from mind, 46; self as knower (vijñātā), 238
Self-awareness, 83, 91, 98, 231, 237
Self-consistency, 116
Self-control, 297, 299
Self-discipline, 263
Self-effulgent light, 88
Self-evident, 112–13
Self-existent, 63
Self-knowledge, 152–3, 203, 230–32, 239, 264–6, 275, 301; virtues conducive to, 263, 267
Self-luminosity, 87, 110, 239
Self-luminous, 63, 240
Self-manifest, 86, 94, 99, 110, 231
Self-manifestedness (svaprakāśattva) of knowledge, 111, 235
Self-realization, or realization of the self, 153, 157, 223, 230, 232, 256, 258, 273, 301–2; obstacle to, 275; three-fold way to, 153, 222–3, 256, 258–62, 264–5, 273, 288, 299; Yōgic and Nondualistic views of, 301–3
Self-validity of knowledge, 112–14
Sen, Keshub Chunder, 287
Sensation, 36, 56–7, 61, 119
Sense-datum or data, 56–7, 75; -knowledge, 56, 142, 221; -object, 42, 57, 71–2, 100, 164
Sense-organ(s), 35–6, 35 n, 40, 42–6, 48–51, 53–5, 71, 73–5, 84, 86, 92, 94, 96, 100, 104, 106, 131, 166, 230, 248 n, 249, 312; composition of, 50–51; different views of, 49–50; how they contact objects, 53–5
Sense-perception, 17–18, 36, 43, 55, 60–1, 64–5, 71, 94, 142, 163, 193, 197, 215, 219; complication of, 96; problem of, 57, 60, 64
Sensible objects, 69, 97
Sensory experience, 44, 48, 53, 55
Sentence, 173–4, 176–9, 181; four conditions of its meaning, 178–81
Śeṣavat, 159 n, 229
Sheath of intelligence (vijñānamaya kōṣa), 248 n
Siddhānta-bindu, 97 n, 98 n, 102, 102 n, 103 n, 104 n
Siddhānta-leśa-saṁgraha, 97 n, 135 n, 261 n, 279 n, 280 n, 290 n, 325, 344; Eng. trans., 327
Siddhānta-muktāvalī, 37 n, 38 n, 95 n, 115 n, 121, 131 n, 166 n, 169 n, 176 n, 178 n, 180 n, 181 n, 183 n, 229 n
Siddhānta-ratna, 329
Siddhitraya, 328
Śikhāmaṇi, 108 n, 159 n
Similarity, knowledge of; (*see* comparison)
Sinha, Jadunath, 69, 69 n, 94, 95, 95 n,, 107 n
Sircar, Dr Mahendranath, 228, 228 n, 341
Śiva, 289 n, 297, 322
Six Systems of Indian Philosophy, The, 309 n, 340
Six tests (ṣaḍvidha liṅga), 197, 221–2, 222 n, 223
Six Ways of Knowing, The (Datta), 49 n, 58 n, 64 n, 89 n, 96 n, 118 n, 148 n, 155, 155 n, 158–9, 159 n, 160, 160 n, 161, 161 n, 178, 178 n, 188–9, 189 n, 212 n, 339
Sleep, dreamless (suṣupti), 52, 62, 65, 79, 82, 86, 88, 236–7, 240–42, 249, 255, 270, 279–80, 295
Ślōka-vārttika (or *Mīmāṁsā Ślōka-vārttika*), 107 n, 141 n, 156 n, 158 n, 166 n, 317–18, 343
Smṛti (scriptures other than the Vedas), 202–3, 217, 224, 227, 268, 293
Smṛti-prasthāna Vedānta, 320
Socrates, 232
Soul(s), free, 254, 283, 300; liberated, 301; illumined, 216, 254
Soul, individual, finite, 79, 98, 204, 246, 248, 252, 303
Source Book in Indian Philosophy, A, 211 n, 226 n, 340
Space, Time, and Deity (Alexander), 138 n, 339
Sphōta, 185, 185 n, 186–7
Spinoza, Baruch or Benedict, 63
Spiritual aspirant(s) (sādhaka), 205, 250, 253–4, 262, 288, 290, 295, 297; their gradation, 205–7, 296–7; (*see also* seekers of liberation)
Spiritual discipline(s), 205, 208, 275–6; gradation of, 205–7, 297–8
Spiritual experience, 250; (*see also* samādhi)
Spiritual Heritage of India, The, 313 n, 341
Śrī-bhāṣya, 328
Śrī Caitanya, 227, 319, 321, 332
Śrīdhara-swāmī, 325
Śrīharṣa, 122, 324
Śrī Jīva Gōsvāmī, 321, 332, 333
Śrī Kṛṣṇa, 43, 203, 208, 217, 254, 267, 294 n, 297, 297 n, 300, 302
Śrī Kṛṣṇa-stava-rāja, 330
Śrīmad-bhāgavata, 79 n, 279 n, 284 n, 298 n, 344
Śrī Rāmakṛṣṇa, 199, 232, 247, 251–2, 254, 275, 284, 285 n, 285–7, 303
Sri Ramakrishna, The Great Master, 252 n, 254 n, 286 n, 341

Śrī Rūpa Gōsvāmī, 332–3
Śrī Sanotana Gōsvāmī, 332–3
Śrī-Vaiṣṇava School, 327–9; the works of, 328–9
Śrōtriya, 265–6
Śruta-prakāśikā, 328
Śruti, 63, 66, 103, 118, 141 n, 152–3, 157, 196, 198, 200, 202–07, 210–11, 213, 215, 219–22, 222 n, 224–8, 230, 232, 236, 239, 246, 256–8, 260–61, 264–5, 268–9, 290–91, 293, 295; authoritativeness of, 207, 222; (*see also* the Vedas)
Śrutyanugṛhīta, 228; Śruti-pradhāna, 227, 316; Śruti-śira, 307; Śruti-prasthāna, 320
Stout, G. F., Prof., 96, 243, 243 n, 341
Studies in Philosophy and Psychology, 243 n, 341
Subhuman level, its distinction from human, 212
Subject (in relation to the object), 46, 60, 62–3, 65, 74, 82, 85, 89–90, 94, 97, 129, 255
Subject-consciousness, 97–8, 101, 104–5
Subjectivism, 68
Subōdhinī, 331, 345
Substance, 48 n, 49 n, 50 n, 63, 169 n, 183
Substratum, 125, 127, 135–6, 169
Subtle, body (*see* body); element(s); (*see* elements)
Śuddhādvaita, 107 n, 321–2, 331–2
Śukadeva, 281
Summa de Veritate, 63 n, 339
Śūnya-vāda (theory of void), 128, 128 n
Superconscious state, 194, 223; experience, 195, 203
Superimposition (adhyārōpa), 124, 124 n, 125 n, 127 n, 139, 248, 258, 280
Supernal vision, 43
Supposition, 160
Supramental truths, 220
Suprarational, 194, 222
Suprasensible, 18, 142, 155, 164, 177, 193, 215, 219, 229; knowledge of, 229
Suprasensuous facts, truths, etc., 18, 36, 177, 196, 203, 218–20, 222, 224, 229; knowledge of, 177
Suprasenuous knowledge, experience, 152, 176, 194, 215, 266
Supreme Self, 18, 41, 65, 79, 79 n, 195, 200, 204, 209, 212, 214, 246, 248, 272, 276, 282, 293; Good, 300; Goal, 204, 277
Sureśvarācārya, 97, 111, 125 n, 219, 231, 233, 235, 238, 242 n, 260, 260 n, 288–9
Suri, Sudarśana, 328
Sūtras (aphorisms), 312
Suvarṇa-sūtra, 332
Svārājya-siddhi (or *Iṣṭa-siddhi*), 324
Svarga-lōka, 141 n, 206, 300
Svarūpalakṣaṇa (intrinsic characteristic), 199
Svasaṁvedya (real to itself), 83, 248
Svataḥ-prakāśa (self-manifest), 110, 112
Svataḥ-prakāśa-vāda (theory of self-manifestedness of knowledge), 111
Svataḥ-prāmāṇya-vāda (theory of self-validity of knowledge), 112
Svataḥ-siddha (intrinsic), 112
Svayaṁsiddha (self-evident, self-established), 89
Śvetaketu, 197, 203
Śvetāśvatara, the sage, 263
Swāmī Akhilānanda, 42 n
Swāmī Brahmānanda, 232 n, 286, 341
Swāmī Jagadānanda, 252 n, 327, 341
Swāmī Mādhavānanda, 314, 318, 326–7
Swāmī Nikhilānanda, 253 n, 325–7, 340
Swāmī Prabhavānanda, 313, 313 n, 326, 341
Swāmī Sāradānanda, 252, 252 n, 253, 284, 286, 341
Swāmī Vivekānanda, 16, 43, 66, 70, 140, 182, 194, 196, 198, 207, 218, 255, 293–4, 303, 341; The Complete Works of, Vol. I, 182 n, 194, 194 n, 196, 196 n, 293, 293 n, 294, 294n; Vol. II, 16, 16 n, 43, 43 n; Vol. III, 140, 140 n, 218, 218 n; Vol. IV, 207, 207 n; Vol. V, 218, 218 n, 255–6, 256 n, 303, 303 n; Vol. VI, 198, 198 n, 207, 207 n, 218, 218 n; Vol. VII, 66–7, 67 n, 70, 70 n
Syllogism, 145–8, 153; Aristotelian, 148; hypothetical, 148; Indian, 147; Nyāya, 146, 147 n
Symbol, visual, audible, 291
System of Vedānta, The, 61 n, 339

Tādāmya-sambandha, relation of identity in essence; (*see* relation)
Taittirīya-bhāṣya-vārttika, 324
Tamas, 51, 51 n, 77, 134, 257, 273; (*see* guṇas)
Tanmātra, 51 n
Tantra-vārttika, 180 n, 317
Tarka (*see* argument)
Tarkabhūṣaṇa, Paṇḍit Pramathanātha, 49 n, 345
Tarka-saṁgraha, 106 n, 108 n, 115 n, 120 n, 121 n, 122 n, 146 n, 150 n, 151 n, 154 n, 181 n, 183 n, 314, 344

Taṭastha lakṣaṇa (extrinsic characteristic), 199
Tātparya-candrikā, 328
Tātparya-jñānam (knowledge of the purport), 179
Tattvacintāmaṇi, 37 n, 314, 344
Tattvakaumudī (Vācaspati), 38 n, 106 n, 154 n, 158 n, 165 n, 229 n, 315
Tattva-muktā-kalāpa, 328
Tattva-pradīpikā (or Pratyak-tattva-pradīpikā), 110 n, 113 n, 325, 344
Tattva-saṁkhyāna, 331
Tattva-ṭīkā, 328
Tattvavaiśāradī (Vācaspati), 77 n, 120 n, 187 n, 316, 345
Tattva-viveka, 331
Tattvōddyōta, 331
Teacher, spiritual guide, the imperative need of, 197, 264–9; and pupil, their qualifications, 266–7; their relation, 267–9
Telepathy, 42 n, 45, 45 n
Tendencies, past, 300
Test of knowledge, of truth, 115
Testimony (*see* verbal testimony)
Theology, rational, 216; dogmatic, 216, 226
Theory of Knowledge, The (George D. Hicks), 16 n, 36 n, 58 n, 73 n, 340
Theory of momentary consciousness, 244
Thilly, Frank, 231 n
Thing-in-itself, the, 62
Thirteen Principal Upaniṣads, The, 326
'Thou art That', 153, 185, 192, 200, 215, 221, 242 n, 246–8, 256–7, 259–62, 269, 269 n, 273, 283, 289; explanation of, 270–72
'Thou art the tenth', 192, 192 n, 260
Thought, 67, 182; and word, 182; speculative, 226
Thought-transference, 45 n, 54
Three Lectures on Vedānta Philosophy, 293 n, 340
Tilak, Balagangadhar, 307
Toṭakācārya, 125 n, 260 n
Tōtā Purī, 285, 285 n
Transcendence, 69–70
Transcendent and immanent, 254–5
Transcendental 83; experience, 18, 278; truths, 219, 222; self, 36, 82, 111, 230, 234, 272
Trayī (the Vedas), 305
Treatise of Human Nature, A, 243 n, 340
Triad (the threefold manifestation of Brahman), 76, 256
Tripuṭī-vilaya, 248
Tṛtīya-liṅga-parāmarśa, 146
Truth(s), 207, 216, 246–7, 266; supramental, 203, 220; suprasensuous, 203, 220, 224, 317; supreme, 200; of truths, 203 eternal, 207; fundamental, 212
Truths (revealed, rationalized), 320
Ṭup-ṭīkā, 317
Turīya, 249, 270, 294–5

Udāharaṇa (example), 145, 153
Udayanācārya, 313
Uddālaka, 197, 203, 268
Uddeśya, vidheya (the subject and the predicate), 107, 174
Uddhava, 297
Udyōtakara, 313
Ujjvala-nīlamaṇi, 333
Unconditioned, Undiversified, 254
Unconsciousness, 249
Uniate, Union (Neo-platonic terms), 251 n
Unillumined, 303
Unity in diversity, 198, 213, 246–7, 251, 255
Universal(s) (jāti), 49 n, 150, 181, 182 ff, 217, 246; (*see also* particular)
Universal duty, 210
Universal law of causation, 209
Universal love, 214
Universal proposition, 147, 149
Universe, 247–8; objective, 132; diversified, 262; sensible, 64, 69, 86; its projection, etc., 199
Unknowingness, unknownness, 100
Unknown and unknowable, 247
Unselfishness, 208
Upadeśa-sāhasrī, 103, 192 n, 233 n, 240 n, 241 n, 242 n, 262 n, 265 n, 268 n, 272 n, 273 n, 278 n, 282 n, 324, 344; Eng. trans., 327
Upādhi-khaṇḍana, 331
Upādhyāya, Gaṅgeśa, 37, 314
Upamāna (comparison), 35, 92, 142, 155–6, 189; different from perception and inference, 154–5
Upamiti, 154
Upanaya (application), 145–6
Upaniṣad(s), 46–7, 69–70, 76, 78, 85, 87, 90, 194, 196, 198–9, 200, 202, 211, 218, 221, 224, 227, 227 n, 228, 230, 238, 243, 245–6, 251, 253, 255–6, 263–4, 269, 272, 279, 283, 290, 295, 299, 303, 306–10, 320, 325–6, 344
— *Aitareya*, 200, 200 n, 248, 248 n, 307, 309, 344
— *Brahma-bindu*, 79 n, 344
— *Bṛhadāraṇyaka*, 47, 47 n, 50 n, 62 n, 78 n, 87 n, 87–8, 91 n, 101 n, 123, 123 n, 153 n, 196 n, 199 n, 200, 200 n, 202 n, 206 n, 210, 210 n,

213 n, 214 n, 221 n, 222 n, 230 n, 238 n, 243 n, 248, 248 n, 250 n, 251 n, 255 n, 256 n, 260 n, 261 n, 264 n, 265 n, 270 n, 274, 274 n, 278 n, 279 n, 281 n, 282 n, 284 n, 288 n, 291 n, 298, 298 n, 300 n, 302 n, 305 n, 306–7, 309, 326, 331, 344
— *Chāndōgya*, 69 n, 128 n, 157 n, 197, 199 n, 200, 200 n, 202 n, 204 n, 221 n, 246 n, 254 n, 268 n, 269 n, 282 n, 283 n, 284 n, 291 n, 292, 292 n, 296, 296 n, 302 n, 305 n, 307, 310, 326, 344
— *Īśa*, 213 n, 214 n, 247 n, 255 n, 270 n, 306–7, 309, 344
— *Jābāla*, 307, 309, 344
— *Kaivalya*, 344
— *Kaṭha*, 17, 70 n, 85 n, 87 n, 199 n, 214 n, 221 n, 230 n, 236 n, 255 n, 261 n, 264 n, 265, 265 n, 270 n, 274, 274 n, 279 n, 282 n, 291, 291 n, 307, 309, 344
— *Kauṣītakī*, 307, 309, 344
— Kena, 47 n, 202 n, 230 n, 236 n, 307, 310, 344
— *Mahānārāyaṇa* (or Nārāyaṇa), 209 n, 307, 309, 326, 344
— *Maitrāyaṇīya*, 309
— *Māṇḍūkya*, 123, 123 n, 199 n, 200, 249, 249 n, 270 n, 292, 294 n, 295, 295 n, 296 n, 307, 310, 321, 326, 344
— *Muktika*, 305, 307, 344
— *Muṇḍaka*, 79–80, 80 n, 85 n, 87 n, 121 n, 200 n, 201 n, 213 n, 221 n, 236 n, 247 n, 248, 248 n, 250, 250 n, 254 n, 261, 261 n, 263 n, 264 n, 265 n, 266 n, 270 n, 272 n, 274, 274 n, 280, 281 n, 295, 295 n, 299, 299 n, 305 n, 307, 310, 344
— *Nṛsiṁha-Pūrva-Tāpanīya*, 199 n, 307, 344
— *Paiṅgala*, 307, 309
— *Praśna*, 210, 210 n, 213 n, 243 n, 290 n, 291 n, 292, 296 n, 305 n, 307, 310, 344
— *Śvetāśvatara*, 43 n, 70 n, 76 n, 85 n, 87 n, 196 n, 201 n, 202 n, 203, 203 n, 236 n, 255 n, 256 n, 263 n, 269 n, 272 n, 296, 296 n, 303 n, 307, 309, 326, 344
— *Taittirīya*, 199 n, 201 n, 209 n; 247 n, 274 n, 283 n, 305 n, 306, 307, 309, 344
Upaniṣad Series, The, 326
Upaniṣads, The, 326
Upapādaka, Upapādya, 156
Upāsanā (meditation), 290–91
Upaskāra, 313
Uttara-Mīmāṁsā, 141, 227, 316, 320; (*see Brahma-sūtras*)
Vāk, 292–3
Vākyapadīya of Bhartṛhari, 107 n, 186 n, 187 n, 345
Vākya-vṛtti, 262 n, 269 n, 271 n, 282 n, 324, 345; Eng. trans., 327
Vaibhāṣika (school of Buddhism), 68 n, 312
Vaidika Dharma, 323
Vaiśeṣika school (of Kaṇāda), 38–9, 154, 176, 225–6, 311–13; texts and commentaries of, 312–13
Vaiśeṣika-darśana or *Vaiśeṣika-sūtras*, 38 n, 175 n, 345
Vaiṣṇava-tōṣiṇi, 333
Vaiṣṇavism, five schools of, 227, 319, 327–34
Validity, of knowledge, 110 ff; of perception, 219; of a sentence, 181; of the Śruti, 226
Vallabhācārya, 107 n, 319, 322, 331–2
Vārttika (Udyōtakara), 313
Vāśiṣṭha Dharma-sūtra or *Dharma-śāstra*, 206 n, 345
Vātsāyana, 35 n, 313, 343
Vātsāyana-bhāṣya, 313, 343
Veda(s), 37, 141 n, 196, 199–200, 202–7, 209, 211–12, 215, 216–19, 223, 264 n, 291–3, 302–3, 305, 307–10; two main parts of, 204, 204 n, 305–6; two sections of, according to theme, 206, 227, 308; universality of, 207; the four Vedas —(1) Ṛk, 70 n, 193 n, 200, 207 n, 209, 209 n, 248, 283 m. 292 n, 305, 308–9; (2) Yajuḥ (White), 200, 306–7, 309; Yajuḥ (Black), 305–7, 309; (3) Sāma, 200, 200 n, 305, 310; (4) Atharva, 200, 305, 310
Vedāṅgas, 264 n
Vedānta, Vedāntins, 43, 48 n, 51–4, 59, 62–5, 69, 73–4, 81, 84, 89, 103, 107, 107 n, 113–14, 127, 129, 144, 181, 198, 214, 219, 223–4, 226–8, 258, 266, 270, 301–2, 307, 311, 316, 320–22
Vedānta-deśika, 318, 328
Vedānta-dīpa, 328
Vedānta-kalpalatikā, 325
Vedānta-kalpataru, 205 n, 257 n, 325, 345
Vedānta-kalpataru-parimala, 257 n, 325, 345
Vedānta-kaustubha, 329, Eng. trans., 330
Vedānta-kaustubha-prabhā, 329
Vedānta-paribhāṣā, 36, 37 n, 42 n, 48 n, 53 n, 54 n, 62, 62 n, 67 n, 77 n, 89 n, 90, 90 n, 92 n, 93, 93 n, 94 n, 98, 104, 104 n, 106 n, 108, 108 n, 122 n, 113 n, 117, 117 n, 118, 118 n,

135, 136 n, 143, 145 n, 146 n, 149, 150 n, 151, 153, 155–6, 156 n, 157 n, 159, 159 n, 160 n, 166, 166 n, 168 n, 169 n, 174 n, 179 n, 180 n, 183 n, 184, 184 n, 196 n, 205 n, 217, 217 n, 223, 223 n, 256, 257 n, 258 n, 259 n, 260 n, 262 n, 300 n, 325, 345; Eng. trans, 327
Vedānta-pārijāta-saurabha, 329; Eng. trans., 330
Vedānta philosophy, 141 n, 212, 220, 225–7, 227 n, 228, 318
Vedānta-ratna-mañjūṣā, 330
Vedānta-sara, 53, 53 n, 62 n, 76 n, 223 n, 256 n, 264 n, 307, 325, 345; Eng. trans., 327
Vedānta-siddhānta-muktāvalī, 325
Vedānta-sūtra, 227 n; Eng. trans., 329; (*see Brahma-sūtras*)
Vedānta and Yōga, 302
Vedānta-tattva-sāra, The, 329; Eng. trans., 329
Vedārtha-saṁgraha, 328
Veda-Vyāsa, 43, 217, 305; (*see also* Vyāsa, Bādarāyaṇa)
Vedic, authority, 225–6; dicta, great, 201, 203–4, 260; religion, a two-fold way, 205; its universality, 207; revelations, 216; schools, 311–12; seers, 282, 308–9, 320; systems (six), 226–7, 311; teachings, supreme, 200, 212; testimony, 37–8, 128, 141 n, 193, 212, 216, 219, 229, 233, 236, 258
Veṅkaṭanātha, 328–9
Venkataramiah, D., 259 n
Verbal, comprehension, 176, 178, 180, 180 n; knowledge, 175–8, 187; its four conditions, 178–81; its distinctive character, 187 ff; testimony (āgama or śabda), 17, 35–7, 44, 142, 164, 173, 175, 177, 188, 191, 193–4
Verification, not the cause of knowledge, 114, 188
Vicāra (reflection and right apprehension), 290
Vidagdha-Mādhava, 333
Videha-mukti (liberation-at-death), 279, 282; (*see also* jīvan-mukti, liberation-in-life), 283–4
Vidhi-rasāyana, 318
Vidhi-viveka, 318
Vidvan-maṇḍana, 332
Vidvanmanōrañjinī, 256 n, 307, 325, 345
Vidyābhūṣaṇa, Baladeva, 107 n, 321
Vidyāraṇya, 45, 48, 48 n, 49, 52, 93, 103, 215, 225 n, 235, 238, 259 n, 262 n, 289–90, 343, 345
Vijñāna (right apprehension), 288–9
Vijñāna-bhikṣu, 43 n, 131, 131 n, 315, 343
Vijñānamaya-kōṣa, 248 n
Vijñātā (knower), 238
Virtue, 208, 210; practice of, 208, 210
Viśeṣa (particularity), 312
Vision or Sight (C. B. Goulden), 55 n, 339
Viśiṣṭādvaita of Rāmānuja, 89, 107 n, 132–3, 227, 321–2, 327–9
Viṣṇu, 297, 322
Viṣṇu-tattva-nirṇaya, 331
Vital principle (prāṇa), 234, 240–41, 249
Viṭṭhala, 332
Vivaraṇa-prameya-saṁgraha, 49 n, 128 n, 225 n, 256 n, 259 n, 325, 345
Vivaraṇa School, 36, 142, 257 n, 258–9, 261, 321
Vivaranōpanyāsa, 259 n
Vivarta (apparent modification), 335
Viveka-cūḍāmaṇi, 191 n, 223 n, 225 n, 250 n, 251 n, 259 n, 262 n, 263 n, 264 n, 267 n, 273 n, 275 n, 276 n, 277 n, 284 n, 296 n, 303 n, 324, 345; (*see* Eng. trans. 327)
Viveka-khyāti (discriminating knowledge), 338
Vivekakhyāti-vāda (theory of non-discrimination), 130
Void, theory of (śūnya-vāda), 128, 128 n
Volition, 42 n; its relation to cognition, 90; disappears in dream, 236
Vyakti (*see* particular)
Vyāpti (*see* invariable concomitance)
Vyāsa, Bādarāyaṇa (commentator on *Brahma-sūtras*), 225, 227. 261, 320
Vyāsa, commentator on *Yōga-sūtras*, 36 n, 120, 181, 195 n, 315
Vyāsatīrtha, 329
Vyatireka-vyāpti (agreement in absence), 144, 149, 151, 159–60
Vyavahārika (empirical), 83, 118

Waking state, 51, 65, 82, 123, 129, 237, 241, 249, 255, 270, 295; experiences of, 129, 242
Ward, James, 58, 59 n, 95, 95 n, 96
Ways of Knowing, The (Montague), 40 n, 190 n, 340
Weber, Albrecht, *Indische Studien*, 293 n
Weber, Alfred, 231 n, 341
Western, logic, 143–5, 158, 160–61; logicians, 148; philosophers, philosophy, 39, 63, 93, 97, 112, 114, 115, 160, 175, 194, 225; psychologists, 57; (*see also* psychologists, modern)

Western, thinkers, 55–7, 142, 228, 247; their views of external perception, 55–6, not satisfactory, 56–7, the problem remains unsolved, 58–60; thought, 46
Whitehead, A. N., 63
Will, unconscious, 80; of God, 181; of the Lord, 74
Witness-self (*see* self as witness)
Woods, Professor James Haughton, 186 n
Word, and its meaning, 181 ff, 217; and thought, 182, 293; primary meaning of, 183–4; secondary meaning of, 184; in relation to universal and particular, 182 ff.
Word of words, 217, 292–3
Words of the Master, 232 n, 341
Works of Śaṅkara, The, 102 n, 343
World, its reality and unreality, 67–8, 77; sensible, 74
World-appearance, 123, 128 n, 169, 199–221
World-process, 70
World-soul, 52
Worship as preparatory to meditation, 298

Yājña-paribhāṣa-sūtram of Āpastamba, 204 n
Yājñavalkya, 87–8, 196, 249, 256, 288
Yājñavalkya-smṛti, 203, 210 n, 345
Yatīndra-mata-dīpikā (text and Eng. trans,), 329
Yati, Prakāśātma, 259, 259 n, 343
Yōga, 194–5
Yōgācāra School (Buddhist Idealists), 68, 68 n, 71–2, 126, 129, 244, 312
Yōga-darśana, 315
Yōga-sūtras of Patañjali, 36 n, 42 n, 45 n, 46 n, 77 n, 82 n, 93 n, 111 n, 120 n, 181 n, 186 n, 187 n, 194 n, 195 n, 196 n, 240 n, 241 n, 295 n, 298 n, 301 n, 302 n, 314, 316, 345
Yōga system, 38, 43, 113, 141, 225–6, 301–2, 311, 314–15
Yōga-vāśiṣṭha Rāmāyaṇa, 258 n, 345
Yōgī, 43, 254, 297, 297 n, 301
Yōgic dualism and Vedāntic nondualism, 335–6
Yōgic insight, 43
Yōgic method of meditation, 337–8
Yōgīndra, Sadānanda, 222
Yudhiṣṭhira, King, 16
Yukti-pradhāna, 226, 316